Praise for

SKIPPER

"*Skipper* is filled with anecdote after anecdote around the most notable in-game decisions over the last half century, with the managers telling the readers about all the complications that framed their choices. The excellent and comprehensive work is not surprising to me, after watching Scott Miller extract details from big-league All-Stars over his remarkable career. In this era when narrative-bending is exchanged for access, Scott is an outlier: He seeks the truth in every situation."
—Buster Olney, author of *The Last Night of the Yankee Dynasty*

"Scott Miller has always been one of the best and most insightful baseball writers in America. But this might be his finest work, because *Skipper* is *the* definitive book on the complicated, new-age world of modern managing. Reading it, I felt just the way I did when I read *Moneyball*. We were all pretty sure we knew what baseball and baseball managers have always looked like. And this isn't it! Once you've read *Skipper*, you'll understand exactly why."
—Jayson Stark, senior baseball writer, *The Athletic*

"Simply, this is the ultimate and definitive book of MLB managers. It's a must-read with Scott Miller brilliantly capturing an unprecedented behind-the-scenes look with today's managers and their predecessors. He takes you into the living room of the Bob Boone house where he is watching his son, Aaron, managing the Yankees. He takes you into the day-to-day grind with Dave Roberts as he leads the Los Angeles Dodgers to the World Series championship. And he takes you into the pain Art Howe endured watching *Moneyball*. Every chapter is absolutely riveting, giving you an exclusive perspective into the complicated world of baseball managers."   —Bob Nightengale, baseball columnist, *USA Today*

"There are certainties in baseball. Sixty feet six inches from the pitcher's mound to the plate. Ninety feet from one base to the next. And Scott Miller at the ballpark, several hours before game time in the dugout waiting for a one-on-one conversation with the manager. And if the manager isn't in the dugout, then certainly they meet in the manager's office. What Miller brings to the page is the insight of the manager, about the players he manages and oversees. The game isn't just numbers and lineups, it is the people who play it, and how they play it under the guidance of the Skipper. The managers and their personalities. Each manager has his own view of his and opposing players and how the game can and should be played. That is the essence of the game. Its heart and its soul. Why baseball managers matter (and always will). Scott Miller is the Skipper of this game."

—Charley Steiner, radio play-by-play, Los Angeles Dodgers

SKIPPER

SKIPPER

WHY BASEBALL MANAGERS MATTER AND ALWAYS WILL

SCOTT MILLER

GRAND
CENTRAL
NEW YORK BOSTON

Grand Central Publishing
Hachette Book Group
1290 Avenue of the Americas, New York, NY 10104
grandcentralpublishing.com
@grandcentralpub

First Edition: May 2025

Grand Central Publishing is a division of Hachette Book Group, Inc. The Grand Central Publishing name and logo is a registered trademark of Hachette Book Group, Inc.

The publisher is not responsible for websites (or their content) that are not owned by the publisher.

The Hachette Speakers Bureau provides a wide range of authors for speaking events. To find out more, go to hachettespeakersbureau.com or email HachetteSpeakers@hbgusa.com.

Grand Central Publishing books may be purchased in bulk for business, educational, or promotional use. For information, please contact your local bookseller or the Hachette Book Group Special Markets Department at special.markets@hbgusa.com.

Library of Congress Cataloging-in-Publication Data

Names: Miller, Scott, author.
Title: Skipper : why baseball managers matter and always will / Scott Miller.
Description: First edition. | New York : Grand Central Publishing, 2025. | Includes index.
Identifiers: LCCN 2024054137 | ISBN 9780306832703 (hardcover) | ISBN 9780306832727 (ebook)
Subjects: LCSH: Baseball—United States—History. | Roberts, Dave, 1933-. | African American baseball managers—Biography. | Baseball managers— United States—Biography. | Los Angeles Dodgers (Baseball team)—History.
Classification: LCC GV863.A1 M53 2025 | DDC 796.357090973—dc23/ eng/20240102
LC record available at https://lccn.loc.gov/2024054137

ISBNs: 9780306832703 (hardcover), 9780306832727 (ebook)

Printed in the United States of America

LSC-C

Printing 1, 2025

To my wife, Kim, and daughter, Gretchen…my heart

To my parents, Alan and Rosemary…my soul

And to my brother Greg, the real writer in the family, and my sister Jennifer, who now can borrow my sweaters anytime she wishes

CONTENTS

SKIPPER

PROLOGUE

PET PROJECTS

In January 1977, the world's first personal computer was taken for a public test drive at the Consumer Electronics Show in Chicago. The Commodore Personal Electronic Transactor (PET) began shipping to the public in June. Clunky, bulky, yet fully functional out of the box, it cost $495 and weighed about twenty-five pounds. It was so cumbersome and so complicated that, in the beginning, Commodore could manufacture only about thirty units a day. The top of the PET popped open for easy maintenance, just like the hood of a car. The screen was only nine inches. Users complained about the small keyboard that made typing difficult. The model came complete with a built-in cassette player in the front for data storage.

It was a start. And the race was on. On January 3, 1977, not long before that Consumer Electronics Show in Chicago, two men named Steve Jobs and Steve Wozniak had incorporated a new company called Apple Computer, Inc. And on April 16, 1977, they introduced the Apple II at the West Coast Computer Faire. Eventually using something called a "floppy disk" for data storage instead of audiocassette tapes, the Apple II would become a smash hit and launch the newly incorporated company into the stratosphere as a worldwide power. Soon, every aspect of our lives—and games—would change. The old Republican campaign slogan from the 1920s of putting "a chicken in every pot" would, by the twenty-first century, morph into the public's basic demand of a Wi-Fi router in every home.

The New York Yankees of April 1977 were still far more powerful than Apple and vastly more advanced than the Commodore PET. With twenty World Series titles and myriad Hall of Famers, they were baseball's jewel franchise and already ranked as one of the world's best-known brands. They had just signed free agent Reggie Jackson to a then-unheard-of sum of $2.96 million over five years. They were coming off a World Series loss to the Cincinnati Reds the previous October but were odds-on favorites to change that this season. But with the expansion Toronto Blue Jays in Yankee Stadium for a game on April 20, what the Yankees were most in need of was a reboot. They had lost five consecutive games and eight of their previous ten.

To address this, their manager approached Jackson before the game and asked him to perform a simple task. Billy Martin had turned his cap upside down, and inside were pieces of paper, each containing the name of a Yankee who would be in that night's lineup. Except the lineup itself had not yet been constructed. This was what Jackson would be doing as he responded to the manager's request to pick the names out of a hat.

"I understood it because I had seen it before," Jackson, the Hall of Famer, says more than four decades later, in a conversation during the 2022 World Series in Houston. "Nobody's hitting, we're not doing well, so make a lineup today, just pick it out of the hat. And I think we won the game."

It was a gimmick Martin had pulled before, once back when he was managing Detroit in 1972. The Tigers lost that game. But in the Bronx on this late April evening in 1977, just as Jackson recalled, it was a success: The Yankees snapped their five-game losing streak with a 7–5 win over the Blue Jays, and Martin stayed with his "hat trick" lineup again the following day as the Yankees beat Toronto for a second consecutive time: Willie Randolph 2B, Thurman Munson C, Jackson RF, Graig Nettles 3B, Mickey Rivers CF, Roy White RF, Carlos May DH, Chris Chambliss 1B, Bucky Dent SS. "I did it to relax the guys," Martin explained to reporters afterward. "Besides, when you don't have any hot bats, it doesn't matter where they hit."

Forty-eight years later, with both the sport and the world awash in a blizzard of bits and bytes, the thought of a major-league manager actually picking his lineup out of a hat for anything this side of a celebrity softball game seems as prehistoric as a caveman carving petroglyphs into a rock formation. Can you imagine today's reaction to a stunt like that? The mocking would commence before the No. 9 hitter's scrap of paper emerged from the cap. The modern and essential website FanGraphs would self-implode. Baseball Savant would turn savage. Statcast would freeze.

With each of the game's thirty organizations having built its own sophisticated, proprietary information system, there is precious little left to chance with lineup construction—or with anything else. Lefties, righties, switch-hitters, setup men, closers, openers…matchups dominate today's game, and matchups are created in the tapping of keyboards to input information and in the whirring of computers crunching that information. It is a game of probabilities, and today's managers are directed to implement them. We see it every night from Los Angeles to Minnesota to New York to Tampa Bay and beyond. We especially see it each October when playoff and World Series games slow down to a freeway-gridlock crawl as the late innings arrive and each matchup brings higher stakes than the previous one.

What the 1977 season offers today is a couple of things: a starting point from which the seeds of so much change sprouted and bloomed, from what would become the tech sector to the way owners conducted their business; and a stark contrast between a time that presented managers at the peak of their powers and today's dilution of those powers. The road map from then to now changes in scenery as starkly as moving from a 1977 Ford Pinto into a 2025 Toyota Prius hybrid.

That Martin, a highly successful if personally troubled manager, would pick a lineup out of a hat—or be allowed to do it—just a couple of weeks after the world's first personal computer was publicly unveiled is both wildly coincidental and altogether fitting.

One of the leading reasons why so many of us who love the sport profess to do so is because, supposedly, baseball never changes. Like the goldening of the leaves each autumn and the twinkling of Christmas lights on cold December nights, it is part of the rhythm of the seasons and helps keep us in touch with time and place. But while the latter may be true, the former is a full-blown myth. Always, baseball has changed. Sometimes with the subtle grace of a new generation of stars, other times with a wrecking-ball sledgehammer, as with the introduction of the designated hitter in 1973, the beginning of interleague play in 1997, and the introduction of the pitch clock and the outlawing of the defensive shift in 2023.

The game has changed as much or more in the past half century than it ever has, and even more rapidly over the past couple of decades. Look in the owner's box: What once were mostly family-financed businesses have become largely corporate. Peek into the general manager's office: What once was one man in charge of building a roster now is a "baseball operations department." Check the dugout: Replacing a somewhat ill-educated group of carousing hell-raisers (particularly in the game's early days) is a largely knowledge-seeking, health-food-eating, private-coach-leaning, video-gaming bunch of players who require wholly different treatment than their forebears.

But most important, look into the manager's office: He (or, perhaps, one day, she?) is the one person who must work, lead, and coexist with all of the above. He is the so-called person in charge yet must walk the fine line between executing the preferences of the baseball ops department and what he thinks is best—both in deploying personnel and in deploying strategy—all while simultaneously maintaining the respect of his players. If they view him as a puppet of his superiors, their respect evaporates and then the manager is finished. Too many losses and the manager is finished. If he doesn't play nice with the front office, even if his results are wildly successful, then he is finished—see Mike Shildt, who managed the St. Louis Cardinals to seventeen consecutive wins in September 2021 in an exhilarating charge to the playoffs and was fired at season's end nonetheless. Then, whatever happened in the game, he must sell it to the public—by way of explaining his own moves, or covering up for the baseball operations mandates if something went wrong that wasn't the manager's idea. This is where the changes in the game—and in society—are most reflected and best understood. It is an office that once consolidated as much power as anybody in an organization. Now, its occupants, in many cases, have been reduced to the role of middle managers as power bases and flowcharts have drastically been reorganized and restructured.

"I don't think the job is different from how I envisioned it," says Craig Counsell, the longest-tenured manager in the National League with Milwaukee before leaving for an enormous contract with the Chicago Cubs in 2024. "It's different because front offices have grown immensely, baseball operations and employees, and it's an exponential jump. That's because they are providing more input to the product on the field. They're more involved in providing information and making player decisions because they've invested more to try to get it right."

When Detroit hired Sparky Anderson in 1979, he blew into Tiger Stadium like a tornado, warning, "It's my way or the highway." He—and, by extension, the general manager who entrusted him with such power, Jim Campbell—wasn't kidding. Within a few years, acquiescing to Anderson's feel and personality, the Tigers significantly shuffled their roster to meet the manager's demands. Sparky had clout.

Among others, they shipped All-Stars Steve Kemp, Jason Thompson, and Ron LeFlore out of town. And in 1984—the Hall of Fame manager's fifth full season in Detroit—the Tigers won their first World Series since 1968.

"Right at the get-go, he put his foot down, and it *was* 'My way or the highway,'" says the Hall of Fame shortstop Alan Trammell, a franchise cornerstone during Anderson's entire seventeen years managing in Detroit. "What we needed was direction. Some of the guys didn't stay that long. Sparky knew what he wanted, and they didn't fit what he wanted. He moved guys along like any manager would like to do."

By and large, managers enjoyed Sparky's autonomy, or, at least, something within a neighborhood play of it, for more than a century after the game's beginnings in the late 1800s. When fans talk about baseball's unbreakable records, pitcher Cy Young's 511 wins often is the first number mentioned. In an era of dominant relievers and hitters now having to face four or five pitchers a game instead of one, Joe DiMaggio's 56-game hitting streak appears as timeless as a Beethoven symphony. Cal Ripken's 2,632 consecutive games played in a current era of "load management" surely appears safe. Nolan Ryan's 5,714 career strikeouts in an age of the five-inning starting pitcher continues to appear as unreachable and majestic as Mount Everest.

All of these are incredible and, almost certainly, unreachable. But the game's two true numbers that are untouchable? Connie Mack's records of 3,731 victories and 7,755 games managed. Tony La Russa is a Hall of Famer and was still managing the Chicago White Sox at age seventy-seven. Yet when he was finally finished and made his unceremonious, health-related exit from the White Sox, he remained second in all-time managerial wins at a whopping 847 behind Mack. Not only is Mack viewed as one of the game's all-time great managers (with an equally memorable nickname; at six foot one he was known as the "Tall Tactician"), but his longevity over the decades as he piloted the Philadelphia Athletics for fifty years was sturdied by one small little fact.

He owned the team.

This explains why his 3,948 losses are more than 1,000 beyond that of any other manager, too. Now, managers are afforded little ownership of even their own offices.

One of the very first dominoes to fall that led to this point also occurred in 1977, and it wasn't simply the advent of the computers that one day would make the manager's job unrecognizable to Martin, Anderson, Dick Williams, Whitey Herzog, Tommy Lasorda, and other strongmen who worked the game's dugouts as skippers that summer. Three weeks after Martin picked his lineup out of a hat early in that 1977 season, an owner again suited up to manage a game. But Ted Turner was no Connie Mack.

Turner had purchased the Atlanta Braves before the bicentennial summer of 1976, and they went 70-92 in his first season of stewardship, losing thirteen consecutive games at one point en route to a last-place finish in the National League West. Though they were supposed to be better in 1977, early in the season they launched a losing streak that was even worse than the summer before, a run that reached sixteen in a row. That was when Turner, whose purchase of the Braves in 1976 coincided with his starting the country's first "Superstation" that distributed programs—and Braves games—via satellite to television stations throughout the country, sprang into action.

"I thought about firing our manager, Dave Bristol, but instead I decided to just give him some time off," Turner wrote in his autobiography, *Call Me Ted*. After telling the press that Bristol was away on a scouting trip, "I put on a Braves uniform and served as the team's field manager."

What Turner planned on was a sort of scouting mission for himself. He told Bristol at the time that he wanted to find out what was wrong with the club. "In the dugout, I really didn't do a whole lot other than crack some jokes and yell encouragement," Turner wrote. "I didn't know the signs, so I had to sit next to one of the other coaches, and when I thought we should steal or bunt, I'd have to tell him so he could relay the signal."

With Phil Niekro on his game that May 11 evening in Pittsburgh, Turner never even had a chance to leave the dugout and walk to the mound. But the Braves still were beaten by the Pirates 2–1. The next morning, Turner said, he received a telegram from National League president Chub Feeney "telling me that my first game would also be my last."

In benching the owner, Feeney cited MLB rule 20(e) that "no manager or player on a club shall, directly or indirectly, own stock or any other proprietary interest or have any financial interest in the Club by which the manager or player is employed except under an agreement approved by the Commissioner." It was a little-known rule installed after Mack's fifty-three-year managerial run ended.

Turner quickly appealed, and Commissioner Bowie Kuhn denied it before the owner had a chance to even his 0-1 lifetime record as manager (Atlanta's seventeenth consecutive loss). Kuhn cited Turner's "lack of familiarity with game operations" and the commissioner used the best interests of baseball clause to double down.

For more than a century, the term "skipper" has been interchangeable with "manager," sometimes as a sign of affection, sometimes as a sign of respect. And sometimes both. The word itself, according to the authoritative *Dickson Baseball Dictionary*, comes from the Dutch "schipper," or "schip"—which, of course, means "ship"—and on the diamond, its usage dates as far back as 1890. A manager acts as the captain of the ship; when professional baseball was in its infancy in the 1800s, the man appointed to the position was responsible for everything from roster construction to team travel logistics to finances. He managed every aspect of the team and its business operations. As a nod to tradition, the classic term "manager" continues to stand the test of time even as the other North American sports developed professionally and their teams named "head coaches."

Famously, in September 1977, Turner would be wildly successful as a different kind of skipper: Off the coast of Newport, Rhode Island, he skippered the United States defender, *Courageous*, to an America's Cup triumph over the Australian challenger. And two months after that, in November 1977, the would-be manager dubbed Captain Outrageous pulled another winning move by hiring as Atlanta's new manager Bobby Cox, a man who had been piloting the Yankees' Triple-A team.

I still remember the month that all finally came together eighteen years later. I was standing outside of the Braves' Fulton County Stadium clubhouse during the 1995 World Series, awaiting postgame entry, as that key 1977 decision was coming full circle that autumn for Cox—then in his second tour of duty managing the Braves—Turner, and the city of Atlanta. The Braves were on the verge of defeating Cleveland and winning the city's first World Series title. A black town car attempting to exit the ballpark postgame slowly inched its way through the mass of people crowding the tunnel. I was on the outer edge of a scrum of reporters waiting for the clubhouse doors to open as we all pushed toward the wall to do our best to make room for the car.

Driving was Captain Outrageous himself. Riding shotgun was his then–significant other, the actress Jane Fonda. The passenger window opened as Turner carefully inched the vehicle past our group. Fonda, cracking a grin, quipped, "Suck it in, boys." From the driver's seat, Turner belly laughed. So, too, did those of us who squeezed in tighter so the car could pass. It was a charming moment.

Memories of the champagne that autumn, it turned out, needed to last an extra-long time. Though the Cox-managed Braves would return to the World Series in 1996 and again in 1999, they ran smack into the buzzsaw that was evolving into the Yankees' latest dynasty. The Braves lost to the Bronx Bombers both times. Atlanta would not win another World Series until more than a quarter of a century later, when Brian Snitker led the Braves past Houston to win the 2021 title. As for Cox, his managerial nemesis in the '96 and '99 World Series, Joe Torre, was awarded his own manager's office just three weeks after Turner spat out the final wad of tobacco that he entertainingly chewed throughout his managerial stint in Pittsburgh's Three Rivers Stadium.

The New York Mets owned the game's worst record on May 31, 1977, and several key players were openly hostile to management when the club fired Joe Frazier and promoted Torre to the role of player-manager—an antique form of managing that disappeared for good a decade later when Cincinnati let go of Pete Rose amid one of the biggest scandals in the sport's history. Star pitcher Tom Seaver was publicly outspoken against M. Donald Grant, the Mets' chairman of the board, and his conservative policies. So, too, were slugger Dave Kingman, left-handed starter Jon Matlack, and others.

In installing Torre, then thirty-six and in his final days as a player, the Mets cited some of the same reasons clubs have employed for more than a century: A change was needed. Maybe the players would listen better to a new voice. Also, with attendance lagging, they hoped the popular veteran player might give them a boost at the box office. Mostly, with Grant getting ripped in the press and by the public and with losses piling up, the Mets wanted to change the subject.

But what Torre said at his introductory press conference foreshadowed the kind of manager he ultimately would become over twenty-nine years of piloting the Mets, Braves (Torre would replace Cox for the 1982 season after Cox left Atlanta to become the Toronto Blue Jays' manager; Cox then returned to the Braves in 1990 and led the most successful era in Atlanta history), Cardinals, Yankees, and Los Angeles Dodgers. "I have the feeling that I can get into the players' heads a little bit," Torre said.

From 1996 to 2007, Torre would manage his greatest years on the game's biggest stage in the Bronx, across town from his entry-level job in Queens. He led the Yankees to four World Series titles in his first five seasons. The Hall of Fame manager's run there perfectly bridges the span from 1977 through today: The '96 World Series title was the

Yankees' first since they won back-to-back Fall Classics in 1977 (under Martin) and 1978 (under Bob Lemon, after Martin was fired earlier in the season). Indeed, Torre's calm manner and fatherly approach to the job did get into his players' heads, in a good, modern way: He was a master at shielding them from the glare of the spotlight and the shrieking headlines of New York's tabloids. He was a genius at buffering his clubhouse from distractions. And then his wildly successful twelve-year run in the Bronx limped to its conclusion when Torre's Yankees missed the World Series in his final four seasons, giving general manager Brian Cashman a natural opening to lean into analytics, just as many other successful teams were doing, deeper than ever. Eventually, the lineage would lead to the Yankees hiring someone straight from the television booth who had not managed or coached at any level: Aaron Boone.

With the Yankees' brand now having been surpassed by Apple, the postmodern era for both the Yankees and for managers everywhere was coming, and it was coming fast.

As Cashman became more heavily invested in analytics, Torre squirmed. Don't forget about the heartbeat of this game, Torre pleaded. Players have a heartbeat. Cold computer numbers do not. It was an argument that Torre, of course, had no chance of winning. Four World Series rings and a guaranteed Hall of Fame induction one day did not shield him from the hard truth that the players, the game, and the world were changing. Torre's time had run its course.

"Joe was old school enough that he kind of blanched with some of the analytics that were starting to force their way into the game," says Don Mattingly, the Yankees' star first baseman who would become a coach under Torre in the Bronx, move with him to Los Angeles in 2008, and then succeed Torre as the Dodgers' manager in 2011. "But on the relationship side, he was probably ahead of his time."

Upon learning of the split between the legendary Torre and the Yankees during the Red Sox's American League Championship Series against Cleveland in October 2007, then–Boston manager Terry

Francona was flabbergasted. How could this be? he wondered. Ten days later, the man who guided the Red Sox to finally smashing the Curse of Babe Ruth in 2004 managed them to their second World Series title in four seasons with a sweep of the Colorado Rockies. But four seasons after that, Francona went the way of Torre. Where the Yankees strategically drove Torre away with an insulting contract offer—one year and a pay cut to $5 million for a man whose salary had reached a high of $7 million to make him the highest-paid manager of all—Boston essentially did the same to Francona in other ways.

"To be honest with you, I'm not sure how much support there was from ownership," Francona said at his farewell press conference in Boston, before taking the 2012 season off and then moving on to Cleveland and, eventually, Cincinnati, one of the most respected skippers of this or any generation. "You've got to be all in on this job. It's got to be everybody together, and I was questioning that a little bit."

Unlike Connie Mack or Tommy Lasorda (twenty-one seasons leading the Dodgers), even the most successful and longest tenured of managers today now mostly can be measured by an hourglass, not by decades. Mike Scioscia (nineteen seasons with the Angels, through 2018) very well may be the last of the two-decades-in-one-place skippers. There was a time when a manager who won a World Series with the Chicago Cubs would have been welcome to keep the job for life. Instead, Joe Maddon lasted only three additional seasons after the Cubs' first title in more than a century in 2016 before he essentially was invited to leave after the 2019 season.

The lifespan of a manager is ever shortening today, squeezed by analytically minded front offices on one side and public saturation on the other. Corporate and complicated ownership groups such as Boston's—John Henry (former Miami Marlins owner) and Tom Werner (former San Diego Padres owner) lead the Fenway Sports Group—in many ways play the role of Wall Street sharks demanding high returns on their stocks, ratcheting up the pressure far more than did the family owners of a generation or more ago. The digital and internet age that led to instant gratification and short attention spans with the general public plays its role, too: Managers today must meet with the media—writers, radio, and television—before and after each game, 162 games a season. That's 324 press conferences a summer, not including spring training, off days, impromptu public remarks when breaking news occurs, and on and on. One manager's appearance in one season on his team's social media feeds alone easily accounts for more in-a-fan's-face time than Leo "the Lip" Durocher's entire career's worth of press clippings. The beast must be fed today, and the beast's appetite is insatiable. Welcomes easily wear out quickly in more instances than not.

When Counsell had occasion to chat with his professional coach colleagues before leaving Wisconsin, one common reaction was that the Green Bay Packers' coaches Mike McCarthy and Matt LaFleur and the Milwaukee Bucks' Mike Budenholzer were astounded at his media responsibilities.

"If you talk to coaches in other sports, that might be the thing they're most amazed about," Counsell says. "How much we talk to the media. They meet with the media maybe twice a week. The Packers' coach has, probably, like forty media sessions a year, total."

Today's managers not only do not own their own teams, many of them do not even fully oversee the nine innings they manage. Over his first eight seasons guiding the Dodgers, Dave Roberts entered 2024 with the highest winning percentage by any manager in MLB history (minimum 850 games managed) at .630 (753-443), yet he freely describes his work as "collaborative" with the Los Angeles baseball operations group.

"Collaboration" is the key word in dugouts and manager's offices throughout the game today. Analytics came roaring into the game around the turn of the century as internet and computer usage rendered the idea of Commodore's manufacturing output of thirty or so computers a day in the summer of '77 historically quaint, just like players once leaving their mitts on the field when an inning ended and they went in to bat. With bandwidth both in computers and in front offices increasing exponentially by the week, the early-2000s Oakland A's led the charge—at least publicly, with the release of the book *Moneyball*. Though visionaries such as Earl Weaver, the Hall of Fame manager from Baltimore, had been using rudimentary forms of analytics as far back as the 1970s, now the movement had a name—and mustered momentum that would bloat baseball operations departments across the game and soon make the job of manager unrecognizable to the lions of the past like the Weavers, Andersons, and Lasordas. Ivy League brainiacs established beachheads in just about every organization and now are far more ubiquitous than, say, the wine refrigerator that once was a trusty companion in four-time World Series winner Bruce Bochy's San Francisco office and helped calm him following losses as he thought through his next moves. It is routine today to see a dominating starting pitcher hooked from a World Series game after two times through the opposing lineup. Had St. Louis had a baseball operations department in 1987, Cardinals manager Whitey Herzog would have popped somebody in the nose at the mere suggestion that he yank John Tudor early from a Fall Classic game.

Times have changed and so, too, have both expectations and ways of doing things. Because there are only thirty of these jobs available, the men managing today tolerate far more interference than their predecessors for one very simple reason: One must navigate the world in which one lives, not the world in which one wishes to live.

It is survival. And increasingly, the world in which we live is becoming only more noisy and more complicated.

Consequently, survival today is impossible without accepting new ways of doing things and adjusting one's thinking to forward, rather than backward, because jobs today rightly come with responsibilities and social ramifications that were too easily ignored as recently as a few years ago. Tony La Russa was harshly critical of NFL quarterback Colin Kaepernick's kneeling for the national anthem. Upon accepting the Chicago White Sox managerial job in 2021, he spoke with Tim Anderson and other Black players on his team in raw, honest conversations and told them he had a better understanding of things now and accepts things today that he wouldn't have a few years ago. Industries beyond baseball are reckoning with better minority hiring practices that are long overdue and with eliminating prejudice and misogyny in the workplace.

Yet even in a different age then, and almost unbelievably for the sport that broke the color line with Jackie Robinson in 1947, the first Black manager in baseball history, Frank Robinson, also was fired in 1977—on, of all days, Juneteenth.

Frank Robinson had come to the Cleveland Indians as a player-manager on April 8, 1975, twenty-eight years after Jackie Robinson broke the game's color barrier. He replaced Ken Aspromonte after Cleveland had compiled six consecutive losing seasons. Robinson got the job because he had been a strong leader as a player both in Cincinnati and in Baltimore; he had managed five seasons of winter ball in Santurce, Puerto Rico; and, with the designated hitter still in its infancy, the Indians figured his 574 career home runs would lead to some on-field help, as well. On the day he was hired as the game's first Black manager, October 3, 1974, Commissioner Bowie Kuhn and Lee MacPhail, the president of the American League, were in Cleveland for the press conference.

"We got something done that we should have done before," Kuhn said.

Gerald Ford, the president of the United States at the time, echoed that sentiment, describing the hiring that day as "welcome news for baseball fans across the nation." Robinson, who was given just a one-year contract upon his hiring, said, "I just hope baseball people don't say, 'All right, Frank Robinson is the first Black manager, we have one, that's it.'"

Robinson didn't even last three full seasons in Cleveland. And when he was fired in 1977 with the club having posted a 26-31 record—after he had guided the Indians to a winning mark in 1976 (81-78)—it left zero Black managers on the bench. The Chicago White Sox would make Larry Doby the second Black skipper in the game on June 30, 1978, just as he had become the second Black *player* in the game after Jackie Robinson in 1947. Nearly five decades later, following the retirement of Dusty Baker, there remain only two Black managers working today, both in Los Angeles: Roberts with the Dodgers and Ron Washington with the Angels.

Managers throughout history have come in all kinds of shapes and sizes, equipped with different personalities and skill sets. There never has been a one-size-fits-all because each organization has unique needs and different groups of players require different leadership styles. And as the seasons change, so, too, do those needs and requirements evolve. What the Yankees needed in 1977 is different from what they required in 1997 and still different from what they need today. But while the job has changed drastically, one thing has not: Managers still don't come in many colors.

The season of 1977 was an expansion year, with the Toronto Blue Jays and Seattle Mariners swelling the number of MLB teams to twenty-six. That, of course, increased the job pool for managers—and, potentially, for minority managers. Cito Gaston would lead the Blue Jays to their only two World Series wins in short order, in 1992 and 1993, becoming the first Black manager to win a Fall Classic. In Seattle, Maury Wills would become the second manager—and first Black manager—in franchise history in 1980. Though, following the familiar pattern, Wills wasn't exactly given a wide berth. He managed the final 58 games in 1980 and then the first 24 in the strike-shortened 1981 season (going 6-18) before his axing. He also received a two-game suspension from the American League shortly before the firing for ordering the Seattle grounds crew to enlarge the Kingdome batter's boxes.

That transgression occurred after Oakland complained that Seattle's Tom Paciorek repeatedly stepped out of the batter's box while hitting. The A's manager that year just happened to be Billy Martin, temporarily working elsewhere in between his multiple Yankees stints. And it was Martin who busted Wills. He suspected that the Mariners would attempt to game the batter's box after his loud complaints and, thus, asked umpire Bill Kunkel to measure it before the game. This wasn't exactly as scandalous as the 2017 Houston Astros' video-cheating, trash-can-banging season that wound up getting managers A .J. Hinch and Alex Cora (coaching for Hinch at the time before managing Boston) suspended for an entire season in 2020. In actuality, it was more like the beginnings of Watergate, the "second-rate burglary" part. While the Astros' scandal had deep ties to multiple perpetrators, Wills's brainstorm came in the days when managers mostly worked alone.

Managers had all the power back then.

"Tony La Russa always used to mention the managers were all one name," says Dave Dombrowski, the Philadelphia Phillies' president of baseball operations who started his career with the Chicago White Sox in 1978 and is destined for the Hall of Fame one day. "You knew who Earl was. You knew who Billy was. You knew who Sparky was. Gene Mauch. You could just call them by their first names. They were much more front-and-center of the organization and making decisions hand-in-hand with the general manager. But when it came to running the game, it was the manager. That was it."

Billy's Yankees won the World Series title in the autumn of 1977. It was their first championship since 1962, when a Bronx Bombers team piloted by Ralph "The Major" Houk—now *there's* a strong Skipper nickname—won a seven-game thriller over Willie Mays, Willie McCovey, and the San Francisco Giants. It was the Yankees' first title under owner George Steinbrenner, and it was the autumn in which Jackson came to be known as "Mr. October"—a moniker that is stenciled onto the Astros cap he frequently wears today as a special adviser to Houston owner Jim Crane. Jackson smashed three home runs in the deciding Game 6 to lift the Yankees in an 8–4 clincher. It was a power display for the ages, and it came just four months after a power struggle of a wholly different sort. In a nationally televised game in Fenway Park that June, Martin had embarrassed his new free agent Superduperstar (as *Sports Illustrated* had dubbed Jackson a few years earlier) by removing him from a game in the middle of the sixth inning, for what Martin judged to be a lack of hustle in right field while Jackson was going after a Jim Rice single that turned into a double. Paul Blair jogged out to replace Jackson, who returned to the dugout and immediately engaged in a shouting match with the manager. The pugnacious Martin and the proud Jackson nearly came to blows until coaches Elston Howard and Yogi Berra intervened.

In the heat of the moment, Martin and the hundreds of others who have sat in managers' chairs sometimes find it difficult to take a breath and remember the instructive words of one of their Hall of Fame predecessors. "The secret of successful managing," Casey Stengel, whose Hall of Fame managerial career included twelve seasons piloting the Yankees, once warned, "is to keep the five guys who hate you away from the four guys who haven't made up their minds."

Among others, Stengel for a time during his Yankees years managed a young, brash second baseman named Billy Martin. Who, as things turned out, wound up on far too many enemies' lists himself.

"I have nothing good to say about him," Jackson says today. "I don't want to have to dance around it. It's not worth it."

Following the newly christened Mr. October's three home runs and the Yankees' first World Series title in fifteen years, on one of the organization's greatest nights, Martin wound up leaving the team's victory party after an argument with his wife and finished the evening drinking alone at his neighborhood bar, the Bottom of the Barrel, across the river in New Jersey.

Managing was a lonely job back then, and despite being surrounded by more "support" people than ever, it remains so today, in a wholly different way. "A manager's job is simple," Weaver once said. "For 162 games, you try not to screw up all that smart stuff your organization did last December."

As usual, Weaver was ahead of his time. If only he knew then how "simple" the job would remain in that vein, as sea changes soon would sweep across the game.

CHAPTER 1

OFFICE SPACES
AND OFFSPRING

Some forty-five years after Billy Martin went after Reggie Jackson in the Yankees dugout in Fenway Park smack in the middle of a game in June 1977, one of his successors spent time in the middle of another Yankees game giving a tour of his home office on an ESPN *Sunday Night Baseball* telecast.

"This has turned into a really cool space for me," Aaron Boone, the manager and tour guide, told Karl Ravech, the TV guy, in a pre-taped bit that ran during the game. Boone talked about how the team photographer picks out pictures to show him and how, over the years, Boone has "added and pulled" framed pictures on the Yankee Stadium manager's office wall. There are various pictures of Boone interacting with current and former players as well as with "Mr. Torre," as Boone respectfully still calls his former manager Joe.

The tour continues with a framed photo from the 2003 All-Star Game at U.S. Cellular Field in Chicago that includes Aaron, then an

All-Star with Cincinnati; his brother Bret, then an All-Star with Seattle; the boys' grandfather, Ray, who was a two-time All-Star; and their father, Bob, a four-time All-Star. The Boone family was the first to send three generations of players to the All-Star Game.

"That's a very meaningful picture," Aaron said. "My granddad actually passed away about a year after that."

The differences between yesterday and today in some ways are as stark as two words: office and space. In your father's time, and in *his* father's time, managers and everyone else did much of their work in *offices*. Offices were utilitarian. Blue-collar. Places where work was simple and straightforward. Today the sons and daughters of these office workers multitask at standing desks or while comfortably reclined on couches in places now referred to as *spaces*. Spaces conjure up thoughts of a place where one simply exists—and of blurred lines between where work ends and outside life begins. It is altogether fitting because in our Digital Age, with social media and the constant temptation to check emails at any hour of the day and night, there is no quitting time. We're all on, or feel like we're expected to be on, around the clock.

Baseball is about generations, and people, and lineages. Boone, both in respecting the past and carrying on his own family's legacy, nevertheless is moving forward doing things in a way vastly different than both Martin in a Bronx Bombers uniform and his own father while Bob was managing in Kansas City and Cincinnati. Bob Boone and Billy Martin, when they weren't orchestrating games in the dugout, could be found working through things in the manager's *office*. Aaron Boone and his peers figure things out in the manager's... *space*? It's apt because the *space* the manager directs from today has changed shape and remains fluid. Discussions are different today in our own families—our fathers kept track of batting averages and RBI, whereas today those are less important than on-base percentages and OPS (on-base percentage plus slugging percentage). It has changed the conversations even within families who are baseball fans, let alone those within the industry.

There have been only five father-son duos who have served as major-league managers since the inception of the sport as a professional league in 1903, and two of those five were carrying on together recently, with Boone managing the Yankees and David Bell piloting the Cincinnati Reds for six seasons until he was fired near the end of the 2024 campaign. Bob Boone managed Kansas City (1995–1997) and Cincinnati (2001–2003). Buddy Bell, David's father, managed in Detroit (1996–1998), Colorado (2000–2002), and Kansas City (2005–2007).

The three other duos were George Sisler (St. Louis Browns, 1924–1926) and his son Dick (Cincinnati, 1964–1965), Bob Skinner (Philadelphia, 1968–1969; San Diego, 1977) and his son Joel (Cleveland, 2002), and Felipe Alou (Montreal, 1992–2001; San Francisco, 2003–2006) and his son Luis Rojas (New York Mets, 2020–2021).

Now retired with traces of infield dirt still in their pores, Buddy Bell, seventy-three, and Bob Boone, seventy-seven, watch everything during the summers. *Everything.* Buddy figured he could count on one hand the number of pitches he missed while David was managing the Reds from 2019 to 2024. Part of that is because he worked in the organization alongside David for many of those years. Buddy was a vice president and senior adviser to the general manager in Cincinnati until he resigned during the summer of 2023 simply because he was tired of the grind and wanted more family time. But most of his rapt attention to the Reds was because David is his son, and the Bells are a close-knit family and baseball is the family business.

"First of all, it's really great to be able to see my son every day," Buddy Bell was saying during a spring training conversation in Goodyear, Arizona, as he entered his last year with the Reds. "To talk to him about not just baseball, but life in general. I'm just so lucky to be able to do that."

Bob Boone watches every Yankees game from his home in the San Diego area, arranging his entire days around first pitches. And though he and Aaron may not talk every day, it's close. The three-hour time difference between the East and West Coasts often plays into their favor, in some ways helping Aaron to unwind after games back east.

"I would say it's actually been one of the neat things about this job that I've enjoyed the most," Aaron Boone says. "Almost every night, especially when I'm at home, I'll call him on the drive home because he watches every out of every game. He absorbs it. He is rooting us on. So one of the ways I connect with him, especially being on the other side of the country, is we just maybe talk about the game. Occasionally, he gives his opinion on certain things but, honestly, it's more him understanding the seat I'm in and having the ability to relate. It's less about the Xs and Os. We certainly talk about the game and the individuals and how they're doing, and, man, this guy, wow, he was great tonight, he's swinging great. But it's more just talking about the game and it allows us to connect. It's more about being a supportive dad, passionate over every detail."

Ray Boone, Aaron's grandfather, broke into the majors with Cleveland in 1948. It was the start of a thirteen-year career that also took him to Detroit, the Chicago White Sox, the Kansas City A's, the Milwaukee Braves, and the Boston Red Sox. He got one at bat as Cleveland won the 1948 World Series, striking out against Warren Spahn in the eighth inning of an 11–5 loss in Game 5. Mostly a third baseman and shortstop, Boone led the American League with 116 RBI in 1955 when he was with the Tigers. A native of San Diego, Ray married his high school sweetheart, Patsy, and they had three children. Son Bob followed Ray into the majors in 1972, beginning a nineteen-year career with Philadelphia that eventually led him to the California Angels and Kansas City. A seven-time Gold Glove catcher, Boone brilliantly handled NL Cy Young winner Steve Carlton, Dick Ruthven, Bob Walk, closer Tug McGraw, and the rest of the staff as the Phillies won the 1980 World Series. Bob's son Bret debuted in the majors with Seattle in 1992, beginning a fourteen-year career that also included stops in

Cincinnati, Atlanta, San Diego, and Minnesota. A second baseman, Bret won four Gold Gloves and was a two-time Silver Slugger. Younger brother Aaron, also an infielder, debuted in Cincinnati in 1997. He also played for the Yankees, Cleveland, Florida, Washington, and Houston during his twelve-year career.

Gus Bell was a center fielder who broke into the majors two years after Ray Boone, in 1950. He helped the Reds win the 1961 pennant and knocked in 100 or more runs four times while producing a .281 lifetime average. He played fifteen seasons with Pittsburgh, Cincinnati, the New York Mets, and the Milwaukee Braves. A native of Louisville, Kentucky, David Russell "Gus" Bell earned his nickname because he was a fan of Gus Mancuso, a longtime major-league catcher. Bell's son, Buddy, broke in with Cleveland in 1972 and over the next eighteen seasons would win six Gold Gloves as a third baseman and earn five All-Star nods. After Cleveland, Buddy played for Texas and Cincinnati, with a brief stop in Houston at career's end. Two of Buddy's sons, David and Mike, then made it three generations of Bells in the majors, just like the Boones. David debuted in 1995 and played twelve seasons with Cleveland, St. Louis, Seattle, San Francisco, Philadelphia, and Milwaukee. He was the Giants' third baseman in 2002 when they lost an excruciating seven-game World Series to the Anaheim Angels. Mike made it to the majors for just nineteen games with Cincinnati in 2000 before moving on to a highly respected coaching and executive career in Arizona and Minnesota. In 2021, he tragically passed from cancer at the age of forty-six. The outpouring of tributes across the game spoke both to Mike's singular, beloved, compassionate personality and to the respect engendered by the Bell family over the generations.

In so many ways, baseball is the same as regular life only with the volume turned up. The decades have provided the Bells and the Boones, like other families, with so much joy, reward, heartbreak, satisfaction, smiles, tears, and, most of all, rich, full lives. Only theirs have played out very publicly on baseball's grand stage. It has been incredibly meaningful to be in the family baseball business, but sometimes uncomfortably so.

"I really struggle answering that question because it is important," Buddy Bell says. "Baseball is, like, huge to our family. It's given us a ton of opportunities not only to make a good living, but the people that we meet, this game has given us so many great friends. So, yeah, baseball is really important for our family. However, I don't back my car out of this lot and drive home thinking about baseball much. You know, it's important, but it's not. I probably go instantly, 'Hey, I wonder what my daughter did today,' so I'll call her. Or call my son Ricky and see how he's doing. I think sometimes people get the wrong impression that just because our family is in baseball, that's all we are. And that's certainly not the case. I don't want to downplay the fact that this game has been really good to us. But we've been good to it, as well."

Not only did David Bell inherit an outhouse situation that was nowhere close to the penthouse suite Aaron Boone was able to walk into, but also unlike Aaron, Bell apprenticed as a manager in Cincinnati's minor-league system from 2009 to 2012, then spent 2013 as the Chicago Cubs' third-base coach and 2015 to 2017 as Mike Matheny's bench coach in St. Louis. Before that, following the 2009 season, he managed the Peoria Saguaros in the Arizona Fall League.

There are so many different paths to the manager's office, or *space*, and so much factors into the equation of whether it will work. Working with typically limited Midwest resources—from 2019 to 2024 the Reds ranked 15th, 11th, 17th, 21st, 26th, and 25th in major-league payroll—Bell's teams nevertheless mostly outperformed projections. The Reds finished over .500 in three of his first five seasons, including 82-80 in 2023 after a disastrous 62-100 finish in 2022. In July 2023, the Reds awarded him a three-year extension that takes him through 2026. But when the Reds fell to fourth place in the NL Central in 2024 at 77-85, they cashiered Bell with just five games left in the season. To replace him, they lured Terry Francona out of retirement.

"I've enjoyed the relationships with our writers," David Bell told me during our extended conversation in the summer of 2023, speaking of one of the aspects of the job that surprised him. "Cincinnati's obviously different than New York. But I've actually enjoyed that part of the job way more than I thought. The game itself is still the best part, the three hours of the game. But the one surprise for me is I'm really loving the challenge of figuring out how to lead. I'd played the game, knew what that was all about. But I'd never done anything like this before. I was kind of thrown into managing a Double-A team, so that process over the years of really searching and learning as much as I can, picking people's brains, learning from all of the experiences, I feel like that's never ending. That could keep me going wanting to do this job for a long, long time. You feel as you learn you're growing for yourself and for all of these people you have a chance to lead and to impact. That's been the bigger part of why I like the job more than I thought. I knew the game would be fun."

David Bell played for an incredible array of championship managers during his career—Mike Hargrove, Tony La Russa, Lou Piniella, Dusty Baker, Charlie Manuel, and Ned Yost among them—and all, of course, were big influences. He took pieces from each. But his father, by far, is his biggest influence.

"This is probably not a great thing, but I'll say it anyway," David says. "There are very few people that I have 100 percent trust in what they say. So there's very few people that I really care what they think. And he's in that very, very small group of people. You get questioned a lot, there's a lot going on in this job, and I only care about what a few people think. Certainly everyone in our clubhouse. But, beyond that, it's my family. As far as baseball goes, if I ask him a question, or if he says something, it just flat out means more than anyone else. I think he's the best baseball man I've ever been around. Not only the knowledge—and one thing he has that I don't have, he does not miss anything on the field, he sees *everything*. Plus, I always know where it's coming from. It's coming from a good place and consistent values."

Though their careers overlapped throughout the 1970s and 1980s, Bob Boone and Buddy Bell don't know each other well. Their families would make their biggest connection with their third generation, when David Bell and Bret Boone were teammates on Seattle's sensational 116-46 team under Lou Piniella in 2001. Boone played second base and led the AL with 141 RBI that summer. Bell contributed 15 homers, 64 RBI, and metronomic defense.

Both were established veterans by then—Boone was thirty-two, Bell twenty-eight—and obviously well aware that they were descendants of baseball royalty. But they didn't talk about that. Instead, with lockers across from each other, they'd mostly keep their quiet conversations in the present.

"We laugh about it because everybody else talks about it," Bret Boone says. "We both are very proud of our families, of course. David to this day is one of my favorite teammates I've ever had. Top ten. We had a really good relationship, he was a really good player. He was the unsung hero of that 2001 team. And I tell him this all the time: 'Do you realize how weird of a person you are, David Bell?'

"He knows he's strange. He's serious as a heart attack as far as being in the moment and taking his job seriously, one of the most serious I've ever been around. At the same time, he has a wry sense of humor. Something would happen in a game and I'd look over and say, 'Did you see that?' And he would say, 'Of course I saw that. You *know* I saw that.'"

From his perspective, Bell remembers having great fun with Boone that summer. Their personalities are different, but they came together in an opposites-attract sort of way. Bell the buttoned-down, organized one. Boone, the casual, free-flowing fun lover. Yet that unspoken family connection always was there.

"Without really speaking about it too often, we had kind of a better understanding of each other, knowing what each other's lives have been like, on some level," says Bell, who recently guested on Boone's podcast with more laughter and memories.

The Mariners in those days had little lights inside their lockers. Each night after they showered and were leaving for the evening, Bell would change into his street clothes and then holler, "Boone! What do you have for me tonight?" Then, once he had his teammate's attention, Bell would very methodically and dramatically make sure that Boone saw him click off the light switch before offering, "I'll see ya tomorrow, Boone," and exiting through the clubhouse kitchen.

"He would turn that light off to leave," Boone says, still chuckling. "And then all was right in the world."

———

The light clicked on for Aaron Boone, somewhat unexpectedly, as the Yankees' manager in 2018. In some ways, for the Yankees to hand the house keys to a man who had never before managed or even spent one day on a major-league coaching staff was shocking. These were the Yankees. This, until now, was not an entry-level job. For the previous twenty-two seasons, the militaristic Joe Girardi, who had managed one season in Florida before moving to New York, and the Hall of Famer Joe Torre had shaped what the idea of a manager in pinstripes *looked* like. But Brian Cashman, who had been leaning harder into analytics for several years, was reshaping and modernizing the baseball operations flowchart. So while bringing in a new manager directly from the ESPN broadcast booth might have been stunning to others, maybe it wasn't so much for a man who had complimented White Sox president Kenny Williams on his hire of the raw Robin Ventura back in 2012 as an "obvious" choice.

"I'm the longest-tenured general manager in the game," Cashman says. "I've been around the block enough. If I believed in it as strongly as I did early in my career, I wouldn't have had the backbone then to push it because of the risk."

But Cashman no longer was early in his tenure. He was two decades down the road from having succeeded Bob Watson as the

Yankees general manager in 1998. He saw where the game was, and he was not about to get stuck in the past.

"I knew he was the right person for the right job at the right time," Cashman says. "He fit all the requirements despite not having any record of managing."

Boone was just forty-five, sharp as a spike, had retired as a player just nine years earlier, and, as part of ESPN's crew, had spent hundreds of hours over the previous few seasons with managers across the game, soaking in a wealth of information regarding leadership, tricks of the trade, and manager-player relations. Furthermore, he was a Yankees hero: It was Boone whose eleventh-inning walk-off homer in Game 7 of the ALCS—the Pedro Martinez–Grady Little game—crushed the Red Sox. Beyond that, Boone's character was irreproachable: Three months after that epic moment, in January, Boone blew out his left knee playing basketball. That injury cost him the 2004 season and his playing career with the Yankees, who released him and traded for Alex Rodriguez that winter. With a $5.75 million deal for 2004, Boone could have lied and made up a story for the Yankees regarding how he was injured that off-season. Instead, he told Cashman the truth and cost himself millions.

"I don't think he gets an interview for the Yankees managerial job without being honest right there," Bret Boone says. "The Yankees released him. It cost him $3 million. How many people, when they're faced with losing $3 million, would fess up to the truth? Not many. That's a Bob Boone move right there. Bob Boone will go through a yellow light and call the police on himself. It's how he's always been. It's a little bit of geekism, but at the same time it's an honorable trait. It's a tribute to how he lived his life. Aaron is in a similar vein."

At the time Aaron interviewed for the Yankees job, he was looking to make a transition out of the broadcasting world and back into the heart of baseball. One of the mantras for ex-players and managers in the broadcasting business is that standard exit line as they leave the stadium following a game: What a joy it is to be involved but not have to worry about the pressure of wins and losses. But by this time, Boone missed the wins and losses. He *wanted* them.

Things culminated as Boone and Dan Shulman worked the radio side of the 2017 Houston–Los Angeles World Series for ESPN.

"We're in our pregame meetings every day with the managers and, with A. J. Hinch, he and I played on the same junior Olympic team," Boone says. "He went to Stanford, and Doc Roberts went to UCLA and played against me at USC. They're my age, and they're not peers—I consider them friends. I just felt like, having conversations with them that fall and having this pull to get back into the game, I felt like in a lot of ways, I was looking in the mirror."

Boone actually was down the road with one team to join their front office at that point. But then, shortly after the World Series, Cashman phoned him about the Yanks manager job.

"So I put on hold that front-office position and, over the next two, three weeks things unfolded, I got the job, and the rest is history," says Aaron, who preferred not to name the club he was close to joining as an executive.

Once he learned that Aaron was interviewing for the Yankees job, at least one man had every confidence that he would get it—even with no managerial experience. That man managed Boone in Cincinnati from 2001 to 2003. That man is his father.

"When he was interviewing for that job, I'd talk to people and say Aaron is going to get this job," Bob Boone says. "He's had a knack his whole life. People love him. He knows how to deal with people. He is tremendous with people. It's the way he was even back in high school. Everybody loved playing with him. He knew how to present himself. You want to see him.

"The art of it is how you handle people. That's all Aaron."

In the eight or so hours he spent interviewing with Cashman and various other departments, Boone impressed one Yankees executive after another. And Bret is correct in one regard: Aaron's honesty about his knee injury years earlier was something that Cashman took into account.

"Without a doubt," Cashman says. "When you partner with some-one…I know we get accused of managing from the front office. None of it is true. So at the end of the day, I want to partner with someone I can trust, someone who can do the job, someone who has similar beliefs and core principles when the bullets start flying, which they will—baseball is a sport and a lot of things can go wrong—I want to know that person is tough enough and strong enough to withstand the temptations of covering his ass and falsely pointing the finger elsewhere."

Character matters.

"Everybody can do kumbaya," Cashman continues. "But in reality, things never play out the way you want them to. There's going to be turbulence. You want who you're partnered with to be there through thick and thin. Without a doubt, the way Aaron Boone conducted himself, when many people wouldn't do what he did, spoke volumes. I think he's one of the best managers in the game. I'm proud of all of our hires, but this one was a lot more controversial and I feel he isn't getting his due because ultimately we're the Yankees and we haven't won a championship. But that's not his doing."

The job Aaron Boone now performs in the Bronx is different from the job Joe Torre performed, even though on paper it looks the same. There is far more media. More noise. The Yankees are far deeper into analytics now. And though they are still owned by the Steinbrenner family, the buttoned-up, corporate leadership of Hal is vastly quieter and less chaotic than that of his wildly emotional (and whip-smart) late father, George.

"The only thing that is consistent is you're managing the New York Yankees and there's a great deal of pressure to be successful and there's no getting around it," Torre says. "Of course, I had George always there, albeit it wasn't the same George as Billy Martin had. I caught George on the back nine. Not that he still wasn't totally in charge. But it wasn't the same George that went back and forth with Billy. The difference is, and I knew Billy fairly well, Billy didn't like to be told what to do and I acknowledged the fact that I had a boss. I'm not sure if Billy ever wanted to have a boss."

When Boone joined the Yankees as a player on August 1, 2003, after the Reds dealt him at the trade deadline, one of the first things Torre told him upon his joining the team in Oakland was to make sure he did not read the papers.

"So now one of the things that I talk a lot about with our players is to be careful with social media," Boone says. "It can get noisy out there, and if it is something you think is affecting your play or you're having a hard time handling it, you need to have the wherewithal to stay away from it. You need to use social media for positive things, whether it's information, getting something out for a charity, or connecting with family members and friends across the country. Try and use it for positive because you can go down a rabbit hole on social media. For us, it was papers back in the day. Now, it's social media."

Derek Jeter once said the worst invention during his career was the cell phone camera, because as soon as selfies became the equivalent of autographs, players had to beware because late-night bar photos—and pictures in other locales—could be misconstrued and put them in a bad light. An innocent selfie could become a nefarious tool for gossip column fodder, blackmail, or worse. That translates across the board, and into Boone's modern warning to players. Facebook was launched on February 4, 2004, less than a month after Boone's fateful knee injury ended his first chapter with the Yankees. Twitter publicly launched two years later, in July 2006. Instagram debuted in October 2010, with twenty-five thousand users, and less than three months later it had more than one million users. TikTok started in September 2016, just before Boone's managerial debut in the Bronx in 2018.

As time marches on, there are other differences. Old-school managers like Torre and Bob Boone had more autonomy in choosing their coaching staffs. In both Kansas City and Cincinnati, the hitting and pitching coaches were in place when Bob was brought aboard as manager, but he was given the latitude to choose the rest of his coaching staff. And when hitting coach Ken Griffey Sr. left Cincinnati in 2003, Boone was able to hand pick Jim Lefebvre to replace him.

In New York, Willie Randolph and Tony Cloninger were already a part of the Yankees staff when they hired Torre in 1996, and he kept them. It was his idea to add Don Zimmer as bench coach "because he managed in both leagues and I had only managed in the National League," Torre says. It was more difficult convincing Zimmer to take the job than people remember because Zimmer was friends with Steinbrenner and was wary that the Boss was foisting him on Torre. The new manager brought Mel Stottlemyre aboard as pitching coach, not realizing at the time that Stottlemyre was on the outs with the Yankees and that had to be patched up. He brought in Chris Chambliss because he had managed Chambliss in Atlanta and the former first baseman was a former Yankee. Stottlemyre remained as the pitching coach for each of Torre's first ten seasons; Zimmer was the bench coach for Torre's first eight years.

"I liked to bring people aboard that I was comfortable with because I liked to delegate as a manager," Torre says. "I felt it was important."

Under Boone, and given the Yankees' modern bent toward the game's conference-room decisions, the team has cycled through several coaches. In fact, the only staff constant from Boone's first season in 2018 to 2024 was bullpen coach Mike Harkey. Otherwise, there was complete staff turnover, and multiple turnovers in some coaching positions.

"I would say most coaching decisions are collaborative," Boone says. "I'm probably as big a driver of it as anyone, in the process. We've had some turnover. When I first came in I hand-selected a few guys, but they all went through the interview process. Everyone signs off on it. We've had some turnover and I've probably had as strong a say as anyone about who we're going to have, but it is something we do as a group, go through the interview processes as a group and try and come up with the best person."

Boone's job also is vastly different in so many ways than the job his father performed while managing the Kansas City Royals in the late 1990s and the Reds in the early 2000s. It has to be, because the game has changed. Aaron is far less inclined to sacrifice-bunt a runner from first to second. One of Bob Boone's biggest managerial influences was the great Gene Mauch, who was the Angels' skipper when Boone signed as a free agent there in 1982 and remained manager through 1987, covering six of Boone's seven seasons in Southern California. Mauch was a devotee of small ball, and if there was a runner on first base with nobody out in the second inning, it was a slam dunk that the bunt was on. Bob managed similarly. Today, of course, Aaron says he probably wouldn't do that unless there was a very specific situation that called for it. The game evolves, and so, too, do the generations—even when it is all in the family.

External pressures Aaron faces are far different from those his father faced, going well beyond the standard talk-radio criticisms. Boone in 2023 managed a team with an overall payroll of $278.6 million, third-highest in baseball, with individual salaries as high as Aaron Judge's $40 million, Gerrit Cole's $36 million, and Giancarlo Stanton's $32 million. These are unique challenges inherent in today's game, especially in the Bronx, and they only ratchet up World Series pressure. During Bob's last year in Cincinnati in 2003, the Reds' total payroll was $59 million, seventeenth overall (and yes, the Yankees' $125.9 million payroll ranked No. 1 that year).

His father's biggest influence on his managerial skills isn't so much strategic as it is force of personality, Aaron says. What could have been an awkward situation when Bob was named as Cincinnati's skipper in 2001, replacing Jack McKeon, never went that way. Aaron already was an established veteran player, and while conventional thinking might have been that his father would be harder on him than the other Reds, Bob wasn't. He treated Aaron just the same as everyone else.

And a beautiful bonus for Aaron was that he got to spend extra time with Mom and Dad away from the field over lunches, dinners, and impromptu visits. Another situation Aaron was concerned with never developed, either: Inevitably in this game, players over the course of a long season will become moody or angry if their playing time isn't what they think it should be—and then they'll begin griping about the manager, who metes out that playing time. Aaron never wanted his teammates to feel like they couldn't be themselves around him with his dad managing, and he says, "Maybe to my teammates' credit, or it may be delusional, but I never felt that way. So for me, it was pretty easy. It helps that, at the end of the day, my dad is a really good guy. So it's not like there's too much hatred there, ever."

Boone never got involved as a go-between when his father was managing, never was asked by another player to talk to his father on the player's behalf.

"I felt like, as one of the team leaders, I had a voice, and I just looked at it as I had a pretty good relationship with our manager," Aaron says.

The Reds went 66-96 in 2001, Bob's first season managing, then improved to 78-84 the following summer before a 46-68 start in 2003 cost Bob his job. What Aaron soaked in from his father and manager during that time, especially in that awful season of 2001, was how very consistent emotionally Bob remained day in and day out.

"There wasn't a lot of volatility with him," Aaron says. "That's one thing I've tried to take with me. We're all human, we have human moments where you get frustrated or whatever. But I would like to think that if you walked in here in the middle of us on a winning streak, or if we've lost five of six and we're going through a tough stretch, hopefully the players coming through the clubhouse know what they're going to get from me. They're not going to be on this emotional roller coaster from me, and that's something I took from him."

Basically, what Boone has attempted to create with the Yankees is a place where, no matter what kind of season a player is having—great, average, or disappointing—and whether a player is going through something positive off the field or something exceptionally difficult, when he walks through the clubhouse doors he can be comfortable and be himself.

"There's a lot of noise, especially here in New York, so we try to strike that balance between this being a place you enjoy and look forward to and can find some kind of refuge while also creating a very hypercompetitive environment," Boone says. "I feel like one thing we've done really well here over the last few years is create that environment where guys compete really hard and also, for the most part, it's a place that guys enjoy being each and every day. That no matter what's going on, you look forward to walking in those doors every day."

It wasn't until his seventh season, in 2024, that Boone finally managed the Yankees into their first World Series since 2009. They were steamrolled by a stronger and much more fundamentally sound Dodgers team in five games, leaving Boone "heartbroken" for his players who "poured so much into this" and, ridiculously, causing some to question whether the Yankees should even pick up the option on his contract for 2025. Always, there are critics—and with more teams and more playoff spots than ever, Yankees fans nevertheless remain the gatekeepers of vigilantly unrealistic expectations—but under Boone, the Yankees now have had two 100-win seasons and three 90-win seasons (and in one other summer, 2020, they played only a 60-game schedule because of the pandemic). He is immensely popular as a leader within the clubhouse, and the players generally respond to Boone. One tiny snapshot in an ocean of moments: During a game in Milwaukee in September 2022, Boone went to the mound intent on pulling starter Jameson Taillon with two out and a Brewer on third in the fifth inning. The Yankees trailed 4-1 at the time, and the right-handed Taillon, who went 14-5 with a 3.91 ERA that season, argued to remain in the game, insisting he could get the lefty Rowdy Tellez. Boone's intent was to play matchups and go lefty-on-lefty. But he read something in Taillon's eyes and left him in the game. Taillon did, in fact, retire Tellez on a line drive to deep center field to end the inning.

"When he left me out there, I was like, I want to make him proud," Taillon says. "I want him to make the right decision. I liked him so much. And I respect him so much. I wanted him to be rewarded for this decision."

Bret Boone sees this in many Yankees.

"He has a way about him," Aaron's brother says. "I think his players really respect him and really want to play for him. That's a huge thing to have as a manager. Bruce Bochy has that. You never met a man who has a negative thing to say about Bochy. You never met a man who has a negative thing to say about Dusty Baker. They both have that It factor. There's not many players I've ever met who don't have something nice to say about Aaron Boone, whether they were a teammate or an opponent, and that's an innate thing he was born with."

Aaron Boone will tell you that he didn't burn to become a manager his entire life. It was only after he was finished as a player and facing that what-do-I-do-for-the-rest-of-my-life question that he took his time to methodically decide. He figured broadcasting would be the natural early avenue as opportunities were there immediately, and that it might open doors to more as his desires changed. He was exactly right.

Bret is not surprised by where the path has led his brother.

"Aaron was a different kid," Bret says. "I was that kid where baseball was everything. I'd eat it and sleep it, all I did was baseball, sports. I'd let Aaron tag along, he was four years younger and it was not cool for a junior in high school to let a seventh grader tag along. But my buddies all liked Aaron. He'd play."

And if not, Aaron would sit on the sidelines and voice play-by-play, channeling an all-time Philadelphia favorite from when the family lived in Philadelphia from the early 1970s until Bob left the Phillies after the 1981 season.

"He was imitating Harry Kalas from the age of five," Bret says. "When he went to the booth, it didn't surprise me because that was innate in him.

Then when he went into managing, with everything that led up to that, I remember talking to him and saying, you know, usually your first job isn't the Yankees. Usually, it's what Dad did—Kansas City, Cincinnati. Or what Mark Kotsay is enduring in Oakland. The way Aaron got that first job, and I see Dave Roberts in LA getting into that position, those are very special, coveted spots. Everybody doesn't get that their first time."

———

It is a Wednesday evening in May 2023, the Yankees are in last place in the AL East to start the night, and frustration is palpable everywhere. But unlike in New York, where manager Aaron Boone was vociferously booed two nights earlier and then savaged in the press for hooking starter Domingo Germán after only 88 pitches with a lead and one out in the ninth only to watch the bullpen blow it in a 3–2 loss to Cleveland, the frustration inside the home of Bob and Sue Boone as the Yankees and Guardians begin their series finale is for different reasons.

We are watching the game in Bob's memorabilia room because one of his nine televisions, the main big screen in the family room, is on the injured list—just like so many of Aaron's players. Aaron Judge, Giancarlo Stanton, Josh Donaldson, pitchers Luis Severino, Carlos Rodón, Frankie Montas, Tommy Kahnle, Bob's giant flat-screen…all out.

"This team gets hurt an unbelievable amount," says Bob, sitting in one of two plush leather recliners. "They don't even say Stanton's name anymore on the broadcasts. And then they shut Judge down. I was hurt a lot and I never missed a game. Gene Mauch would always ask, 'How are you? Can you play?' I'd tell him, 'I can't run very fast but I can play.'"

Clarke Schmidt is starting tonight in a game the Yankees—and their manager—badly need. The Guardians are countering with ace Shane Bieber.

It is a nightly family link, these Yankees games. As Aaron works under the spotlight of wherever the team is playing, Bob and Sue are right here in front of their flat-screen in suburban San Diego. Bret, who lives a short drive from his parents, perpetually is paying attention and often phones his father for check-ins during the games.

It is routine family life for the Boones.

To this point, by the way, Aaron has 27 ejections in 738 career games as manager. Bob had only 8 in 815 games. I kid Bob about being the best-behaved Boone.

"Aaron is very passionate," Sue interjects. "Bob and him are so much alike. I'm surprised Bob was not thrown out more. Aaron is very even keel. He cares about every guy on that team. But if you push him, the clouds come out. I have to say, even though I'm his mom, he's usually right. When he has a legitimate beef, I think he's generally right."

When I relay this comment to Cashman later, he laughs knowingly and agrees wholeheartedly.

"I love the fact that he lets loose on behalf of his players and our organization," Cashman says. "I *love* that. I think it's fantastic. MLB's really come down hard on trying to rein him in. I don't want him to change. That's stuff you can't get in an interview. I had no idea what that was gonna look like. It seems like he's got a lot of Bobby Cox in him. He essentially launched Jomboy Media with his tirades. That's what made Jomboy famous, when he unpacked that whole thing and unleashed the reading of the lips."

My guys are bleeping "savages" in that bleeping box, Aaron Boone screamed at plate umpire Brennan Miller on that July day in 2019. A hot mic picked all of it up. Jomboy put words to the video and it played like a lovely, unforgettable symphonic harmony across the internet. Legendary.

Sue is in and out of the room during the game, I assume because without use of the main television and with Bob and me occupying the two recliners in the memorabilia room, space is tight. Or she may just have other things to do while she multitasks and watches the game on her cell phone in the kitchen. Later this summer, she and her husband will celebrate their fifty-sixth wedding anniversary. So many of those nights are spent just like this.

Bob, he watches everything. Details, such as how each Yankees hitter picks up his front leg as he steps into the ball, do not escape him. Bob was into his thirties when he learned a few things about that, he says. Fascinatingly, he learned from watching the late Hall of Famer Tony Gwynn, one of the game's all-time good guys, great hitters, and a man Bob somehow never got the chance to meet. But what he learned from Gwynn, he says, pushed him along to a career-high .295 batting average in 392 plate appearances at age forty in 1988, and then he hit .274 in 469 plate appearances in 1989.

Six years later, Bob was named Kansas City's manager, and he and Aaron have one thing in common: Just like his son, he never managed in the minor leagues.

"It was easy for me," Boone says, smiling. "I invited Gene Mauch to be my bench coach. He's the smartest baseball guy I've ever been around. He was with me early in a game and we were watching the pitcher and I was thinking, 'Gee, should I take him out?' I turned to Gene and asked, 'What do you think?' And he said, 'I'm not managing, you are.'"

As a father, that is the attitude Bob mostly takes with Aaron. When Aaron took the Yankees job in 2018, he was all in in every way. Following several years of living in Southern California and Scottsdale, Arizona, the Aaron Boone family decided to move back to Connecticut. Now, during those late-night, postgame phone calls that keep the bonds tight as Aaron drives home and digests things with his father, Bob tries to listen more than talk.

"If I've got a little question, I might ask him why did you do that? And he'll tell me," Bob says. "I could irritate him if I tell him here's what you should have done. That won't work. But if I have a thought, I'll tell him."

Spoils from a wonderful life are on display all around us as we talk. There is a small World Series trophy replica from Bob's 1980 Phillies team and a full-size replica of the World Series trophy Washington won in 2019 when Bob was a special assistant to general manager Mike Rizzo. On one wall is a giant print of Aaron following through during his Game 7 walk-off homer against Boston in 2003. An eye-catching, blown-up baseball card of Ray Boone, the family patriarch, keeps watch over things. There are presidents: a photo from the 1976 All-Star Game with President Gerald Ford shaking Bob's hand in Veterans Stadium, another featuring manager Bob and player Aaron in Cincinnati uniforms with President George W. Bush.

Three TVs line one wall. Tonight, the Yankees game is on the middle one while the two on either side remain dark. Sometimes, multiple sets are required to spring into action: This summer, Nick Allen, engaged to Bret's daughter Savannah, will play 106 games for Oakland and 33 for Triple-A Las Vegas; and Bret's son Jake, twenty-six, is a middle infielder for the Windy City ThunderBolts of the independent Frontier League. Bob watches each of their games daily, too.

"Jake is Bob's heartbeat," Sue says of their grandson.

In New York, Cleveland touches Schmidt for two runs right away in the first inning ("Come on, Schmidt!" Bob beseeches), but the Yankees tie it at 2–2 in the fifth on solo homers from Willie Calhoun and Jake Bauers ("Attababy!" Bob cheers).

At home, the father doesn't question the son's decisions. But, ever the manager, Bob will confide to Sue at certain junctures that he would leave the pitcher in as his son goes to the mound to remove him. Or he'll tell Sue when he would pull a pitcher when Aaron is still pondering in the dugout. But he understands and knows the score.

"Aaron follows things that already are in baseball," Bob says. "The number of pitches, they get real nervous about that. When I managed, the pitchers would go deeper. The third time around the lineup is a huge thing now. I'd let them pitch longer. Now, they count. Aaron has to do it different than the way I did it. I tended to watch how he was throwing a little more. I would go more on how I thought they were pitching. They take them out earlier now than I ever did."

Bob understands that Aaron's relationship with his boss, Cashman, is vastly different from what Bob had with Herk Robinson in Kansas City and Jim Bowden in Cincinnati. Because now, analytics drive everything. And Bob admires Aaron's deftness in this area.

"It's not just him," Bob says of Cashman. "It's the whole world. You have to be able to speak to them and not argue. A manager has to deal with that and agree with them, but then also say, 'Here's the change I would make within that…'"

There are certain things Boone and other modern managers simply must do today if they want to hold on to their jobs. It's about more than wins and losses. Now more than ever, it's also about how a manager arrives there. And to the inevitable question of how much input he gets from the club's baseball operations department regarding lineup structure, Aaron says he rolls his eyes when that comes up.

"I've never not made the lineup," he says. "I know there are some places where guys do not have autonomy, necessarily, and that's not the case here. I've never made out a lineup that wasn't mine. Now, I look to different people at different times. Reach out on their thoughts on something I'm thinking about, or, there are certainly suggestions that come from time to time on certain things. But for me, I make the lineup."

It is a question that never would have arisen with Bob Boone or Buddy Bell at the helm. But things change, just as the generations do. Old School melts into New School as sons grow up to become fathers.

"He still has a lot to offer, but I've gotta smack him down sometimes and say, 'Dad, it's not 1986,'" Bret says endearingly of his own father. "I see it from the older generation. I saw it a lot with my granddad, one of the greatest men in my life. He'd be seventy, meet me after a Padres game and point something out, and I'd laugh and say, 'Gramps, this is not 1956.' But that's what grandpas do. I loved my childhood watching my dad play for the Phillies in the '70s, those are some of my fondest memories. But the game has changed. I loved my era. I'm not a fan of every time you get a hit, throw a party at first base. But this is these kids' generation. Whatever players are currently playing, they get to decide what the rules are."

In the recliner as the game approaches the middle innings and Aaron goes to his bullpen with one out in the fifth, Bob needs a little relief himself. His recliner comes equipped with a touchpad that instantly moves it back or forth, up or down, the back, the legs. But he hasn't yet mastered the buttons, so he cheerfully calls to Sue for help. The touchpad is the equivalent of his own version of PitchCom, another new development that he never had to worry about when he was calling pitches behind the plate the old-fashioned way, with his fingers.

The good news tonight in New York is that outfielder Harrison Bader was activated from the injured list a night earlier, so there's one weapon to deploy while so many Yankees are hurt. But with two out and none on in the top of the ninth in a 2–2 game, Aaron calls for closer Clay Holmes, which completely mystifies the Cleveland broadcasters. Why now?

"Absolutely" it's a good move, Bob says. "Aaron knows way more about it than me. They're counting pitches. He knows who he can trust."

But, disaster: Holmes surrenders a Myles Straw double and then an RBI single to Oscar Gonzalez. Worse, Bader and Isiah Kiner-Falefa collide in the outfield on the play and Bader exits the game. Again.

Immediately, Bob's cell phone rings. It's Bret. They commiserate together over the Yankees' latest misfortune as Bader is helped off the field. When they hang up, Bob laughs.

"I knew he was going to be hot," Bob says. "We didn't leave games. Bret never would have left. The trainer used to ask me, 'You hurt?' And I'd say, 'Yeah, it hurts but I ain't coming out.' All of the Boones were raised that you don't get hurt in this game."

Today's Yankees do, and quite often. But what could be another dismal evening takes another turn when the Yankees rally to tie the game at 3–3 in the bottom of the ninth and then walk it off in the tenth on Jose Trevino's RBI single. Bob claps animatedly in his recliner. Frank Sinatra blares through the television speakers with "New York, New York."

"Shoot, I never used to watch games like I do now," Bob says before exclaiming: "We won!"

Sue joins us to watch Aaron's postgame media conference. He explains decisively that after his reliever Ron Marinaccio retired consecutive lefties to start the ninth, he wanted Holmes in to face the right-handed-hitting Straw. Plus, rain was on the way, another reason for the aggressive move. His principles were sound. It just did not work. But the Yankees won anyway. Baseball is a sport that simply can never be tamed. Mom and Dad watch Aaron's answers with pride. They grumble more about injuries after the press conference is finished. It's been a high-stress night. And there are five months to go.

"And we're playing Tampa Bay, what, seven of the next nine games?" Sue says.

At its heart, baseball is a generational game, and no matter how you crunch the statistics (then) or data (now), no matter how different things are or how differently they are done, the past, in one way or another, stays with us. You can use it as a foundation as you keep moving forward, or you can become stuck in it like quicksand.

CHAPTER 2

IT'S ONLY A GAME

It was the middle of the ninth inning in Game 7 of what many still argue is the greatest World Series ever played. The Twins and Braves were deadlocked at 0–0, two future Hall of Famers—Jack Morris and John Smoltz—had been dueling, and the 55,118 fans stuffing Minnesota's Metrodome on this Sunday evening in 1991 were bringing the thundering volume and vibration of a freight train.

While Braves manager Bobby Cox had summoned reliever Mike Stanton to replace Smoltz with two on and one out in the eighth inning, Morris had just roared through the top of the ninth and was sitting on the end of the Twins' bench when manager Tom Kelly did the responsible—and reasonable—thing. He walked the length of the dugout to reach Morris, whose odometer was at 118 pitches.

"That's all, can't ask you to do any more than that," Kelly told the ace right-hander.

Morris insisted he was "fine," said there was "no game tomorrow night," and pleaded—no, demanded—to go back out for the tenth inning.

Kelly, with pitching coach Dick Such standing there and siding with Morris, stared at the pitcher for a beat, threw his arms up, and said those immortal words: "Ah, hell. It's only a game."

So after Paul Sorrento struck out swinging, Morris went back out for the tenth and zipped through a 1-2-3 inning on eight pitches, running his count up to 126. That was where it would stay as Gene Larkin singled home Dan Gladden in the bottom of the tenth with the series-winning run.

It's only a game.

That simple statement belied the bold, autocratic way—with a dash of benevolent dictatorship and a touch of democracy—in which Kelly operated. And, most important, a way in which he was *allowed* to operate. He was entrusted by the front office to fully and solely manage the game—Game 1 of 162 regular-season contests or Game 7 of the World Series, one and the same. There were no probability charts demanding that he remove a starting pitcher before facing the opposing lineup a third time, or after one hundred pitches, or after some other random pitch-count number or arbitrary highway marker.

With his decision, Kelly made the "smart stuff" his organization did the previous winter—namely, signing Morris to a one-year free-agent deal with two options—stand up, a Twin Cities exclamation point on Earl Weaver's sharp definition of a manager's job. He also made one of the gutsiest decisions in World Series history with full autonomy. There was no bloated baseball operations department and no pregame blueprint delivered regarding how to use the bullpen. It was Minnesota's second World Series title in five years, and it cemented Kelly as one of the greatest masterminds of his generation.

Twenty-nine years later came another pivotal moment in another World Series: It was in the COVID season of 2020, and Tampa Bay's Blake Snell was dominating the Los Angeles Dodgers in the sixth inning of Game 6, throwing a two-hit shutout with the Rays clinging to a 1–0 lead while attempting to force Game 7. Snell had thrown just

73 pitches when manager Kevin Cash hooked him with one out and one on to prevent him from facing the Dodgers lineup a third time.

Standing in the on-deck circle at the time, Mookie Betts felt a surge of confidence. "Man, it was kind of like a sigh of relief," the Dodgers outfielder said of Snell's exit. "Had he stayed in the game, he may have pitched a complete game. I don't know exactly what would have happened, but he was rolling. He was pitching really, really well. That was the Cy Young Snell tonight. Once he came out of the game, it was a breath of fresh air."

At home in Minnesota on that October evening, a retired Tom Kelly was doing what you might expect. He was watching another World Series with great interest in his living room. And like many of us in these digital days of remote controls and incessant commercials, when the national broadcast cut from the action at Texas's Globe Life Field—where the World Series was being played in a pandemic-induced "bubble"—to advertisements, he briefly clicked away to another station.

"My wife wanted to watch something else, or see something else," Kelly says. "So whatever his last inning was that he pitched, I thought he did really well. I don't remember what it was she wanted to see. But there was no thought in my mind when I turned that channel that he would not be in the game.

"When I turned it back, he was out of the game. I couldn't believe it. I said, 'Son of a bitch!'"

Not far from Kelly's Twin Cities home, in another living room in front of another flat-screen, the man who completed one of the most famous starts in the history of the Fall Classic also was slack-jawed—if not disbelieving, given where he had seen his game go. Had Morris been shielded from facing Atlanta's lineup for a third time on one of baseball's highest of holy days, that long-ago Sunday evening in 1991, Kelly would have gone to get him with one out and one on in the top of the fifth inning of a scoreless game. Atlanta's No. 8 hitter, Mark Lemke, had punched a single to right field to start the fifth inning, and light-hitting shortstop Rafael Belliard followed with a sacrifice bunt. Morris was at 63 pitches when Atlanta's leadoff man, Lonnie Smith, stepped into the batter's box to begin the Braves' third turn through the lineup.

At that point, the game had barely begun.

"You've got to understand, I have a lot of respect for the Tampa Bay manager," Morris, now a Hall of Famer, says today. "I really like the guy. But I was raising my eyebrows. It's a kid that's got it rolling. Why would you mess with that? I don't get it. Maybe that's why I'm not managing. I'd never manage scared. Today it's 'He's thrown two balls, I've got to get him out of there.' Jesus. Maybe he's setting up the hitter, did you ever think of that?"

Today's managers, it is accurate to say, with the help of their armies of data scientists and analysts, have considered every possible angle you can think of, and dozens more you probably never thought of. The game is broken down, strip-mined, and then put back together again long before that night's first pitch is ever thrown. Managing always has been the industry's loneliest job. It's just lonely today for different reasons. The game *looks* the same today as it did in 1991, or in 1981. Its skeletal system is the same. But the challenges that managers face today in so many ways are vastly different. Then, a manager lost sleep at night because often that evening's win or loss stemmed directly from a strategic decision he alone made. Now, the loneliness emanates from being the front man and public face for group decisions. Baseball operations departments that help author processes do not publicly explain those decisions after a difficult World Series loss. The manager does.

Before every postseason game, the national broadcasters—both television and radio, separately—are granted time to debrief each manager to glean the latest information regarding his team. Some of the subject matter in these meetings is on the record, much of it is off the record. Combined, it offers essential background so that the broadcasters can put things into context and explain nuances as the national telecasts unfold. Before Game 6 of the Tampa Bay Rays–Los Angeles

Dodgers World Series, Hall of Famer John Smoltz, the analyst for Fox television, asked Cash a question in advance regarding how much of Snell's outing later that evening already was predetermined.

"I know you have twenty-five different scenarios already planned out, I get it," Smoltz remarked to Cash during the television broadcaster's pregame access. "And you do this as well as anybody. But of those, which is your nightmare scenario tonight?"

In a remarkable revelation of how exact some of these preplanned scenarios often are, Cash's answer brilliantly and eerily foreshadowed what was to happen a few hours later to the outrage of many and to the understanding nods of those steeped in Sabermetrics.

"A 1–0 game, two outs in the sixth, and I've got to take out my pitcher," Cash responded.

"So when it happened, there was nothing I could do or say, no matter what I felt was right or wrong," Smoltz says, recalling the signature turning point of the 2020 World Series. "I had to say this is what Kevin Cash was afraid of, and he has not deviated. He easily could have deviated. But that was not their playbook. So when your playbook is so scripted, it's going to be harder for you to get fired if you stay with the script."

Seventeen years earlier, in Game 7 of the 2003 American League Championship Series in Yankee Stadium, then-Boston manager Grady Little made an egregious error by leaving ace Pedro Martinez in the game too long. He was fired four days later. The script was far less formal at that time. Analytics were in their embryonic stage. The book *Moneyball*, which pulled back the curtain and described in rich detail the Oakland Athletics' operating system under Billy Beane and his then-assistant, computer whiz Paul DePodesta, was published that year. Little's gut decision to leave Martinez in the game against the Yankees was one of the last flickering embers of the Old School campfire.

When Smoltz was on the mound against Morris in Game 7 in 1991, though the internet was not yet up and running, Kelly and Atlanta manager Bobby Cox sure were.

"It's not something Bobby could have done," Smoltz says of removing a starting pitcher who is throwing the game of his life. "His eyes would have seen something, he would have trusted his eyes and said, 'I'm staying with the guy.' So what seems elementary to everybody else who blew up my phone that night saying 'You've got to be kidding me' was something I couldn't go crazy about because there's no doubt the percentage of the chance of them losing that game went way up when he came out. But it is what it is, and it would have been different had he never said anything to me verbatim: 1–0, two outs, and I have to go get him."

According to the Baseball Reference website, Tampa Bay's odds to win Game 6 and, thus, force Game 7, stood at 60 percent when the sixth inning started. The Rays' probability to win increased to 64 percent when Snell retired outfielder A. J. Pollock for the first out. When light-hitting No. 9 hitter Austin Barnes coaxed a base hit off of Snell, the Rays' win probability reduced a bit, back to 60 percent.

Clearly, the Rays' internal probability charts disagreed with Smoltz in the moment and dictated that their chances of winning improved when they removed Snell before facing Betts a third time. Reliever Nick Anderson had been great during the pandemic-shortened season, but the Rays had used him frequently in the playoffs and he was fatigued. When Betts ripped a double, Tampa Bay's win probability was reduced to 45 percent. When Anderson wild-pitched Barnes home to tie the game at 1–1, it dropped to 35 percent, and by the time the Dodgers took a 2–1 lead on Corey Seager's fielder's choice, it was down to 26 percent.

Blake Snell had not yet been born when Morris threw his masterpiece. It would be roughly fourteen months after that raucous evening in the Metrodome, on December 4, 1992, when Snell came into this world with a left arm that one day would become a lightning rod in another World Series. As for Cash, he was just thirteen and a schoolboy in Tampa, Florida, on the night Kelly allowed Morris to go the distance. He, too, was watching the game on television.

"If I could pick a result, I'd much rather have Blake throw ten innings and us win the game, looking back at it," Cash says. "I do think, look, the game has changed. It goes back to, was there somebody in that bullpen who was better than Jack Morris? After seventy-five, eighty pitches? After a hundred pitches? Maybe not right then.

"But I'll bet you in this game, there's pitchers who are better. Not with all of them. Pitching staffs are built differently. It's just the way the game has evolved."

———

Now seventy-four and more than two decades into his retirement, Kelly was a young manager when Twins executive Andy MacPhail tabbed him to replace Ray Miller in 1986. Kelly, thirty-five when he took charge, guided the Twins for the next sixteen seasons, stepping away from the job following the summer of 2001 at the still-young age of fifty. He had a couple of nibbles to return over the next few seasons—Boston and the Los Angeles Dodgers were among those who called—but declined to interview. The game and the players were changing. But more than that, he missed something during a game early in that 2001 season that alarmed him. Nothing major, nothing game-changing, just a minor detail. At a time when managers worked from the hard drives in their heads, committing everything to memory, it ate at him. Then…it happened again that August. Just another small thing, like a hand-scribbled note that gets away in the wind. And he decided that was it.

For more than a decade, through the World Series wins and more 90-loss seasons than he cares to remember as the game's economic structure changed and the Twins sank in the small-market quicksand of financial squeezes and endless rebuilding, nothing had slipped past Kelly and his loyal, longtime coaches. Above all else, he taught his players to respect the game and keep things simple. Even during their down years, Kelly's Twins were known as perhaps the most fundamentally sound team in the game.

"We had a saying: Let's make the plays we're supposed to make, and somebody make a good play every now and then," Kelly says. "And then if somebody makes an error, now the pitcher has to pick you up. That was something we said a lot.

"Everybody wants to hit, hit, hit, blah, blah, blah. We understand that. But we wanted to focus on defense first, then we go hit. Taking good at bats, baserunning, recognizing when to go first to third, recognizing a hit in the outfield, and not letting the runner take an extra base, there's so much there to try to single out. There's a big umbrella that encompasses so many facets of the game and the people who are playing it that it's hard to lump them all into one sum. There's so much that goes on."

From the beginning, Kelly designed his spring training programs to focus on defense first. He thought the Twins had been sloppy under Miller; with experience managing in the minor leagues, and with a heavy emphasis on player development, Kelly blanched at a game that wasn't played "right." In his heart, Kelly is a baseball purist, someone who appreciates the artistry of the game more than the sizzle of the big moments. When the Twins won, he was criticized for staying in the dugout and not showing outward signs of emotion. But if you know him, there's a simple answer. He thinks the game and the moments belong to the players. And he is such a purist that he found as much joy in spring training drills on the back fields in Florida as he did in anything else. That's what was most important to him as he honed his managerial philosophy, and why he so clearly and continually broke the game down to its simplest terms.

"We never got too fancy with bunt plays. We didn't get too fancy with giving signals and signs," Kelly says. "We tried to keep it simple enough to where it didn't become a burden. I dealt with coaches when I was playing, and managers, that when it came to even getting a sign from the third-base coach, you needed a Harvard degree to try and understand it. I coached third enough and understood when you are trying to hit, run the bases, and play, and now you've got to dissect whether the third-base coach put the sign on or erased it, it was 'Aww, enough of this.' It became a challenge.

"The game is hard enough to play. We tried to eliminate where there could be any problem. We tried to focus on keeping the mind clear and playing the game, and not on some of the other stuff that goes on. I figured if we pitch good enough, catch it, and make a good play every now and then, you could be in the game with a chance to win."

He learned several things, some the hard way, as all managers do. The Twins had taken a fifteen-game winning streak into Baltimore one day in 1991 when Kelly ordered an intentional walk to Cal Ripken Jr. at a key moment with closer Rick Aguilera pitching. Next, Aguilera threw two splitters "that missed by a foot and a half" to a burly right-handed hitter named Randy Milligan, as Kelly recalls, implying that Aguilera lost his release point after throwing four consecutive balls to Ripken Jr. Then, on the third pitch, Kelly says, Aguilera "threw one that stayed up over the middle of the plate and he hit it off the damn wall and we lost. It ended the streak. I said to myself, 'I'm never going to have my closer walk anybody again, because I have to think he's better than this guy coming up.' And I never did that again. It bothered me a lot."

When Kelly took charge in Minnesota, he entered a managing world that was filled with colorful, strong characters who created teams in their own image and, for the most part, had full authority to rule over—and shape—their kingdoms as they saw fit. In St. Louis, Whitey Herzog presided over "Whiteyball," a fleet of jackrabbit-quick everyday players, led by Vince Coleman, Willie McGee, Ozzie Smith, and others, that won more than its share by turning games into track meets. Under Herzog, the Cardinals won the 1982 World Series, lost a controversial Fall Classic to Kansas City in 1985 that turned on umpire Don Denkinger's infamous blown call, and soon would run into Kelly's Twins in October 1987. In Detroit, Sparky Anderson was just off of the 1984 title that solidified the Tigers as a team for the ages following their record-setting 35-5 start that summer. Tommy Lasorda was bleeding Dodgers blue in Los Angeles, Davey Johnson was guiding the Mets to the 1986 World Series championship, and Earl Weaver was toward the end of his Hall of Fame run in Baltimore.

"We found out when we got to the big leagues that keeping fans interested was really a priority," says Kelly, who managed five seasons in the minor leagues before joining the Twins' big-league staff as a coach in 1983. "If ownership isn't happy with the number of people in the seats, things can get unpleasant. So we always tried to make it somewhat interesting. If you don't keep them interested, they aren't going to be there."

Kelly's Twins made it interesting immediately. After replacing Miller for the final twenty-three games in 1986, Kelly piloted the Twins to an unlikely World Series title over Herzog's Cardinals in 1987. The Twins in 1988 became the first team in American League history to draw three million fans. Yes, they did it before the Yankees or the Red Sox. Ten years earlier, in 1978, the Dodgers had become the first team in MLB history to cross the three-million-fan threshold.

"When there's a lot of people in the seats and you're winning some games, obviously, from the president of the club to the people working in the ballpark, whether they're ticket or security guys, whatever it is, everybody is a lot happier," Kelly says. "Keeping people in the seats is a very good thing. If you're not playing the game properly, it's hard for people to go in and watch, I believe. I don't blame them.

"So whether you're winning or losing, presenting the game in the proper fashion is a big, big thing for keeping attendance up and people happy. You might lose 4–3, but if it was a hell of a game, I think people appreciate it. Yeah, we wish we would have won and we have to live with it, but you don't go away from the ballpark mad. Playing solid was important to me. Of course, it didn't happen all the time. When we were getting our asses handed to us for a few years there, I'm sure we made some miscues along the way, didn't hit as well or pitch as well, but I think the players in general hustled and tried. I was always content with that. I didn't like losing, but if the players put forth the effort…"

It was a small moment, but one of the more memorable compliments of Kelly's career came one day in Baltimore when the team was losing and losing big. Everything that could go wrong was going wrong when Andy MacPhail, the general manager, popped into the manager's office one night after another loss.

"You know, I haven't given you the best team," MacPhail told Kelly. "I know that. But there hasn't been any discontent with pitchers complaining about hitters, or hitters complaining about pitchers. They all seem to be playing hard, trying hard, and I just wanted you to know I see that."

The lines of demarcation throughout were clear: From MacPhail, who hired Kelly in 1986 and stayed through 1994 before leaving to become the president of the Chicago Cubs, to Terry Ryan, who replaced MacPhail as Minnesota's GM and held that role until Kelly retired, the front office did the roster building and Kelly retained full clout to run the clubhouse, the dugout, and, most important, the games.

"I don't belong in the clubhouse, that's your department," MacPhail told Kelly. "I'll do mine and you do yours."

It was the way the game operated, for the most part, for more than a century: The GM would acquire the players. The manager would do the best he could with them. And if the lines of communication remained open and the mutual respect continued to flourish, the organization had a chance to accomplish some pretty special things.

First MacPhail, and then Ryan, "would ask what do you think of Johnny Joe and I would say I don't know if I care for him," Kelly says. "But that didn't mean he wouldn't ask six others. He'd ask some coaches what they thought. I always told him, you get your information and if you deem the player will fit with us, that's fine. I'll do the best I can with him. Even though I may not care for him. But if two of the coaches like him and Andy likes him and somebody else does, maybe I'm wrong. That's very real. My ego's not that big to where I can't be wrong. I make a lot of mistakes."

When he was working in the Florida Instructional League for the Twins in the early 1980s before getting the big-league job, Kelly had a team of, like, thirty-two players, with maybe fourteen pitchers and eighteen position players. Attempting to be fair with every player, he settled on an every-other-day playing rotation to make sure everyone got equal chances. This was over a two-month schedule in which they played about sixty games. They were a fair bit into it when Rick Stelmaszek, who coached for Kelly and the Twins for more than thirty years, approached him one day.

"Don't you think this Puckett guy could play a little more?" Stelmaszek asked. It was one of the first conversations they had about the future Hall of Famer Kirby Puckett.

"He dropped a Puckett on me," Kelly says. "I said, 'He's doing fine, Stelly. I'm trying to give everyone a chance.' As we thought back on that later, it was pretty humorous.

"You listen to your coaches. That's why you have them. You try to be fair. The worst thing you can hear is, 'You never gave me a chance.' I tried to give everybody a chance."

More often than not, the manager retained the final word. And there were players who didn't fit, or who didn't think the organizational philosophy fit them. The most notable over the years in Minnesota was David Ortiz, who wound up being nontendered by the organization after the 2002 season and went on to smash 483 home runs and win three World Series rings with the Red Sox before landing in the Hall of Fame in Cooperstown. Ortiz grew up in the Twins organization and to this day maintains the close bonds of brotherhood with his former Minnesota teammates Torii Hunter, LaTroy Hawkins, Jacque Jones, Matt Lawton, and Eddie Guardado.

But those early steps in his career are not all happy memories.

"The way they did me over there, I never understood what was going on," Ortiz told me in the spring of 2016. "It seemed like they didn't know what to do with me."

More than just the release, Ortiz was particularly chapped at the early pause in his big-league career. After showing promise over eighty-six games as a rookie with the Twins in 1998, Ortiz broke the hook of his hamate bone and was optioned to Triple-A the following spring; he played only ten games in the majors in 1999. At the time, Kelly didn't think Ortiz was working hard enough defensively, and the manager also felt that he was focusing too much on being a pull hitter rather than a complete hitter with the tools to use the entire field.

"I think the way they used to make decisions was wrong, but you can't complain to Tom Kelly about anything because he was the one who ran the show," Ortiz told me. "It was a take-it-or-leave-it situation."

He was the one who ran the show. From Kelly to Dick Williams to Billy Martin to so many others during previous generations, that was the way of the world. Authority figures had the clout, including—and especially—on the field and in the dugout. Those who worked or played under them didn't ask questions, they simply bit their tongues and changed their ways. Or they moved on.

Kelly was not warm and fuzzy. He was adept at commanding attention as a natural leader, especially when ratcheting up his already booming voice to chainsaw level. He could zero in on a target with the best of them, and his razzing could thicken the skins of the most sensitive souls in his clubhouse—or make them wilt. But he also did have a softer side, and the road map to it was pretty straightforward: Respect the game—put in the work, do things right, be a good teammate—and he had your back regardless of the teasing zingers.

"He had a reputation of being rough on young players, but a high majority of them, at the end of their careers, said that whatever direction T.K. took them in, or put them in, was in the best interest of the player and the team," says Paul Molitor, who finished his twenty-one-year Hall of Fame career by playing for Kelly from 1996 to 1998 and later managed the Twins from 2015 to 2018. "They might not have seen it at the time, but most did in the end."

Especially poignant to Kelly is a story that involves Jacque Jones. The outfielder, who went on to play for the Cubs, the Tigers, and the Marlins, was part of a young wave of prospects who brought winning baseball back to Minnesota in the early 2000s. But Jones, Ortiz, Torii Hunter, Matt Lawton, Doug Mientkiewicz, and others still had some maturing to do in those early days. Jones in particular had a penchant for wrestling with teammates during pregame stretching and getting scolded by Kelly. Eventually, Jones didn't fit in to the plans anymore and went to the Cubs.

"So we're playing the Cubs in the Dome and here's Jacque, and I had to do something on the field," Kelly says of the pregame batting practice encounter. "Jacque waved over at me, and the next thing I know, I came off the field and started up the steps in the Dome toward the clubhouse and here comes Jacque running up the steps beside me."

Jones was on a mission.

"I want to say hello, and thank you for all the things you did for me," Jones told Kelly. "I didn't know how good I had it over here until I left."

"I thought that was pretty good," Kelly says.

Jones remembers that vividly.

"I told him that we didn't understand it at the time, but the further we got away from his teachings, the better we all did," he says. "At the time it was like, 'This guy's crazy.' But he was teaching us to play the game hard, play it the right way, and don't take anything for granted."

Kelly was like that stern teacher you had who helped shape and mold you, and at the time you were scared to death…and then, years later, the understanding and appreciation kicks in.

"Of all the people I've been around as a manager, player, coach, and executive, he's at the top of the list of probably the guy I learned the most from about the game, how it should be played, attention to detail, how to deal with various personalities on the twenty-five-man roster," Molitor says. "When I became a manager, he talked to me about the meetings when I sent players down, and he told me to take a photo of myself and stick it in my drawer, and when you feel run-down look in the mirror and then at that photo and if you see a big change, you need to slow down and hit the pause button. Even if it was more symbolic than real, it was a metaphor that you needed to be cognizant of how to deal with things when the game beats you up."

More often than not, as it does with players, this game of failure has its way with managers, too. Strange as it may sound, there is an easy comparison between managers and presidents of the United States: From the first day in office to the last, following the day-to-day stress, the crises managed, the fires doused, the key decisions made, and the final scorecard of wins and losses, both usually look shockingly older at the end of their terms than at the beginning.

As the 1990s ticked along and the game's economic divide widened, which increasingly put the Twins and other small-market teams at a disadvantage, the gruff skipper's competitive zeal always was readily identifiable even when his teams were outmanned.

"He would always downplay how much he had to do with the outcome of a game," Molitor says. "But I do know when he went up against the so-called high-IQ managers, he took it personally. He knew which cards were in their deck and how to counteract them. Part of the makeup of a guy who wants to sit in the manager's chair is an ultra-competitive component when you're in a position like that."

Kelly and Tony La Russa, in particular, staged many intense battles over the years, especially before divisional realignment when Minnesota and Oakland both were in the American League West. Kelly, who never went to college, was all baseball, greyhound racing (and later, horses), and infield-dirt-beneath-the-fingernails. La Russa had a law degree, oozed California confidence in his Oakland green-and-gold, and befriended rock bands like Styx. They could not have been more different, this managerial odd couple. Kelly was a cigar-smoking, batting-practice-throwing, Zubaz-pants-wearing East Coaster originally from New Jersey. La Russa was a vegetarian who devoted time to his Animal Rescue Foundation. But the two greatly respected each other and developed a lasting friendship.

"We always kind of considered Tommy and La Russa and Sparky the guys that really seemed like they didn't make any mistakes," says Kent Hrbek, the Twins' anchor in the middle of the lineup and at first base in both the '87 and '91 World Series wins. "They managed the game. There was something special about it when we played those guys. La Russa, especially. It seemed like a battle going on between those two in the dugout. Gary Gaetti and I always talked about that. You could see it in the first, second innings, they were already setting up for the sixth and seventh innings, knowing which pitcher they wanted to use, which matchups, before all this analytics crap that's going on now. It was all about who was pitching well and who wasn't. They respected each other and they wanted to outmanage each other. I just got that vibe."

There were times when the Twins were facing other teams, Hrbek says, and Kelly would mutter to himself in the dugout, "I can't believe this guy is managing," or point out a move the other guy made that was going to backfire for a specific reason. Often, it did. But then the A's would show up, and Kelly and La Russa would eye each other from across the field like lions sizing each other up across the carcass of a zebra.

During one game in Minnesota, an Oakland pitcher was tipping his pitches and the Twins deciphered it. The Metrodome had a unique design underneath the stands in which the Twins' and the visitors' clubhouses actually were connected by a common area that was used by the athletic trainers and medical personnel. After this particular game, La Russa waited for the players to leave and then quietly walked through the training area over to the Twins' side.

"We knew what pitches were coming, and not that we did great against him or anything, but he came into my office one day after the game, sat down, and closed the door," Kelly says, chuckling. "I said, 'Oh boy, what's this about?' He said, 'You know what pitches are coming, don't you?' I said, 'Wellll…'"

"We still had to play him again. I didn't think I should tell him, but we could tell what was coming. I didn't answer him. I wouldn't. Didn't do it. He sat there for a long time."

———

Like Kelly, La Russa's first managerial job was in the minor leagues, though he was fortunate in that his time there was brief. La Russa managed just 280 games at Double-A Knoxville and Triple-A Iowa before being promoted to the White Sox, when he was just thirty-four, as Don Kessinger's replacement midway through the 1979 season. For Kelly, it was 709 games at Class A Visalia, Double-A Orlando, and Triple-A Tacoma before taking over in Minnesota.

This was not an anomaly. At that time, managers were viewed just like players: Management thought they should pay their dues in the minor leagues until they were seasoned enough for promotion. The Show was not for learning on the job. Future Hall of Famers or not, almost to a man, they rode the buses, ate the crappy food, and slept in the fleabag minor-league motels just like everyone else.

Earl Weaver managed in 1,509 minor-league games over eleven seasons in places like Aberdeen, Fox Cities, and Elmira before piloting the Orioles through 2,541 games between 1968 and 1986. Bobby Cox managed in 846 minor-league games before moving on to a Hall of Fame career with Atlanta and Toronto. For Tommy Lasorda, it was 941 games in the bushes. Sparky Anderson (690), Billy Martin (145), Bruce Bochy (489), Buck Showalter (467), Dick Williams (294), and Whitey Herzog (50) all served apprenticeships on the farm, as well. Terry Francona managed 563 minor-league games, including being the man in charge during NBA superstar Michael Jordan's moonlighting stint at Double-A Birmingham.

Jim Leyland's 1,402 minor-league games managed over eleven seasons seems incredibly exorbitant given his baseball-sage-like acumen, but it is nothing compared with Atlanta's Brian Snitker, who managed a whopping 2,714 games in the bushes before replacing Fredi González in 2016 (and, in one of the more emotional championships in recent vintage, guiding the Braves to the 2021 World Series crown).

"Leyland was a lot like Sparky and T.K.," says Morris, who pitched for Leyland very briefly in the minors before watching him work up close in Detroit when Morris was a television analyst there. "He deserved a chance. The problem with Leyland in Detroit is he was behind Sparky. He kind of got a raw deal. He should have been a manager long before, like Tony."

Leyland managed in Detroit's system from 1971 to 1981 before leaving the Tigers to become a coach under La Russa with the White Sox. He clearly deserved a chance in Detroit, but Anderson wasn't close to leaving, and Leyland didn't get an opportunity to manage in the bigs until he was forty-one, in 1986 with Pittsburgh.

By the time Cash was hired by Tampa Bay for the 2015 season, times were vastly different. Between 2013 and 2015, major-league teams hired eighteen managers. A total of twelve, including Cash, had never managed at any level. There were two chief reasons for the dramatic change. One, of course, was the rampant proliferation of analytics into every corner of the game: With so much data available, now every team had a full-blown baseball operations department that wanted someone pliable in the manager's seat, someone who would be more of a conduit between the baseball scientists upstairs and the players in the clubhouse downstairs. A *middle manager*, so to speak. The dividing wall between the executive office and the clubhouse had come tumbling down.

A second reason for the change was a result of both the exploding revenues and skyrocketing salaries in the game. Unlike the days when

Martin, Bochy, and Francona played, the recently retired players mostly made enough money during their careers that they had little motivation to cut their teeth by returning to the minors to manage. First-timers such as Molitor (roughly $40 million earned as a player), Dave Roberts ($23 million), Craig Counsell ($21 million), and Aaron Boone ($16 million) were comfortable enough to choose a less demanding way to stay in the game, such as broadcasting, rather than learn to manage in the minors. These two facets set the stage for the stampede of the first-time managers.

"It's a function of the financial success that players have had," Counsell says. "Aaron Boone has made too much money to go spend time managing in the minor leagues. It's not a job he's going to do. It's got nothing to do with earning your stripes. He's not going to do that job. There would be no former major-league players, successful former major-league players, as major-league managers if you had to go manage in the minors. They just wouldn't do it. That's not trying to be arrogant. It's just a function of your financial state. I'm not trying to be flip, but who would do it?"

Cash put together a nice career as a backup catcher for Toronto, Tampa Bay, Boston, the Yankees, and Houston between 2002 and 2010. Razor-sharp, personable, and a natural leader, he was just thirty-seven when the Rays tabbed him to replace Joe Maddon, who had left for the Chicago Cubs after the 2014 season. Cash's pedigree was impressive: He signed with Toronto as an undrafted free agent after playing the infield at Florida State, during which time he volunteered to switch to catcher in the Cape Cod League in 1999 when two of his team's backstops went down with illness and injury. With the Blue Jays, he was tutored by Ernie Whitt and made it to the majors almost as if by force of will. When the Rays needed a manager, Cash fit the profile of a recently retired player who knew the game and could command respect in the clubhouse and communicate well with his players.

So after serving as Cleveland's bullpen coach for two years under Francona, Cash became only the fifth manager in Rays franchise history, following Larry Rothschild, Hal McRae, and Lou Piniella, and, of course, Maddon, who was the only one of the bunch who compiled a winning record.

Cash and Piniella crossed paths briefly in Tampa Bay, in 2005 after Cash was traded there by Toronto for pitcher Chad Gaudin. It was Piniella's final season with the Rays. By then, the fiery Piniella, who never met a trade deadline as manager at which he wouldn't publicly lobby his bosses to go get him more bats, was flat out of patience with losing and with the penurious ways of the Rays.

"He came into a situation in Tampa where I don't know if it was the perfect match for Lou," Cash says. "Where Lou has been, he's been on very veteran-based clubs that won a lot. Tampa was floundering, looking to rebuild, trying to keep its head above water. That's not Lou. Lou's a winner. He expects to win every single night."

Cash saw the old-school side of the game via Piniella: the clubhouse food spreads turned upside down after particularly infuriating losses, postgame pies and cakes slung across the room, lemon meringue and whipped cream staining the carpets.

"He might have been the last to do stuff like that," Cash says. "But you learned a lot from him, and anytime you run out of stuff to talk about in conversation, as soon as Lou's name is brought up, anybody who played for him or worked for him can all appreciate it, because they witnessed it. He was consistent at being him.

"Lou asked me if I had holes in my bats. He second-guessed me as a catcher: 'Why did you call a fastball? If I wanted a fastball, I wouldn't have brought so-and-so in throwing only ninety. I would have brought this guy in.'

"It was constant. But I certainly appreciated the experience with him. He's one of the game's better characters, better personalities."

That a man named "Cash" would lead a franchise with a chronic shortage of it is another example of baseball's twisted yet consistent sense of humor. The Rays are routinely at the bottom of the barrel in terms of player payroll. And Piniella was simply in the wrong place at the wrong time: Wall Street investor Stuart Sternberg became the franchise's principal owner following the 2005 season and hired Andrew Friedman as general manager on November 3, 2005.

Sternberg had started his professional career trading equity options part-time at the American Stock Exchange in 1978—incidentally, one year after the births of the Apple II and Commodore PET. In short order after entering baseball, with the help of tools unavailable to owners of previous generations, he began constructing an organization that encouraged experimentation and supported new ideas.

"You want to know why they have so many innovative strategies?" wrote John Romano, the award-winning and longtime columnist at the *Tampa Bay Times*. "Because owner Stu Sternberg is not constantly looking over their shoulders, tallying up every success and failure."

Cash now is the longest-tenured manager in the American League. Other managers sometimes quiz him about exactly how the Rays manage to pull off what they regularly accomplish.

"You try not to dive into too much detailed information, but there are certainly questions, and there are questions I ask anytime I'm stumped on something," Cash says. "I talk to Tito [Terry Francona] fifty times during the season, constantly."

There is envy of the Rays and what they've built, Cash admits, but it goes both ways.

"You look at a guy like Aaron Boone, handling a market like that and handling a superstar-caliber player" like Aaron Judge, Cash continues, speaking of the division rival Yankees. "We've got really good players. I don't think we have the Stantons, the Judges, the Gerrit Coles. It takes unique people to be able to manage those groups of people."

In Tampa Bay, Cash and his coaches must be fully open, honest, and transparent with their players because the Rays ask and require the unconventional, be it targeting certain pitchers as "openers" to pitch the first inning and then turn the game over to another pitcher who will give them "length"—pitch more innings—or moving players around to different positions. Operating in this manner can be especially sensitive, because while putting restraints on some players and reducing the role of others may help the whole become greater than the sum of the parts when it comes to winning, it also reduces the earning potential for many players. Cash is tasked with selling this philosophy to the clubhouse.

Mostly, the potential for clashes comes with the pitchers. The Rays invented the "opener," were mocked for it initially, and then wouldn't you know it: Other organizations began copycatting. The Rays were at the forefront of preventing a starting pitcher from facing the opposing lineup a third time, which especially requires tact with type A personalities such as Alex Cobb or Tyler Glasnow. Until this generation, starting pitchers were developed to have the mindset that today is my day to start, I will take the ball until I no longer can lift my arm, I will do everything I can to give my team a chance to win while giving the bullpen a day off.

"Well, we said, 'No, that's not what we're doing,'" Cash says. "We said, 'You're going to get us to a point in the game.' And then our information tells us we can make a lot of good decisions from there. We'll be a little more aggressive about getting the bullpen involved."

Twenty years ago, Cash says, a rival team's goal was to get to the bullpen "because they were considered the lesser pitchers until you hit the closer. That's not the case anymore."

Indeed, pitching is so different today as to be, fundamentally, nearly unrecognizable from the past. Executives hunt power arms, line them up, and deploy one after the other, each going as hard as he can for as long as he can. One common topic whispered about in today's game is that a guy like Hall of Famer Greg Maddux, who excelled in location while not throwing very hard, likely would not even draw much interest as an amateur in today's world. Baseball operations personnel identify relievers early. Starting pitching is diminished, and it is not developed.

"Back in those days, most pitchers were starters," Kelly says. "They all were starters pretty much in the minor leagues. Now, they pull the plug, they see a guy throw for a year or two and decide he'll be a reliever. We didn't do it that way, baseball in general. It was more, 'Let's give this fellow every opportunity to be a starter because they're so hard to come by.' You explored every avenue before you put them in the bullpen. You certainly gave them a chance to try and flourish as a starter. Now, OK, it's not working out so now you go to the bullpen and we hope to find a spot, or you figure out whatever your niche is in the game. Is this guy capable of pitching three innings out of the bullpen? Can he get through the lineup once? Or pitch two innings?"

As the Rays developed and refined their novel plan based on volumes of proprietary intelligence and information, the misunderstanding, Cash says, was that the organization would treat every starter the same.

"No, we're not," he says. "If we had Gerrit Cole, we wouldn't pull him. Tyler Glasnow, Shane McClanahan, we're not pulling those guys. Your elite starters can still go out and be elite. But if there's a way to prevent maybe that fourth and fifth guy from being overexposed and handing the ball to somebody that now turns into, well, this is like an elite pitcher for three batters, why wouldn't we do that?"

Radically imagining a new way of doing things is a science of its own, and difficult enough. But disrupting the way things had been done in baseball for more than a century? Others don't take kindly to that. There is a natural fear of anything new, whatever one's lot in life, and there too often is a knee-jerk reaction to mock new ways of thinking. Cash's early conversations were difficult, and not with just one or two of his pitchers.

"The whole fucking staff," Cash says, chuckling. "Every one of them. I applaud all of them because it was Alex Cobb, it was Matt Moore, it was Chris Archer and Nate Karns. Drew Smyly. There were a lot of them. And it was a tough time. I was a year into this, and I probably didn't have the best sense of what the hell I was doing, I was very much learning on the job, a year or two into doing this. And I'm trying to look at these established major-league pitchers and saying it's not a knock on you, we just think the guys we're bringing in to face the eighteenth through the twenty-third batters have a better chance of helping us win.

"That's a gut punch to really good pitchers. But I applaud them all, the way they handled it. Did they like it? No. And we wouldn't expect them to."

———

Snell had not worked six innings in a start in more than a year, since July 2019. And now it was crunch time in the sixth inning of Game 6 in the 2020 World Series.

For his career to that point, Snell was allowing a .742 OPS the third time he faced hitters, and in a small sample size of just twenty-four hitters in the COVID-shortened 2020 season, right-handers were scorching him for a 1.042 OPS.

The Rays led 1–0 with one out in the bottom of the sixth when light-hitting catcher Austin Barnes lined a single up the middle. In the on-deck circle was Betts, who represented two things that were an anathema to Cash and the Rays despite the lefty Snell's dazzling performance.

Betts bats right-handed. And worse, he was the start of the third time around the order for Snell.

It was agonizing, but Cash had won too many games in Tampa Bay not to trust the Rays' process. So out came Snell, and in came reliever Nick Anderson.

Enter disaster.

Betts doubled, Anderson wild-pitched home the tying run, another run scored on a Corey Seager ground ball, the Dodgers zipped ahead 2–1, and three innings later secured a 3–1 win and their first world championship since 1988.

Snell had grown up in the Tampa Bay organization. It was all he knew. Kyle Snyder was one part pitching coach, one part psychologist, and one part father figure to him. And he trusted Cash implicitly.

"He always instilled confidence," Snell, a Cy Young winner in both 2017 and 2023, says. "Every time I had a good start, he was always there. Always there. He was always positive and uplifting. Just really easy to play for."

When he saw Cash coming, Snell didn't want to believe it. But it was the way of the Rays. Snell insists today that he's moved past what could have been the greatest, most triumphant night of his life. He still has difficulty working more than five or six innings in any given start, yet he has two Cy Youngs.

"That's my manager at the time," Snell says. "I respect everything else he did, and I'm on the same team. I'm with him. He did what he thought was best for the team." He adds, "We'll never know" what would have happened had he been allowed to stay in.

Anderson had been Tampa Bay's best reliever all season, except recently. The Rays had leaned heavily on him that October, and he had surrendered at least one run in six consecutive postseason games leading up to the fateful World Series Game 6.

And by putting limitations on Snell for so long, the Rays seemed to have cost themselves a chance to win. It's one strong argument against leaning so heavily into analytics: Generally, they emphasize what a player cannot do rather than what he can do. They do not coach him, or allow him, to grow and develop as a player.

"Doesn't matter if a guy has balls the size of an elephant now," shrugs Hrbek, who was at first base as Morris mowed for ten innings against Atlanta in Game 7 in 1991. "If the computer spits you out, you're gone."

The Dodgers, of course, were relieved. As Betts quickly said postgame of Snell's departure on that long-ago October evening.

"Thanks, Mookie," Cash says today, the sarcasm in his voice thicker than the summer humidity in Tampa, of an evening that will never leave him.

Over the years, he's heard all about how Tampa Bay is simply run by the computer. Cash's reaction is, let everyone think that.

"It's comical," he says. "I'd be the first to say we pride ourselves on having as collaborative a process as we can. But there has never been a situation where this guy is pitching against this batter, and the computer says you're pinch-hitting at this time, or here's your lineup for the day. Never. And if there was, I'd tell you."

Maybe it would make it easier if that were the case. Because as it is now, the probabilities calculated by the computer are still not certainties. Unless or until Tampa Bay wins a World Series, the Snell decision will continue to shadow Cash every single day. And it still may even if the Rays one day do win it all.

"I think about it probably every time I make a pitching decision as it's coming up," Cash admits. "I mean, it will sit with me forever because of so many factors. Probably the biggest is, Blake still has to answer those questions. He didn't make that decision. And that's going to be stuck with him."

When the Padres advanced to the National League Championship Series against Philadelphia in 2022, Cash says, he was leading the cheers hoping that San Diego would win the World Series.

"Because then people will stop talking to him about that. That, in a way, is unfair to Blake," Cash says. "The questions coming to me? That's fair. I ultimately made the decision and we all know that the result was not what I was looking for. But I mean, yeah, that's a perfect one that was scripted out."

In a sense, what Cash and many of his peers do today is Conference Room Managing. Collaborative, with input from many, emanating from far more daily meetings than ever before. In some organizations, baseball operations personnel have even moved into lockers in the clubhouse or coaches' room, violating what once was the inner sanctum, eroding the personal space that a manager and coaching staff have earned over careers in uniform.

But it is the manager alone who must face the public, take ownership of decisions, and be judged by history.

Internally, the Rays debated the Snell decision afterward, reviewing their process well into the winter of 2020–2021. Whether Cash should have allowed Snell to keep going, whether it would have been better had he removed Snell at various other mile markers in the game, whether it should have been his game to lose regardless, given that he had fanned nine of the eighteen batters he faced.

"A lot of healthy discussions," Cash says. "But it still didn't take away from the fact that, yeah, I think about it all the time. It's gut-wrenching. Were we going to win the World Series? I don't know, had he stayed in there and kept performing the way he was. Maybe it would have given us a better chance. That's for other people to write."

Five years earlier in a different World Series, then–New York Mets ace Matt Harvey, working on a 2–0 shutout in Game 5 in Queens, talked manager Terry Collins into allowing him to start the top of the ninth inning against Kansas City. When Collins went to speak with him at the end of eight innings and tell him his night was finished, Harvey's lips could be read on televisions everywhere: "No way! No way!"

Harvey was at 101 pitches; Collins relented, and it backfired spectacularly. Harvey issued a leadoff walk to Lorenzo Cain, Cain stole second, and Eric Hosmer followed with an RBI double.

At that point, Collins removed Harvey, but it was too late. The Royals tied the score in the ninth and plated five runs in the twelfth to win the championship.

"Sometimes you let your heart dictate your mind," Collins said afterward.

It burned him.

Meanwhile, Cash was determined that his mind was going to overrule his heart, and that burned *him*.

In Minnesota, Kelly's phone rang after the Harvey game, too.

"Harvey was doing a terrific job, no question," Kelly says. "But he certainly doesn't have the résumé Jack Morris had. You're comparing two guys that I don't know should be compared. Jack is in a different class. The situation might have been somewhat similar, but you're comparing apples and oranges. No disrespect to Harvey, he had a good couple of years and deserved the accolades. But when he talked his way in, he certainly didn't back it up."

Comparing Snell and Morris is apples and oranges, as well. The left-hander was throwing the game of his life that night, but in the years since, even after adding a second Cy Young Award to his collection in 2023, he's yet to prove he can consistently go deep into games.

When Morris trotted out for the tenth inning on that long-ago night in the Metrodome, the Twins had an All-Star closer in Rick Aguilera, but their bullpen ranked sixth in the AL with a 3.53 ERA and had the eleventh-lightest workload in the league at 448.2 innings pitched.

The bullpen Cash was deploying in 2020 ranked second in the AL with a 3.37 ERA and had the second-highest workload at 262.2 innings pitched (in a sixty-game, pandemic-shortened season).

"You don't know everything, that's the problem," Kelly says of an outsider's view of Cash's in-the-moment decision. "You can form an opinion, but you really don't know. You just don't. The manager certainly knows his people better than I did, that's for sure."

Old-school or new, there is so much to weigh when these decisions come racing at a manager, and in no way, shape, or form do any of them come with guarantees. It is a high-wire act, and the only correct decisions are the ones that happen to work out. So many more decisions made for the right reasons still blow up because it is baseball, famously a game of failure.

As for the rest, as Kelly says, so much of it depends upon how the game is presented. Current preferences in our Digital Age—power arms that do not work deep into games, nightly conga lines of relief pitchers, no sacrifice bunting, no hit-and-runs, strikeouts are acceptable for hitters—in many respects are vastly different from the preferences of previous generations. But it is not universal. What is cutting-edge to some in the industry, and to a segment of fans, is an insult to others.

"The thing you have to keep in your mind is that the Tampa Bay Rays have been terrific," Kelly says. "They put together teams at a low budget, per se, and they have done terrific. With their minor-league people, the way they do things, the way the manager has been able to keep those groups together and get the most out of those people, you have to take your hat off to them."

CHAPTER 3

THE AUTOCRATS

Though Tom Kelly was seventeen years younger than Sparky Anderson, they had several things in common. One was their razor-sharp baseball acumen. Another was the fact that both men were in complete control of their baseball worlds. Still another was that in winning World Series championships just three years apart, each enjoyed the gift of a young and talented nucleus of players who were ready to be shaped and molded as they came of age.

In Minnesota, Hrbek, Kirby Puckett, Gary Gaetti, Chuck Knoblauch, Shane Mack, and Kevin Tapani were among the groups that will live forever in the collective hardball memories in the Land of 10,000 Lakes.

In Detroit, Morris, Alan Trammell, Lou Whitaker, Kirk Gibson, Lance Parrish, and Dan Petry matured into winners under Anderson and in 1984 sent the entire state of Michigan toward doing what the old Motown song by native Detroiter Martha Reeves and the Vandellas suggested, "Dancing in the Street."

Kelly and Sparky had one other thing in common, as well: In 1987, after Detroit's rousing comeback to seize the AL East title from Toronto to position itself to pounce on its second World Series title of the Sparky Era, the Tigers ran smack into a Twins team that played mistake-free baseball and pitched well enough to shock them in the 1987 AL Championship Series.

"The thing I learned about Sparky, and it didn't take me long, was when you don't expect anything to happen, that's when it's going to happen," Kelly says. "You're sitting in the dugout thinking that everything is going along hunky-dory, that's when you'd better be aware. He was going to try something. He was very crafty that way."

Anderson came to Detroit in 1979 after being fired in Cincinnati, where he had led the Big Red Machine to back-to-back World Series wins in 1975 and 1976. The Tigers were rebuilding and had hired a longtime organizational man named Les Moss to replace Ralph Houk, who was in the midst of a long and respected run managing the Yankees—he led them to two World Series titles—the Tigers, and Boston. Moss was barely into his first big-league job, leading the Tigers to a 27-26 mark, when he was sacked by GM Jim Campbell. Though Campbell felt bad for Moss, his reasoning was sound: Anderson was available, and he surely wouldn't be on the market for long.

So the move was made and Anderson rolled into the grand old cathedral that was Tiger Stadium with every bit the bravado of a man entrusted with the keys to the kingdom. "My way or the highway" was real as the Tigers moved players in and out like lawn chairs in a garage sale. Plus, before La Russa came to be known as the Godfather of the Modern Bullpen by reinventing and redefining the closer and late-inning specialist roles, Anderson already was delving into that territory. As he handled his pitching staff in Cincinnati, he had earned the nickname "Captain Hook." And it wasn't because he favored pirate clothing.

"He scared me to death," says Petry, who was twenty and made his major-league debut on July 8, 1979, less than a month after Sparky's

June 14 arrival in Detroit. In fact, Petry said he always told Roger Craig, the Tigers' pitching coach under Anderson, that he never wanted to talk with Sparky.

"Never," Petry says. "If you talk to him, it's one of two things: You're going to the minor leagues, or something is wrong. He never called you into his office just to say you're doing well. He never patted you on your back. He always said that your reward is your paycheck. If you were in his office, something was wrong. Sparky always used to laugh at that. We didn't."

Today's postmodern managers are hired specifically to maintain frequent and smooth communication with each player on their roster as baseball operations departments figure they can help steer the schematics of a game, or that the paint-by-numbers strategy will be obvious at a particular moment in a game given the data spreadsheets. While one key to success for leaders like the Dodgers' Dave Roberts, the Rays' Kevin Cash, and the Orioles' Brandon Hyde is to nurture relationships with their players, Anderson frequently voiced his desire *not* to become close with his players. The way he viewed it, the time would come when he would have to trade or release just about every one of them, and he knew those players had wives and families. And if the manager allowed himself to become close with a player, it would hurt too much when the tie with the team was severed.

Some of the things that went on behind closed doors were breathtaking.

"We would say things to each other that probably never should be said between a player and a manager," Morris, who was notoriously cantankerous in his prime, says. "He presented it his way. He would say come, make your complaints if you have something to get off your chest, but be ready to get it right back. Lance, Gibby, and me would go in and give it to him, get our two cents' worth in. And there were times he would admit he was wrong. To me, that was healthy. It's got to be both ways. But we all understood that no matter what was said, he was still the boss."

Anderson and Kelly were very similar, says Morris, the Game 1 starter who launched World Series titles for each man. Both were students of the game, demanded respect for the game, and expected their players to play it properly. In an effort to keep egos in check, Anderson always reminded his teams: This game has been played for one hundred years and is bigger than any one man. No matter how big of a star you become, he told them, when you fade away, the game moves on without you. It's just the way it is.

In many ways, Anderson was as much Philosopher King as manager. In Plato's *Republic*, the Greek philosopher and great teacher espouses the idea that the very best leaders come when philosophers are placed in charge because they possess both knowledge *and* wisdom. Anderson could philosophize with the best of them, channeling the legendary Casey Stengel, who came before Sparky, and possessing similarities to a couple of managers who would follow Anderson, Felipe Alou, and Jim Leyland. All were wise, plainspoken, and filled with common sense.

One of Anderson's key tenets, developed during the Big Red Machine days and useful again when the Tigers were rolling: If you have a bunch of good players, tuck your feet under the bench and don't trip anybody. Stay out of their way.

Unlike Kelly, Anderson enjoyed bantering with the media. And given his gift of gab, his lovable knack for mangling the English language, and his extraordinary baseball IQ, the media loved him back. Who else would rave about one of his favorite restaurants in Boston, Lethal Seafood? He was right, to a point: The fish was—and is—very good at *Legal* Seafood.

As he developed his Tigers, he naturally became a father figure (he was fifty in 1984 when they won it all). And he passed along lessons from his own father. He was relentlessly nice to almost everybody he encountered, to the point where people around him marveled. He was cheerful even when fans interrupted him during dinner. "My daddy always told me it don't cost a nickel to be nice to people," he would say. And then he would pass that on to his players.

One lesson that Petry remembers vividly came shortly after the right-hander's debut in the majors.

"Everybody would request his autograph, he'd sign it, they'd say thank you, and he would say, no, thank *you*," Petry says. "He thanked everybody."

So one day Petry asked him about it. And Anderson, employing his habit of using a player's full, given first name, answered.

"Daniel, my boy, it's a true honor for people to ask for your autograph," Anderson told him. "And one day, it's not going to be there."

"That stuck with me," Petry says. "He's right."

His hyperbole sometimes got him into trouble. Kirk Gibson had an especially rough start in getting a firm foothold in the major leagues. The fact that Anderson had an early habit of publicly comparing him to a "young Mickey Mantle" didn't help. Gibson felt the pressure build until he was ready to explode. Finally, he confronted Anderson about it and the manager backed off. Today, one of Gibson's most treasured possessions is a letter Anderson wrote him after they were retired.

"It was a handwritten letter and I have it framed in my office," Gibson told me in 2015. "It basically says, 'I just want you to know, though you were a challenge, the memories that we made together are unforgettable.' And that his favorite part of managing all those years were those types of memories where he built a relationship.

"And we went through some tough-ass times. Ooohhhhh."

But as that group matured—Gibson, Morris, Trammell, Whitaker, Parrish, Petry—the walls began to slowly come down. Over time, Anderson could not help but develop a great affinity for them, and they for him. He often referred to Trammell as his "Huckleberry Finn"—his dirt-on-the-trousers, fresh-faced, sunny kid who remains forever young.

"I don't know exactly the year when he loosened the reins," says Trammell, who, like his old manager, is enshrined in Cooperstown. "Obviously, when we won in '84, he had come in with a five-year plan and we win it in his fifth year, but we needed direction. I didn't think it initially. I'm a young player, we're studs. But we didn't know diddly compared to what we needed to learn.

"Sometime in the mid-'80s, he started loosening the reins. Maybe he felt that he would lose guys if he continued to be overbearing. I can't really pinpoint it, it was just a transition that happened over time."

One of the flashpoints came behind the plate. Parrish, an eight-time All-Star who was one of the best catchers of his generation and, as such, an extension of the manager on the field, became very close with Anderson. Yet for the longest time, the manager continued to direct Craig, the pitching coach, to call all of the pitches.

"Lance was like, wait a sec, what am I, chopped liver?" Trammell says. "That was part of getting to the level we needed to get to. We thought we were there, but we weren't. After Baltimore won the 1983 World Series, we knew we were good, but we came out of the gate 35-5 and that took us to another level. And we had the same nucleus for a few more years. That was all Sparky, lining things up, teaching us what he thought was the right way, all of us buying in."

It was the best forty-game start in baseball history, and it set the stage for the rest of the summer for Anderson: tension and stress. Anderson often said it was the toughest season he ever managed because he knew if the Tigers blew the AL East lead, he would be run out of town.

In Detroit, Anderson enjoyed many riches, chief among them the serendipity of Trammell and Whitaker emerging at the same time. They comprised the longest-running double-play duo in major-league history, playing together in 1,874 games (third all-time for teammates) over nineteen seasons, almost all of them with Trammell at shortstop and Whitaker at second base. They were dependable as Opening Day each April and as productive as Detroit's Big Three automobile manufacturers during their heyday.

Anderson became the first manager to win a World Series in both the National and American Leagues, and the first skipper to manage teams to 100-win seasons in each league. The professional collateral he had stockpiled over the years emboldened him even further to stick to his principles, and when the players went on strike in August 1994, and the owners responded the following spring with their cynical and shortsighted plan to forge ahead with "replacement players," Anderson was the only manager who declined to participate. He went home to California to wait out the end of the strike, saying he would forfeit whatever portion of his $1.2 million salary his stance would require. Unlike today, there was no "collaboration" between himself and his team's front office. He refused to participate in the insulting charade in which major-leaguers would be replaced by scabs, a bunch of former lower-level athletes recruited from current jobs busing tables or clerking at sporting goods shops.

"Please let's don't think of such a horror story that we're going to have baseball with replacement players," he told reporters at the time. "I don't like my intelligence insulted by telling me this is the Detroit Tigers."

The stance cost him his relationship with the Tigers and, essentially, his career. Though he returned when the strike was settled and managed the 1995 Tigers to a 60-84 record, his relationship with ownership was irreparably strained. Economics were changing the parameters of the game, and there were limits even for an iconic "my way or the highway" manager.

Meanwhile, in Cleveland, Buddy Bell, the five-time All-Star and six-time Gold Glove winner, was now a coach on Mike Hargrove's staff and was involved in organizational meetings laying out how the replacement-player scheme would work.

"All of them could play a little bit because they all had played before," Bell says. "But once the game sped up, we're not very good. Like, bad players. So we were having a meeting after three or four days of this, trying to figure out how we should do this. And I stood up and said, 'Listen, this shit ain't going to work. This is terrible. You're asking us to make these guys players that they have no chance of being.'"

What Bell didn't realize was how much time and effort then–Indians executives John Hart, the general manager, Dan O'Dowd, one of Hart's assistants, and others had been required to put into the project. And they didn't exactly love it, either—they were simply following marching orders from the commissioner's office.

"So that was a little bit of a lesson in knowing your audience," says Bell, who immediately received an angry lecture from the executives in the room informing him that he had no idea what was going on. Hargrove looked sideways at Bell later and said, yeah, you didn't handle that very well.

"Next time you're going to say something like this again, run it by me first," Hargrove told Bell.

"It was just a terrible time," Bell says.

When the season was finished, his legacy secure, Anderson resigned after eighteen seasons in Detroit. And Bell was named as his replacement.

"What a super person," Bell says of Sparky. "He was really, really kind to me."

Anderson, then sixty-one, hoped for one more managing assignment so he could finish his career with a contender. But there were no more offers. He passed away in 2010, at the age of seventy-six, as a result of complications from dementia. His 2,194 career victories rank sixth on baseball's all-time list.

"I always smile when I hear people say he didn't get along with younger players," Trammell says. "I say, wait a second. Our group. The Big Red Machine. Johnny Bench had a few years under his belt when Sparky took over in Cincinnati but, believe me, I've talked to Johnny Bench and those guys felt the same way about him. I was so happy to hear that because I wasn't sure. But it was 100 percent."

———

Bench was the Most Valuable Player of the 1976 World Series, the Big Red Machine's second consecutive championship under Anderson and a thorough, four-game sweep of Billy Martin's Yankees. It was Martin's first full season in the Bronx and, following varying degrees of success—and self-destruction—in Minnesota, Detroit, and Texas, it was the first time the fiery and troubled skipper managed a team to the pennant.

The Bronx was the fourth managerial stop for Martin, a scrappy onetime Yankees infielder who played on five pinstriped World Series winners from 1950 to 1957. An acolyte of manager Casey Stengel and a great friend and nighttime running partner of Hall of Famers Mickey Mantle and Whitey Ford—the "Three Musketeers," as they became known—Martin was a volatile mix of pure, unadulterated baseball genius and feisty, quick-triggered alcoholic.

Yankees owner George Steinbrenner, who found him irresistible partly because of Martin's Yankees pedigree and partly because of his take-charge, bare-knuckled macho swagger, would fire him five times and yet keep bringing him back between 1975 and 1988.

A showdown between Martin and the right-handed pitcher Doyle Alexander in 1976 was instrumental both in understanding Martin's modus operandi and Steinbrenner's attraction to him. It also was just one of innumerable such incidents during Martin's torch-and-burn tenure in an era in which the alpha dog manager ran his team with a steamroller mentality. It was on Old-Timers' Day in New York against Earl Weaver's Baltimore Orioles, and Alexander was hit for four runs and seven hits in four innings. Martin had seen enough.

Alexander, who had come to the Yankees as part of a ten-player trade with the Orioles in June 1976, had developed a pattern of pitching well early in a game before running out of steam in the later innings. On this day, according to Peter Golenbock's *Wild, High and Tight: The Life and Death of Billy Martin*, Alexander was livid when Martin arrived at the mound, snarling: "Those were horseshit hits. My arm's as good as the last time."

Martin snapped: "I decide how your arm is, not you."

Afterward, Martin held a team meeting.

"A player *never* talks back to the manager, not in front of the other players," Martin raged. "I have an office with a door for that." Later, he threatened: "If anyone does that again, I will kick the crap out of him right there in front of the team."

Nobody doubted it—at least, that Martin would try, if not succeed. A ubiquitous barroom brawler whose involvement in a fight with patrons at the then-trendy Copacabana supper club in 1957 sealed the end of the Yankees portion of his playing career, Martin was fired after just one season managing Minnesota in part because he knocked out one of his own pitchers, Dave Boswell, in a barroom fight at the Lindell Athletic Club in Detroit. That season, 1969, Martin managed the Twins to a 97-65 record before losing to Weaver's Orioles in the first expansion-era divisional playoff. It was his only season managing in Minnesota. The Twins refused to tolerate his behavior despite the winning.

Martin was direct, confrontational, and unyielding. He battled umpires, his own players, fans, and his bosses. When Detroit hired him for the 1971 season, he was ejected twice in the first ten games for arguing strikes while backing his players. Later, he would yank beloved star outfielder Willie Horton from a game for lack of hustle—something he would more famously do with Hall of Famer Reggie Jackson with the Yankees in Fenway Park in 1977. In the spring of 1973, Martin and Ike Blessitt, a Tigers minor-league outfielder, were arrested for using profanity in public during an altercation with another customer at a bar in Lakeland, Florida, during spring training. Then, a few days later, Martin abruptly resigned as manager during a disagreement in general manager Jim Campbell's office only to return a day later.

Despite his guiding them to the American League East title and a five-game AL Championship Series loss to Oakland in 1972, the Tigers finally fired Martin in September 1973. They were exhausted by and disenchanted with his alcohol-soaked, antisocial behavior. He was drinking. He was womanizing. He had blown off a team charter flight from Oakland to Chicago in order to take a side trip to see a girlfriend in Kansas City, then was forty minutes late to the start of a game in Chicago. When Campbell asked him about being late—and it happened on other occasions as well—Martin's stock reply was, "I'm here for the game, ain't I?"

The final straw came when he was suspended for three games for ordering two of his pitchers, Joe Coleman and Fred Scherman, to throw spitballs one night against Cleveland. Gaylord Perry, the well-known Hall of Fame spitballer, was pitching for the Indians; Martin was doing a slow burn and wanted to force the issue into the open. On the third day of his suspension, the Tigers axed him.

"There was a breakdown on company policy matters," Campbell told reporters. "There were misunderstandings. Foul line to foul line, he did a darn good job."

If managers were listed in dictionaries the way words are, that would perfectly define Martin.

He was a wreck even before then.

"Being a baseball manager is a terrible job," he said. "You have to be father, mother, babysitter, and policeman to twenty-five guys. Things got so bad I had to take a drink all the time, to settle my nerves. It's a hell of a thing to go home and say hello to your kid and wobble."

At times, it seemed as if he was equally addicted to baseball and alcohol. He won, and he self-destructed, and then he won again. Lather, rinse, repeat.

If his on-field success didn't immediately speak for itself, a later study by the Elias Sports Bureau certainly presented grist for debate: Elias analyzed his record over sixteen seasons and twice, in 1988 and again in 1992, ranked him as the best manager of all time.

"Billy Martin happens to be the best manager in the history of Major League Baseball," the bureau proclaimed near the end of the twentieth century, based on statistical modeling that revealed Martin's teams won

7.45 more games per year than they should have, according to predictive analysis. That number was higher than any other manager.

Fans loved his passion and style. Managers fueled imaginations in that era, and the best were viewed as modern-day miracle workers. Martin certainly was seen as that, and his frequent outbursts at umpires only excited the fans even more. In Minnesota, attendance increased by some 200,000 in 1969 from the year before. After Martin's firing, it decreased by 100,000 in 1970. On Martin's first Opening Day in Detroit, on April 6, 1971, 54,089 fans jammed Tiger Stadium—more than for any game of the 1968 World Series and Denny McLain's return after a long suspension, and even more than for Al Kaline Day.

You cannot name one manager in today's bland world of corporate-speak who is a hit at the box office.

All of this—and a stint with the Texas Rangers—was just a prelude to the run that would take Martin national as a manager.

If his heart was stitched together with the red seams of a baseball, his soul was covered in pinstripes. After Martin's death from a drunk-driving accident on Christmas Day 1989, his close friend Bill Reedy revealed that for much of his managerial career, the manager carried with him an old Casey Stengel jersey.

Many Roman Catholics today wear crucifixes around their neck as a constant reminder that there is a higher power. Ancient warriors carried a leopard's claw or a shark's tooth for luck. In Cajun and Creole communities in Louisiana, the gris-gris is believed to fend off evil spirits.

Martin used Stengel's jersey as his secret talisman while working dugouts from coast to coast.

He received his chance to return to the Yankees when he was hired to replace Bill Virdon in August 1975, in a move that had every indication it was a George Steinbrenner production. The only technicality when general manager Gabe Paul made the announcement was that Steinbrenner was serving a two-year suspension at the time after being convicted of and fined for violating federal laws on contributing to political campaigns—a thread from the Watergate scandal. The suspension was ordered by Commissioner Bowie Kuhn. Still, Steinbrenner was allowed access to the stadium and had watched the Yankees get shut out in both games of a doubleheader against Boston from a club box just a week earlier. That Paul was dispatched to Colorado the following week, where Martin was fishing after being fired by the Rangers, seemed more than a mere coincidence. Already by then, Steinbrenner's tight grip on his team was alienating those who could not tolerate it. Virdon's predecessor, the highly respected Ralph Houk, had quit at the end of the 1973 season, telling the players of the Boss, "I have to quit before I punch the guy. I don't want to leave the game of baseball by punching an owner." Not exactly the "collaborative" method that serves as the working conditions for today's managers. And as the merry-go-round that is baseball spun that winter, it was the Tigers who hired Houk—to replace Martin.

The Steinbrenner-Martin union in 1976 was the start of one of baseball's longest-running soap operas, complete with star power to rival anything running on Broadway in the late 1970s and early 1980s. After getting swept by the Big Red Machine in that 1976 World Series, Martin's 1977 Yankees, featuring a cast of characters for the ages, went 100-62 and then defeated Tommy Lasorda's Dodgers in a six-game World Series, the only one Martin would win. Most of the characters returned in 1978 and were memorialized by closer Sparky Lyle in his book *The Bronx Zoo*. They were trivialized in third baseman Graig Nettles's classic line: "Some kids want to play big-league baseball, and other kids want to run away and join a circus. I'm lucky; I get to do both here." Mostly, they were edgy, talented, and unforgettable.

It was June 18, 1977, a nationally televised Saturday afternoon game on a sweltering day in Fenway Park, when Martin and Jackson came within a whisker of a fistfight in the dugout. The Hall of Fame outfielder had signed a $2.9 million free agent deal with the Yankees during the winter and was still adjusting to his teammates, who were not necessarily all enamored, anyway, with the self-proclaimed "straw that stirs the drink" in a *Sport* magazine article published that May. Jackson later denied making the comment—or, at least, said it was written out of context, in his 2013 book, *Becoming Mr. October*. Catcher Thurman Munson, the target of some of Jackson's zingers in the magazine article, was among those who despised Jackson.

As the Yankees and Red Sox battled, Jim Rice roped a double into right field that Jackson tracked either with caution (his version) or lazily (Martin's version). The ever-angry manager walked to the mound to replace Mike Torrez at that point—and sent Paul Blair to right field as a defensive replacement despite the fact that Jackson already had a double and a single to extend his hitting streak to fourteen consecutive games and was due to bat the next inning. Humiliated and enraged, Jackson confronted Martin in the dugout. Elston Howard, a Yankees coach, stepped between them. Two more coaches, Yogi Berra and Dick Howser, intercepted Martin when he attempted to chase Jackson up the runway leading from the dugout to the clubhouse.

Had there been streaming at the time, the incident would have gone viral in a heartbeat. But the Apple II, the first microcomputer to be widely distributed, had just been launched in April at a price of $1,298. Bill Gates and Paul Allen were still in the early days of Microsoft and were roughly three years away from striking a deal with IBM that would help produce IBM's first personal computer. As it was, on this Saturday afternoon in June 1977, national television caused enough of a ruckus as news of the Martin and Jackson fight went national.

It was a scorching and tense summer. Son of Sam, the serial killer, was terrorizing New York City. The blazing heat contributed to a twenty-five-hour blackout in July when lightning from a thunderstorm struck a substation and zapped power, during which time looters pillaged the city. From Manhattan to Queens to the Bronx, everyone was on edge.

Martin was overwrought by insecurity with Jackson aboard and Steinbrenner favoring his newest toy, and the manager knew he had to control Jackson because the Boss would now naturally side with the outfielder. Meanwhile, in the midst of the tension, Martin confided to Munson that Steinbrenner was attempting to dictate lineup changes to him—two decades before analytics, data, and computers would overtake the old-school baseball men and front offices would routinely make lineup suggestions throughout the game.

At season's end, Torrez and Jackson would play key roles in another, happier game, when the Yankees clinched the World Series title with an 8–4 trouncing of the Dodgers in Yankee Stadium. Torrez started and pitched a complete game, but it was Jackson who stole the show. It was his three-homer game, the night on which he was branded for once and for all time as "Mr. October."

The scars from that tumultuous time remain. "I don't even want to bring it up," Jackson says of Martin. "I don't want to go through it."

A year later, Goose Gossage would join Reggie in the Bronx and the Yankees would win a second consecutive World Series. It was 1978, another summer in which Martin's drinking and self-destructive behavior would break him. On the night of the 1977 World Series triumph, the greatest night of his baseball life, Martin finished his evening drinking alone in a bar in New Jersey. In the thick of the pennant race in July 1978, tension again bringing out his worst, Martin could hold his bitterness no longer. He told reporters Murray Chass and Henry Hecht, speaking of Steinbrenner and Jackson, "The two of them deserve each other. One's a born liar, the other's convicted." Martin tearfully resigned before he could be fired. The Yankees named Bob Lemon, with a personality of sugar to Martin's vinegar, to replace him. And Lemon was there when the 1978 Yankees staged a rousing comeback in the AL East, won the Bucky Bleeping Dent one-game playoff game over Boston, and went on to take down the Dodgers in another six-game World Series.

The Yankees trailed Boston by 14.5 games at one point in July and were 10.5 back when Lemon took charge.

"Lem comes out of his office for a meeting and says, 'Hey, boys, you guys are the world champions. Basically, we have the same team, a hell of a team. I'm going to give you the bats and balls, you guys go play, and I hope I make the right pitching changes. You guys go get 'em,'" Gossage, the Hall of Famer, says. "Handling a pitching staff, that's how I gauge them. It's not manipulating players, you only have so many players. But handling that pitching staff, and that's where the worst managers came in."

Gossage pitched under Martin in the first half of the 1978 season, then again in 1983 when Steinbrenner named Martin as Yankees manager for the third time.

"Billy was one of the worst managers I have ever played for," says Gossage, who played for a veritable Who's Who of impressive skippers in Chuck Tanner, Paul Richards, Buck Showalter, Lou Piniella, Yogi Berra, Tony La Russa, Dick Williams, Gene Michael, Roger Craig, and Bobby Valentine. "What a joke. Nastiest drunk you've ever been around in your life. It was out of control. And he hated pitchers. How do you hate pitchers? They're your bread and butter.

"He thought we were the dumbest motherfuckers on the planet. Which we may be, but you need us."

In May 1988, with Martin's drinking, womanizing, and paranoia of losing his job peaking, he was badly beaten in another bar fight, this one in Arlington, Texas. Three weeks later, in the midst of another tantrum while arguing a call, he repeatedly kicked dirt at umpire Dale Scott before reaching down, grabbing another handful of dirt, and heaving it at Scott's chest. Three weeks after that, a cold war ongoing between Billy and the Yankees brass, Martin left reliever Tim Stoddard in during a close game even though the right-hander had nothing on the ball, had no command (he walked five of eight hitters during the extended appearance), and was getting shelled.

Martin had not wanted Stoddard on the roster, and the manager refused to remove him on this night because he wanted to drill home his point to Steinbrenner and the front office. It is one lever available to managers in any era: If this is the roster you're going to give me, then these are the players I will play. And I'm not hiding anyone.

Four days later, Martin was fired by Steinbrenner for the fifth and final time. The Yankees were 40-28, and Lou Piniella, who had resigned as general manager during the chaotic start of the season roughly a month earlier, was named to replace him. The Yankees finished 85-76 and fifth place in the AL East that season—but only 3.5 games behind Boston.

"If Billy had stayed as manager, we'd have won the pennant," Yankees designated hitter Jack Clark said at the time.

So...one of the worst managers, as Gossage said? Or the absolute best, as Elias Sports Bureau maintained?

Both, at times, can be true. But before he manages others, a manager must manage himself. If he cannot do that, it is impossible for him to manage his clubhouse. Martin was a brilliant baseball man beset by demons that doomed him to failure.

One man's trash is another man's treasure.

———

Martin and others retained power, sometimes through more chances than they deserved, because it was a different game—and a different world—in the late 1970s and 1980s. Ownership consisted mostly of individuals and families, all of whom had different needs, agendas, and personalities. Like the sixty-four different colors in a box of Crayola crayons, men like Steinbrenner, the inimitable Charles O. Finley (Athletics), Carl Pohlad (Twins), John Fetzer (Tigers), and Edward Bennett Williams (Orioles) all were smart and successful businessmen with their own hues. The economic stakes in the game were nowhere close to where they are today, so the days in which ownership tilted toward syndicates and corporations were still far off in the distance. The Sternbergs and the Wall Street influence could not yet even be imagined.

The concept of free agency did not begin until 1976, and it was in its embryonic stages for years after that. Part of the chain reaction from outfielder Curt Flood's suit against baseball and its reserve clause following his trade from St. Louis to Philadelphia in 1969, free agency started when arbiter Peter Seitz declared Andy Messersmith and Dave McNally as such before the 1976 season. Owners, panicked, negotiated free agency into the next Collective Bargaining Agreement with players and were still unsure of—and undervaluing—what they had done.

Until then, and even for many years afterward, ball clubs were often run like mom-and-pop shops, fun side diversions for the owners from their "real" businesses. The chain of command was pretty simple: An owner installed a general manager to run the club—both the business and baseball sides. The GM hired the manager to run the team. That doesn't mean the manager was never questioned. Some owners were notoriously more meddlesome than others, and the same with GMs. But by and large, the managers ran the clubhouses, the games, and everything in between.

Dick Williams managed for owners Tom Yawkey in Boston (inherited family money earned in the lumber and iron ore industries in the Midwest), Gene Autry in California (the Singing Cowboy, star of radio, film, and television), Charles Bronfman in Montreal (heir to the Seagram's liquor empire), Joan Kroc in San Diego (married the founder of McDonald's), George Argyros in Seattle (real estate investor), and Charles O. Finley in Oakland (insurance salesman).

He was crusty and irascible, and he quickly wore out his welcome wherever he worked. But he excelled at turning losers into winners, and for a time, with every bridge he burned, more avenues opened up for him. He guided the 1967 "Impossible Dream" Red Sox to within one win of a World Series title before being fired late in the 1969 season—and today he remains considered, along with Francona, as the best to ever do it in that town. He won two World Series with the Athletics in 1972 and 1973, then quit because of conflicts with Finley before the A's went on to win a third title in a row under Alvin Dark. He managed the Padres to their first-ever World Series appearance in 1984, where they lost to Sparky's Tigers, but then was a no-show on the first day of spring training in 1986, picking that day to make a grand gesture of resigning following a simmering clash of egos with general manager Jack McKeon.

"I guess a lot of guys around here were uptight around the guy," Nettles, back in a circus with the Padres following his earlier quip about the Yankees, told reporters at the time. "I don't know who the new manager will be, but most of the guys are happy."

Williams was a proven winner. And a proven fighter who had no hesitation in calling his players out publicly—such as starting pitcher Andy Hawkins, whose underperformance early in his career so frustrated Williams that the manager began referring to Hawkins, a native of Waco, Texas, as the "Timid Texan" to the media. Hawkins finally responded with an 18-8, 3.15 ERA season in 1985.

"Dick Williams is the best manager I've ever played for," Tim Flannery, a key utilityman on the 1984 Padres NL title team, once said. "But as soon as he gets out of baseball, I'm going to run him over with my car."

"I said that just to show how demanding he was," Flannery says today, chuckling. "He would tell you that you were the worst player he's ever had. And if you don't move the runners over tonight, I'm looking for somebody else. I mean, he was vicious. They all made more money than anybody at that time, and that's how most of them managed. But, you know, he was great. And I heard him in my head my whole life from managing through the minor leagues to coaching in the big leagues."

Williams wound up visiting Flannery one day when Flannery was managing at Class A Rancho Cucamonga in the 1990s and Williams happened by the area.

"And he told all my players that I had threatened to run him over in a car," Flannery says, eyes twinkling. "All of it. We laughed. It was great. It was cool, but it was a different time back then."

As Charles O. Finley himself famously said, "Dick Williams is the best manager I've ever had. I ought to know. I've fired enough of them."

One of those was Jack McKeon, who managed for Finley in both Kansas City and Oakland. Just as Williams would after him, McKeon became accustomed to taking phone calls at all hours of the day, especially in the early mornings in California, from the Chicago-based owner.

"We brought up this kid named Chris Woodard from Jersey City, and he's a rabbit," says McKeon, who first managed at age twenty-four in Fayetteville, North Carolina, in the old Carolina League. In 2023 as a special assistant to Washington Nationals GM Mike Rizzo, he was celebrating his seventy-third year in professional baseball. "Charley's term for fast guys was rabbits, and guys who were slow were trucks. So if a truck got on base late in the game, I had to get him out of the game and put a rabbit in the game.

"Well, we bring this rabbit up, Woodard, and Charley says, look, he can only play second base. If you have to use him late in the game he can only play second because he's not very good anywhere else. So we were in Oakland, it's the bottom of the eighth, and Wayne Gross gets on base. Well, he's a truck. So I put in the rabbit, which is Woodard. But now I don't have anybody else, so he has to play."

McKeon kept his double-play combination, Mike "Pee Wee" Edwards and Rob Picciolo, intact and inserted Woodard at third base, and Oakland wound up winning by 4–3 as Woodard started a key double play.

Next morning, 6 a.m., McKeon's phone rang.

"McKeon? Finley. Dammit, I'm trying to help you become a good manager. I told you not to play this guy anywhere but second base, and you went and played him at third base."

The manager explained he put Woodard at third only briefly, in a pinch, and that the A's won.

"Then there's a ten-, fifteen-second pause on the phone," McKeon says. "And then he says, 'Well, I guess you think you're a goddamned genius now.'

"This was every day. Something like that every day."

McKeon went on to manage the Padres, Cincinnati, and Florida. At seventy-two, he guided the Marlins to a second World Series title in 2003 with one of the most brassy decisions of the past few generations, when he elected to start young ace Josh Beckett on short rest in Game 6 at Yankee Stadium. Probabilities be damned. Not only did that unconventional move go against nearly every statistic in the book suggesting that pitchers going on three days' rest is a losing bet, but McKeon didn't even move toward the bullpen. Beckett was brilliant in throwing a complete-game shutout in the clincher, scattering 5 hits, striking out 9, and walking 2 over 107 pitches in the Marlins' 2–0 win.

"Who made that decision? Me," McKeon says. "And when I made it, I went around as a courtesy to check with people."

It was one of the last gasps of a skipper managing by instinct and intuition. And it was not a coincidence that it coincided with Grady Little's similarly unilateral move with Pedro Martinez in that same postseason. The book *Moneyball* had been published four months earlier, and soon the era of analytics and Conference Room Managing would take hold. But as McKeon revealed his plans to Marlins owner Jeffrey Loria (who made his fortune as an art dealer), president David Samson, and GM Larry Beinfest, there were no directives, printouts, or interference.

"I made that decision because when I looked at the situation, it was Mark Redman's turn," McKeon says of the soft-tossing left-hander. "He had been blasted by the Cubs in the playoffs, he pitched the second game of the World Series and the Yankees tore him up. I know the mystique of the Yankees. You don't go to a seventh game with them in Yankee Stadium, because something happens."

As McKeon said so eloquently at the time, "Historically don't matter against the Yankees."

McKeon told Beckett what he was thinking, and asked how the right-hander was feeling. At twenty-three, the swaggering Texan was just beginning a career that would wind through Boston and help the Red Sox win a World Series four years later. During his talk with the manager, he said he would see how he felt during a between-starts throwing session.

At the time, Beckett was 18-19 in his career, yet McKeon's reasoning was simple. He wanted no part of chancing a Game 6 loss that would force the Marlins to face a Game 7 in Yankee Stadium. He just needed to get the cocky Beckett on board—and it didn't take much.

"He came back and said, 'I'm your guy,'" McKeon says. "That's all I needed. And if he doesn't win, I'm going with Carl Pavano the next game and he's got three days' rest. I was not going to give the fucking game to the Yankees."

As another Florida team, the Rays, would experience with Snell in a World Series seventeen years later, had the Marlins directed McKeon not to allow his starting pitcher a third trip through the rival lineup, they very well might have lost Game 6 and been in trouble in Game 7. And perhaps the Yankees would be sitting on twenty-eight World Series crowns rather than twenty-seven.

———

That spring of 2003, a man whose career path eventually would take him into the seat McKeon occupied as the manager in Miami was working as special instructor in the Yankees camp.

Don Mattingly, one of the most beloved Yankees ever, had been a young first baseman just summoned to the majors in 1983 when, during a Yankees game in Minnesota's Metrodome amid one of Billy Martin's turns as manager, he was the cutoff man on a ball hit to the outfield on which there would be a play at home plate.

"I thought the runner is probably going to be safe," Mattingly says.

Nevertheless, he played it conservatively anyway and allowed the throw to pass by him and continue to the catcher. But he figured he would attempt to hold the batter at first by faking as if he was going to cut the throw from the outfield. Possibly because Mattingly impeded the catcher's vision with his deke, the throw home got away from the catcher and the runner advanced to second anyway.

Back in the dugout, the young first baseman got an intimidating earful. Immediately. He had barely stepped into the dugout before Martin was in his face.

"Billy was like, 'He was going to be safe. Just cut the fucking ball,'" Mattingly says. "And you just kind of went, 'All right.'

"We didn't say anything back then, you know? There was no talking back. Now in my mind, as I processed it, I thought, well, that wasn't awful, because I did everything right except the ball getting away. I did think he was going to be safe, but I wasn't 100 percent sure. And I felt like I had the runner stuck. I knew he wasn't going anywhere. But the fact that the ball got away, things changed. I don't know if it was the result, or if it was necessarily the wrong play."

Contrast that with another manager and another superstar another decade-plus down the Yankees' timeline. Derek Jeter was in his first full season in the majors in 1996 when he attempted to steal third base with two out in the eighth inning of a tie game. Cecil Fielder was at the plate against the White Sox, and Jeter was thrown out to end the inning. The Yankees lost 3–2 in ten innings.

One of the most basic, fundamental aspects of the game that baserunners are taught early on is that you never make the first or third out in an inning at third base. By violating that cardinal rule, Jeter took the bat out of the hands of one of the Yankees' big RBI men that season in Fielder. Manager Joe Torre, who had never played or managed in a World Series to that point and was still unproven and under pressure in the Bronx, was livid. He had a brief, in-the-moment conversation in the dugout with his bench coach, Don Zimmer.

"I was mad at myself, basically, for probably giving him too much credit, knowing what he should do there," Torre later wrote in his book, *The Yankee Years*. "And I was mad—more mad at myself. I said to Zim,

'I'm not going to talk to him until tomorrow. We've got the rest of the game to play.'

"What does Derek do? He comes in off the field and sits right between me and Zim. Just came right over to us. He knew what he did. I hit him on the back of the head and said, 'Get out of here.'"

Two Yankees managers. Two New York superstars. Two completely different ways of handling things.

Eventually, Mattingly would serve as Torre's Zimmer, in a sense, when the two moved to Los Angeles and worked together for the Dodgers from 2008 to 2010. Though veteran Bob Schaefer was Torre's bench coach during all three years while Mattingly served as hitting coach, Mattingly was Torre's handpicked successor and would manage the Dodgers after Torre's retirement, from 2011 to 2015, before becoming the Marlins' manager in 2016.

Outside of the Bronx and those antique beauties Wrigley Field, Fenway Park, and Tiger Stadium, the game was dominated by bland, soulless, multipurpose stadiums at the time. The games no longer were played in those baseball-only cathedrals of the 1940s and 1950s that fueled the imaginations that engineered a return to that style in the 1990s and beyond, beginning with the 1992 opening of Camden Yards in Baltimore. Home runs did not dominate as they do today, largely because it was pre-steroids and the ballparks often favored the pitchers, especially the round, cookie-cutter, artificial turf–covered facilities such as Riverfront Stadium (Cincinnati), Busch Stadium (St. Louis), Three Rivers Stadium (Pittsburgh), and Royals Stadium (Kansas City). Managers mostly had free rein to play the angles before owners became corporate and played the angles themselves—or hired Ivy League numbers gurus to do so. Front offices were slim, and marketing departments generally consisted of some guy with mismatched clothes who sometimes helped out in the ticket office when things were busy.

It was not uncommon for teams to be constructed in the image of the manager—the Whiteyball era of the Cardinals that emphasized stolen bases and small-ball strategies that are mostly gone today was the guiding principle; the Billyball era in Oakland that leaned heavily into—and burned out—the A's starting rotation.

Whitey Herzog had succeeded McKeon in Kansas City and guided the Royals to three first-place finishes in five years between 1975 and 1979. His Royals were eliminated in the playoffs by Martin's Yankees in 1976 and 1977, then he was fired after a disappointing second-place finish in 1979. So he set up shop in St. Louis in 1980 and managed the Cardinals for the next eleven years. During that run, he won three NL pennants and one World Series.

"When I got to St. Louis and managed in that big ballpark with the artificial turf for a year, I decided right away we needed to build a team that had speed and defense," Herzog told author Peter Pascarelli in his 1993 book, *The Toughest Job in Baseball: What Managers Do, How They Do It, and Why It Gives Them Ulcers.* "Hell, if I had been in Fenway Park, I would have built a different team."

Behind the fleet feet of Vince Coleman, Willie McGee, Ozzie Smith, Lonnie Smith, and others, and stalwart starting pitching in arms like Joaquin Andujar, Bob Forsch, John Tudor, Danny Cox, and Hall of Fame closer Bruce Sutter, Herzog built an empire by day and entertained by night. He became an institution, emphasizing speed, on-base percentage, a bopping cleanup hitter, and good pitching, and the Cardinals offered him a lifetime contract. He looked at owner Gussie Busch, then eighty, and quipped, "Your lifetime or mine?" Like Sparky Anderson and Earl Weaver, he preferred to keep his distance from the men he would write onto the lineup card. "I'm not buddy-buddy with the players," Herzog wrote in *White Rat: A Life in Baseball.* "If they need a buddy, let them buy a dog." When he finally resigned in St. Louis in 1990, he was replaced by Torre.

As it usually does, money changed things in a hurry. As free agency took root and contracts swelled not just in size but in length, the game's wave of autocratic managers began to recede. It had to, just as the GMs upstairs soon needed support to crunch numbers as rapidly increasing payrolls and decisions made with emotion rather than cold analysis began to make owners uncomfortable.

One thing managers always controlled was playing time. And one commonality among all players throughout time, whether a group that traveled by train in 1920 or players who swipe their way through social media today, is that they all want to play. To the degree that managers control playing time, they retain the power.

But two things have tilted that. One is the lucrative, long-term contracts signed by free agents. Now, if there is a clash with the manager, those players know they can simply wait things out until ownership sours on the manager. The power dynamic shifts when a player knows he will be around longer than a manager. He knows the repercussions will be few, if any.

The other variable that has siphoned power from some managers is: Who writes the lineup card? Is it solely the manager? Or is it a collaboration between the manager and the baseball operations department, as has become custom in many organizations today?

If the manager is writing the lineup card, his authority is far-reaching. Players want to play. But if he is taking suggestions from the front office, that authority is now diluted. Dynamics change when a manager does not have authority, or when a player does not have security.

The days of Whiteyball and other managers crafting teams that suited their styles and personalities were going, going...

"See, today you couldn't do that because you couldn't turn over a roster that quickly," says longtime executive Sandy Alderson, the original mentor to Billy Beane in Oakland and a man who has run the A's, Padres, and Mets since 1983. "I remember when Dick Williams took over as manager of the Seattle Mariners, they were in the Kingdome, which at the time basically was a Homerdome. He said, 'We're going to remake the Mariners into a defense and speed team,' and I thought to myself, 'Are you crazy? In the Kingdome, that's what you're going to do?' I smiled at that and thought, 'That will take care of the Mariners for the next three or four years.'

"The point is, with contracts the way they are now, eight, ten years, you couldn't turn around a roster that quickly. It's different when you're going to have someone buy into the notion that they're going to change the basic nature of your roster to pursue a different sort of strategy. But therein lies the issue with managers. There has to be some sort of continuity. If you turn over your organization to someone who is only going to be around three or four years, that's not how great organizations are built. It's not just an arrogance of someone in the front office. It's, look, great organizations are a product of continuity, consistency. You have to have the right philosophy and right direction, but ultimately that success is continuity and consistency. You can't just turn that over to someone different every couple of years or so. It doesn't work."

In Oakland, where Martin was between Yankees stints and managed the A's for three seasons beginning in 1980, it was Billyball—and the fans loved it. In 1979, the year before his arrival, the Athletics drew just 306,763 fans. Martin's presence in the dugout increased that by half a million in 1980, up to 842,259. Then it was 1.3 million in 1981, when the A's advanced to the ALCS before losing to the Yankees, and 1.7 million in Martin's last season in Oakland. The Bay Area was seeing exactly what they had seen in Minnesota and Detroit in terms of Martin as a box-office draw.

Billyball was built around Martin turning loose his 1980 rotation and allowing it—pushing it—to throw an astounding 94 complete games. By the time Martin was fired following the 1982 season, Rick Langford, Mike Norris, Matt Keough, Steve McCatty, and Brian Kingman combined to finish 93 of their 159 starts. All in their twenties and all showing great promise early, by the end of that 1980 season, all were fried and, essentially, done.

Not unlike poor Mark "the Bird" Fidrych after his rookie season in Detroit in 1976. Through a combination of living in the uneducated dark ages and bowing to public pressure and gate receipts that increased exponentially each time he pitched, the Tigers, managed by Houk with Jim Campbell as the GM, criminally overused him. He threw an incredible 250.1 innings during his rookie season, led the AL with a 2.34 ERA, and started the All-Star Game. He threw more than 44 innings in a season just once after that. But in 1976, the lowly Tigers averaged 33,649 fans for each of the Bird's starts, and just 13,843 in their other games.

Checks and balances, it turns out, can be a good thing in an organization. Despite much of today's griping about pitch counts and micromanaging.

"There are sort of regulatory constraints imposed on a manager today that didn't exist before," Alderson says. "But that's also part of being incorporated into a larger, organizational, corporate environment."

As the Red Sox built a state-of-the-art analytics department in the early 2000s, one of the things they examined was the disappearance of the workhorse starter, and the reasons behind it. They traced it back to Martin's 1980s Oakland staff. Throughout the industry, everyone noticed the shredded arms of those poor fellows. Their tale was told and retold. And everyone vowed never, ever to allow that to happen to the arms in their own organizations.

"That was the inflection point, when those guys were on the cover of *Sports Illustrated* and they all blew out," says Theo Epstein, who built that Boston analytics staff. "Bill James talks about this. It's why pitch counts now are down, innings are down, it was all a reaction to that and everybody was like, 'We don't want to get fired.'

"But all that's happened since is pitchers are pitching less. They're still getting hurt. All we've accomplished is using more pitchers to get through a season. We certainly didn't figure out how to keep pitchers healthy. A lot of the teams that do well, it's because their starting pitching stays healthy all year. The more innings you get out of your starting pitchers, it's great for your whole team because it's really good for your bullpen."

The regulatory constraints of which Alderson spoke to guide managers can be helpful guardrails. But as the doctors getting rich performing Tommy John surgeries can attest, the game—managers and executives—still has eons to go. Developing and protecting pitchers successfully and productively remains more elusive today than ever.

———

Autumn was settling upon Baltimore on the first Wednesday of October 1979, when future Hall of Famers Jim Palmer and Nolan Ryan matched up for Game 1 of that year's ALCS. In New York earlier that day, Pope John Paul II had finished his tour of the city by saying Mass at Shea Stadium and then Madison Square Garden before traveling to Philadelphia. The presidential campaign between Jimmy Carter and Ronald Reagan was just around the corner.

In Memorial Stadium, when Palmer threw the first pitch of the game to Angels center fielder Rick Miller, a rudimentary system of analytics continued in the Orioles dugout, its own Pony Express to today's point-and-click digital delivery system.

Earl Weaver was ahead of his time in preferring the three-run homer over the bunt. He was ahead of his time in a lot of things. Since replacing Hank Bauer as Baltimore manager a decade earlier, and without access to a computer, a hard drive, or anything more exotic than a No. 2 pencil and an eraser, Weaver intuitively and exhaustively began to develop his own system of what, eventually, would come to be known as analytics. They were elementary then, and they were concocted by Weaver himself, not a research-driven baseball operations department. Interns in the media relations office were tasked with painstakingly producing spreadsheets before they were known as, well, spreadsheets.

The system was this: There was an 11 x 17 envelope assigned to each team in the AL. Inside was a stack of individual sheets of paper or index cards containing the names of each pitcher on that team. And on, say, the Ryan sheet, the name of each Orioles hitter was listed, alphabetically, with columns for runs, hits, doubles, triples, homers, RBI, strikeouts, walks, and so forth. A new idea then, they were something that even the most casual of fans takes for granted today: batter vs. pitcher matchup numbers.

So Weaver could quickly scan through his players—Baylor, Belanger, Bumbry, Crowley, all the way down through Murray, Brooks Robinson, Singleton—and check matchups instantly. The statistical sheets were updated at the end of each series and filed away, ready for use when the Orioles next played that opponent.

"It was pretty progressive for baseball back then," says the Hall of Famer Palmer, who today is an Orioles television analyst. "I don't know how long it took him to get the stats, but it just made sense. Wouldn't you want to know what the batting average is, and so on? I mean, now, you've got all that with StatsPass, Baseball Savant, you get a lot of help. If you're a manager, you've got to figure out what your players do best. I think that stats made him feel a little bit more comfortable about platooning."

Indeed, in winning the AL East in 1979, every move Weaver made seemed to carry the mark of genius—especially his outfield platoon of righty Gary Roenicke and lefty John Lowenstein. The two combined that summer for thirty-six home runs. It was smart, productive, and cutting-edge.

In his third year of doing statistics for Weaver that season was a twenty-year-old University of Maryland student named Charles Steinberg. Over time, Steinberg would ascend to vice presidency positions with the Padres, Red Sox, and Dodgers. He would become one of the game's premier marketing minds, a sort of Forrest Gump–like figure with a knack for appearing in historical moments. He planned and executed the wonderful closing ceremonies in Baltimore's Memorial Stadium in 1991 and the memorable hundredth anniversary of Fenway

Park celebration, and he helped market the Padres back to relevance following Tom Werner's fire sale of the early 1990s. The nightly fan favorite "Sweet Caroline" in Fenway Park was his brainchild. Jimmy Buffett played the first concert ever there, and when the evening reached the approximate time of the seventh-inning stretch had there been a baseball game, it was Steinberg who played the organ as Buffett led the crowd in singing "Take Me Out to the Ball Game." He is credited right there in the liner notes in Buffett's *Live at Fenway Park* CD/DVD package.

But during Game 1 of the Orioles-Angels series in 1979, Steinberg was under a different kind of pressure. Brought back from Maryland for the playoffs, the city buzzing, phones ringing off the hook, and in the eye of the postseason hurricane frenzy, Steinberg was sitting in the third row of the Memorial Stadium press box, counting pitches for each pitcher (yes, Weaver did that, too) and tracking other assorted stats. It was the seventh inning, Palmer and Ryan were locked in a matchup for the ages, and Weaver, as all good managers always are, was two, three moves ahead of everyone else.

As the bottom of the eighth started, a forgettable reliever named John Montague replaced Ryan. Weaver consulted his matchup sheets and could not find Montague. So pitching coach Ray Miller phoned the press box.

The Angels had acquired Montague in an under-the-radar trade with Seattle on August 29 for a player to be named later. In those days, as is the case now, to be eligible for the postseason, a player must be on the roster by the end of August. Montague barely made it for the Angels…but in his return to college, Steinberg missed it. Montague was absent on the spreadsheet. The top of the Orioles lineup—Al Bumbry, Mark Belanger, and Ken Singleton—was due to face Montague, and Steinberg could see the end of a short-lived career in baseball from where he was sitting. Panicked, he called and asked a colleague to race to his office and locate the Seattle stats packet. She pulled Montague's sheet, copied it, and immediately delivered the original to Weaver in the dugout and the copy to Steinberg in the press box.

"As long as Montague did not pitch the last time we faced him, I'm OK," Steinberg says.

But, alas. In late July, Montague had faced twenty Orioles hitters over three innings in two games, and the Birds had torched him. So now it was the top of the ninth inning, still 3–3, and Steinberg was frantically updating Montague's numbers against the Orioles. Finally, in the top of the tenth, he called Kim Hollenbeck, a member of the Orioles' Base Belles who also happened to be Weaver's stepdaughter and was friends with Steinberg. He beseeched her to get his updated numbers to Weaver.

It was still 3–3. Hollenbeck raced through the Orioles clubhouse, and she still recalls the sight of Palmer, the future underwear model who had been removed from the game after nine innings, emerging from the shower wrapped in a purple towel. When she reached the dugout with Montague's updated numbers, the ex-Mariner was still pitching. There was one out; Doug DeCinces was on second base, and because of his uncanny ability to reach base (.357) against Ryan—again, Weaver with the matchup numbers—Belanger was hitting second, moved up from his usual ninth spot for this game.

Rich Dauer, the Orioles' Game 1 nine-hole hitter, was due to hit. Instead, Weaver sent pinch-hitter Terry Crowley to the plate.

"I'm like, 'Oh, God,'" Steinberg says. "So I call Kim and ask, 'Did you get the stats to Earl?' She said, 'Yes, I gave them to him myself.' Earl was a genius. He wanted Crowley to get an intentional walk with first base open. But [then–Angels manager] Jim Fregosi double-crosses him and later says, 'I wanted to pitch to a cold bat on a cold October night.'"

So after Crowley flied out, the intentional walk was given to Bumbry with two out. Belanger was due to hit next, but since Ryan was out that was not going to happen. In came Lowenstein, who had belted a three-run homer against Montague in Seattle in May—evidence that now was available to Weaver via the freshly obtained, updated matchup sheet. And in the bottom of the tenth inning of Game 1 of the 1979 ALCS, he did it again: another three-run homer to help launch the Orioles to a four-game series win over the Angels.

In the chaos of victory, Bob Brown, the old Orioles publicity director, noticed Steinberg's joy was muted. Steinberg told him, Well, I'm thrilled we won, but the manager is going to throttle me. Then he proceeded to tell Brown all about the mixup and the tension-filled last few innings upstairs in the press box to make sure the manager had the information he required.

"Wow, what a story!" exclaimed Brown, who would pass away in 2020. "That's how an organization comes through under pressure! Everybody plays a part, everybody knows where everybody is, that's the way an organization runs. I'm so damn proud!"

Says Steinberg: "So I figure I'd better go see Earl, and his office is downstairs all the way in the back of the clubhouse. It's like I'm walking a plank. I see Ray Miller and ask, 'Is he in there?' And Ray says, 'Yeah, but he's OK.'

"So I go into his office and it's full of writers. And I say, 'Mr. Weaver, I am *so* sorry.' And he says, 'No, I got the stats in time, you won us a ball game, get a beer!'"

Near the peak of Disco Fever and in a season in which the White Sox forfeited a game when their Disco Demolition Night backfired into a chaotic riot, the We Are Fam-A-Lee Pirates would thwart the Orioles in the World Series. But Weaver, a Hall of Famer who built his teams around pitching, defense, and the three-run homer, managed Baltimore to five one-hundred-win seasons, four American League pennants, and the 1970 World Series title.

Before a game with the Red Sox in 1978, Weaver had rather brusquely placed another packet of statistics in front of Steinberg and demanded: "Is this right?"

Luis Tiant was pitching for Boston that evening. What concerned Weaver was the statistical line for his first baseman, Lee May, who was something like 3 for 31 with no homers and 17 strikeouts against Tiant. The manager thought something was off. So Steinberg, then just nineteen and a second-year intern, went back, hauled out all the score-books in the Orioles archives, and recalculated May's numbers from each previous game against Tiant. He then went back downstairs to find Weaver, who was holding court with the Boston writers before the game. Yessir, Steinberg told him. I've triple-checked and those numbers all came out the same way. They are correct. OK, Weaver said, and bumped May down to seventh in the lineup.

"Now, twenty-five years later I join the Boston Red Sox, and I get to meet Luis Tiant," Steinberg says. "And I'm on a bus one afternoon telling Tiant that story. And Tiant, with his great manner, says, 'You know why he no believe your stats? The Orioles were at Fenway Park one night, I'm doing the pitching, and third inning, Lee May hits a home run off of me all the way over the Green Monster. In the fourth inning. It rained. Game no happen.'"

Weaver recalled the homer but not the rainout. And that illustrates so much. Weaver remembered everything. But sometimes, as with even the most perfect of our memories, details become fuzzy with time.

Ironically, after their early start with numbers and data under Weaver, as an organization, the Orioles were among the industry lag-gards in building out their own analytics department. Even as late as 2016, their last postseason appearance under Buck Showalter and more than a decade after the game's Analytics Revolution, Baltimore employed fewer than half a dozen people in its research and develop-ment department. It wasn't until after the 2018 season, when the team hired Mike Elias as general manager and executive vice president, that it started to play catch-up and modernized its operation. Today, a full decade after Weaver's death and more than three decades after he man-aged his last game for the Orioles, they are so seriously advanced that they even employ one assistant general manager, Sig Mejdal, who for-merly worked at NASA as a biomathematician.

CHAPTER 4

CRIBBAGE AND SKUNKS: THE PLAYERS' MANAGERS

*N*oon. *Terry Francona's office in Boston's clubhouse, Fenway Park, June 2009. Game time was still seven hours away. But the daily cribbage games involving the Red Sox manager, second baseman Dustin Pedroia, third baseman Mike Lowell, and outfielder Mark Kotsay were just starting.*

"He had a nickname for me. 'Neal,'" says Kotsay, now managing the Athletics, formerly of Oakland, and one of seven current managers who played under Francona at some point in their careers. "I'd get skunked. I wouldn't get my pegs to the skunk line, and he started calling me Neal, like, zero."

Neal? Zero?

"You're going to have to ask him what the definition of 'Neal' means."

I didn't have to. A few days later in the spring of 2022, Francona's Cleveland Guardians were scheduled to play Kotsay's Athletics in a Cactus League game. In preparation for setting his own lineup for the day, Francona texted Kotsay twenty-four hours ahead of time: "Hey Neal, who's pitching for you tomorrow?"

Kotsay texted back with his plans and, almost as an afterthought, added: "Why Neal?"

In the manager's office at Cleveland's complex in Goodyear, Arizona, Francona howled with laughter.

"After fucking years of calling you that, you don't know?" Francona taunted in his text back.

Indeed, more than a decade later, Kotsay finally learned the answer from Francona himself: The outfielder's lifelong nickname as a player, naturally, had been "Kots." Working in the Chicago White Sox bullpen in 2008 and 2009 was a relief pitcher named Neal Cotts. So during their cribbage games in Fenway, Pedroia dryly started referring to Kots as Neal. Francona picked it up immediately and, some fourteen or fifteen years later, Kotsay was still "Neal" to Tito.

"I texted Pedroia and I said, 'Hey, dumbass here doesn't even know why we've been calling him that,'" Francona says, still laughing.

———

The best managers perform an alchemy that makes the whole of the team greater than the sum of the parts, and that goes well beyond strategic decisions in the dugout. At its heart, managing is a people business, more now than ever as data and numbers dictate so much of the strategy. And just like in the office where you work or in the school you attend, some have that It factor when communicating with others. Some folks are just naturals. They're genuine. It is a good day when you interact with them because they bring out the best in you, put a smile on your face, leave you ready to take on anything.

Francona was an all-timer when he retired following the 2023 campaign, and remained so when he cut short that retirement to take over the Cincinnati Reds in 2025. Through twenty-three seasons leading Philadelphia, Boston, and Cleveland, this ability enhanced his managerial brilliance because the communication skills dovetailed with his stellar in-game strategy and his deployment of personnel. And those personnel blossomed because of his communication. Gabe Kapler, one of his former players who went on to manage in Philadelphia and San Francisco, says, "I felt like we had good rapport, I understood how he wanted to utilize the roster from player one to twenty-five, and I *really* understood how he wanted to use me as a Red Sox player."

Kapler was the right fielder on the 2004 Red Sox team that broke the eighty-six-year-long Curse of the Bambino to win Boston's first World Series since 1918. He was right-handed, and his role was well defined: He started in the outfield when Boston was facing a lefty, and on days when he did not start, he often was used as a late-inning defensive replacement for Manny Ramirez.

The Red Sox were a veteran-heavy team that was not easy to manage in a baseball-mad city where no detail was too small to blow up into a major news story. Ramirez, Pedro Martinez, David Ortiz, Curt Schilling, Jason Varitek, Johnny Damon, and the gang gave Francona the talent to win in his first year on the job, but also the personalities to risk stepping onto a land mine of perceived disrespect or outright mutiny at any time. Yet Francona held it together beautifully.

Eighteen years later, in another city with a team that was the polar opposite of those Red Sox, Francona managed the 2022 Guardians to an American League Central title. They did not win a World Series. The Yankees—Francona's nemesis during his years piloting Boston from 2004 to 2011—ousted them from a division series after the Guardians beat Tampa Bay in the wild card round of the expanded playoffs. But with Francona in charge, it was a magical summer in Cleveland regardless. The Guardians were the youngest team in the majors, with an average age of twenty-six. They were an afterthought when the season started. Deservedly, Francona earned his third AL Manager of the Year award—and deep into that winter, people were still trying to figure out how he did it.

"Unbelievable feel," Steven Kwan, the Cleveland outfielder, says. "If he thinks a guy is down, he'll talk to him. If the team is sluggish, he'll have a team meeting. But he never overloads on meetings. The feel in him is truly amazing."

Over his career, Francona excelled at being both a leader of veterans and a whisperer of rookies. The latter always is impressive, but Francona was forty-five when he led Boston to the 2004 World Series title and sixty-three when managing Cleveland's Kiddie Corps further past the graham-crackers-and-milk stage than it had a right to go. Something about that seems backward. It takes a special person to relate seamlessly and on a modern level with twenty-somethings into his sixties.

"They don't play like a young team," Mike Chernoff, Cleveland's general manager, said near the end of that 2022 season. "And I attribute that all to Tito. Tito sets the standard."

Surveying the landscape during the spring of 2022, Francona called two of his veteran leaders, third baseman Jose Ramirez and shortstop Amed Rosario, into his office. If I'm going to hold all these young guys to this standard, Francona told them, then I'm going to need you two to hold yourselves to that standard first. I need you to run out every ball, back up every base, teach the kids by setting a perfect example.

"Jose almost walked out of the office because that's just how he plays," Chernoff says. "He said, 'Tito, I got it.' From that day on, those guys set the example and everybody just follows it."

A young player named Will Brennan, twenty-five, was fighting to establish himself in the Cleveland outfield in 2023. He had been called up to the majors the previous September, got a taste of big-league action in eleven games, and now was soaking in as much information as he could. The fact that Francona played the game at this level, understands how much failure occurs, and yet shows compassion and empathy goes a long way toward closing the age gap between the veteran manager and the young team.

"He evaluates how you react to failure," Brennan says. "That's why we run the bases so hard. It's why we work so hard to put the ball in play. He's an absolute legend. And he's coached and managed some unbelievable teams."

The young Guardians appreciated all of that about Francona, as well as his fatherly, or grandfatherly (depending on the day and moment), approach. Gearing up for his first team charter flight late in the 2022 season, Brennan went out and bought himself a new suit. As he was boarding that flight, his manager happened to be walking behind him and suddenly called out to him, "William, I need you over here."

"Uh-oh, I'm already in trouble," Brennan thought to himself.

Instead, Francona reached around behind his neck and snapped off a tag that was sticking out.

"Don't worry," Francona said with a wink. "I won't tell anyone."

To those who know Francona well, that interaction is especially funny. He is not challenging for the cover of *GQ* magazine anytime soon with his own wardrobe. One of baseball's endless charms is that it is the only game in which the manager—or head coach, as it were—dresses out in full uniform. Nobody loves the ritual of the double-knits more than Tito.

"I'm sure people probably think, 'God, a [sixty-six-year-old] man showing up in full uniform,' but that's all I've ever done," says Francona, whose 1,950 managerial wins ranks thirteenth all-time, between Leo Durocher (2,008) and Casey Stengel (1,905). "It's normal for me, right?

"I'd rather wear a uniform than wear a suit, I'll tell you that. But if they allowed us to wear a sweatsuit, I'd probably be OK with that. I never understood why coaches in other sports wear a sport coat and tie for games. That's the last thing I'd want to wear. I'll be in the grave first. I'll be in a fucking casket. I don't want to have a sport coat on, or a suit."

Not only does Francona suit up with a belt and proper shoes in the dugout, but before he pulls on his baseball pants, he tugs on his sliding shorts.

"I'm not going to slide," he quips. "But it's a baseball uniform. And that's what I've always worn. So I do it."

———

When Tito broke in as a player under Dick Williams in Montreal in 1981, texting had not yet been invented and there certainly were no early-afternoon cribbage games in the manager's office. His skipper did not gently reach out to tug a price tag off of his jacket.

Summoned from Triple-A Denver, he arrived in Houston's Astrodome in the middle of a game on August 19. He, of course, was bubbling over with joy. He was enthusiastically greeted by the handful of Expos who were friends of his. The first words from his first manager: "Get a fucking bat," Williams growled. "You're leading off next inning."

Hitting for pitcher Elias Sosa, Francona grounded to first base for an unassisted putout. It was the first of 1,827 plate appearances in the majors over ten years. Francona would finish his career with 474 hits, 16 homers, and 143 RBI during stints with Montreal, the Cubs, Cincinnati, Cleveland, and Milwaukee.

"I pinch-hit that night, then I pinch-hit the next night, and then I played the next game in Atlanta," Francona recalls, before saying of Williams, "I don't think he ever sat down and talked to me. There was no talking to you."

He is not registering a complaint.

"I didn't play for him very long, but he was ahead of the game," Francona continues. "Like, his thinking. You knew a couple of innings ahead you were going to pinch-hit. You could tell he was good. He just wasn't real warm and fuzzy. But he knew baseball."

There is no man alive today who knows more baseball or more enjoys his job than Terry Jon Francona. The "Tito" part came easily: His father, Tito, was a good-hitting first baseman–outfielder over fifteen major-league seasons. The son earned the nickname "Little Tito" while shadowing his father around major-league parks as a young boy. Little

Tito was a clubhouse rat not long after he learned to walk. He grew into a star at the University of Arizona, and as a junior in 1980 won the Golden Spikes Award, given annually to the nation's top amateur player. He was Montreal's first-round pick in 1980 (twenty-second overall) and went on to play ten years in the majors, though significant injuries to both knees short-circuited his career. He bounced from the Expos to the Cubs to Cincinnati, Cleveland, and Milwaukee. He played for four managers in five seasons in Montreal (Williams, Jim Fanning, Bill Virdon, and Buck Rodgers) and then for Jim Frey (Chicago), Pete Rose (Cincinnati), Doc Edwards (Cleveland), and Tom Trebelhorn (Milwaukee).

Baseball dugouts have been filled for more than a century by managers of various shapes, sizes, and dispositions. The "Players' Manager" archetype is time-honored but easily misunderstood. Clearly, they get on well with their players. But there is a fine line between relating to players and simply being a patsy, someone who is easily taken advantage of and allows too much freedom in the clubhouse.

"A Players' Manager, simply put, realizes how hard the game is and understands the ebb and flow of a season," says John Smoltz, who started eight games for Francona's Red Sox near the end of the Hall of Fame right-hander's career in 2009 after two decades playing for another ultimate Players' Manager, the Hall of Famer Bobby Cox.

"When your job is on the line and you're connected to wins and losses, it's easy to lose faith in people," Smoltz continues. "But a Players' Manager understands that losing faith in someone, it's not part of the DNA. You may try to help that person get back on his feet and gain confidence, but a Players' Manager is not letting a player do whatever he wants to do. That's kind of a misconception.

"It's understanding the moments over 162 games, and correcting over the long haul if they happen multiple times. A Players' Manager, you have to be pretty bad to get in their doghouse and not get out. Because, again, he's understanding the scope of leading men in a game of failure."

Maybe because of the battles he watched his dad fight to build his own major-league career, perhaps because of the knee injuries that prevented him from living up to his own potential as a player—likely a combination of the two and more—Francona has never forgotten how hard it is to play the game. Decades after he tagged along with his father throughout the American and National Leagues, he still couldn't get enough. He loves the game and the uniform and the players in his clubhouse the way kids love ice cream and birthday parties. And at sixty-six, with a rebellious body that has suffered through more than thirty surgeries, Francona still has it.

But it's about far more than likeability and feeling good. Francona elicits results because the relationships he builds result in improving the want-to in his players. By and large, they are fully invested under him and pay attention to the details that win games. They stay sharp and ready for situations because he prepares them for those moments before they happen, as Kapler says. And it extends beyond the players: Coaches are better under Francona because of his all-encompassing ability.

The first year Carl Willis worked as pitching coach under Francona, there was an in-game miscommunication that cost the then-Indians a loss because the wrong reliever was warming up at the wrong moment. The confusion involved left-hander Oliver Pérez and right-hander Danny Otero.

"We called Danny 'O.T.' and Ollie 'O.P.,'" Willis says. "I heard him say, 'Get O.T. up.' But he said 'Get O.P. up.' It was a pretty large mistake. We lost the game. We both came in and were upset. The irony of it is, he felt like it was his sole responsibility, and I felt it was my sole responsibility. And the bench coach, Brad Mills, felt it was his sole responsibility.

"Regardless, I begged Tito to let me address the team and he would not allow it. He said, 'It's my responsibility. I'm in charge, I did it.' At the same time, his trust in me never wavered, our relationship never suffered. There was no giving me funny looks. I'll never forget that because it means a lot to me."

When Francona got sick and had to take leaves of absence in consecutive seasons in 2020 and 2021, this loyalty from Willis, bench coach DeMarlo Hale, and others on the Cleveland staff was the glue that held things together and, really, what allowed Francona to return and continue doing what he loved when he healed in 2022.

Hale, who is African American, was with Francona for fourteen years before moving to the Blue Jays organization after Francona's retirement. Together in Boston, they formed a powerhouse Fantasy Football League team called Ebony and Ivory.

"He wanted to change the name to Ivory and Ebony, and I said, 'That ain't happening. The lyrics are Ebony and Ivory,'" Hale says, laughing. "The other thing is, in 2010, he told me to draft a tight end. I said, 'I am not drafting a tight end in the second round.' He said, 'I'm telling you, we need to.' I was like the general manager and he was the president. I was like, 'Who drafts a tight end in the second round?'"

Ebony and Ivory had a solid season in 2010 and went to the championship game. But as the season unfolded, every time the tight end that Hale did not draft scored, Francona would agitate him via text. The tight end's name? Rob Gronkowski, who went on to become one of the NFL's greatest tight ends of all time and helped lead the New England Patriots to four Super Bowl titles.

At the time of the draft, Francona had texted Scott Pioli, then New England's vice president of player personnel. Pioli texted back: Is it important? Yes, Francona assured him, it is.

"So he calls me, and I ask: 'Is Gronkowski going to make the team?'" Francona says. "And he says, 'I'm in a fucking meeting and you called for *that*?'"

After bypassing Gronk and watching the rookie excel as the NFL season played out, Hale says, "It was like, Lord, just let us win." Ebony and Ivory did reach the championship game and had a chance to split the overall pot that was for significant money—somewhere, Hale recalls, around $30,000 or $40,000. But Hale told Francona, Since we did all the work, forget any agreement to split the pot, let's just go for it all. So they did. They lost in the championship. And their big payday disappeared altogether.

"So he wore me out again," Hale, sixty-three, says. "He said, 'You've been wrong all year. You didn't want to draft the tight end, you didn't want to split the pot.' That's why I can't be his teammate now. That stopped right there. Ebony and Ivory was done. I couldn't take it. I was scared to be wrong."

Says Francona: "He fucked everything up. He's not a good partner. It was perfect: If we lost, I could yell at him. And if we won, we won."

On team charter flights, Francona would cue up the Paul McCartney and Stevie Wonder song on his phone as Hale walked down the aisle: "*Ebony and Ivory live together in perfect harmony, side by side on my piano keyboard, oh Lord, why don't we?...*"

"He's like a brother to me," Hale says. "He really is."

Time freezes and teams bond in moments like those.

Cleveland is a forward-thinking, cutting-edge, analytically minded group and has been since club president Chris Antonelli's predecessor, Mark Shapiro, moved the franchise into the Digital Age in the early 2000s. The Guardians thought so highly of Francona, and his ability to bridge the analytics with relationships, that they deferred to him on most baseball decisions (though not necessarily on roster moves). Owner Paul Dolan essentially gave him a lifetime contract. It was an interesting dynamic and spoke highly to the respect engendered by Francona, as many in the industry predicted during Tito's final years that the moment he retired, Cleveland's baseball operations department would lean into the manager's office far more than it had. Sure enough, when the day did come, the Guardians hired Stephen Vogt, thirty-nine, who had one season of coaching experience (Seattle, bullpen coach, 2023), had retired as a player just two years earlier, and had never managed. But baseball ops figured that the coaching staff brought 150 or so seasons' worth of experience that would set a nice foundation from which Vogt could work. As with so many other organizations, now there would be far more collaboration between baseball operations and the manager, a new day in Cleveland.

In the Guardians' defense, from 2013 to 2023 they had a once-in-a-lifetime gem as a skipper. Where do you even go from there?

"It's not just the incredible tactical decisions he makes," says Chernoff, quickly bringing to mind the brilliant way in which Francona deployed left-hander Andrew Miller in all sorts of key moments from the fifth inning on during the 2016 postseason. Miller was named as the MVP of the ALCS against Toronto. In the World Series, the underdog Indians nearly knocked off the Cubs to win what would have been their first title since 1948 until falling short in extra innings in Game 7. "It is the small things with guys he runs into in the clubhouse, or how he brings in a guy for a conversation who needs it. He has the energy to do it at a high level."

Francona excels at handling situations and instructing his players on the finer points of the game no matter who is involved or how big the star. Long before Ortiz, Ramirez, or Martinez came under his watch, Francona was beginning his managerial journey with Double-A Birmingham in the Chicago White Sox system when a raw player named Michael Jordan, taking a break from his storied basketball career, joined the team. Francona historically has stressed being aggressive on the bases as a way to play and win; Jordan may have been an NBA champion but he did not understand the nuances of baseball. Birmingham led 11–0 one day when Jordan, after a double, broke to steal third. Rival manager Dave Miley screamed from the other dugout, asking what the hell Francona's team was doing, trying to run up the score? A flustered Francona hollered back that Jordan didn't understand what he was doing.

"So we get Michael into Tito's office after the game and Tito said, 'What the hell are you doing? You can't be running in a game when we're up 11–0!'" says Mike Barnett, who was with Francona then as a coach and served as Cleveland's video coordinator under Francona. "And Michael says, 'I didn't know any better. In the NBA, we get up by thirty points in the third quarter and then we try to get up by forty in the fourth.'"

In any other environment, Francona would have been intimidated by Jordan. But after a lifetime in the game, Francona had become more comfortable and confident in a dugout or clubhouse than anywhere else in the world. To this day, some twenty-five years or more down the road, as Francona has passed through life-threatening blood-clot issues, ulcers, a gastrointestinal disorder, gout, staph infection, and toe, knee, and hip surgeries, Jordan still checks in on Francona.

"I've tried to be real careful with him, because I've seen people, this poor guy," Francona says of the many directions in which the megastar gets pulled. "But I saw a side of him maybe not a lot of people did, when he lets his guard down. He doesn't do it very often, because he can't. But if I text him, I get one back, I'd say, within thirty seconds."

———

Entering the 2022 season, the Terry Francona Managing Tree was flourishing with a total of nine of his former players pulling the levers in their own dugouts from sea to shining sea: Kapler (Giants), Kotsay (A's), David Ross (Cubs), Torey Lovullo (Diamondbacks), Dave Roberts (Dodgers), Alex Cora (Red Sox), Rocco Baldelli (Twins), Chris Woodward (Rangers), and Kevin Cash (Rays).

By then, Francona was more than two decades into his career. His first job was in Philadelphia in 1997, the youngest skipper in the majors that year at thirty-eight. Unlike his own first manager, Williams, and the Sparky Andersons and Earl Weavers, Francona did not distance himself from his players. Times change. By the late 1990s, players across the board had little tolerance for direct orders and iron fists. In college basketball, even Indiana University deemed its legendary, hotheaded coach Bobby Knight outdated, firing him in September 2000 after he had one too many altercations with players and students. (An avid college basketball fan, Francona maintains courtside seats at his alma mater, the University of Arizona.)

Instead, those player relationships were part of the draw for him—and, over time, would become the secret sauce in his genius.

"Torey Lovullo was the last cut one spring in Philly," Francona says. "He had played his ass off. It was the last cut and it was awful. Not that he didn't handle it good, but it was hard for me. He knew it hurt me."

Francona had big dreams and, other than a starter by the name of Curt Schilling, little pitching. Especially in his bullpens. The 1997 Phillies staff ranked twelfth of fourteen National League teams in ERA, the 1998 Phillies ranked dead last, the 1999 Phils were thirteenth, and then in 2000 they improved to eleventh. But after four losing seasons, he was shown the door.

"I had a lot more energy then," Francona says. "I could throw BP. I knew I was learning on the run. But I also knew how I felt about the players. Then when you get with teams that maybe have a little deeper roster but you still know how you feel about the players, it has a chance to get pretty special."

The nucleus of those rebuilding Phillies teams included such up-and-comers as Scott Rolen, the future Hall of Famer; catcher Mike Lieberthal, who was replacing Darren Daulton, one of the heroes of the 1993 Phillies' NL pennant winners; a fleet center fielder acquired from the Cubs named Doug Glanville; and a slugging first baseman named Rico Brogna.

"Young guys who were still finding their way in the league, and I felt like it was my responsibility to help protect them a little bit and help them learn how to get there even if it meant taking a few bullets," Francona says. "I still feel that way. I'd rather someone from the media think I don't know what I'm doing than throw a player under the bus. I just think it works better that way."

Says Francisco Lindor, the Mets shortstop who debuted under Francona in Cleveland in 2015: "He acts not intelligent, but he's very intelligent. He's brilliant."

Philadelphia paved the way for the Boston job even though Francona's Phillies were a cumulative 78 games under .500 during his four seasons. Francona spent 2001 as a special assistant to baseball operations in Cleveland under Shapiro and Antonetti, then he was Jerry Narron's bench coach in Texas in 2002, and he filled the same role for Ken Macha in Oakland in 2003. He battled more health issues. But the year in Oakland was pivotal to his future success in a way that Francona at the time could not even begin to appreciate. It was the year that *Moneyball* was published, and he was able to peek under the hood at Oakland's analytics operation without the responsibility of being the manager.

"I got kind of an indoctrination and could see what I liked," Francona says. "And what I didn't understand, I could ask. It was really good. *Really* good. It taught me a lot of things I thought maybe I believed."

That October came the Grady Little and Pedro Martinez debacle in Game 7 of the American League Championship Series, a job opening in Boston, and a neophyte Red Sox general manager who had a clear idea of what he wanted.

"I really didn't want to hire any first-time managers, period," says Theo Epstein, Boston's top baseball man from 2003 to 2011 before he moved on to run the Cubs from 2012 to 2020. "One of the reasons I hired Tito is because I felt like he had learned a lot in his four years in Philly. He was a hot young managerial prospect when the Phillies hired him and then suddenly was a bad manager? No. He just had bad bullpens. I felt like he had really learned from that experience."

The pairing was as perfect as chowder and oyster crackers. Epstein was remaking Boston's baseball operations organization, building out a research and development department as the Sabermetrics revolution was taking root. Bill James, the godfather of Sabermetrics (and, at that point, author of several *Baseball Abstract* annuals), was hired. Francona was enough of a player at heart to relate well in the clubhouse. Yet, especially after his education in Oakland watching Billy Beane crack the analytic whip on Macha, he was learned and open-minded enough to accept and implement the data and information sent to him from the team's burgeoning analytics department.

As would be the case later when he was running the Chicago Cubs and hired Dale Sveum, Rick Renteria, and then Joe Maddon as managers, Epstein and his group valued experience, open-mindedness, and collaboration.

"We didn't want somebody who you could just control," Epstein says. "You will not go anywhere if your players think the manager is controlled by the front office. We wanted guys with some backbone but who were also collaborative, wanted to work with us, but also would stand up for themselves and make it clear to the players that the authority rested with them."

Under Francona, not only did the Red Sox—and, then, Cleveland—flourish, but it is indicative that players who play under him sharpen their thinking, anticipate situations, and execute. And win.

"Tito, for me, stands out as one of the more passionate, caring, loving managers in the game," Kotsay says. "He really, truly, shows that to his players. He left an impact on me when I played for him in Boston. If I could have half the career Tito's had in managing and have half the impact on players, I'll leave this game really happy."

Francona says he was especially hard on Cora, who ultimately would join him in Boston's lineage of managers, "because I felt he had the ability to be a leader. I told him, 'I'm probably unfair to you.' He helped Pedroia like nobody's business."

The Red Sox picked up Cora as a utility infielder in 2005, with ticker tape still floating through the breeze in the heady days following their 2004 World Series title. Cora played for Boston for two and a half years with a very well-defined role: He was a backup second baseman to start, behind Mark Bellhorn and Mark Loretta. But beginning in 2006, he also was given a very specific duty: to help bring along a twenty-two-year-old future second baseman named Dustin Pedroia.

Today, the current Boston manager chuckles and nods knowingly when I tell him the old Boston manager cops to being extra hard on him in part because Francona identified Cora as a future manager.

"It was just the role and the expectations and everything that he wanted me to be as a twenty-fifth guy on the roster," Cora says. "You know, taking care of Pedroia and all that stuff. I think he understood that I was very important and he pushed me to be that guy. I had a role."

Cora says Francona was "straight up" with him immediately, and as such Cora knew "where [his] feet were in the clubhouse, and in the dugout," knowing exactly what was expected of him. Toward the end of Cora's time in Boston as a player, Francona gave it to him straight, that he thought the infielder would manage in the big leagues one day.

"His advice was like, you have to delegate, you have to trust your coaches," says Cora, who easily can be classified as a Players' Manager today. "I started paying attention to the way he relied on Millsy and DeMarlo and [then–pitching coach] John Farrell at that point. I was like, there's a lot of stuff that goes on, in that city especially. They pull you from one side to the other. You have to deal with the media and expectations, and if you don't surround yourself with capable people, people that you trust and can do a job, then you're going to be in trouble."

Cora and Mike Lowell were nearing the end of their playing careers in Boston and were "the bridge guys," Cora says. "We were bilingual, we can deal with the Latino guys and the American guys and kind of, like, unite everybody."

The parameters of Cora's job have changed since he led the Red Sox to their fourth World Series title in fifteen years in 2018. He was hired by Dave Dombrowski, an old-school executive who worked for years with Jim Leyland and allows his managers wide latitude. Eccentric Red Sox owner John Henry stunningly fired Dombrowski in 2019, less than a year after he and Cora built that 2018 World Series winner. Boston replaced Dombrowski with former Tampa Bay executive Chaim Bloom, who lasted just four years before he was fired. So, when Cora returned from a one-year suspension in 2021 relating to his involvement with the Houston Astros' cheating scandal (he was a coach there under manager A. J. Hinch), he stepped into a world in which he had to operate with far more constraints than he once did. Unlike Dombrowski, who spends freely in old-school fashion, Bloom clearly was hired to plug back into Henry's cold-blooded spreadsheet—and less expensive—way of constructing a team. The plug-and-play Bloom Sox traded Mookie Betts and installed Enrique Hernandez at shortstop, among many other moves in de-emphasizing stars—and de-emphasizing defense.

"The roster is the roster," Cora said tersely during one 2023 stretch in which his Red Sox were getting drummed by the Yankees, Rays, Orioles, and Blue Jays. Translation, straight from the Manager's Unwritten Handbook: I've got no input in the roster. All I can do is play the players they give me.

Henry made his fortune at the age of thirty-one in 1981, when he developed a mechanical, trend-following method for managing a futures trading account. His company managed money via a system that removed human emotion and subjective analysis. It was to asset management what *Moneyball* would be to baseball two decades later: a bloodless data-reading way of doing business that was ruthlessly efficient. It decided which assets to trade based on a proprietary, objective system that studied various market trends.

That same year, on August 12, 1981—exactly one week before Francona stepped into a major-league batter's box for the first time—IBM announced the release of the first IBM Personal Computer, which quickly became the first dominant personal computer in the world. Henry and his partners, Tom Werner and Larry Lucchino, completed their purchase of the Red Sox two decades later, in 2002. In short order, Epstein and his assistants were green-lit to build out a state-of-the-art baseball analytics system in Fenway Park. Henry's estimated net worth is $4 billion today, and he did not get there by allowing the Dombrowskis of his business or baseball worlds to spend unchecked and with emotion.

Henry does not like confrontation and is exceedingly awkward in person. He didn't even bother to show at the Fenway Park press conference announcing Francona's departure despite Tito having played a pivotal role in making Henry even more rich and famous via baseball by winning two World Series. When Henry does choose to communicate from behind his closed doors, email is his preferred method. But even Francona's emails went unanswered after the Red Sox dumped him.

Which is how it came to be that Cora, in two tours of duty managing the Red Sox (pre- and post-suspension), is tasked with maneuvering his way through wildly different administrations. Dombrowski, hired in August 2015, lasted four years and was fired just ten months after the 2018 World Series. But the players—star or not—respond well to Cora. So do the media and the tough Boston market in general. It is easy to see some of the tricks he learned from the genial Francona.

"It's different, you know?" Cora, who aspires one day to be a general manager or president of baseball operations, says of the pressures and stress that are unique to Boston. "Early in the [2023] season, Tampa Bay had a twelve-game winning streak, and when you walk past their dugout, there's three beat writers. And here, it's a packed house every day. One thing for sure is, I've kind of learned how to control the narrative. At the end of the day, I'm the one talking twice a day, and the way I conduct myself and talk about the team is how people see it. And you've got to make sure you're consistent with it. What you said on February 14 about the team, you better say it on June 14 unless something has changed."

Before they went head-to-head in the AL East and compared the disparate sizes of their daily media, Cora shared a bench seat with Cash on most nights in Boston in 2007 and 2008. Like Francona, Cash has an infectious personality and an improv-ready sense of humor. But the Rays, of course, are one of the organizations most steeped in putting the numbers ahead of the player. Just ask Snell. Cash has the unique ability of administering heavy doses of analytics to his players without them taking it personally.

"The biggest thing about him is, he's always relaxed," says slugger Luke Raley, another of the Rays' on-the-cheap, smart analytics pickups when they acquired him from the Dodgers in a minor-league deal in March 2022. "And he does such a great job of keeping us relaxed."

Part of his method for doing that is delivering one-liners with the expert timing of a comedian. Before the Rays traded Raley to Seattle in 2024, Cash frequently told him before games that Yu Darvish, or Gerrit Cole, or whomever that night's rival starting pitcher was, was thrilled when he saw Raley's name in the lineup. Raley's family owns a Christmas tree farm in northeast Ohio, and another of Cash's entertaining motivators was to tell the slugger that the enemy starting pitcher that night also has a Christmas tree farm, and that his is better than Raley's.

In their own ways of reaching players, Roberts shares similar traits in Los Angeles, as does Baldelli in Minnesota. Like Tampa Bay, both of those organizations lean heavily into analytics. So, like Cash, their job is as much interpersonal communications and preparation as it is brainstorming creative strategy.

———

A Players' Manager classifies naturally under Torre's description of the game having a heartbeat, and that those in positions of responsibility should never forget it no matter what the computer spits out and the algorithms dictate.

Charlie Manuel was able to forge a special bond with his players, first as a hitting coach for winning teams in Cleveland and then as a manager both in Cleveland—before the then-Indians waded into the deep end of the Sabermetrics pool—and Philadelphia, where he led the Phillies to a World Series title in 2008. As a hitting coach in Cleveland, he literally would wrestle with slugger Manny Ramirez to get Ramirez's blood pumping enough to go into the batting cage to do his work—and keep his concentration where it needed to be. The team would be preparing for its pregame activities and there would be its six-four, 195-pound hitting coach and its six-foot, 225-pound slugger rolling around on the clubhouse carpet, each attempting to put the other into a headlock. A different way of motivating, sure. But Ramirez led the AL in both slugging and on-base percentage in 1999 when Manuel was Cleveland's hitting coach, and again in 2000 when Manuel was the manager. He also led the majors with 165 RBI in 1999 and, under Manuel in 2000, the Indians won ninety games and just missed the AL wild card spot. Hall of Famer Jim Thome also grew up and thrived under Manuel's tutelage, coming to view him as a father figure when he played and, still, today.

"From the moment I met Charlie Manuel as a wide-eyed kid in the Gulf Coast League, I knew this was someone I could connect with instantly," Thome said during his induction speech on a warm 2018 summer's day that was perfect for slugging in Cooperstown, New York. "Charlie took a scrappy young kid who was anxious to hit a million home runs and actually encouraged those crazy dreams. He told me that I could hit as many home runs as I wanted to."

That is baseball as art. Creative and imaginative, driven by emotion, coupled with smart instruction. It is the opposite of analytics, which is zero emotion and, essentially, caps a player's ability by identifying what he doesn't do well and, instead of teaching and developing those areas, finds a second puzzle piece that simply plugs in to overcome the first player's shortcomings.

"If you'd be standing at the cage or in the dugout listening to me, I joke and kid with the players and you'd look at me as good old Uncle Charlie," Manuel says. "But I was totally different from that when it came to being a manager."

Indeed, he still *could* be good old Uncle Charlie at times, but not if a player pushed him. He benched a young Jimmy Rollins a couple of times for not running balls out in Philadelphia before Rollins blossomed into the 2007 National League Most Valuable Player and then helped lead the Phillies to the 2008 World Series title.

"I think structure counts in the clubhouse," Manuel says. "And it starts when you run balls out and be on time."

Torre, who was able to facilitate tremendous relationships with almost everybody except Alex Rodriguez when he was in the Bronx, was so good he lasted twelve years managing the Yankees—the longest stretch of any pinstriped manager since Stengel (1949–1960). Torre, who led the Yanks to ten AL East titles in those twelve years, had feel. One small example: One day he went to the mound for a talk with Bob Tewksbury when they were both in St. Louis. Tewksbury thought Torre was coming to remove him because the manager never came to the mound unless it was for that reason; usually it was the pitching coach who visited to discuss strategy. Consequently, Tewksbury, expecting the hook, let down his mental guard and wound up getting hit hard after Torre's visit. Torre recognized the issue and, from that point on, made this adjustment: When, as a manager, he was going to remove a pitcher, he walked to the mound. When he wanted to go to the mound to get a feel for the pitcher, he jogged. This signaled the pitcher that Torre's mind wasn't yet made up. It was seemingly a small thing, but something that helps a player retain his mental edge, rather than relax, is far from a small thing. More often than not, it led to successful results.

Tewksbury, a former All-Star pitcher, talks about this in *Ninety Percent Mental*, the book we co-authored during his nearly two-decade run as a mental skills coach for the Boston Red Sox, San Francisco Giants, and Chicago Cubs. And during subsequent conversations for this book, Tewksbury emphasized that managers who earn the respect of their players *always* will matter.

"Players want to know where they stand," Tewksbury says. "They can deal with the hard facts, but not the ambiguity of not knowing. It is important that the manager cares about them as a player. The old 'I don't want to get too close to the players' comment is crap, at least in today's game. Bobby Valentine is a great example of a manager who the players didn't respect when I was with Boston in 2012. Joe Torre, Tito, and Bruce Bochy are at the other end of the respect spectrum. Good managers pay attention to their entire roster, not just the stars. Jim Leyland and Joe Maddon are good examples of this. They roamed the field during batting practice and talked to players instead of hanging at the cage."

Trust is a by-product of this communication. When a player trusts that a manager cares about him, then it becomes easier for a player to give himself what Tewksbury calls "permission to succeed": The player's confidence soars as unfounded doubts are released. And at that point, he also becomes more receptive, Tewksbury says, to "hard conversations" a manager may need to have with him.

One of the many areas in which Torre's genius at managing people was evident was in his ability to hear a player out on a sensitive subject while also during the conversation leading the player to understand that a teammate, a coach, an executive, or a manager may have a different point of view. Little-known fact: Insecurity abounds in big-league clubhouses. Players almost always view a particular moment through the prism of how it immediately affects them. But a Players' Manager builds strong enough relationships in which—not always, but often—he can convince a player to move off one position and take another after explaining the trickle-down effect on the team.

Failing that, when disagreements arise or something comes up that isn't the way the manager wants it done, the best will recognize that maybe the message is better coming from someone else. During his Yankees' glory years, Torre leveraged Derek Jeter beautifully: Jeter was Torre's chief conduit in the clubhouse; sometimes if the manager felt a message needed to be delivered to a player such as, say, Chuck

Knoblauch or Johnny Damon, but felt that message would be better absorbed coming from a player instead of the manager, Torre sent it through Jeter.

Similarly, it's what Francona did in using Cora and Lowell as an extension of his own leadership…and what he did in Cleveland by deploying veterans such as Jason Giambi and Mike Napoli (in 2016, Napoli became such a cult figure that Indians personnel and fans both wore PARTY AT NAPOLI's T-shirts all around town).

"Me and him hit it off right from the beginning," says Napoli, who was thirty-four during his one season in Cleveland and now is a coach on Counsell's Cubs staff. "I was in his office every single day. He always made me feel good about stuff, always reassured me when I was struggling. He would sometimes go through me to get a message out to a player, and it made you feel good to be thought of in that way, to be a lifeline for him."

Along with pitchers Josh Tomlin and Bryan Shaw and outfielder Michael Brantley, Napoli was part of the almost-daily cribbage games in the manager's office in Cleveland. Out of those would come team-related discussions, bonding ideas, and more. When Napoli left the manager's office with a message, it often "was just trying to get on a guy, maybe get a little more pep in his step, or if he was getting off the path, get him back on. Little conversations like that."

Specifically, Napoli spent time with outfielder Tyler Naquin.

"He was a young guy, and just making sure he was not too hard on himself," Napoli says. "Don't worry about all the outside noise kind of stuff. I was really close with Naquin already, so it was an easy conversation to have. He knew it was coming from a good place. I tried to approach it how I would want to hear it. Be honest. Like it was coming from me. I left Tito out of it. That was the whole point."

It's not dissimilar to having children. Sometimes kids are more apt to listen to their peers than their own parents. You pick and choose your battles.

At the same time, things are not always what they seem, especially from the outside. Given the size and length of player contracts today, it isn't as easy as it once was for a manager to crack the whip. Billy Martin and Dick Williams held the ultimate power because they could leverage playing time. Now, many players have longer contracts and more financial security than do the manager. Consequently, even if a manager benches a player, in most cases it will not wield the impact that it once did. So managers at times must be wily and political, and tread carefully.

Before things blew up on Little in Boston, there was a game in which Manny Ramirez tapped a one-hopper back to the mound and then barely ran as the pitcher threw to first base for the out. It was so egregious that the talk radio screamers, a large segment of fans, and even some in the media were calling for Little to teach Manny a lesson for not running by delivering some punitive measure. Little did not.

"When the season was over, he came into the office and we happened to sit down and we were talking," Steinberg says. "He says, 'You remember that game when everybody was calling for my head to bench the guy?' Well, there are three things you've got to know about that. One, when he came back to the bench, he came right down the line and apologized to every player for not running out that ball. Two, he got the game-winning hit. And three, if you bench a guy in his situation, he's liable to sit out the rest of the year. You're out of postseason contention. So what's the consequence to *him* when he doesn't play?"

Furthermore, Little explained, before the coaches and manager jump in and discipline a player, there has to be a guy on the team whose statistics, stature, and credibility allow him to approach a player like Ramirez and say flatly, "We don't do that here." Jeter in New York for Torre. Giambi for Francona in Cleveland. Chipper Jones for Bobby Cox in Atlanta. Little had a leader, but he hadn't quite established the credibility yet. That player was Jason Varitek, and he would naturally step into that role as the Red Sox ascended under Francona.

Pedro Martinez and Manny Ramirez remain the two most difficult players Francona has ever managed. Martinez was nearing the end of his time in Boston during Francona's first season there in 2004. He was jealous of Schilling's acquisition and felt disrespected by management over that and for contractual reasons. One of Francona's rules was that a starting pitcher, after being removed, cannot leave before the game ends. Well, Pedro was the starter on Francona's first Opening Day in 2004, threw six innings in a 7–2 loss in Baltimore, and guess who was long gone from the clubhouse by the time the game ended? He also was late to the ballpark on several other occasions that summer.

"He's a sweetheart whenever I see him now," Francona says. "But when I got to Boston, he was already set in his ways. And I had to either swallow my ego or, if I tried to instill my will, that wasn't necessarily going to help us win.

"Manny, he was *hard*. I don't think people understand, he has an extremely sweet side to him. But when you're in charge, when things go off the rails, it can get challenging with him.'"

Manny Being Manny moments were far more voluminous than the rabid Red Sox fan base realized. He heard things nobody else heard, saw things nobody else saw, and presented daily challenges for which traditional paths to managing simply were incapable of preparing a man. Beyond their hardball doctorates, those who managed Manny at times needed to draw from skill sets that included psychiatry, babysitting, child psychology, negotiation, elementary education, secondary education, kinesiology, and outright bribery. Manny could barely remember which hamstring he said was sore yesterday, let alone today. He took days off. He was keenly aware of what others were doing, afraid somebody was getting treatment that was far more special than his. And each time he failed to run hard to first base elicited more groans.

"I was told when I came to Boston, 'Keep Manny on the field, and win,'" Francona says. "There was one time I think I called eight of the veterans into my office. We were going through a bad period with

Manny. I had been there awhile. I said, 'Hey, I see what you guys see. I'll handle it if you want me to. But David, just know, he ain't hitting behind you then. And Tek...' And they were all like, 'Hey, we'll take his numbers and keep him out there.' I just didn't want them to think I didn't care."

Besides, what was Francona going to do, wrestle Ramirez?

"That's a hard one," he says. "There are a lot of games I probably swallowed and turned the other way and didn't feel good about myself. But if you try to instill your will, at what cost? I remember telling Theo after '04, 'Hey, I think we can win and do it in a better way.' Because Manny in the batter's box, it was special. But when he left the batter's box, you didn't know what the hell was going to happen. And we're playing the Yankees and Jeter is doing something in between innings to beat you. It was hard for me to take."

———

When he managed the Red Sox in the summer of 1977, Don Zimmer had a series of clashes with a handful of his players. In later years, Zimmer, who was eighty-three when he passed away in 2014, became well known as Torre's congenial consigliere of a bench coach. But as a manager, he was an uninspiring 114-190 for four different organizations—San Diego, Boston, Texas, and the Cubs. He was in charge when the 1978 Red Sox blew an eight-game AL East lead down the stretch and lost a one-game playoff to the Yankees in the unforgettable Bucky Bleeping Dent game.

Left-handed pitcher Bill Lee, nicknamed the "Spaceman" for good reason, dubbed Zimmer the "Gerbil" in 1977. Players were already beginning to distrust the system by the early 1970s (Jim Bouton's revealing *Ball Four*, published in June 1970, offered a vivid peek into the changing times), and that mushroomed as the decade progressed. This was during the post-Vietnam, post-Watergate, "Don't trust anyone over thirty" days of youthful rebellion.

Managers, who always had taken their authority for granted, not only were slow to recognize the culture change—those in charge, comfortable in their positions and adverse to change, usually are—but increasingly struggled as it was happening. Respect for authority figures quickly was eroding. Lee famously said he sprinkled his breakfast cereal with marijuana. Zimmer most certainly did not. A *Chicago Tribune* columnist, John Schulian, had memorably described Billy Martin as "a mouse studying to become a rat," so someone asked Lee, if that was the case, then what was Zimmer? That's where the "Gerbil" line came from.

Lee wasn't Zimmer's only nemesis. In 1976, Lee, Ferguson Jenkins, Rick Wise, Jim Willoughby, and Bernie Carbo dubbed themselves as the "Royal Order of the Buffalo Head" after Jenkins told a reporter that "the buffalo is the dumbest animal known to man. The Indians used to hunt them by driving one off a cliff. All the rest would follow."

Nevertheless, Zimmer's four-and-a-half-season run in Boston was his longest managerial tenure. He fought back, and he survived. By 1979, Zimmer's last year as Boston's manager, the Red Sox had systematically shed themselves of Jenkins, Wise, Willoughby, and Carbo.

"You can see fear," Gossage says of managing in general. "It's like a parent. If kids see frightened parents, they're going to be ten times worse.

"It's like life. You've got to let life come to you. That's why baseball and life parallel. Both are filled with failure, and you've got to deal with the shit coming at you."

Lou Piniella mostly was enormously popular with his players in New York, Cincinnati, Seattle, and Tampa Bay as he straddled that line between Dictator (early in his career) and Players' Manager (later). Yet even he charged into his Reds' clubhouse to fight reliever Rob Dibble in September 1992. He was hotheaded, as evidenced by any highlight video you see of him ripping a base off its mooring and heaving it through the air during an ejection. And he was fiercely competitive. He managed Paul O'Neill in Cincinnati. Then, when he was leading

Seattle and Tampa Bay, he sometimes made sure his pitchers dusted O'Neill because he knew the hitter was emotional and sometimes could be thrown off his game with a knockdown pitch.

"When I was young we almost went to fisticuffs on several occasions," says Bret Boone, the former infielder, who played for Piniella in Seattle in 1993, when he was twenty-four, and again in 2001, when he was thirty-two and the Mariners went 116-46. "Now, fast-forward to 2001, when I had my best year, and Lou was always sarcastic and funny. He came to me one day and said, 'Boonie, you've played fifty or sixty games straight, I need to give you a day off.'"

Well, managing players on hot streaks isn't always a day on Easy Street, either. Yes, the player generally is in a good mood. Yes, he is producing. But knowing what might be best for a hot player and implementing it are two different things.

"No way in hell you're giving me a day off," Boone told Piniella. "I'm on fire."

So on what was supposed to have been a day off for Boone in Oakland, Piniella relented.

First at bat: strikeout.

Second at bat: pop to catcher.

"Everybody's in a good mood because we're leading the division by twenty games," Boone says. "We're losing 2–0. As I come back to the dugout, Lou turns to the entire dugout, throws up his hands, and says, 'If you guys are depending on Boone to come through for you today, you're going to have to wait a long time. He's 0 for 2 and was supposed to have had a day off.'"

Boone laughs.

"Your first impression is, 'F you,'" he says. "But it was funny. I go 0 for 4 and, after the game, I go to Lou and I say, 'Skip, you son of a bitch, I'll give you this: In the future, the next time you give me a day off, I will accept it.' He laughed, we hugged, and he said, 'Boonie, you got a deal. I want to give you a breather this week. You pick the day.'"

Rare is the manager with the singular ability to combine knowledge, feel, instincts, and textbook decision-making with the deep human touch required to keep a player confident, productive, and happy.

When Torre's tenure with the Yankees ended as algorithms encroached upon space formerly reserved for heartbeats in the Bronx, he finished his career by managing three years in Los Angeles (2008–2010). By then, the public relations maestro Steinberg had left the Red Sox and was working for the Dodgers. And at the trade deadline in 2008, the Dodgers and Red Sox completed the blockbuster deal that sent a familiar, slugging man-child west. Everybody in the Red Sox orbit was familiar with him, and relieved to see him go.

Ramirez.

The baggage was substantial by then. Everyone wondered how Torre, whose Yankees were the epitome of class and professionalism, would handle the flighty Ramirez, who too often was neither of those things. It was another fly-on-the-wall moment for Steinberg, who happened to be in the clubhouse and witnessed Torre greeting Ramirez for the first time.

"He extended his right hand and shook Manny's right hand," Steinberg says. "But as he did, he put his left hand on Manny's right shoulder and said, 'Hi, son.' And I watched Manny just melt.

"It was something."

Manny was thirty-six by then, and still productive enough to help power the Dodgers to consecutive NLCS wins against Philadelphia in 2008 and 2009. As with so many Manny things, though, it came with an asterisk: He was suspended early in the 2009 season when he tested positive for performance-enhancing drugs. The Dodgers waived him in 2010. He would play in only twenty-nine more big-league games afterward, with the White Sox and Tampa Bay.

As the culture changed, the "my way or the highway" dictum became a relic from a bygone era. Managers with good bedside manners with their players, such as Torre and Atlanta's Bobby Cox, ascended with great success. But time keeps moving: One small procedural move that the two Hall of Famers Torre and Cox shared was that each had a clubhouse rule that players must listen to music via their headphones or earbuds. They each disallowed clubhouse stereos. Their reasoning was simple and based on common sense: Different players come from different cultures and, thus, enjoy different styles of music. Consequently, music could lead to needless arguments. The Latin players in the room don't necessarily want to listen to country music. Players from rural America don't necessarily get salsa or merengue. And everyone but the heartiest metalheads may lose it when Guns N' Roses is cranked up to 10.

One of the seminal moments in Wrigley Field history came on the final day of the Cubs' disappointing 2004 season, when Sammy Sosa begged out of the lineup and left the ballpark fifteen minutes after the first pitch of Chicago's game with Atlanta, and, by day's end, a still-unidentified Cub took a baseball bat to Sosa's boom box in the clubhouse. The badly beaten boom box, broken and muted, signified the end of Sosa's usefulness to the Cubs. The players had had it with years of DJ Sammy blasting music to wall-shaking degrees in the clubhouse, ignoring requests to turn it down, his diva behavior finally reaching the point of no return. And that incident occurred under the charge of music lover Dusty Baker, one of the greatest and most perennially hip of all the Players' Managers.

"I will set the record straight by saying there were twenty-four guys upset with what happened," Cubs pitcher Kerry Wood told me in 2015, speaking of Sosa's early departure while declining to say whether he was the one who took the first swing at the boom box. "There are things that need to be kept inside the clubhouse."

By the 2010s, as iPods and cell phones and then streaming services became ubiquitous, earbuds had turned nearly every baseball clubhouse library-silent before games. When they weren't hitting early, on the training table, or attending another in an endless stream of scouting meetings designed to digest more information sent from the analytics gurus, many players listened to music or watched videos at their lockers, lost in their devices, the outside world just a rumor.

Soon enough, the music came after games, when teams began celebrating every routine victory with postgame clubhouse dance parties—like the 2016 World Series–winning Cubs, long after the echoes of Sosa had disappeared. Now, managers had to figure out—and coexist with—the whims and wants of young players who came of age in the "every player gets a trophy" Little League generation. Epstein, then the Cubs president of baseball operations, said following a disappointing 2018 season that teams now were dealing with "ultramillennials" and that "if you're not making adjustments, you're falling behind."

That was why, at baseball's annual winter meetings in Las Vegas that December, with the Cubs coming to a post–World Series crossroads and Joe Maddon's expiration date as manager beginning to move into view, the ever-with-it skipper showed up with a copy of the book *Managing Millennials for Dummies*.

"You always think this 'for Dummies' thing is really rudimentary written—but it's really well written and researched," Maddon said of the book authored by Hannah L. Ubl, Lisa X. Walden, and Debra Arbit. "I'm learning about traditionalists, baby boomers, the Xers, the millennials. And I'm really starting to understand this a little bit better."

Maddon preceded Cash as Tampa Bay's manager in 2006. He was an unconventional hire at the time by then–Rays general manager Andrew Friedman, who later would take charge of the Dodgers and hire Dave Roberts. Maddon, then fifty-two and even at the time considered on the older side for a first-time skipper, replaced Piniella after having served as a coach in the Angels organization—majors and minors—for three decades. He was an erudite choice, someone who bicycled by day and managed by night, a Renaissance Man sort of leader who loved classic rock, Motown, and reading. He broke up the tedium of spring training by bringing in zoo animals. He made the grind of the road more tolerable by designing themed road trips. When Jake Arrieta tossed a no-hitter in Dodger Stadium in 2015, for example, the Cubs were all dressed in pajamas for the late-night charter flight home. In Tampa Bay, the Rays traveled in grunge wear, 1950s-style clothes, and letterman sweaters. Earl Weaver would have blanched.

Now, the man who rhapsodized over the virtues of his favorite author, Pat Conroy—Maddon once told me he would rescue the discarded, crumpled-up, typewritten pages of Conroy's out of a trash can and read those, he enjoyed the author so much—was doing his best to dumb down.

"Whether anybody here agrees or disagrees with the generation and how they process things doesn't matter, because that's the way it is," Maddon said. "And if that's the way it is, just like my dad, that generation thought we were a bunch of babies, the boomers. The traditionalists thought they're all soft. And then you think the Xers are soft. The Xers think the millennials are soft. It doesn't matter. You have to figure out how to communicate and extract the best out of this group and make sure that you're always on the same page."

Maddon was still on top of the world following the Cubs' World Series title a couple of years earlier, but even that was a narrow escape. Francona's Cleveland team rallied for three runs in the eighth inning of Game 7 to knot the score at 6–6 and send the home fans into a frenzy that was briefly paused when the rains came following the ninth inning, causing a short delay. Cubs outfielder Jason Heyward called an impromptu, players-only meeting that took place in a room just off of the clubhouse, a gathering that carried a defiant tone as the angry players felt that Maddon had mismanaged closer Aroldis Chapman, and they vowed not to let those mistakes or anything else take the title away from them. The issue was that the manager used Chapman for twenty pitches during a 9–3 Game 6 rout instead of saving him for Game 7. Chapman was the Cubs' chief bullpen weapon and had only so many bullets. To use him in Game 6, many felt, was shortsighted.

Then, by bringing Jon Lester in from the bullpen in the fifth inning of Game 7, it meant that the Cubs had to call upon aging catcher David Ross, as well. The trickle-down there: When Chapman entered in the eighth, he had to throw only fastballs because at that point in his career, Ross couldn't handle Chapman's breaking pitches. Rajai Davis smashed Chapman's fourteenth consecutive fastball for a two-run, game-tying homer. Things became a mess in a hurry for the Cubs, the rains came, Chapman was in tears after blowing the lead, and the players were not happy with the way events played out. Then, they won it in the tenth.

As the culture and geopolitical landscape of the world shifts, so, too, do the generations—which reduces the odds that Players' Managers will remain successful over time. Once, a man who led the Cubs to their first World Series title in a century would have been Manager for Life in Wrigley Field if he so chose. Instead, Maddon and the Cubs parted ways following the 2019 season. He was snapped up by the organization in which he grew up, Arte Moreno's Los Angeles Angels. His first season was shortened by the worldwide COVID-19 pandemic. The Angels went 77-85 in 2021 and then Maddon, at sixty-eight, was fired in June 2022.

Almost always, through nobody's fault, voices get old and tired, and new ones are needed. Players who find zoo animals fun one spring view the same thing as gimmickry by the third, fourth, fifth time around.

Rules of engagement change because life is fluid. And one unavoidable, biological fact for managers is that while they become older each year, the basic age of the players remains roughly the same. So it is that Francona, at sixty-four, was managing the majors' youngest team, with an average age of about twenty-six, again in 2023. The big difference was that things in Cleveland are more muted than they were in Boston.

"I tell people, there was a fire to put out every day and if there wasn't one, somebody would make one up," Francona says of his big-market Boston days. "You've got to be young and energetic to be doing that and I'm not young and energetic anymore. So, I look at Cora. He's young and can do it. I couldn't do that anymore."

One component of the magic trick he continues to perform, Francona reveals, is that coaching staffs are bigger today than they were even a decade or so ago. Now there are two or three hitting coaches, and two or three pitching coaches, and he does not hesitate to delegate. He retreats to his office before pregame batting practice to sneak some rest. He has no choice: He has to manage his health while managing his players. Though it is survival, he feels bad even doing that because he worries it may cause him to miss out on a conversation or two that could be important.

When he was younger and more spry, he kept daily "office hours" by making the rounds in the outfield and talking with his players during batting practice. The conversations ranged from a play in the previous night's game to a hitter's slump to what was going on at home with a pitcher. They evolved organically, the best way. He never liked to call players into his clubhouse office for conversations because the rest of the team would see that and think something was wrong. Think back to your school days, when a classmate was summoned to the principal's office. All eyes would be on that student afterward, with lots of whispering and conjecture about what was up.

With the Red Sox in 2010, ace Josh Beckett's four-year, $68 million extension came partly because of one of these on-field, batting practice conversations. Everyone knew that Beckett was heading into the last year of his deal, and different players react differently to the uncertainty of impending free agency. The business of baseball may be out of the purview of the field manager, but keeping a finger on the pulse of each player's physical and mental health is not. Above all, a manager must protect his team. And a Players' Manager does that in ways that aren't necessarily within everyone's skill set. When Francona and Beckett talked that day, a simple manager-player check-in resulted in a conversation in which the pitcher mentioned to the manager a rough salary figure he was looking for, and Francona thought it was reasonable enough that he passed it on upstairs to Epstein. The deal soon was done, the pitcher and club were happy, and the season moved along.

"It seems like with Tito, just like with Davey Martinez, Clint Hurdle, Bob Melvin, all of their doors are open," says Josh Bell, ticking off his big-league managers in Cleveland, Washington, Pittsburgh, and San Diego. "They're quick to ask you how your weekend was. Their demeanor, they keep things very comfortable."

Lindor vividly remembers both his first day in the majors and his first playoff game under Francona.

"When I first got called up, he told me, 'Hey, just understand that somebody lost a job today by you getting called up. Respect your peers and show them that you are here to help us win,'" Lindor says, still appreciative of the moment.

The next October, in the time leading up to Game 1 of the World Series in 2016, the shortstop had another moment with the manager.

"You have butterflies right now?" Francona asked.

"Yeah," said the twenty-two-year-old budding star.

"Me, too," responded the two-time World Series–winning manager, fifty-seven at the time. "Enjoy."

At their roots, Players' Managers are natural, and genuine. Players sniff out phonies in an instant. That's why the good ones last.

"A Players' Manager, I hope, is that you ask more of the guys on the field than maybe they've been asked," Francona says. "But at the same time, you care about them more."

As legacies go, that's a pretty good one.

"You want guys to enjoy playing the game, but you want them to enjoy playing it in the right way," Francona continues. "So I think there's a difference between just being silly and enjoying yourself, or enjoying competing and then trying to do it right."

CHAPTER 5

AMERICAN SKIN:
THE MARGINS

Dusty Baker earned the two thousandth win of his managerial career on May 4, 2022, guiding the Houston Astros to a 4–0 win over the Seattle Mariners—and in doing so became the first Black man ever to reach that threshold as a manager. The win sealed what already should be a Hall of Fame induction: Each of the eleven managers who reached that milestone before him was inducted into the Hall of Fame except Bruce Bochy. And Bochy's exclusion is only due to a technicality: He hadn't been retired long enough for his name to be up for a vote. (Then in 2023, at sixty-seven, Bochy unretired to manage the Texas Rangers.)

Six months after that memorable win over Seattle, Baker earned his first World Series ring as a manager when his Astros beat Philadelphia. Now, he stands atop an even greater mountain as the only Black manager to win both two thousand games *and* a World Series.

It was a life-changing experience even for a man with fifty-six years in the game as a player, coach, and manager. And, even for a man who is as comfortable in his own skin as anybody you will ever meet, a proud man who long ago had reached the point where he would match his career against anybody else's even had he never entered the World Series throne room.

Baker has three Manager of the Year awards on his résumé and, the way he figures it, probably should have three more because he knows he did the best job of managing in those particular years, too.

"I don't use America's accolades, I don't read the newspapers, I don't read the internet and other things," he says. "I've dealt with some other managers who were affected by what was said about them.

"I've refused to let other people's opinions affect my self-esteem."

Call that a survival tactic. Call it a good life lesson. For Baker, it's certainly been both.

While win No. 2,000 was a great moment and the Astros players presented Baker with a bottle of Dom Perignon champagne, which they all autographed, it should have happened at least a few years earlier. Over a winter conversation leading into the 2022 season at his wine-tasting room in Sacramento, California, Baker was happy yet slightly—and understandably—hurt. The delay in win No. 2,000 was because of multiple unwanted breaks between jobs. When the Chicago Cubs fired him in 2006, he sat out the 2007 season before Cincinnati hired him in 2008. When the Reds fired him after the 2013 season, he was in exile for two years before Washington hired him in 2016—and that only came after Bud Black rejected a paltry, insulting one-year offer from the Nationals. Then, when the Nats let Dusty go after the 2017 campaign, he was forced to sit out two more seasons before Houston hired him in 2020—and that came only after the digital sign-stealing scandal that caused the Astros to fire both general manager Jeff Luhnow and manager A. J. Hinch.

"He definitely should have been a guy who should have been able to call his own shots like the La Russas and Leylands," says Jerry Manuel, who has spent a lifetime in the industry as a player, coach, and manager.

He now works with the MLB Youth Development Foundation, a joint initiative between the league and the Players Association designed to improve the accessibility to and caliber of amateur baseball and softball for minorities who may otherwise be shut out because of expense.

Manuel, who, like Baker, lives in the Sacramento area, continues: "Guys like Dusty, I know that when he was out, if he made a phone call to somebody, it wasn't the same as some of those other guys in his stature making phone calls. Those are great managers, I'm not denying that. But I also feel the same about Dusty."

By any measure, Baker is one of the greatest managers ever. He had done everything there is to do except manage a team to a World Series title, and now that box is checked. He will be going into the Hall of Fame one day soon. He connects with players better than nearly anyone who has ever managed. Four of the five teams he's piloted had winning overall records during his term (only the Cubs, at a .497 winning percentage, were slightly off). Cincinnati has reached the expanded playoffs only four times in the past twenty-seven years, and three of those came when Baker was managing. He has guided five different franchises to the playoffs, an MLB record since 1901.

And yet.

He has had to scratch and claw for everything he's gotten, and it is difficult not to believe that the color of his skin, in keeping with the history of this game and this country, has made it more difficult for him than it should have been. He only got in the door of his last two jobs as a break-the-glass-in-case-of-emergency hire.

"Something's rotten in Denmark, but there's nothing you can do about it," Baker says. "You can't hire yourself. There are some towns in America that are more conducive to hiring an African American manager than other towns and you realize that" those who do the hiring "have to answer to whatever society says in the town or they have to answer to guys at the country club or whatever, you know. So you just keep the faith.

"Even I had some other guys, minority guys, asking me how I keep getting these opportunities when they can't get them. I don't know, man. You've got to have somebody that likes and trusts you and is not worried about what's going to be said in society about you being hired. And there aren't that many kind of people around."

Baker was raised in Sacramento heeding the lesson that his mother drilled into him from a young age: As an African American, you must be twice as good as everybody else to accomplish the same thing. His father, an Air Force sheet metal technician, taught him all about Jackie Robinson and focused especially on Robinson's ability to turn the other cheek. At times, young Dusty did that. But he will tell you he is not a turn-the-other-cheek kind of guy. And as he earned his place in the game, one thing he learned was a man must stand up for himself, whatever the pigmentation of his skin—and, too often in his case, because of it.

Forty-nine years after Frank Robinson broke the game's managerial color barrier and after Baker's retirement, there were still just two Black managers working in 2024: the Dodgers' Dave Roberts and the Angels' Ron Washington. Both are in Southern California, one area of the country where, to put it in Baker's words, the guys doing the hiring wouldn't have to answer many questions at the country club about hiring a Black man.

It is a battle that has been going on for decades. On Opening Day in 1987, twelve years to the day after Robinson's managerial debut in Cleveland, then–Dodgers executive Al Campanis went on Ted Koppel's ABC *Nightline* program and said of the paucity of Black managers back then: "I don't believe it's prejudice. I truly believe that they may not have some of the necessities to be, let's say, a field manager or perhaps a general manager." Campanis was summarily fired, and in 1992, Cito Gaston managed the Toronto Blue Jays to the first of back-to-back World Series titles.

And yet.

After the Jays let him go following the 1997 season, Gaston did not return to a major-league dugout until 2008, when Toronto brought him back to manage for another two and a half seasons. Men like Jerry Manuel (New York Mets, Chicago White Sox), Willie Randolph (Mets), Don Baylor (Rockies, Cubs), and Lloyd McClendon (Pirates, Mariners) had moderate degrees of success and yet were banished.

"It's not easy to take, either," Baker says. "You try not to harbor any bitterness."

Because one man alone, or two, cannot fight the system. As Baker says, you cannot hire yourself. And if a baseball man wants to stay in the industry to which he has devoted his life, well, the best way to keep hope alive is to accept that job on someone else's coaching staff, work hard, and hope an enlightened executive will grace him with another opportunity. But, as Manuel says, historically, for Blacks, that job on the coaching staff often was that of first-base coach. Which is the least influential job on a staff and comes with the fewest responsibilities.

One of the game's greatest managers ever—whatever his ethnicity—came to his postplaying career by accident. As a kid, Baker loved basketball more than baseball. He began playing more baseball after his parents divorced. That led him to the majors. Then he got divorced and that's the reason he started coaching after his retirement. He had the time and, obviously, the skill and the passion. He was San Francisco's first-base coach and then hitting coach when the Giants fired Roger Craig and named him as their skipper before the 1993 season.

"I didn't request this," Baker says. "Al Campanis is the one that got people talking, and after Campanis is when baseball came look-ing for some newly retired Black ballplayers, namely Cito, Hal McRae, Don Baylor, and myself. And then within a few years after that, within maybe five years, all of us were hired. And that's why I believe that as much as Al Campanis was wrong, out of the rubble and out of the ashes came the opportunities for us, because of what Al said. So out of a negative statement came a positive occurrence for us, but it took a white guy to say that, because Black guys had been crying about opportunity for a long time and going unheard. Other than Maury Wills and Frank at the time."

When the 1993 season started, Baker was managing in San Francisco, Gaston in Toronto, Baylor in Colorado, and McRae in Kansas City. There were a couple of other minority managers as well: Felipe Alou in Montreal and Tony Pérez in Cincinnati. Because of baseball's heightened sensitivity following Campanis's explosive remarks, ever so slowly, doors were beginning to open.

Baker stepped through the one leading to San Francisco. In his first season, he managed the Giants to a 103-59 record—five games better than the Pythagorean win expectancy's 98-64 projection—and a second-place finish. It was an epic NL West race, one of the most exciting ever. But the Giants went home after the season, because Atlanta's 104-58 mark was one game better, and in those days there were no expanded playoffs. The NL East winner played the NL West winner in the NL Championship Series, with the victor going to the World Series.

He managed the Giants for ten years, winning two NL West titles and the 2002 NL Wild Card. That team he managed to the World Series before a heartbreaking loss to the Anaheim Angels. His original intent might not have been to manage but, as they say, life has a way of happening while you are making other plans.

"Some of the doors were open for me, and I just took it to a different level because of the amount of time that I've been in the job," Baker says. "I took it to a different level because of the number of towns and the number of jobs I've had. Like, Cito Gaston was in Canada. And Toronto had a totally different outlook on things that Americans really didn't pay attention to." Over time, Baker says, "a lot of the guys asked me, 'Man, how do you keep getting these opportunities?' I mean, you look at Lloyd McClendon. He's been looking for an opportunity. Look at Willie Randolph. And most of the time, you're going to get a second division team that you have to rescue. Until I got to Washington, and since then Houston, they were the first good teams that I inherited. And Houston was because they were in trouble."

On the other end of his managing career from San Francisco, Houston was a different entity altogether. By then, for whatever criticisms were aimed at Baker—*He can't manage a bullpen! He runs his starting pitchers into the ground!*—he had established himself as a manager beloved by players and media alike wherever he went. And the hated Astros needed every ounce of goodwill they could muster. Really, it was the perfect hire by owner Jim Crane, and it was borne out with the 2022 World Series title.

From his home in Dunedin, Florida, Gaston was watching and rooting and, finally, phoning his congratulations to Dusty for winning the big one. It took Baker a few days to work his way through the messages and get back to everyone. When he reached Gaston, their talk was emotional and meaningful.

"I mean, I've been talking to Cito since I was eighteen years old," Baker says. "Cito was there with me my first day in the minor leagues and then the next year when I got to Atlanta."

Gaston was twenty-three when Baker, Atlanta's twenty-sixth-round pick in the 1967 amateur draft, joined him at Double-A Austin later that summer. In one of his first minor-league games, Baker dropped a fly ball in Little Rock, Arkansas. Fans jeered him, calling him a bunch of names, "and I wanted to cry and go home," Baker says. "And Cito told my mom then that, hey, man, he had me, he would take care of me, which he did."

The Braves made sure that Baker's support system was strong. Uncertain he would even sign when they drafted him because Baker had trepidation about playing in the Deep South for racial reasons, Atlanta assigned Hank Aaron to speak with both Dusty and his mother. Aaron assured each that he would care for Baker as if he were his own son. He told them that with his skills, Baker would land in the major leagues before his college class would graduate. As Baker matured and grew in Atlanta's system, both Aaron and Gaston kept their words. And each man would become like family to Baker.

"You know how you can tell your father some things but you can tell your uncle other things?" Baker says. "Cito is more like my uncle. You can tell him anything. Where Hank, I could tell him most things."

———

Only three Black men have managed teams to the title through 119 World Series dating back to 1903: Baker, Roberts, and Gaston. Worse, those are three of only four Black men (Ron Washington, Texas, 2010 and 2011) who have ever even managed in a World Series.

Over the years, Gaston told Baker a few things, too.

"We talk a lot," Gaston says. "I remember when he was going to interview in Cincinnati he said, 'What do you think?' And I said, 'Well, if you want to get back in the game, take the job.' He did, and he finally won. But he's won a lot of places and then gets fired and I can't really understand that. Dusty's a good man, a good manager, a good leader, and a good friend."

The Reds had finished 72-90 in 2007, their seventh consecutive sub-.500 finish. Jerry Narron and Pete Mackanin had split the job in 2007—Narron was fired about halfway through the season; Mackanin finished—when then–general manager Wayne Krivsky made the move. Cincinnati was a small-market team with a small payroll, an aging Ken Griffey Jr., and not much beyond Joey Votto and Brandon Phillips. Things were unsettled under owner Bob Castellini, evidenced by the fact that he fired Krivsky before the end of April during Baker's first month in town. Baker became the first African American manager in Cincinnati history—and the Reds have been fielding teams since becoming a charter member of the National League in 1890.

His dream job, it wasn't. But as Baker says, when you are a Black manager hoping to stay in the game, you take what you can get. And most of the time, what you get are unattractive rebuilds that are going to be difficult roads filled with potholes and losses. The hope is that the owner is patient enough and that the wins begin to come soon enough. Sometimes, they do. Usually, it's a losing proposition.

But Baker heeded Gaston's advice with Cincinnati because he knew his mentor was right. It certainly wasn't going to take a PhD in Sabermetrics to see that. Gaston's path remains one of the most inexplicable of all. He was hired by the Jays when they fired Jimy Williams thirty-six games into the 1989 season, and the team immediately clicked under him, going 77-49 the rest of the way and then 86-76 in 1990. Then, the World Series titles in 1992 and 1993 with luminaries like Joe Carter, John Olerud, Roberto Alomar, Dave Winfield, Jimmy Key, Jack Morris, Dave Stewart, Paul Molitor, and more.

"He was a man who gave respect and commanded it in return," Molitor says of Gaston. "With the personnel we had in Toronto, he didn't have to overmanage that team. It was a veteran team, heavily talented, and he just knew when to sit back and be kind of the guiding rudder of that team. When we needed to be addressed, when we were being lax, overconfident, letting our guard down collectively, he would never hesitate. I thought he was a man's man. Stood like a pillar every day in the dugout. He never changed his outward appearance and made it really joyful to walk into that clubhouse as a player."

Morris went 21-6 with a 4.04 ERA over thirty-four starts in that 1992 title season and remains mystified as to why Gaston wasn't in demand by other organizations after Toronto cut him loose.

"He didn't get the credit he deserved," Morris says. "It's not always easy when you have personnel, a lot of egos, All-Stars. He kept us on the right track. I love Cito. I told him years later, 'Cito, I had no idea what a good guy you are.' He laughed and said, 'Jack, I never realized you were OK, too.'"

When Gaston's teams fell below .500 for each of the next three seasons following the titles—and Toronto's average attendance dropped from around 4 million to 2.5 million during that time—he was cashiered near the end of the 1997 season. He was fifty-three at the time, still young, two World Series rings…and he would get one more managing job, period. It came eleven years later. And it was back in Toronto after the Jays fired John Gibbons nearly halfway through the 2008 season. Gaston would manage two more full seasons. Then he was done after the 2010 season at sixty-six.

As Baker would after him, Gaston learned firsthand that even successful African American managers have shorter leashes and the opportunities afterward are fewer and farther between than for many of their white counterparts. It's difficult to think that racism is not playing into that.

"Oh, absolutely," Gaston says. "I didn't get a job for ten years and I won two World Series. So I know exactly. It does. I hate to say that, but it does. Look around now, what do you have, two African American managers managing in the big leagues? It plays a part. And it seems like when they get fired, they don't get an opportunity to manage again. Where other guys still manage. I know some guys who have been managing for years and never won a thing. Maybe one division title. And they're still managing."

Gaston hoped to manage again after the Jays fired him the first time. He interviewed in Cleveland and thought he had a good chance there, but he told them he had a "couple of irons in the fire" and wanted a bit of extra time before making a decision. The then-Indians moved to hire Charlie Manuel (2000). He interviewed in Milwaukee and thought he had a chance, but Davey Lopes got that job ("I really do think they were trying to hire an African American manager," Gaston says). He interviewed for the vacant Anaheim Angels job after the 1999 season but his now ex-wife told him she wasn't going to move to Southern California. The Angels hired Mike Scioscia.

"A year later we were no longer married anyway, so that was a mistake on my part," Gaston says, noting that some of the lost opportunities were partially his fault, while others were simply mirages "just to say they interviewed an African American."

One of those "checking a box" interviews, he says in hindsight, was in Cleveland, even though he thought at the time he had a good chance at the job.

"I used to live in Toronto and Florida, and I still live in Florida now," Gaston says. "I remember interviewing for that Cleveland job and I had told them, 'I'm going to fly back to Florida until Tuesday, then I'm going to Toronto. So if you don't call me by Tuesday, call me in Toronto.'

"They called and left a message in Florida after Tuesday, when they knew I wasn't there."

Gaston says he was close to getting the Chicago White Sox job in 2004 after they fired Manuel, but Ozzie Guillen was the pick. As Gaston says, Sox owner Jerry Reinsdorf is "really, really great with his ex-players. He really has the tradition in that city, they're like the Yankees where they care about their ex-players. Ozzie got the job and he won. I was teasing him one day when I ran into him later. He said, 'Cito, you know I had to take that job.' I said, 'No problem, but I would have won the first year. You didn't win until the second year.' Him and I got a laugh out of that."

Not only is laughter the best medicine, but it also can help paper over the emptiness. At least, for a time.

Gaston lays out his interview path, but the question all these years later continues to flash as brightly as a neon sign at midnight on a deserted main street: How can a man win two World Series and become a free agent, and no other organization is interested?

"Sometimes, it depends on who you work for and what they say about you when you leave," Gaston says. "It's about likes and dislikes, too, and it shouldn't be that way. I never would not play a guy because I didn't get along with him. If he's going to help the team, he's playing. If you get a manager who can help you win, take the guy and go with him. No one gets along with everybody. But I think sometimes general managers don't get along with the manager, and other GMs call and say what do you think and they might not put in a good word for him. That's the way it works sometimes."

Is that the way it worked for Gaston?

"Well, some of that must have happened somewhere, because I couldn't get a job," he says. "I have no proof of it, no more proof than I couldn't get a job. Then when I did get a job, I went back to the same team I was managing before."

The pattern remains over the years, as consistent as Opening Day pageantry and red, white, and blue October bunting. McClendon took charge of the Pirates in 2001 after the Gene Lamont–managed club had gone 69-93 the year before. The cupboards were bare—classic start for a Black manager—and, after enduring a 62-100 season in 2001, McClendon's Buccos improved significantly over the next two seasons, going 72-89 and 75-87.

"Quite frankly, that was the only job I could get," says McClendon, sixty-six, who today lives in Valparaiso, Indiana—where he went to college—and plays a lot of golf while hoping he is not shut out of baseball completely. "A bottom feeder at that time. We just didn't have the forces. That job was not very appealing to many people, but you take what you get and make the best of it. I think we did a pretty good job. I remember Jim Leyland telling me, 'You're going to get fired.' I said, 'What are you talking about? We're getting better every year.' He said, 'Exactly. You do, and upper management is going to start expecting it.' He was right."

McClendon joined Leyland's Detroit Tigers staff in 2006 as bullpen coach first, then hitting coach. In four of McClendon's seven seasons as hitting coach, a Tiger won the batting crown. Miguel Cabrera won the Triple Crown in 2012.

"What was really frustrating was, it took nine years to get another opportunity to manage," McClendon says. "You look at my résumé, I managed all those years, worked for arguably the best manager in base-ball at the time in Leyland, we went to two World Series, I started out as bullpen coach and we had the best bullpen in baseball. He moved me to hitting coach and we set every franchise record, Tigers won batting titles, home run titles, a Triple Crown, and none of it equated to another job. That was tough. To hear television commentators talk about the pitching coach in Cleveland [Mickey Callaway] and how intelligent he was and how he deserved a chance…why doesn't that equate to Black coaches? I couldn't have done a better job than I did in Detroit."

Finally, Seattle hired McClendon as manager in 2014 under then-GM Jack Zduriencik—to take over a team that had, of course, fin-ished 71-91 the year before under Eric Wedge. In McClendon's first sea-son, a franchise that hadn't qualified for the postseason since 2001 went 87-75 and was in the race until season's end. The Mariners went 76-86 the following year but fired Zduriencik and hired Jerry Dipoto in Sep-tember. According to McClendon, he and Dipoto talked as that season ended, and the GM told him, go home, enjoy your family, and in a few days we'll talk about some things we're going to do next year. That Fri-day, McClendon was at the golf course when he saw a news crawl across the bottom of a television screen that he had been relieved of his duties.

"I got fired with a winning record [163-161 in two seasons in Seat-tle] and one year left on my contract," McClendon said. "His quote to the press was 'philosophical differences.' I was never asked what was my philosophy. But that quote is damaging enough to me because here's the guy who obviously is an analytical guy, a Sabermetrics guy, and his quote led everybody to believe that I didn't believe in analytics. We've all been operating under the same roof for years. We all need information. It was damaging to me. I never got another opportunity as a result."

The beat goes on.

Like Baker, Gaston wasn't even seeking to become a big-league manager when the position suddenly came to him early in that 1989 season. He had constructed a nice, solid, eleven-year playing career as an outfielder for Atlanta and San Diego that ended in 1978. He roomed with Aaron, was named as an NL All-Star in 1970 for San Diego (his .318 batting average that summer was the Padres' highest until a fellow named Tony Gwynn came along), and then finished his career with the Braves in 1978. It was in 1981 that Aaron convinced Gaston to take a job in Atlanta's organization as a minor-league hitting instructor.

Gaston wasn't sure where his path would lead at that point, but it was clear he was a relationships person. As Gaston moved into coaching, he was working with Atlanta's Fall Instructional League team, taking tips from Aaron, and rooming with another young Braves Instructional League coach named Brian Snitker. That was when, aside from helping young hitters, he proved adept at matchmaking, too.

"He's responsible for hooking my wife and I up," Snitker says, four decades later. "We were living together, Cito and I, and we were having a great time in the Instructional League. He and I were like the roving coaches that year, and roommates, and we'd sit around in the evenings and drink beer and talk baseball. It was awesome. He became a really, really close friend. I still talk with him quite a bit. He is an awesome, awesome, wonderful guy."

Snitker and Ronnie, a friend of a friend of Gaston's, were married about a year later. By the 1982 season, Gaston was already gone from the Braves organization. Team owner—and erstwhile manager-for-one-night—Ted Turner fired manager Bobby Cox after the 1981 campaign. The Blue Jays pounced to hire Cox, who brought Gaston along as the major-league hitting coach.

And that was what Gaston did until then-president Paul Beeston and then-GM Pat Gillick made the move in 1989 to fire Williams and asked Gaston to succeed him.

"First of all, I didn't even want the job," Gaston says. "I lived in the same area as Jimy in Mississauga [Ontario], I had lived there for twenty years, and they came to my house and said, 'We want you to manage.'

I said, 'You know, it's not too often that you go to work and you love your job, and I love being a hitting instructor.' Beeston looked at me and said, 'Well, you've got it.'"

So that was how Gaston became manager. As the Jays turned around their season, players approached him privately and said, "You've got to take this job." Detroit manager Sparky Anderson urged Jays executives in that direction, as well, to make Gaston's hire permanent.

"I'm glad Paul made me take it, and the players twisted my arm, because we came back and won our division," Gaston says.

It was the beginning of the most special era in Toronto hardball history. What helped galvanize the team and put Gaston into a comfortable position immediately was that he had long-established, strong relationships with many of the position players that he had instructed in hitting for so long. In that respect, his beginning in the manager's office paralleled that of Baker.

"As a manager and as a coach, it's like Dusty said with Hank and me," Gaston says. "Players will tell coaches anything, but they won't tell the manager everything. I had an advantage that year. I don't think I ever knew my teams as well as I did that year."

Then as now, Toronto boasted a diverse population and a cosmopolitan experience for those who lived and worked there. A Black manager didn't garner quite as much notice in the capital city of the Canadian province of Ontario as he would have in other cities.

"All kinds of people in Toronto are from all over the world," Gaston says. "It was like New York. You're going to find racism everywhere you go in the world, but you couldn't see it up there as badly as certain places you'd manage in the States, or even living in the States, at times. That part was good. But people don't realize, people talk about the New York and Los Angeles press, we had three newspapers in Toronto and one in Hamilton. We had all kinds of people writing all the time, whereas you'd go to St. Louis and there would be maybe only one newspaper."

The press always was the most difficult and uncomfortable part of the job for the quiet, gentlemanly Gaston. He knew the battery of reporters he faced every day in Toronto often was attempting to squeeze information from him that he couldn't—or shouldn't—divulge, and as different reporters asked their questions in different ways with different angles, Gaston was uncomfortable more often than not. One knock on him was that he failed to cultivate relationships with young players such as John Olerud, Shawn Green, and Carlos Delgado. Like most managers, he was skewered when certain decisions didn't work, and as the Jays started to go south after their glory days and attendance declined, the voices became louder. When Gaston finally was fired, Gord Ash had replaced Gillick (who had become Seattle's GM) and Beeston was working for MLB.

Other Black managers, or Black coaches who hoped to become big-league managers, watched Gaston disappear almost without a trace after he was fired in September 1997, not to return until the Jays needed a calming and familiar voice in 2008. Then, after three years, he was gone again, with no other organization biting, ever. And they could only shake their heads.

"That's really probably at the precipice of this whole thing, you know," Manuel says. "That's kind of the impetus of where this all seems to have gone. If he can't get it, you know you're not going to get it. You know you've got to fight to get what you need to get, or prove yourself when you get the opportunity. And if he can't get another shot, why are you crying? That kind of really is looking in the mirror and saying, 'Hey, man, that's Cito Gaston. That's two world championships back-to-back, and he don't have a job? Wow. That's interesting.' That's where it hits us, right there. That kind of tells the story. I don't know Cito as well as I know Dusty. But I've admired and respected who he is."

As it happens, times changed during Gaston's decade away from the managerial merry-go-round, and when he returned to the Jays for his brief second tour, it just wasn't the same. Not even close.

"'The difference was the players," Gaston says. "They were making a lot more money. I had seven guys who had their own jets at one time or another. They didn't use them all the time. You could just see it in guys and their attitudes and the way they spend their money. It was just different. Some guys cracked me up. They had so much money coming in they would go dye their hair, dye it blond or purple. They had so much they didn't know where to spend all the money."

And this was in the embryonic stages of the Analytics Revolution that was beginning to seed the game.

"I don't believe a lot of managers write their lineup out these days, I really don't," Gaston says. "I believe those people write it out for them. It's not all bad. But people are really sensitive about where they hit in the lineup no matter what people think, and if it bugs them, they are going to have trouble playing. You've earned your way into where you're hitting in the lineup."

He points to when Delgado was breaking into the majors in 1994 and 1995. Olerud was still entrenched at first base and the Jays moved Delgado to left field. That was wholly uncomfortable for the future star, "bugging him so much," Gaston says. "If you're not comfortable with where you're playing, it really messes with your game. You have to really be careful where you play people to get the best out of them."

But now he is retired in Florida at eighty-one, and these are memories and reminders. They are not scars and abrasions. Gaston fought the battles, tiptoed through the minefields, celebrated his successes, and gracefully accepted his defeats. He is not bitter or resentful. In October 2023, he was named as one of eight managers, executives, and umpires up for induction into the Hall of Fame on the contemporary baseball–era ballot, essentially up for review by a veterans' committee. For a guy who could not land another job after winning two World Series titles, it was deserved and a long time coming. Maybe next time he appears on the ballot, he'll be voted into the Hall.

He remains not at all surprised at the continued paucity of Black managers, but he is disappointed.

"Like Dusty talks about Hank, and Hank was like my dad, too, he taught me a lot of things," Gaston says. "I was so lucky I roomed with the guy who was my childhood idol, and he's also the guy who got me back in the game when he was working as scouting director for the Braves. He called me three times and asked me to work *with* him. He never asked me to work *for* him. The third time I said OK. He taught me a lot. If you have a good day, enjoy it and don't bring it back the next day. If you had a bad day, you look and see what you did wrong and don't bring it back the next day.

"That's the kind of attitude I have. You can't make them hire you, so I just kind of went on and enjoyed my family, traveled a lot, went to a lot of nice places, and had a good time. I always said this: You think about being bitter and angry, those people are not thinking about you. You're the one thinking about them, and you're the one who is upset."

One of the things Baker planned on doing after winning the 2022 World Series was rounding up Gaston and Roberts for a photo of the three of them, the only Black men in history to manage teams in the World Series—and to titles. At his home in Florida, Gaston often looks at a framed picture he has from a long-ago All-Star Game, him in the middle, Baker to his right, and Don Baylor to his left.

"I have that, and I'd like to have the one Dusty's talking about, too," Gaston says.

On a bucolic swath of land some twenty-five minutes or so northeast of his hometown of Sacramento, when the games stop and his world slows down, Dusty Baker tends to a small vineyard in the backyard of his spacious and elegant home. Though he has plenty of help, this isn't some showplace where Baker hires everything out.

In an area behind a sign reading BAKER FARMS, he prunes his vines. He tools around on his trusty Kawasaki Mule, a small all-terrain vehicle he uses to load and haul away all of those clippings. He knows the soil and the sun patterns, and he's learned how they affect his grapes, their growth, and, ultimately, the annual vintages of his Baker Family Wines business.

While I spend time with him in the vineyard one January morning in 2022, Baker pauses to show me how the north side of one particular vine is cut shorter than the south side. This is so the north side can bask in the morning sun. The south side is allowed to grow more because by the afternoons in sweltering hot Sacramento, the sun is too intense and the longer vines act as a shield for the fruit.

"It's called an umbrella," Baker says. "Too much sun, then you get raisins. And I don't want no raisins."

It is a beautiful, serene spot that for years has allowed Baker a refuge from the noise of a lifetime of endless baseball seasons. It is an outlet for his curiosity. A muse for his creativity.

Inside his home is a warm mix of art, memorabilia, and sneaky humor that, in all directions, suggests a life lived to the fullest. Autographed guitars from his late buddies B. B. King and John Lee Hooker hang high on one wall just off the entryway. Another one from Carlos Santana. Down the hall is a custom-built wine room. Over the toilet in the guest bathroom hangs a sign shaped like home plate with the suggestion: "Players with short bats please stand closer to the plate."

Upstairs is a space that is one part game room, one part sports bar (thanks to the enormous televisions), and one part museum. Here is a display of memorabilia from Baker's five decades in the game in which a person could get lost for days. There are uniforms from every team for which he's ever played or managed. Framed letters from United States presidents congratulating him on this or thanking him for that (George H. W. Bush, Bill Clinton). Enough autographed bats to rival a storage area at Louisville Slugger, and enough autographed balls to rival the same at

Rawlings. Autographed boxing gloves personalized to Dusty from Leon Spinks. Framed lineup cards. Framed photos of Braves, Giants, Reds, Dodgers, Nationals, Astros, crossing the decades, smile after smile, sheer unbridled joy and love permeating the frames. There is a classic photo of J. T. Snow scooping up little Darren Baker—Dusty's son, just three at the time—during that scary play at the plate in the 2002 World Series when the little batboy almost got trampled. The photo is classic enough, but this one is autographed by all of the participants: Snow, Darren Baker, Angels catcher Bengie Molina, and plate ump Mike Reilly.

It all is a testament to a life well lived, a career well played, a beloved family member, teammate, and friend who collects and nurtures relationships with the care and tender touch of a master gardener.

"Dusty is a tremendous people person," Manuel says. "Tremendous. Off the charts. He seems to have a reservoir of time for everybody. He stays in touch."

What a beautiful description for a human being, let alone one who happens to be a baseball manager. *A reservoir of time for everybody.* Baker is genuine, which is part of the secret that, over his seven-plus decades, allows him to move comfortably and easily from a baseball clubhouse to a nightclub in order to hang with Hooker to the partnership with his winemaker, Chik Brenneman. Without question, it is one enormous key to team building and to his success as a manager.

And yet.

Triumph and longevity over time have done a lot to camouflage Baker's scars, but they are there. Always, the words of his mother, *You have to be twice as good as everybody else to accomplish the same thing*, have been bouncing around in his mind, right there with lineup card possibilities, pitching options, and self-survival, all of it tossed together as if tumbling in a dryer.

"Everything is magnified," Baker says. "The second-guessing is magnified. Most of my life, I've even been told that 'You're a smart Black man,' or that 'You're the most intelligent Black in the game today.'

And it's like, why is there a difference between intelligent Black and intelligent white? That has always been there, and it becomes prevalent."

Baker's ears have been singed time and time again by second-guessers, vicious, vitriolic sharpshooting that goes well beyond anything that successful white managers like Tommy Lasorda, Tony La Russa, and Bobby Cox ever heard.

When Baker's Giants held a 5–0 lead over the Angels and needed just five outs to win Game 6 of the 2002 World Series and clinch what would have been his first title, he removed starting pitcher Russ Ortiz and handed Ortiz the baseball as he exited the mound so the right-hander could have a souvenir. After the Giants blew that lead and then lost Game 7, Baker was ripped for years as if he singlehandedly lost the game. And when he left the Giants for the Cubs after that season, essentially a mutual parting of the ways, accompanying the split was a nasty leak into his personal life that he was behind on his taxes. That eventually was sorted out, but the timing and clearly malicious intent of the news leak coming right after the World Series was devastating and hurtful to Baker.

When his Cubs in the 2003 NLCS against the Florida Marlins pulled to within five outs of reaching their first World Series since 1945, it was only a setup for more heartbreak. That was when Steve Bartman appeared, Moises Alou couldn't catch the ball, and the Cubs lost that night and again in Game 7. Worse, neither of the Cubs' co-aces, Kerry Wood and Mark Prior, was ever the same again, and insidious accusations that Baker had ruined them began to take root, fueled by those coconspirators who were in the early stages of becoming part of our lifeline to the game, the internet and the analytics movement.

Never mind that, all these years later, both Prior and Wood steadfastly refuse to blame Baker for their woes. That was the only year Prior ever threw more than 200 innings (211.1). Wood only reached that level twice in his career, in 2002 (213.2) and 2003 (211), and never again. Under Baker, the Cubs would never reach those heights again, either. He lasted three more seasons, as the savage and racist attacks in Chicago got worse and worse, and he parted ways with the Cubs after a 66-96 season in 2006.

Now the Dodgers' pitching coach, Prior calls that level of criticism for Baker "unwarranted" and says simply, "Kerry and I got hurt." How? Why? Injuries are unpredictable and not easily explained. And two decades down the road, despite twenty more years of data, study, and knowledge, pitchers break down today more than ever.

"The front office constructs rosters during the offseason, and you're trying to play, and now maybe as a starter you have 170 innings and I don't think there was any reason to think that I wouldn't throw another 200 innings the next year, or that Kerry wasn't going to throw that," Prior says. "When you have some big injuries and you don't have depth underneath to kind of boost everybody up, it doesn't matter who's managing, you're going to struggle."

After Prior finally retired as a player in 2013 following multiple comeback attempts, he sought Baker out when the Reds came through San Diego to talk about his future. They got Mexican food for lunch in San Diego (Dusty's choice, Prior says, chuckling, "because Dusty knows where the food is.") Prior sought advice for his future and Baker told him to take a coaching job soon "because you have a connection with the players and, if you wait, all of a sudden the next generation is here."

"Granted, that's weird coming from a guy who's in his seventies now but who keeps bridging that gap," Prior says. "But I had never thought about that before."

Not long after, Dodgers assistant general manager Josh Byrnes reached out to Prior about a pitching coach job. The former right-handed ace had his thoughts in order, talked it over with his family, and accepted. If not for Baker, Prior says, he probably would have told Byrnes to try him back in a year or two after he took some time off, and then who knows how things would have turned out?

"That meant a lot, especially when people were trying to blame me for hurting his career," Baker says of Prior seeking his counsel. "There's certain guys that you think would be good coaches, even though you don't want them to start thinking about coaching, you know? You want to exhaust playing first, and then think about coaching."

Baker looks forward to hearing annually from Wood, getting newsy Christmastime updates, eager to hear all about how Wood's family is growing.

"We talk all the time, me and Dusty," Prior says. "I tell him I wouldn't change anything. Yeah, I mean, look, I'm coaching now, honestly, because of him telling me and encouraging me."

But after the Cubs' near miss in 2003, the Chicago experience became as ugly as anything Baker has endured. Boos. Catcalls. Jeers. Hate mail. Racist mail. Sometimes, he would share it with Andy MacPhail, who was president of the Cubs at the time. Baker, who knows his history, too, would tell MacPhail about the Ku Klux Klan's historical early stronghold beginning in the 1920s just south of where they were, in Indiana.

"He got some awful hate mail in Chicago," MacPhail says. "I think Dusty felt the racism and my perception is he had every right to feel it."

Outfielder Jacque Jones, who later would work briefly for Baker as an assistant hitting coach in Washington, talked through some of it with Baker when they were together in 2006 because Jones also was on the receiving end of much racial hatred, just as Corey Patterson, LaTroy Hawkins, and Milton Bradley—all Black—had been when they passed through Wrigley Field. Among other things, Jones says it reached the point where security routinely would walk Baker to his car in the parking lot after home games, just to be safe.

"Dusty always deals with bile in grace," Jones says. "It was sad to see him go through that. It was sad to see it happening in the 2000s. He always took it in stride, handled it."

While Baker grows defiant when the topic turns to whether he needs to prove himself to anybody ("I've refused to let other people's opinions affect my self-esteem"), he also was acutely aware every day that he carried a responsibility because of his race that other managers did not have, a feeling that the more he succeeded, the more chances he could create for other potential Black managers. And if he failed…

"There were a lot of people who needed me to win it for my race," Baker says. "Black America and certain Latin America and certain white people. You don't know how many people have told me they cried when we won the World Series."

There are precious few people who have been in Baker's cleats and know exactly what he's talking about. Gaston. And, in Los Angeles, Roberts.

"I don't look at it as pressure," says Roberts, who led the Dodgers to the 2020 World Series title during the pandemic-shortened season. "I try to put it in the responsibility bucket. But I do know if I screw up people will say, 'See, there's a man of color. A Black manager. He screwed it up. See. I told you so.' I do feel that sense of I have to do it the right way and win. And the thing is, and this is a different topic, but I talk to Dusty and Dusty is a Hall of Fame manager. The thing is, when they talk about Dusty, they say, hey, he's great with players, he's a Players' Manager. But they never say he's intelligent. They say he's a great baseball guy. But there's a lot of white managers who haven't won close to what Dusty's won and they say he's a baseball savant, he's a great baseball mind. And Dusty's like, 'You know what, Doc? Nobody's ever told me I'm a great baseball mind. That's great, but that's not everything. For me, I want to be looked at as a great Players' Manager and also a great manager of the game itself.'"

The Astros' World Series win in 2022 should have solidified that for Baker, once and for all. Of course, in the noisy world in which we live, there seemingly are no universal truths left anymore and, undoubtedly, Baker always will have his detractors. And even carrying the weight during the journey to the World Series title was different for Baker. The

Astros have been on the leading edge of the analytics movement for more than a decade. It is a deep part of their DNA. And while Baker and other old-school managers like Bochy, Showalter, and Francona all will tell you they crave information, and they all become agitated when it is suggested that maybe they don't want everything their analytics departments have to offer, only Baker and Roberts wrestle with the larger picture of doing things their way as they work to keep the doors open for other Black managers against the backdrop of the baseball scientists above them applying pressure regarding lineup decisions and in-game strategy.

In other words, as one of the more accomplished managers ever and after more than five decades in the game, even Baker isn't completely free to paint his own masterpiece.

"When I first started managing, the manager had some say-so on personnel," Baker says. "That's a major difference. I mean, they would say, OK, we came down to between this kid and that kid, who do you want? And I would say I want this kid."

Baker remembers long ago talking to the Touchdown Club of Columbus when another of the speakers was former Michigan coach Bo Schembechler. When the two of them spoke about coaching and managing, Baker says, Schembechler told him you can see things in a player's face. It left an impression.

"And I've used that, like with Jeremy Peña," Baker says of the Astros' rookie shortstop who earned the 2022 World Series MVP award. "He's out with the other young players and, like Bo said, you can see fear, you can see anxiety, or you can see that the kid doesn't have a scared bone in his body. Or you can see his intelligence and you can see his heart. You can see it all by looking at his face."

In the pivotal fifth game of the 2022 World Series, with the Astros and Phillies at two wins apiece, Baker looked into ace Justin Verlander's face, did a quick read, and also allowed his empathy and gut to factor into a decision. Verlander, despite his Hall of Fame career and eight starts over five World Series, had never been the winning pitcher in a Fall Classic game. He was 0-6 with a 7.05 ERA in the World Series. In Game 1, the Astros staked him to a 5–0 lead, and the Phillies torched him for five runs over the fourth and fifth innings on their way to a 6–5, ten-inning win.

But now, in Game 5 against the Phillies, Verlander was clinging to a 2–1 lead in the fifth inning. The critics who have dogged Baker for poor pitching decisions over the years were howling loudly in the distance. The snipers who accused Verlander of choking on the big stage were ready to fire more zingers. Many were expecting Baker to lift Verlander after the fourth inning, as the meat of the Phillies lineup was due up in the fifth. Instead, Baker sent Verlander out for that fifth. Following two strikeouts, Bryce Harper laced a double. Then, Nick Castellanos battled Verlander in an epic ten-pitch at bat before ending the inning with a fly ball.

The Astros wound up winning the game—and the series the following night. Verlander got a W. And Baker finally got his ring.

The decision could have backfired, and undoubtedly if it did, the vitriol would be flowing in full force even today. But here was where Baker had learned not just from Schembechler but from his own experiences. A "gut feeling," something the *Moneyball* A's never dared utter in the early 2000s because GM Billy Beane never wanted to hear that term, doesn't mean a snap decision. Rather, a gut feeling for a manager like Baker means an informed decision that takes into account the sum of his years of experience.

Because of the Game 5 victory, Baker says, he never heard from the Astros' baseball operations department regarding his in-game decision with Verlander. But he heard from them throughout the series.

"Nobody wanted Yuli Gurriel to play," Baker says. "Nobody wanted Maldy [Martin Maldonado] to catch. The operations people didn't want Peña to bat second, either. But I've got to do what I think is right. You know, I'm a numbers man, too. I've always used numbers.

Always. But I don't use them 100 percent. There are no absolutes in this game, period. Whether I go with my feelings or whether I go with numbers, there are no absolutes because the opposition can change your absolute formula by a homer or blooper or walk or whatever it is."

In the case of Verlander, Baker in the moment was recalling what the old pitcher Tommy John used to tell him when they played together with the Dodgers: A good pitcher can get out of trouble twice, a great pitcher three times, a so-so pitcher maybe once. Baker swore after the game that he did not purposely allow Verlander to continue simply to get him the personal win. But, Baker allowed, "It was in my heart." And that's why so many players reward managers like Baker with their trust.

But despite the successes of Baker and Roberts over the past few seasons, the outlook for more Black managers remains distressingly worse than even in the immediate aftermath of Al Campanis in 1987. A study by the Institute for Diversity and Ethics in Sport at the University of Central Florida found that Black players represented just 6.2 percent of Opening Day rosters in 2023, a record low. That was down from the previous record low of 7.2 percent in 2022, and both of those numbers are the lowest recorded since the study started in 1981. Then, 18 percent of MLB players were Black.

In the face of these declining numbers, baseball has turned more and more proactive over the past several years with programs incorporated into the commissioner's office designed to engage and recruit inner-city kids and minorities into the sport. Though he was boxed out of managing jobs long ago, Manuel today works under MLB's Youth Development Department. As part of that, he works scouting combines, the annual Dream Series over Martin Luther King weekend in Arizona (a camp for pitchers and catchers who are elite high school athletes, especially minorities), the Andre Dawson Classic (featuring Historically Black Colleges and Universities) that helps kick off the college baseball season, and many other events.

"I think this is my lane, really, to be honest with you," Manuel says. "Helping promote baseball in the Black community like it used to be. Like I grew up with. It feels good to be in this lane."

Where that leaves the next generation of Black managers remains the unanswerable question. With the percentage of Black players in today's game at a record low, what would be the natural feeder system into the job is nearly evaporated. So many ex-players who eventually graduate into big-league managerial jobs—men such as Aaron Boone, Skip Schumaker, Rocco Baldelli, Mark Kotsay, Torey Lovullo, Kevin Cash, and so many more—are not going to be Black simply because of the paucity of the numbers. As such, it is difficult not to see Black representation remaining at bleak levels in managing circles in the near future.

Under Commissioner Bud Selig, baseball instituted a mandate that whenever there is an opening for a managerial or general manager's job, unless they fill the job with a promotion from within, clubs must interview minority candidates. The rule is well intentioned, but, as with so many other industries, in reality it is little more than window dressing.

"I would take that Bud Selig rule and throw it out the window," Red Sox manager Alex Cora, who is Puerto Rican, says. "You get an interview because you're capable, and when we start looking at everybody being capable, that's when we will get more chances to manage. But if you're interviewing somebody because you have to, it doesn't work that way."

There is a long list of those who can tell you all about it.

"We had our little blip on the radar with the Black Lives Matter thing, after the George Floyd incident, and as soon as that quieted down it went away again," McClendon says. "It's frustrating. But it is what it is. I tell all the people I've known over the years, look, I have nothing to complain about. I had a great ride, I was in baseball for forty-two years. It afforded me opportunities that otherwise would have never happened, financially and everything else. But at the same time, we're talking about equality, we're talking about baseball diversity, we're doing this and that…but we're not. There's no substance to it. It's not a personal thing. It's the truth."

It is why, in Baker's final years in Houston and in Roberts's current chapter right now in Los Angeles, they have been managing for more people than just themselves. As if the job is not difficult enough, they have the added strain of feeling a personal responsibility to further the cause. It is why so many people cried those hard tears when the Astros won in 2022, and why it took Baker days to reply to all his well-wishers.

When he finally retired a year later, after a Game 7 loss to Texas in the 2023 ALCS to fall just one win short of leading the Astros to a third consecutive World Series appearance, Baker was seventy-four and took a role with San Francisco as a special adviser to baseball operations. He still had plenty to give, he said, and anybody who knows Baker figured that part out already. Friends, smiles, memories, and time pruning in his beloved vineyard will help cover whatever scars at one time threatened to poke through. So, too, will the title he won as a manager and those 2,183 wins.

"Know something?" Baker says. "If I hadn't missed six years, I'd be way over that. But I wouldn't have experienced everything that I've experienced—my daughter's wedding, my brother's funeral, my dad. I guess I am where I am supposed to be in my life and in my career."

There is deep pride in his status as the only African American manager ever to win more than two thousand games and a World Series title.

"And I'm hoping that I can help convince other owners that me and Dave Roberts shouldn't be the last" Black managers, Baker says. "That we should have a lot more."

CHAPTER 6

LAPTOPS AND LAPDOGS

During the first five years after Apple Computer incorporated in 1977, revenues doubled roughly every four months. With the Apple II and its software and accessories as the sole products of the new company, annual sales exploded from $775,000 to $118 million just in the period from September 1977 through September 1980. By 2021, with iPhones, iPads, iBooks (and, alas, a fond farewell to the iPod), the company's estimated worth zoomed to more than $2 trillion. Only seven *countries* had annual GDPs higher than that. Those ranking just below Apple in GDP were Italy, Brazil, and Canada.

The company's headquarters in Cupertino, California, stand only forty-three miles south of the Oakland Coliseum. It is a mere coincidence that Apple essentially was only a long bicycle ride from one of MLB's least valuable franchises (only Miami ranked below Oakland's estimated value of $1.18 billion in 2023, according to *Forbes* magazine).

Yet the two are inextricably linked—computers, at least, if not Apple directly with the Athletics—thanks to Billy Beane, Art Howe, Ken Macha, Michael Lewis, Brad Pitt, and Hollywood. Though baseball men have been dissecting statistics and drawing clues for conclusions going back to Earl Weaver and beyond, the Computer Age and Beane's ascension into a baseball management role were serendipitous in Oakland, pushing the Athletics onto the national stage as the model for a raggedy, financially challenged franchise figuring out how to exploit baseball's inefficiencies and hang with the big boys through spreadsheets and data.

The inspiration is—and has been—in the air that they breathe going back to when Beane's predecessor in Oakland, Sandy Alderson, was hired by then–A's owner Roy Eisenhardt as the club's general counsel in 1981. In May 1983, Microsoft announced something called "Multi-Tool Word," which would become what we know today as Microsoft Word.

"You can make the argument that Silicon Valley was essentially the modern-day Florence," Beane says of the Italian city considered to be the birthplace of the Renaissance. "All the ideas in the world were coming out of this place. It's sort of created a stimulus, just being around it, creatively. I mean, it could have been just serendipitous, or is it a part of the environment?

"Listen, all I know is that those are the type of guys we were trying to hire, and they were trying to hire the same people. So I think there's something synonymous with it, that's for sure."

Beane, incidentally, always has worked on Apple products and still favors them today. The proprietary statistical analysis the Athletics famously developed is powered by non-Apple products.

Two things happened in 2003 that would forever change the job of the field manager. The book *Moneyball: The Art of Winning an Unfair Game* was published on June 17, Lewis's insider account of how the Little Engine That Could Athletics under Beane used numbers and data to exploit inefficiencies in the system and chop down rivals with far greater payrolls and resources. Four months later, on October 16, then–Boston manager Grady Little left ace Pedro Martinez in too long in Game 7 of the ALCS in a foaming-at-the-mouth Yankee Stadium. The Red Sox blew the pennant. It was, for all intents and purposes, the last time a manager would be afforded that much autonomy to make a "gut call."

But the seeds for what was to come arrived in those embryonic days of Apple and Microsoft, and they were planted by Alderson. A Dartmouth graduate who then joined the United States Marine Corps and served a tour of duty in Vietnam, Alderson earned a law degree at Harvard in 1976 before going to work for a San Francisco law firm.

That led him to Eisenhardt and the A's, and two years later, in 1983, he was named as the club's general manager.

"Analytics made complete sense to me as early as 1983, 1984, but you have to remember two things," Alderson says. "I didn't really have an alternative means of evaluating players. I hadn't been a coach or scout. I hadn't been in the game for a long time. I hadn't played professionally. So I was kind of a blank slate. Secondly, you have to remember back in those days it was more of a hypothesis than a proven theory because there was very little data. It's hard to have analytics if you don't have data."

What happened over the next two decades, between then and the so-called Moneyball Era, was that Silicon Valley continued to do its thing, computers became as essential in our lives as our daily bread, and the crude, erudite theories being developed by Bill James in his early writings while working night shifts as a security guard at a Stokely–Van Camp pork and beans cannery in Kansas were proved to be not so crude. As more data became available, the numbers showed that James and his small handful of disciples, once viewed as oddballs and misfits by the establishment, in reality were on to something.

Under Alderson, the A's won three consecutive AL pennants as the decade turned, losing the 1988 World Series to the Kirk Gibson Dodgers, sweeping San Francisco in the 1989 earthquake-interrupted World Series, and then getting stunned by Lou Piniella's upstart Cincinnati team in 1990. Easily forgotten today but of absolute importance is this: As Alderson was employing some early, rudimentary analytics skills in constructing those teams, Oakland also ranked in the top half of MLB payrolls during those seasons. And in 1991, Oakland's $33 million payroll ranked No. 1 in MLB. The A's were firing on all cylinders, including with their manager. Alderson had hired Tony La Russa in 1987, and he was a perfect partner in this early analytics laboratory. Before long, La Russa's specialized use of relievers would earn him the nickname "the Godfather of the Modern Bullpen."

"The first manager interview in which I was ever involved was finding a replacement for Billy Martin, who had been the manager in Oakland and kind of self-destructed, purposely, and went to New York," says Alderson, speaking of the winter of 1982–1983. "We were looking for another manager and Roy Eisenhardt, who was the team president at the time, and owner Walter Haas may have been involved, as well, we interviewed a number of individuals without really having any idea what we were looking for. That's how naive and inexperienced we were. We ended up hiring a guy named Steve Boros and, honestly, the only qualification recognizable to us as the uninitiated was that he had a degree from the University of Michigan. Which obviously had nothing to do with his managerial skills."

The A's interviewed a young, up-and-coming coach named Jim Leyland at the time, as well as Jimy Williams, Hal Lanier, and Jim Fregosi—"Some pretty good people with some pretty good track records," Alderson says. "We just were not experienced in recognizing potential manager talent or even what questions to ask."

Three and a half years later, it was a different story with La Russa —sort of.

"That was less an interview than it was a recruiting effort," Alderson says. "He had been fired by the White Sox. Why were we initially attracted to him? He was a lawyer for one thing. And Roy and I were both lawyers."

Time was, all a manager needed to write the lineup was a working pen and a sweet pipe. Hall of Famer Sparky Anderson shows how it was done. *(Photo by MLB via Getty Images)*

he game's first African American manager, Hall of Famer Frank Robinson holds up the literary document prove it. He would last fewer than three full seasons in Cleveland and, incredibly, was fired on Juneteenth 1977. *(Bettmann via Getty Images)*

A historical relic from May 11, 1977, the last time a team owner managed a baseball game. Ted Turner was no Connie Mack, but after the Braves lost their sixteenth in a row, he banished Dave Bristol from the dugout. Commissioner Bowie Kuhn ended that idea after one night. *(AP Photo/R.C. Greenawalt)*

A rare photo in which Billy Martin, George Steinbrenner, and Lou Piniella all smile at the same time. The three Yankees legends often were at odds, but Piniella carried some of Martin's influence during his time managing the Yankees, Reds, Mariners, Devil Rays, and Cubs. *(Photo by Keith Torrie/ NY Daily News Archive via Getty Images)*

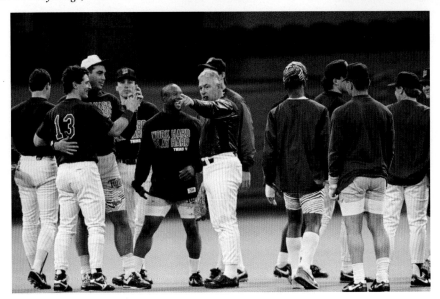

Kent Hrbek and Mike Pagliarulo appear to slow dance as manager Tom Kelly conducts what would be Minnesota's second World Series win in five seasons in 1991, a title ending with Jack Morris's historic ten-inning complete game shutout. Kelly remains one of the game's most underrated managers. *(AP Photo/John Swart)*

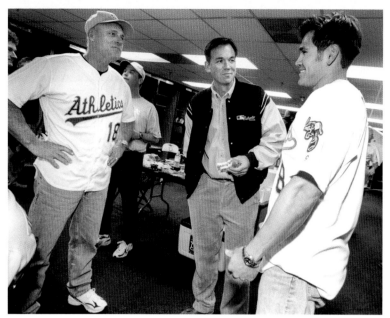

Of the many battles waged between Art Howe and Billy Beane during the "Moneyball" era in Oakland, one of the few the field manager won—eventually—was over where to play outfielder Johnny Damon during his one year with the Athletics in 2001. *(Arleen Ng/Digital First Media Group/Oakland Tribune via Getty Images)*

Grady Little exiting the mound in the eighth inning, having decided to extend Pedro Martinez's leash during the fateful Game 7 of the 2003 ALCS. It was the last gasp of the good, old managerial gut decision before analytics swept into the game for good. *(Photo by Jim Davis/The Boston Globe via Getty Images)*

You don't see managers carried off the field much anymore, but things were different when lovable cartoon character Jack McKeon was brassy enough to buck the odds and start Josh Beckett on short rest in the Marlins' stunning takedown of the Bronx Bombers at Yankee Stadium in 2003. *(Photo by Jed Jacobsohn/Getty Images)*

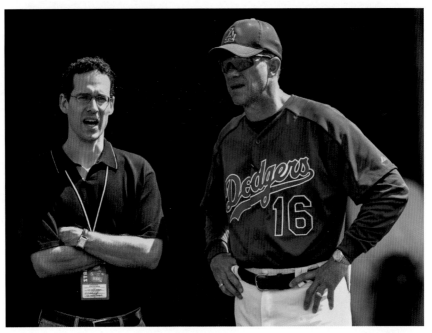

In 2004, the Dodgers went 93-69 and won the NL West with Jim Tracy managing. In 2005, as second-year GM Paul DePodesta took more control, the Dodgers went 71-91, their second-worst season since 1908. Here, the two chat during the spring of 2005. Eight months later, both would be gone. *(Photo by Jon Soohoo/WireImage)*

When the Chicago White Sox and baseball head Kenny Williams hired Robin Ventura to manage in 2012, it ushered in the era of the entry-level skipper, men who had recently retired and never before managed. *(Photo by Jon Durr/Getty Images)*

You bet Ned Yost noticed being called a "dunce" in a 2014 *Wall Street Journal* headline. A year later, he laughed last after guiding Kansas City to a World Series title and hanging out with President Barack Obama as the White House toasted Royals who played hardball. *(John Sleezer/Kansas City Star/ Tribune News Service via Getty Images)*

Counter to the Jack Morris game in 1991: Rays manager Kevin Cash and starter Blake Snell in the moment of truth during Game 6 of the 2020 COVID World Series. Cash still thinks of this moment often, even during pitching changes he makes today. *(Photo by Tom Pennington/Getty Images)*

Great moment from Atlanta's trip to the White House after winning the 2021 World Series. President Joe Biden appears to have just been told that Brian Snitker managed a whopping 2,714 minor-league games before piloting the Braves to their first title since 1995. *(Photo by Win McNamee/Getty Images)*

For all of the second-guessing Dave Roberts has endured over the years—especially in October—his .627 winning percentage (851-506) was the best of any manager in history (minimum one thousand games) entering the 2025 season. The late, great Vin Scully approves. *(Photo by Harry How/Getty Images)*

The first man to manage five different teams to division titles, Dusty Baker became only the third African American manager to win a World Series with this title in Houston in 2022. You should check out his Baker Family Wines, too. *(Photo by Carmen Mandato/Getty Images)*

Having already won three World Series titles in San Francisco, Bruce Bochy was searching for new ways to pop the champagne cork after coming out of retirement and leading Texas to its first World Series title in 2023. See you in Cooperstown, Boch. *(Photo by Steph Chambers/Getty Images)*

Three generations of Boones—Aaron, Ray, Bret, and Bob—celebrate their baseball lives at the 2003 All-Star Game at Chicago's U.S. Cellular Field. This is the treasured photo that hangs on Aaron's wall in the Yankee Stadium manager's office. *(AP Photo/Mark Duncan)*

They took Karl Kuehl, their director of player development, to Chicago with them to sell La Russa on a farm system that included Jose Canseco, Mark McGwire, Terry Steinbach, and others. La Russa would manage the Athletics for the next nine seasons before moving on to St. Louis in 1996. By then, Beane's playing career was finished, and Alderson had brought him on as an assistant GM. Silicon Valley was riding the dot-com bubble as commercial use of the internet grew sharply in 1995 and startups like Amazon and eBay emerged. Microsoft introduced Windows 95 in 1995. Microsoft partnered with NBC to create a new, twenty-four-hour cable news television channel, MSNBC, in 1996. And upon La Russa's departure from Oakland that year, this time, with a practical analytics system being developed and improved upon daily, rather than rough, early elements of it rumbling around in his mind, Alderson had a far better idea of what he was looking for in a manager. Especially because, by the mid-1990s, the game's economic ground had shifted, making it dramatically more difficult for the smaller-market teams that earned less local media and advertising revenue, like Oakland, to compete.

Following the game's soul-crushing strike in 1994–1995, Oakland quickly went from maintaining the game's highest payroll to plummeting to one of its lowest.

"I was quoted in *Moneyball* in all of about two or three pages, but if you look at those pages, what I said about managers is that they are there to implement basic company philosophy, not to purvey their own," Alderson says. "It certainly is true today. But it also made sense. The organization is the one that endures, or should endure, beyond any individual who is a part of that organization. The successful teams are ones that are successful in marrying quality people in an organization with quality systems and philosophy. A lot of that philosophy and those systems come from continuity. One of the things that, for example, you've seen in Oakland is continuity. Basically, there were two people in charge of that baseball organization since 1984. That's almost fifty years."

Before handing the keys to the department to Beane in October 1997, Alderson made one more managerial hire ahead of leaving Oakland to work in the commissioner's office under Bud Selig. Under the sharpened parameters of what now was Oakland's postmodern philosophy, Art Howe was chosen as La Russa's replacement. The A's were rebuilding, attendance had plummeted from 2.9 million in their third World Series season of 1990 to 1.1 million in La Russa's last campaign, and they would play in the summer of 1996 to the backdrop of jackhammers and construction as the Oakland Coliseum was remodeled for the return of the NFL's Oakland Raiders.

In Howe, Alderson and Beane were confident that they had found the perfect conduit through which to channel their gospel of analytics. He played eleven years in the majors as an infielder and was coming off of a five-year run as Houston's manager. The results were steady, but not spectacular—three seasons over .500 in five years, with two third-place finishes in the rugged NL West. Howe was well respected, got along with everyone, and had a naturally sunny disposition. The A's, who would lose 97 games in Howe's second season, were rebuilding and were not expected to contend for several years. It was the perfect laboratory for Beane and his lieutenants—chief among them over the years Paul DePodesta, then Farhan Zaidi and David Forst—to fill beakers and test probabilities.

"We were going from the top payroll to the smallest payroll in a very short amount of time so, yeah, I figured that would be accurate," Beane says. "We did have a great opportunity and a great sort of petri dish, so to speak, to do that. We were convinced it was the right way to go—I mean, Sandy and then, certainly, myself. So it became objective versus subjective. And for us, the more we investigated, the more we saw it play out. It made us convinced. I'm still convinced."

By the time Howe's seven-year tenure in Oakland was finished after the 2002 season—the summer in which Lewis hung around the organization while researching material for his book—the specs of the managing job in Oakland and in dugouts nationwide from Boston to Los Angeles would never be the same.

Initially, Howe found managing in the AL far easier than in the NL because of the designated hitter. There were no difficult decisions surrounding a starting pitcher who was steamrolling the opponent but due to bat in the late innings of a 1–1 game. In the NL, of course, managers had to decide whether or not to pinch-hit. AL managers, with the luxury of the designated hitter, could stay with the starting pitcher as long as he was effective.

Howe had more autonomy to manage as he saw fit early in his Oakland tenure simply because the teams were bad and, as such, both the expectations and the stakes were low. He managed his first two seasons under Alderson, then his next five under Beane.

"They were very similar in a lot of ways," Howe says. "Sandy had a temper. He was very competitive, but I don't think he displayed it as much as Billy did. Billy played for me in Puerto Rico in winter ball. That's where I first got to meet Billy. Probably, that's what helped me get the job. Billy was familiar with me. Sandy didn't really know me."

Howe says, "[Me and my coaches] went in and I ran the game the way I felt I should have. In time, it changed. Sandy didn't get involved in a lot of stuff. In time, Billy got into analytics and when Paul came in, they started going in that direction the last two years I was there. I had my debates with Billy."

Following the percentages, Beane hated the bunt. He did not like the stolen base. All the stuff that analytics over the years would eradicate from the game. Howe was old-school enough to protest, and the debates raged with the power shift now in full progress.

"Billy made the comment to me, maybe my second-to-last year I was there, he hated the bunt, hated to give up an out," Howe says. "The theory was there was a big study and it found out you score more from first base with no out than from second base with one out. I tried to explain to him that it depends on the pitcher we're facing, number one, and number two, the baserunner at first base. If he's a guy who can steal a base, you don't have to give up an out. He can steal second. And also who's coming up. If you're in the bottom part of the order, yeah, you roll the dice and see if you can score a run. But if you're in the top part of the order and you have the 3-4-5 guys coming up with one out and a guy on second base, I like my chances of scoring that run. Because they're your best hitters. They're your RBI guys, and that's where they're supposed to thrive, and you have to give them that opportunity to drive that run in. We just didn't see eye to eye on that. I liked stealing bases. I knew if I had an 80 or 90 percent chance to steal the bag, I gave the guy the green light. And I liked the hit-and-run and he wasn't too big on that, either. That's just the way it was. Slowly but surely, that's basically why I left there. There were too many disagreements as far as how the game should be played."

The Athletics turned the corner in Howe's fourth season at the helm, going 87-75 in 1999. They won the AL West the following season by going 91-70, finished second in 2001 despite a 102-60 record, and won the division again in 2002 at 103-59. With Lewis embedded in the organization, the A's reeled off their historic twenty-game winning streak. At season's end, with Oakland's Sabermetrics movement in full force, Howe walked away from the 103-win team to take charge of the New York Mets.

Something else coincided with the Athletics' on-field improvement in 1999 under Howe: The club hired Paul DePodesta, another Bill James acolyte, as Beane's assistant GM. DePodesta, who graduated from Harvard with a degree in economics, had worked in Cleveland's organization for three seasons and clearly was a rising star. That stardom would take a unique turn when he became a central character in Lewis's *Moneyball*—or when he sort of became a central character. More accurately, "Paul's Computer" is what became the central character. "Paul's Computer said this." "Paul's Computer said that." It popped up enough—and turned DePodesta into the embodiment of a computer nerd caricature—that by the time of the book's theatrical release, he did not approve the use of his name for the movie. Instead, his character, played by Jonah Hill, was given the generic name of Peter Brand.

Slowly but surely, Howe says, Beane and Co. started asking him to play certain players in certain positions. The team was beginning to win. Both expectations and stakes were rising. The baseball operations department was growing ever more confident in its methodology. And with one of the game's lowest payrolls, Beane and his team knew they had to do things differently, follow what their data told them, and follow the cold calculations, not the emotions of the heart.

On January 8, 2001, the A's acquired Johnny Damon and infielder Mark Ellis from Kansas City in a three-way deal that sent outfielder Ben Grieve from Oakland to Tampa Bay and infielder Angel Berroa and catcher A. J. Hinch from Oakland to Kansas City. (Tampa Bay also sent pitcher Roberto Hernandez to Kansas City in the deal.) The A's already had speedster Terrence Long in center field, and the plan was to play Damon in left field because, as was no secret throughout the game, he had a poor arm.

"But Terrence wasn't the center fielder that Johnny was," Howe says. "I'd see certain balls I knew in my heart Johnny could have run down and caught. And I said, well, I'm not doing my job if the right guy isn't out there. I said, if Billy doesn't like it, he can always let me go. So I made that switch, moving Damon to center. When I did that, that's when we took off."

Damon was installed as the regular center fielder on June 24, with the A's struggling along at 35-38. From that point on, they went 67-22. Damon that summer batted .228 with a .297 on-base percentage over 68 games in left field, and .283 with a .348 OBP in 84 games in center field. Long played a lot of left field the rest of the way and some right field. Jeremy Giambi was in the mix, too, as well as a young Eric Byrnes. And, later in the year after the trade deadline, Jermaine Dye.

"Johnny started to thrive in his normal position, and our defense improved," Howe says. "It helped us both offensively and defensively."

Beane vividly remembers the final Damon-Long conversation with Howe that June when the decision was made to shift Damon back to his comfort zone in center field. It was the "early days of Starbucks," Beane says, and he was driving there to get his caffeine fix when he and Howe spoke.

"And he was absolutely right," Beane says. "I knew Art wasn't comfortable making that call, but he made it with conviction. He had analyzed it. One of the reasons we wanted Terrence in center at the time was that he was a younger player who we thought was going to be with us for a number of years. Johnny was probably just this one year before leaving for free agency. We wanted Terrence to establish himself. The organization was thinking about the long haul."

It was a classic example of what so many ball clubs struggle with each year: long term vs. short term. What's best for the organization in the big picture vs. what's best for individuals right now, this season. This is especially dicey for field managers because the wins and losses go on their own personal scorecards, and so many of them are managing for their jobs. Few outside of the legends have the luxury of not worrying about next year. And next season is not guaranteed to even some of the legends—see Baker, Dusty.

Even given his fervent belief in Oakland's developing system, Beane saw Howe's point that June with the team's slow start.

"It was kind of like, hey, we can move Terrence back to center field next year if you really think we need Johnny there now," Beane says. "In fairness, it's exactly what he said. He was the one who suggested it. It was the right move. It was a good move. And I like to think that was a situation where my ego was checked at the door when I said, 'You're right, let's do it.'"

As much as Beane and Howe clashed in the manager's later years, this was an example where both men were right: Howe in lobbying for the move, and Beane for acquiescing.

But in the last couple of years of Howe's tenure, the clashes began to outnumber the agreements. Making things more frustrating for all were Oakland's early playoff exits. In 2000, the A's were knocked out by the Yankees in a pulsating, five-game AL Division Series. In 2001, following their 102-win season, the A's again were stymied by the Yanks in a five-game ALDS. This time, they blew a 2-0 series lead, with Game 3 turning in Oakland on Derek Jeter's legendary flip play to nail Jeremy Giambi at home plate. In 2002, following the 103-win season, Oakland was knocked off by Minnesota in the ALDS.

"He would come down and ask me to play this guy, pitch this guy, pitch that guy," Howe says. "I didn't do it, but I didn't appreciate him coming down and trying to influence who I was going to play. Through time, it happened more often. One thing Billy was big on was to take the first pitch of an at bat. It hurt us because we did incorporate that a lot into our offense. When you're in the postseason facing Roger Clemens and you're taking the first pitch and it's strike one, you're in trouble. That's a lot of the reason why we weren't as successful in the postseasons, I think, against other good pitching staffs. Our poor guys were in the hole a lot. Billy was big on the leadoff hitter seeing a lot of pitches, which I understand. The more pitches you make a guy throw, the sooner you get him out of the game. But if he's a quality pitcher, you're not going to see a lot of pitches. Seven to ten pitches and you're out of the first inning and that's not good."

Though his teams won a lot of games over his last couple seasons, the relationship between Howe and Beane deteriorated. Much of it was understandable: With the team dominating, Howe naturally was going to think his imprint from the dugout was a key reason. Beane, DePodesta, and the number crunchers upstairs naturally were going to think their system was a key. When things went off track, when the A's lost because of what Beane perceived as a tactical error or when Howe did not follow a suggestion, storm clouds brewed quickly. The GM often would blow into the manager's office after the game and things would get heated.

When the team was losing, the front office would dial back their program to a degree. But when it was winning, they would crank it up.

"Billy would lose his temper, fly off the handle, and probably afterward kick himself for doing it," Howe says. "I told him, Billy, if you have an issue with me or with any of my coaches, go home, sleep on it, and call me in the morning if it's still bothering you. And if it still is, let's have lunch and discuss it. But don't fly off the handle in front of everybody because you're losing respect and credibility with the coaching staff and with your players. But it was his team and he said he could do what he wants and that was it."

From the vantage point of his early sixties today, Beane probably appreciates Howe more now than he did at the time. Then in his early forties, cocksure of himself as he carved out his new front-office identity while grinding to blaze new trails, it was a different time for Beane.

"The great thing about Art is that he's able to give an opinion, sort of aggressively and without putting you on the defensive," Beane says. "I was kind of lucky to have a guy like that, right? It takes a lot to get Art really upset and, now, he may show it so that's why he was great with that incredibly talented team. And the thing about Art is that everybody likes him. Everyone on the team liked him. He had the ability to manage stars. Had I been in that situation with a different type of personality, maybe it would have been even more volatile. Most of the volatility at that point was coming from my end. If it came from both ends, it may have been more chaotic."

As the Sabermetrics Revolution progressed, it would become very chaotic for managers throughout the game—some more than others—as baseball operations groups staged power plays that diluted the autonomy of the manager's office and resulted in a power shift in the entire structure of running a baseball game.

Howe was riding high from two 100-plus-win seasons but becoming increasingly disenchanted with his situation. His professional relationship with Beane was growing more and more unfulfilling and his frustrations with Oakland's offensive approach—taking pitches, not bunting runners over, the hit-and-run being frowned on—was at its peak. The three consecutive ALDS eliminations were wearing on everybody. The 2002 season—the twenty-game win streak, the 103 wins and first-place finish—should have been a triumphant moment. Instead, it was the end for Howe in Oakland.

"I thought I was coming back," says Howe, who had a year remaining on his contract at the time. "Billy came in and said the Mets are interested in you, would you consider going? To be honest, I was getting fed up with what was going on in Oakland. We had won 100-plus games my last two years there and here I am getting offered a deal with a team that lost [86] games the year before. But I knew it would be a matter of time before Billy let me go and I knew I would have a multi-year deal if I went to the Mets. And I knew it would give me another opportunity to help put a team together, and I liked that challenge."

Even though Howe was under contract, Beane gave his manager permission to talk with the Mets.

"I tested the waters but knew if not I was coming back for another year with a playoff contender," Howe says. "That was the hard part for me, leaving guys whom I felt were like my own family. Now we were finally in position to contend every year. I knew if I was leaving that my bench coach would get the job and it would be great for Ken Macha to get the opportunity. After I talked to the Mets, they won me over, so to speak. I felt like we were on the same page."

But in an ever-changing game, the ground would shift quickly under Howe in New York. In his first season, the Mets went 66-95. Worse, the general manager who hired him, Steve Phillips, was fired that June 12, less than three months into Howe's New York tenure. Then they went 71-91 in 2004. That September, Phillips's replacement, Jim Duquette, saying simply, "It wasn't working," fired Howe with two years and $4.7 million left on his deal. Ever gracious and classy, Howe agreed to manage the final seventeen games of the 2004 season anyway.

"I was really looking forward to working with Steve and I think we would have done a heck of a job," Howe says. "We were on the same page. Then, within a couple of months, he's gone. Jeez. All of a sudden the guy you came over there to work with is gone and that changed the whole dynamic.

"If I'd have known that was going to happen, I probably wouldn't have gone, to be honest with you. I'd have stayed with Oakland and probably become a free agent. But I don't think Billy would have re-upped me even if we won the World Series. The handwriting was on the wall."

———

It was perhaps the Last Gasp of the Managerial Gut Decision ever allowed on the October stage.

It was October 2003. *Moneyball* was rocketing to the top of the bestseller lists, Oakland's secret was out, and Howe's first Mets team had face-planted with 95 losses. That autumn, in the visiting dugout of old Yankee Stadium late in Game 7 of the ALCS, Boston manager Grady Little and ace Pedro Martinez became forever linked amid the wreckage of a Red Sox season.

And a future generation of executives worshipping at the altar of cold, hard, and unemotional data—starting with Little's own boss, Theo Epstein—would make sure nothing like this October surprise would ever happen again to their teams.

With a 4–2 lead following a highly stressful seventh inning in which Martinez allowed a solo homer to Jason Giambi followed by two singles before an inning-ending strikeout from Alfonso Soriano, Martinez emotionally pointed at the sky as he exited the mound. It was the universal signal of a pitcher who had done his job, was emotionally spent, and had no bullets remaining. Pitching coach Dave Wallace hugged Martinez as he exited the field. But then…Little asked Pedro for more. And when Martinez took the mound to start the eighth inning, what was heard over the din of the Yankee Stadium feeding frenzy was the thundering hooves of the coming Sabermetrics Revolution.

Little, a Texas native with an endearing, folksy manner, was considered a good manager, he was well-liked and respected by his players, and, in the way it Used to Be Done, he relied on his experiences and instincts. But the Red Sox at the time also had the beginnings of a burgeoning analytics department that was producing more data than Little was comfortable digesting in the moment. So the Red Sox in 2003 worked out a system in which they delivered some of the advanced information to Little, some went directly to pitching coach Dave Wallace, some to hitting coach Ron Jackson. It wasn't nearly as structured or routine oriented as it soon would become—especially after the Martinez debacle. But Epstein would figure out ways to get Little certain nuggets of information that he felt would be important to the manager. During the 2003 postseason, those informational sessions became more formal. The Sox would conduct long meetings involving the coaches, the front office, and the analytics department in hotel ballrooms. Audio, visual, everything. PowerPoint demonstrations. The whole shebang, including sessions with catcher Jason Varitek regarding pitch-calling for each game.

The key with Martinez, thirty-one in October 2003, was this: At that time, the data showed he was incredibly effective through ninety-five pitches in a game. But after that marker, he fell off significantly. It was dramatic, far more than the normal, late-in-game decline. In a pregame meeting the day of Game 7, Epstein, wading gingerly into the pitching plans, asked Little how he saw this one playing out. Well, Little told him, I see Pedro taking us as long as he can take us. Then Mike Timlin, Alan Embree, and those boys in the bullpen will help out. As they talked, Wallace, assistant GM Josh Byrnes, and a few Red Sox coaches and other personnel wandered in and out of the manager's office. But from his chair, Little did not have much trust in what by then was a tired bullpen. And that ninety-five-pitch milepost be damned, Martinez had led all of baseball with a 2.22 ERA that summer and had three Cy Young Awards in his trophy case. There was still comfort in that. And there were not yet any mandates from the front office to the manager. There were no color-coded charts telling Little what he must do.

Heading into Game 7 and with the Red Sox still not having won a World Series in eighty-five years, the distrust in his bullpen was something Little had been fretting about all day.

"It's about two o'clock in the afternoon in Yankee Stadium, Grady is there in his long johns, and he and I are standing on the mound along with a bat boy named Sparky," Charley Steiner, then a Yankees radio broadcaster and today the Dodgers' radio play-by-play man, told me during a 2018 interview. "Grady and I are talking, and he's not a happy camper.

"He's not happy for a lot of reasons. One, his contract status was uncertain [Little was not signed beyond 2003] and it was getting to him. What more must he do to be appreciated by ownership? We talked about that.

"And then he said, in that old, slow drawl—and I had no idea how prescient and clairvoyant he would be—'We're fucked tonight. I got nothing in the bullpen. Nothing. I even called Derek Lowe in his hotel room this morning and said, "Can you give me an inning?" and he said, "I can't even brush my teeth."'

"One of his pitchers, I don't even remember which one, Grady said, 'He's so nervous he's got canker sores in his mouth.' I hadn't heard the term 'canker sore' in I don't know how long.

"'*I got nothing.*'"

It was Scott Williamson who had the canker sores, which Little read as: He is scared to death of this moment.

"So now fast-forward to six thirty," Steiner continued. "We'd seen the Red Sox so often, and I'd known Grady for so long, I went downstairs to wish him good luck. And then he said, 'Sit down.' So in that tiny old Yankee Stadium visiting manager's office, I sit down and he closes the door."

There, Little delivered a stunner.

"Grady says: 'Let me tell you what's going to happen tonight. We're going to win this game. We're going to win the World Series. And then on the morning of the parade, I am going to go from one talk radio station to the next and tell them they're a bunch of freaking geniuses, and then I'm going to retire.'"

Howe, Little…the managers at the dawn of baseball's Digital Age were becoming disenchanted, confused, and resentful as the lines of demarcation between the front office and the field manager's office cracked like fault lines in an earthquake corridor.

"He had the backing of his team," Steiner said. "The players liked him. It was an hour and a half before the first pitch of the seventh game, and he was sad, he was motivated, he was angry, he was excited, and he said, 'Sit down,' and he just vented. I'll never forget that. I was really lucky to have known him, to be doing the game in that moment.

"So now the game unfolds, and Pedro is pitching his ass off, one of the most dramatic playoff games between these two ancient rivals. And now, what we had talked about at two in the afternoon is coming home to roost: what to do about Pedro. He is clearly on fumes. Very few people outside of the Red Sox players knew of Grady's dilemma. He had nobody to go to."

Little asked Martinez if he could start the eighth inning, with Nick Johnson due up. In his book *Pedro*, written with Michael Silverman, Martinez says that Little told him, "Embree's never gotten him out. So far, you've handled him pretty well."

So after David Ortiz's homer in the top of the eighth pushed Boston's lead to 5–2, Martinez induced a pop-up to shortstop from Johnson on his 107th pitch.

Aaron Boone, who was then about an hour from stepping into Yankees lore with the eleventh-inning walkoff homer against the knuckleballer Tim Wakefield, told me in 2018 that he did not "recall a sense in our dugout where we were shocked he stayed in the game. I definitely felt we sensed he was tiring and we had a chance to get to him. But it wasn't, 'Oh, they're leaving him in?'"

After the Johnson out, in short order, Derek Jeter drilled a double, Bernie Williams added an RBI single, and then, with two out and on Martinez's 123rd pitch, Jorge Posada rapped a game-tying double.

In his seat in Yankee Stadium, Epstein uttered one angry epithet as he watched: "Fuuuuck!"

Around him, Red Sox front-office men—particularly owners John Henry, Larry Lucchino, and Tom Werner—were livid.

At this point, Little called for Embree to replace Martinez. But it was too late.

"If I had it to do all over again…we had an outstanding bullpen down there, outstanding bullpen of *setup* men," Little told me during our 2018 conversation. "And that's mostly what my decision hinged on. We went through that season with no closer."

And Lowe, the one man Little did trust, had worked in five games that postseason, starting three, and his arm was so shot it couldn't even deliver the Colgate to his teeth.

"Later that day things started getting exciting, and I went with what I thought was the best I had," Little said. "And they recently put him in the Hall of Fame."

The final pitch of the Yankees' 6–5 win was recorded at 12:14 a.m. on Friday, October 17. On Monday, the Red Sox fired Little.

Today, at seventy-four, he continues working as a scout for the Pittsburgh Pirates, based at his home in North Carolina. He did land one more managing job in the majors after Boston, with the Los Angeles Dodgers in 2006, when he led them to an NL wild card berth following an 88-74 finish. Then, his Dodgers went 82-80 in 2007, the team hired Joe Torre that winter, and Little's managing days were finished. Today, though the visits are infrequent, he does occasionally return to Boston to see old friends. When he does, he says folks in restaurants and other public places are cordial.

"For sure," he says. "You know, these jobs in baseball come and go, but good friends that you develop, that lasts. This was a few years after 9/11 when this blunder was made, and after I made that decision, there's probably a small percentage of people in the New England area who had me on the most hated list right underneath Osama bin Laden. Know what I mean?

"It might have been 5 percent of the people, and that's not very many."

Working within today's parameters, Little likely would have been saved from himself because there would have been strict front-office directives on Martinez's ninety-five-pitch limit. And to take it a step further, the Red Sox's World Series drought perhaps would have ended in 1986 were analytics humming along at that time, because then–Boston manager John McNamara surely would have had a defensive replacement (likely Dave Stapleton) in at first base for Bill Buckner in the bottom of the tenth inning of Game 6, with the Red Sox leading the Mets 5–3 and just three outs away from clinching the World Series in Shea Stadium. But this was another case where emotions overtook reason: McNamara wanted Buckner, then thirty-six, on the field for the final out as a sort of a cherry on top of his long career. It was not unreasonable. But that final out never came. The Mets stunningly won Game 6 when Mookie Wilson's slow roller went through the creaky Buckner's legs for an error, and then New York won the title with an 8–5 Game 7 win two nights later.

What emerged from historic moments like these smacking headlong into the Digital Age, from the standpoint of baseball operations departments, was the need to eliminate, as much as possible, emotions from the decision-making element of games.

"There was a little bit of realization that we can't risk everything we put into that season," Epstein says of the ugly aftermath of the

Grady-Pedro game. "All the blood, sweat, and tears, all the resources and everything else."

While Epstein personally liked and respected Little, the ultimate takeaway from 2003 could not have been more crystal clear to him. There now were tools available via research and reams of data that had not been available even a few years prior. In a sport in which even the slightest edge represents the difference between victory and defeat, it is irresponsible not to employ every possible advantage.

Despite the searing memory of its ending, 2003 remains one of Epstein's favorite seasons. The Sox were building something strong, they were tilting at windmills and chopping down rivals, and so many winning decisions went into it. That was the year the Red Sox acquired David Ortiz, Bill Mueller, Kevin Millar, Mike Timlin, and others.

"So when we started the manager search," Epstein says, "we were looking for someone who not only was open to information—Grady was open—but someone who would be a real partner and with whom we could figure out a system we could use to bring the coaching staff and front office together with thoughtful, robust systems to get the right information to the coaches and the players in the right way to help us win and make sure our decision-making was recognizable across all aspects of the organization."

The manager search, of course, led to the hiring of Terry Francona. And in 2004, the team of self-named Idiots—hat tip to the inventor of the nickname, Howe's old buddy Johnny Damon—finally broke through and won the franchise's first World Series since 1918. No small part of it was Francona's magic touch. But a year after the Pedro debacle, the Red Sox also had fine-tuned their analytics operation, from research to information to delivery. Francona was the right man at the right time in part because he had spent 2003 as Ken Macha's bench coach in Oakland.

"They were very progressive," Francona says of what essentially was his one-season, postdoctorate education with the Athletics. "It was after *Moneyball* and everything and so as the bench coach, I got it kind of as an indoctrination. And I got to learn and pick and choose and see what I liked. And when I didn't understand something, I could ask. It was really good. *Really* good. It taught me a lot of things that I thought I maybe believed. So when I got to Boston, it wasn't a shock. When Theo or the guys would say we want to do something, it was just like, that's part of it."

From October 2003 to October 2004. One organization. Two managers. Two dramatic and diametrically opposed season endings.

And one sport that now was unhesitatingly racing into new frontiers.

"At the time we were playing the seventh game of the ALCS in Yankee Stadium, when I made this thing that's gonna dictate my legacy forever: I left a pitcher in a game a little bit too long," Little told me during our 2018 conversation. "I think about it every once in a while, and every once in a while I'm reminded of it.

"People who remind me, I tell them: 'At that moment in time, I was sitting in the dugout in Yankee Stadium. Where were you sitting?' I've been asked about it by kids who weren't even born yet. That's the way it is."

———

Like Grady Little, Kevin Cash made a key October pitching decision that quickly blew up and, by game's finish, ended his team's season. But unlike Little, when Cash pulled Blake Snell in Game 6 of the 2020 World Series, this "blunder"—to use Little's self-descriptor—was not even universally viewed as a blunder. In a post-*Moneyball*, high-def Sabermetrics world, it had plenty of defenders, too, because the decision was defensible with data. And, unlike as with Little, even the tar-and-feather crowd who disagreed was not chasing Cash to hang him in effigy.

While Cash still wears that decision in 2024 as the Rays continue their quest for their first World Series title, he is not as intertwined with it as Little is with Pedro. Most everyone watching the game being played that night in the neutral-site, COVID-19 bubble of Arlington, Texas, knew that Cash was carrying out a game plan based on scads of research and data produced by one of the smartest baseball operations units in the game. It did not make the end result easier for Cash to stomach—no matter how much his job description has changed, the manager still is the guy who makes the move after listening to front-office input all day and then goes home alone that night and must live with himself. It's part of today's delicate balance of power, and Cash and most of his peers not only have been conditioned to accept that, they're good with it.

"As manager, I think it's OK to have people discuss and help with decisions," Cash says. "There's some really, really smart people in this game that might not be in uniform. Shame on me if I'm not going to listen to them."

Even Hollywood could not concoct a championship ending for the A's when *Moneyball* went to the silver screen in September 2011. Instead, the movie had to settle for focusing on the incredible twenty-game winning streak from August to September in 2002 because the A's lost in the first round of the postseason that autumn—one of four consecutive times those A's were bounced in the first round.

When it happened again in 2003, the competitively volcanic Beane raged in a quote for the ages, speaking to the utter randomness of a short postseason series: "My shit doesn't work in the playoffs. My job is to get us to the playoffs. What happens after that is fucking luck." Many analytics-heavy teams over the years, most recently the Dodgers and Rays, know that all too well.

What the game and its changes have taught us over these two post-*Moneyball* decades is that budget-challenged teams who are whip-smart, efficient, and creative—the Rays, the A's, the Guardians, the Twins, and more—can figure out successful paths through the 162-game schedule and win. But it also is a fallacy, as evidenced by the randomness of October, that this system is foolproof.

As the computers whir upstairs, delightfully breaking down so many wonders that heretofore were deep mysteries—we now know why one pitcher's curve breaks so sharply, and it has everything to do with measurable spin rate—the game continues to demonstrate to the Ivy League brainiacs that they do not—and cannot—know it all. The game continually sends reminders that it is all too human, as well, that it has a heartbeat and a soul, and that, yes, it retains a place for skilled and versatile managers. You know whose shit does work in October? Bruce Bochy, who won his fourth World Series ring, with the Texas Rangers, in 2023. In fact, into the 2024 season, the last three World Series champions were managed by brilliant, veteran baseball men who are geniuses in combining human relations with cutting-edge information—Bochy, Baker, and Snitker. Computers and iPhones are essential to so many in our modern lives. But even they do not contain everything we need. They alone are incapable of unlocking certain mysteries of life.

Today, the best examples of the marriage of analytics and heartbeat are the Red Sox teams that won it all in 2004, 2007, 2013, and 2018, and the Chicago Cubs of 2016. Three of those teams were run by Epstein ('04, '07, and '16). It also is enormously instructive that in both cases, Epstein (and then his successors in Boston, Ben Cherington and Dave Dombrowski) managed player payrolls that ranked as the game's highest ('18 Red Sox), second-highest (Red Sox in '04 and '07), fourth-highest ('13 Red Sox), and sixth-highest ('16 Cubs).

What made the whole *Moneyball* idea so riveting in its infancy was that it provided a path for a mighty underdog. But once other organizations boarded the express, especially those that were well-heeled financially, that advantage dissipated and the search to exploit other inefficiencies in the game commenced.

Over the first two decades of the 2000s, the Sabermetrics Revolution thoroughly and completely moved the game into the era of specialization. From it came even more matchups (lefty-righty batter vs.

pitcher). The shift, the bane of lefty hitters' existence. It changed the way players are developed, or not developed: Analytics does not necessarily make players better, rather, it targets what they do well and emphasizes that skill—or skills—and eliminates others. Certain hitters with a skill for launch angle—called "uppercut" in the old days—honed in on that and began booming home runs in the era of the juiced ball. Pitchers with a high spin rate are asked to throw a greater percentage of sliders, or sweepers, or curveballs. Generally, the players are all-in on this because if they are successful with these changes, it means they will be financially rewarded.

But at what cost? In an industry that has grappled for years with significant injuries to pitchers, Tommy John surgery now is routine, rather than an outlier, especially for pitchers who spin the ball. As a whole, the industry is failing to consistently develop starting pitchers—see the "bullpen games" now even routine within the World Series. Even championship teams are short on starting pitchers. Hitters who worship at the altar of launch angle sacrifice so many other offensive skills to get there—strikeouts, in particular, are accepted offensively and have made for an overall less aesthetically pleasing game. Analytics does not help develop the overall skills of players so much as it emphasizes computer numbers to decide what a player can or cannot do. Managers now are tasked with implementing the end result of what management wants and selling it to the players they must work and coexist with for six months. It is the main reason why managers are viewed, profiled, and valued differently today by front offices than they were in the days of Tom Kelly and Sparky Anderson.

The Beane-Howe partnership was a featured dramatic arc in the movie *Moneyball*—the push and pull of the turf war between the front office and the manager—though the Howe part was grossly distorted, much like the Jerry West character in HBO's recent *Winning Time* series featuring the late-1970s and 1980s Los Angeles Lakers. Howe was one of the nicest men in the game, and that he was portrayed cinematically as a temperamental bastard was incredibly hurtful to him and outrageous to those who knew him. It also is illustrative of how the era has been misrepresented.

"That has been proven to be fictional," Buck Showalter says. "It made for a good movie and people watched it. But it was a Hollywood thing and it didn't happen that way."

For one thing, the A's of that period were powered by their starting pitching—Tim Hudson, Mark Mulder, Barry Zito, and even Cory Lidle—not by the Scott Hattebergs of the world. And yet they barely got a mention.

Howe was finished managing by the time the movie was released in September 2011, and says he saw the film only because he had so many calls from former players and reporters, all of whom were angry over the way he was portrayed.

"There's one scene in there where I'm in the hallway asking Billy for an extension," Howe says. "I had another year on my contract, and I had an agent and my agent took care of my contracts. There was *so* much in it that was false. It made Billy look like the good guy and made me look like the bad guy. They did a pretty good job of that."

Dramatic tension is the currency of Hollywood films—good guy vs. bad guy, hero vs. villain—so it was bound to happen. Nobody knows at the time of the writing which books or movies will become smash hits. Out of the frenzy comes the collateral damage, and Howe certainly was that.

The movie premiered in Oakland on Monday, September 19, 2011, during an A's homestand. It was an off day between games against Detroit and Texas, and it was three months after the club had replaced Bob Geren with Bob Melvin.

"I remember going, *whoa*, after I saw that movie," Melvin says. "I was there, with Billy, and Brad Pitt, and I was like, wow. I hadn't gone through a lot of those things I'm seeing. I'm thinking to myself there's no way that's the way it is. It was kind of surreal. It was surreal in the fact that here I am, taking a job and I'm watching Philip Seymour Hoffman do that job and this is how he's treated."

———

Melvin would become the longest-tenured manager under Beane, and it easily was the best and most comfortable pairing. Melvin's decade-long run from 2011 to 2021 resulted in six Oakland playoff appearances and a partnership that smoothly melded Melvin's old-time baseball acumen with his intelligence and eagerness to follow new paths to knowledge.

There were times when Melvin did encounter Emotional Billy, "but in a healthier way than portrayed in the movie," the manager says.

Melvin attended Cal Berkeley, interned at the investment bank and brokerage firm Bear Stearns during the offseasons when he was catching for the San Francisco Giants, and managed in Seattle (2003–2004) and Arizona (2005–2009) before replacing Geren in Oakland sixty-four games into the 2011 season.

Beane and Melvin both paid attention to the stock market. They both enjoyed dining out, which led to restaurant comparisons and suggestions when the team traveled. They both watched *Billions* on Showtime, a show built around a hedge fund manager who accumulates wealth and power. Both in baseball and beyond, they spoke a similar language.

In Seattle and Arizona, Melvin's game preparation with the front-office staffs mostly was basic scouting, digesting the reports filed by advance scouts and evaluating what his eyes told him. The Hall of Fame executive Pat Gillick, who was running the Mariners at the time, sometimes would stop by his office with statistical printouts and say, hey, these are some numbers that are starting to get some legs in the game, on-base percentages, things like that. Maybe take a look at them.

"Oakland was, look, here's some stuff we're giving you, it's all matchup-based, lineup-based, pitcher versus batter stuff," Melvin says. "We expect you to be pretty disciplined with this, yet you don't have to know how it's baked in. Now you know about some of those things—OPS [on-base percentage plus slugging percentage], wOBA [weighted on-base average, a way of measuring a player's overall contributions per plate appearance], WAR [wins above replacement, which measures a player's value by calculating how many more wins he is worth than a replacement-level player at his same position].

"With Oakland, they didn't bog you down with, this is what you need to know. It was more, this works for us. Here's what you need to look at and we expect you to be disciplined with it, and it was how they ran their organization. Right, wrong, or indifferent, they had their way of doing things. These are conclusions and this is what we need you to do. It actually was pretty easy to balance. Farhan would kind of explain to me, hey, look, this is how we come to these numbers."

From the point of view of Beane and Zaidi, Melvin was a skilled collaborator.

"There were times where Bob would say, 'I know the numbers say this, but this doesn't seem right. Can you check this out?'" Beane says. "And then we would go back and either, hey, there's something to what you said so maybe we do it this way, or not. But, ultimately, the curiosity as to why it was working, that was why he learned it and not only eventually did it, but understood it."

There were other times, especially in 2012 as the Athletics were beginning to fire on all cylinders during a 94-68 season, when they clashed. The A's had finished 74-88 in 2011, and most statistical models projected them to lose 100 or more games in 2012. Instead, everything came together beautifully. And, as it did, the baseball operations department started ratcheting things up—as was its custom.

"There were certain instances during the games when I had information and didn't apply it at times when they thought I should have," Melvin says. "Billy was always present the next day: 'We're doing this wrong, why did you not hit for this guy?'"

Melvin would explain, and Beane would counter: "I get why you did it this way, but it's not right."

"There were some contentious conversations," Melvin says. "The expectation in Oakland is, their managers have to do things a certain way."

Beane had cut his Sabermetrics teeth on Howe, Macha, and Geren in his single-minded zeal for ruthless efficiency. By the time Melvin arrived in 2011, most of the battles had been fought and the power base in Oakland was clear. Though nothing was changing in October—the postseason losses were still racking up—Oakland's Little Engine That Could persona became a source of envy throughout the industry.

Macha took over from Howe, won two division titles, and had four winning seasons, yet was fired after Detroit swept Oakland in the 2006 ALCS.

"For me, Macha was a super-nice guy, but I would say his hands were completely tied," says former first baseman Eric Karros, who played the last of his fourteen seasons with Oakland in 2004 and today broadcasts for Fox. "I remember having a discussion with Billy and him telling me they were running algorithms that could determine within three or four games what their record would be before the season started. I had never heard of anything like that. This was in the infancy of analytics. That was no joke who was writing out the lineups there. Macha wasn't writing the lineups. That wasn't happening. I felt bad. But he was bench coach to Art Howe, so he knew what he was getting into. It was different.

"I should have read the *Moneyball* book before I signed there, I would have had a better idea of what I was getting into."

At some point Howe traveled to Oakland to attend a reunion of one of his teams and was in the trainers' room in the clubhouse when Beane appeared.

"Billy came in and said, 'I just want you to know, I'm sorry for the way I treated you,'" says Howe, who thanked his former boss for that acknowledgment as they shook hands.

Then Beane, always quick with a quip and a smile, added: "Macha thinks I'm tough on him. He should have seen how I was with you."

"That made me laugh," Howe says. "Billy just wanted to win so badly that it kind of consumed him. He's a smart guy. I'm sure in most cases he probably thought he was smarter than any manager he had. And he probably was."

Today, Beane says that his experience with Howe "actually helped me going forward because I like to think I was at least self-reflective and self-aware. Like, all right, listen, I still believe in what I was doing, just the presentation could have been better. Let's put it that way."

By the time Geren replaced Macha, Beane says, he literally told the manager that he would never even call him unless there was a player move to be made. I won't go into your office after games. I will leave you alone.

"Look, anytime you're an agent of change, it's not always going to be comfortable," Beane says. "I'd like to think that, beyond the jobs, we're always continuing to grow. Not just as general managers, but also as people. There's a difference between being sixty years old and doing a job and being in your early thirties. That's a long time. So if I haven't evolved over that time, then shame on me."

With Melvin, the battles were not necessarily over the batting order, which has become shorthand around the game and in the eyes of so many fans for the extent to which the front office controls things today. Melvin says he always had a say in the batting order and, "for quite a while, they didn't really worry too much about how the lineup was constructed. It was more *who* was in the lineup. What I got was, OK, you can write out the lineup, but if you talk with this analyst, you're going to figure out who should be in the lineup anyway. And if a guy's numbers are so big against a particular pitcher, you need to get him to the plate as much as you can. It wasn't even one through nine, it was who one through nine were."

Eventually, Melvin says, the lineups were the least of it. Once he understood the A's system, he notes, the lineups became pretty obvious, anyway.

"The brilliance of Bob is that, first of all, he's a smart guy," Beane says. "And he's good in both worlds. The reason he's adapted so well and is one of the best managers, if not the best manager, in the game is, number one, his intelligence and his open-mindedness to sort of embrace the analytics. But the other thing he does so well that maybe the analytics-side people don't quite appreciate is that Bob also understands the human side of managing that, really, arguably, is his most important job. Really. I mean, Bob's got twenty-five young people who are incredibly talented, incredibly wealthy, and in many cases twenty-five different personalities. And he has the ability to pull that together."

After ten full seasons and part of another, Melvin left Oakland for San Diego ahead of yet another Athletics teardown under owner John Fisher in 2022. On paper, it appeared to be a perfect match: one of the game's most skilled skippers and a built-to-win Padres team with a club-record payroll. But it blew up after only two seasons, an NLCS run in 2022 and a failure to make the playoffs in 2023. The outside view going in was that, for Melvin, after a decade of working for the controlling Beane, the Padres would be a piece of cake. Instead, Melvin encountered more drama in his brief stay in San Diego than in a decade in the Bay Area. Where the system was refined and structured in Oakland, it was chaos in San Diego. There were a handful of occasions in which the manager learned that what he thought were private conversations with A. J. Preller, San Diego's president of baseball operations, instead had been relayed to certain players, which threatened to undercut Melvin's authority. Poor roster construction became an issue. There were directives from the baseball operations department that Melvin put his veteran team through extra work on various things as the season deepened. Finally, Preller, whose previous managers in San Diego had no experience and, thus, little choice but to listen to him, wanted Melvin out. In the end, it said far more about Preller and the Padres after failing miserably in two previous managerial hires, Andy Green and Jayce Tingler, than it did about Melvin, who immediately signed with the Giants—and Zaidi, his old Oakland colleague—for the 2024 season. Of course, the world keeps spinning and that 2024 season was a debacle in San Francisco, resulting in Zaidi's firing one year after he cashiered Gabe Kapler. Now Melvin will be under the spotlight in 2025. Meanwhile, Preller's Padres won 93 games under Mike Shildt before being eliminated by the Dodgers in a Division Series. And so it goes.

The lasting legacy of what came to be known by the catchall term "Moneyball," of course, is with the owners. Had they not bought in, analytics would not have taken over the game to the degree in which it did, and the job definition of the manager would not be nearly so different today as it was back when Earl Weaver and Whitey Herzog were in charge. The combination of Oakland's winning and doing so under a rigid economic plan piqued the attention of owners across the game—especially once they all read Lewis's insider account that told one part of the fascinating story (Paul's computer!) while mostly ignoring the engine (pitching!).

"To me, the stuff that Oakland had been doing that was revealed during *Moneyball* wasn't proprietary and it all kind of made sense," Alderson says. "But when people read it, it made complete sense and resulted in a sort of top-down revolution. I think owners read that book and said, you know what, this business isn't much different than my own. These are the types of businesses that made me a lot of money and we're going to run our baseball team the same way."

And those who subsequently would enter the game as new owners also had read the book, were well-versed in the concepts, and used parts of it as their own architectural rendering upon becoming members of the game's exclusive ownership club.

"Then what they did was hire front offices that thought the same way," Alderson says. "Ultimately, the GM is picked by the owner, whereas the manager isn't always picked by the owner. But the GM certainly is, and so then front offices began to resemble ownership rather than traditional baseball communities. Then when those front offices were in place, they started hiring managers that looked more like them. We see this in politics all the time. Like attracts. That's not good in a lot of political arenas and so forth, but that's unfortunately what I think *Moneyball* demonstrated. So now what you have is, managers are extensions of front offices, which themselves are extensions of ownership. And we've ended up with a very homogenous group of managers."

As he navigates his fifth decade in the game, Alderson has seen the industry grow toward producing record revenues (just under $11 billion in 2022). He does not think that things are necessarily more corporate, but he thinks they are more financially driven than ever. Owners still buy teams for their love of the game, he believes, but they now view their stewardship of franchises "as a financial enterprise, not a club."

Others agree.

"The biggest change in ownership from thirty years ago to now is that it is more sophisticated," Epstein says. "Teams used to be held as kind of trophy assets by the rich. They weren't run necessarily as businesses. They were held as these trophies to display. They didn't necessarily have the most dynamic management teams or business plans. Now, by and large, it is a different breed of businessman. It's almost a private equity business. Management teams put in place are really high-powered, with really sophisticated business plans that have created a really demanding environment and more accountability. Not just for results, but for process. That's why I think not just managers, but GMs, too, are not always safe in the aftermath of a World Series. It's not just about one result, but the arc of the organization and the process and making sure everybody is growing and getting better and continuing the health of the franchise."

More broadly, the way the industry now operates, there is access to more information than ever before. People can watch every single game, break down every single play, access every single statistic. As such, goodwill for everybody—managers, players, executives—does not last as long as it once did.

"Good thing is, there's more of a chance to prove yourself," Epstein says. "There's more meritocracy now. When you're really good, you get rewarded."

In two decades since *Moneyball* was published, the Rays, with their consistently low payrolls, have played in two World Series (2008 against the Phillies, 2020 against the Dodgers) and lost them both. They also produced a one-hundred-win team (2021) and a ninety-nine-win team (2023) that each was eliminated early in the playoffs. The Dodgers, another model team for how to best deploy analytics but one that also does it with heavy spending, won ten of eleven NL West division titles into the 2024 season, brilliantly constructing five one-hundred-win teams during that span, but won just one World Series, in the pandemic-shortened 2020 season. And Oakland, despite its groundbreaking Sabermetrics usage, has not played in a World Series since 1990, when Dennis Eckersley, Rickey Henderson, Dave Stewart, Mark McGwire, Jose Canseco, and company were stunned by Lou Piniella's Cincinnati team in a four-game sweep.

But Houston, on the analytical cutting edge for more than a decade, advanced to seven consecutive ALCS through 2023 and parlayed those into four World Series appearances—and two titles, including the 2017 crown, which was tainted by the sign-stealing scandal.

What happened in the industry between the book's publication in 2003 and the movie's release in 2011 was the beginning of a fierce power struggle between managers and baseball operations departments throughout the game. The battles were fought to varying degrees across thirty franchises. Some of the clashes came with more urgency than others because some clubs moved more quickly into the Sabermetrics Revolution than others. Eventually, even the last of the holdouts, clubs like San Francisco and Detroit and Baltimore, moved in that direction.

In managers' offices from Philadelphia to Los Angeles, there would be permanent repercussions.

"When the book came out, that's when it sort of felt like there was World War I trench warfare," Beane says. "Where you dig your trench and we're just going to basically butt heads the whole time. The years immediately following the book were where people sort of chose sides and that's where it really was the most divisive, in my opinion.

"You had front office versus manager or coaching staff. You had writers on both sides. You had old-school writers, you had Baseball Prospectus making fun of the old-school writers. It happened in every part of the industry. Television announcers. And I just think a lot of it was, when the book came out, you were forced to choose a side, and it didn't have to be that way. So I think there was more conflict. It hasn't completely evaporated, but I think over time it became less divisive because if you look at managers now, like Kevin Cash, he came up through the system as a former player and so you have guys like him who have been exposed to both sides. And the creation of a lot of the managers working now came organically through analytics-driven organizations."

CHAPTER 7

THE UPSTAIRS VS.
THE DOWNSTAIRS

The sprawling brick house sits just off the seventeenth green of a leafy country club north of Cincinnati, miles and miles away from the dugouts that once served as his summer home. Overstuffed leather chairs in the basement are surrounded by framed pictures and other relics from Jim Tracy's eleven-year managerial career in Los Angeles, Pittsburgh, and Colorado. As Ohfer, the family's big yellow Labrador retriever, chases a stuffed hedgehog through the basement before being "coached" to take his toy outside, the old manager is a world removed from the trenches he occupied from 2001 to 2012. But reminders of a rich career abound, from the pictures on the wall to the framed uniform jerseys to the flat-screen television.

Each time he clicks on a baseball game, Tracy sees things that take him straight back to the highs, the lows, and, frequently, the "trench warfare" that consumed the game in the decade after the publication of *Moneyball*. As the Upstairs armies of rapidly growing baseball operations departments advanced deeper and deeper onto the turf of the Downstairs managers who, suddenly and without warning, were badly hemorrhaging both authority and autonomy, Tracy during this time was protecting his flank on multiple fronts.

DePodesta, the game's new whiz kid, moved from working as Beane's right-hand man in Oakland to the Los Angeles Dodgers on February 16, 2004, where, at thirty-one, he became the game's youngest general manager. Tracy had managed the Dodgers to winning records in each of his first four seasons, including twice winning more than 90 games. But in 2005, with a roster that had been reshaped under DePodesta's analytic plug-and-play vision, the team imploded to a 71-91 finish. It was a twenty-two-game turnaround in the wrong direction: In 2004, Tracy's Dodgers had finished 93-69 and won the NL West title for the first time in a decade. Tracy was apoplectic—and powerless—as his roster was systematically disassembled, a carefully built team and clubhouse culture suddenly being swallowed whole by the soulless numbers on DePodesta's computer screen. One day after the 2005 season ended, Tracy, with a year left on his contract and no indication that it would be extended, agreed to part ways with the Dodgers. A month later, the Dodgers would fire DePodesta, ending his chaotic and controversial tenure after just two seasons. Afterward, DePodesta would find safe harbors when Alderson brought him aboard as a special assistant in San Diego and then with the New York Mets. In 2016, DePodesta changed sports entirely, becoming the chief strategy officer for the NFL's Cleveland Browns.

Seven years later, in 2012, Tracy was managing in Colorado when the Rockies baseball operations department decided unilaterally to change pitching philosophy three months into the season. They ordered a four-man rotation and that the starters throw no more than seventy-five pitches. Tracy vehemently disagreed. He had worked to build dominant pitching staffs in Los Angeles. He was terrific at managing bullpens. And now, suddenly, he had zero input into the Rockies' pitching program? It was insulting. Then, when the Rockies relocated a baseball operations man into the clubhouse around this same time, Tracy was livid at the encroachment onto turf that for a century or more had been occupied only by those players and coaches in uniform. And when the organization piled one more log onto the already lit bonfire, informing him after the season that it was going to fire three of his coaches, well, that was a bridge too far.

With one year and $1.4 million left on his deal, Tracy walked away. It was a resounding statement in a tumultuous time. As the lines of demarcation were changing between the Upstairs and the Downstairs during a fierce power struggle, Tracy firmly planted his flag, standing in favor of integrity, and managers, everywhere.

"Jim had been with us since 2009, he had been the Manager of the Year and I enjoyed playing for him," says Jeff Francis, one of Tracy's starting pitchers that season. "I loved Jim Tracy. We could sense the tension, and sense that was the reason he left. I think he had been given an indefinite, almost lifetime sort of contract, one of those 'as long as you want to manage the team, you can.' That was the word. The fact that he didn't stay gave us an indication that he didn't like how things were being run."

Tracy first became a major-league manager when the Dodgers hired him as Davey Johnson's replacement in 2001. By then, he had managed seven seasons in the minor leagues. He had served as Felipe Alou's bench coach in Montreal, and in the same capacity for Johnson in Los Angeles. One of the greatest compliments of his professional life came when Johnson sat him down for a conversation on a Dodgers charter flight sometime during the 2000 season, a glass of wine in one hand and unfiltered honesty in the other. Johnson clearly sensed that his time with the Dodgers was about up and now he was telegraphing it to Tracy.

"When I took this job and they told me you were going to be the bench coach, I had no goddamn idea who you were," Johnson told

Tracy. Johnson then praised his entire Dodgers coaching staff, talked about how well everyone worked together, before continuing: "You're as good a coach as I have on my staff. I trust you with anything. If, in fact, they ask me about filling the job with an internal candidate, I'm going to tell them that you're the best guy."

The conversation continued at thirty thousand feet, the wise old sage Johnson, who had managed the New York Mets to the 1986 World Series title, dispensing wisdom and his still-young coach eagerly lapping up every drop. Johnson called Los Angeles, New York, Chicago, and Boston the "Big Four" in terms of big-league managing jobs. Most first-time managers will get a job in another market, Johnson told Tracy, and when things don't work out—as inevitably happens—perceptions will vary, some people will say the manager wasn't given the tools to win, and often there is an outside chance that the manager will get another chance to manage again elsewhere.

But, Johnson told Tracy, if your first job is managing a team in one of the "Big Four" markets and you wind up getting fired, the outside opinion will veer toward, "He effed that up about as bad as he could. He was overmatched." In that case, Johnson told Tracy, you will have the opportunity to coach again on a major-league staff, but you'll certainly never manage another team. That, Johnson said, is a decision you will have to make if the time comes.

Near the end of that disappointing 2000 season—their fourth consecutive summer missing the playoffs despite an NL-high $90 million payroll—and with a deep divide in the relationship between Johnson and GM Kevin Malone, the Dodgers fired their manager. When they offered the job to Tracy, he replayed Johnson's advice in his mind and again threaded his way through the pros and cons. And then he bet on himself and said yes.

He was sure the seven seasons of managing in the minors, from Class A to Triple-A, had given him a solid base. He recalled the 1992 season in particular, leading a Double-A Harrisburg Senators team that included players like Kirk Rueter, Cliff Floyd, Miguel Batista, Rondell White, and Gabe White to a 94-44 record. Then there were the three years of seasoning as Alou's bench coach in Montreal, 1995 to 1998, working with luminaries such as Pedro Martinez, Moises Alou, Vladimir Guerrero, Carlos Perez, Ugueth Urbina, and more. Sitting next to Alou, one of the all-time greats, was like obtaining a doctorate at the feet of Socrates.

"What an education that was for me," says Tracy, who led the Dodgers to an 86-76 record in his first season, outperforming the computer projections of 79-83. "And yet, today, you're qualified to run a major-league club with no managerial experience? How do you do it? If you got that opportunity and you're left to do it on your own, you're going to be a miserable failure. You've never run a bullpen in your life. You don't have any idea how bullpen pieces are put together. You don't have any ideas of how to implement them strategically in relation to what's going on in front of you and a specific situation in a game. Somebody better be doing it for you.

"I'm not saying that disrespectfully. You know why? That you've never taken the opportunity blows me away. It blows me away. People think that they can sit in a radio booth or television booth and next thing you know, they're considered a candidate to become a manager. On what qualifications? Because you've sat and watched 162 games and you get to comment or voice your opinion after the fact of what's happened?"

Here in Tracy's basement, there is a poster-size, autographed print of Eric Gagne, Guillermo Mota, Paul Quantrill, Tommy Martin, and Paul Shuey, his beloved 2003 relief corps that set the stage for the 93-69 romp in 2004. "Best Bullpen in Baseball" reads the caption, and that speaks for well beyond 2004, too. Any discussion of the best ever includes this unit. It is the only bullpen in the past thirty years to rank among the game's all-time top twenty bullpens in ERA (2.46). It was the season in which Gagne, while racking up 55 saves, struck out 137 hitters and walked just 20 while surrendering only 37 hits and 11 earned runs over 87.1 innings pitched. Yes, Gagne years later would be referenced in the Mitchell Report for steroids, complicating his legacy—but what he did in the Steroids Era of 2004 still stands out on that playing field. Mota threw 105 innings in *relief*, striking out 99.

Tracy is justifiably proud of this group to this day. He and pitching coach Jim Colborn designed and constructed that pen, built a pitching staff that allowed the Dodgers to overachieve in four of Tracy's five seasons, and artfully deployed those relievers nightly. Years of managing and coaching fed his knowledge. Tracy understood pitching, how much of a leash to allow his starters, when to open the bullpen door, and which arms to bring into which matchups. When he had it going, in many ways, 2003 was not much different from today's analytics dictum of not allowing the starting pitcher to face the lineup a third time. Nightly, he asked his starters to obtain at minimum the first fifteen outs—five innings' worth. After that, decisions would be made according to the game, situations, and individual personnel.

"We told them we need fifteen outs, and the look on some of their faces," Tracy says of the starters. "Then I said, 'Now let me finish. I'm not saying that after the fifteenth out, you're done, which is just five innings—five and dive, right?' I said, 'Depending upon where you're at, how things are going, what the scoreboard says…are there days when you're going to get the chance to get the sixteenth, seventeenth, eighteenth out all the way through the twenty-first? Or finish the game? Yes. But: Once we get through the fifteenth out, now we're going to take it an out at a time and see where it all goes.'"

Tracy continues: "What I learned over the course of seven years of managing in the minor leagues is that you manage your people, you manage the game, you manage your people who are involved in the game in relation to situations that are in front of you and also to what the scoreboard says. The scoreboard, to me, it's not out there anymore."

Example: A 7–1 game and the rival lineup is turning over for a third time. "And let's say we're going to the fifth or sixth inning," Tracy says. "I've never seen anybody hit a home run that accounted for six runs with nobody on, never have. So what they say is probably we don't want any traffic out there right now. But how do you determine this reliever you're bringing into the game isn't going to get into trouble? And how do you know that the starter who was out there might get four or five more outs and entirely change the complexion of how you would run your pitching staff from there? You don't."

It was a far different Dodgers organization when Tracy was hired than it is today. Following the legendary pioneer Walter O'Malley's death in 1979—it was O'Malley who moved the franchise from Brooklyn to Los Angeles in 1958—his son, Peter, and daughter, Terry Seidler, took charge of the franchise until 1998, when the family-owned ball club went corporate with a sale to the Fox Entertainment Group. Compared with the peace and tranquility of the O'Malley era—they even served ice cream to Dodgers employees every day that the team was in first place—it was a chaotic time. But it would get far worse in 2004 when the corporate behemoth sold to Bostonians Frank and Jamie McCourt.

Under Fox, traditional baseball men ran the baseball operations side of things—Kevin Malone was the GM from 1998 to 2001 (taking over from interim GM Tommy Lasorda), followed by interim Dave Wallace (2001) and then Dan Evans (2001–2004). Tracy and his staff worked well with each of those fellows. The chain of command was clear and just as it always was: The GMs formulated the roster and did front-office things, and Tracy and his staff were in charge of the clubhouse, games, and the overall baseball program—like running the rotation and building strong bullpens. An unknown when he was named to replace Johnson, Tracy immediately proved himself and, remarkably in Hollywood, this Midwesterner who practically oozed corn on the cob exceeded expectations in the beginning and kept on doing so.

But from the beginning of their stewardship, the McCourts were overleveraged and underequipped for running a major-league baseball team—and that lasted until, mercifully, under heavy pressure from Commissioner Bud Selig, they finally sold the team in 2012 to the current owners, Guggenheim Baseball Management. One of the McCourts' very first moves upon purchasing the Dodgers was to hire DePodesta as GM and fire Evans.

Essentially, DePodesta walked into the NL West title upon taking the job in 2004. The Dodgers had the game's best bullpen, solid starting pitching, third baseman Adrián Beltré laser-focused in his walk year before free agency (48 home runs and 121 RBI in 2004), an emerging Jayson Werth, and so much more. Tracy, now in his fourth season, was supremely confident pulling the levers.

"To be quite frank with you, there never was a time where Paul ever told me how to run my pitching staff or do this or do that," Tracy says. "He never did that."

Instead, DePodesta focused on tinkering with the roster, and with the Dodgers steamrolling through their 2004 schedule, a turning point in the careers of both Tracy and DePodesta arrived with that July's trade deadline. The Dodgers led the NL West and were in Colorado as the deadline approached when club personnel met in DePodesta's Denver hotel suite to assess trade proposals and make final decisions in the last hours leading to the deadline.

The new GM tossed out one idea: What would you think of us dealing Paul Lo Duca, Juan Encarnacion, and Guillermo Mota in a blockbuster deal?

"I can't imagine how he perceived the look on my face as he was looking at me," Tracy says. "I didn't say anything. I just sat there speechless for a period of time. And he kind of broke the silence in the room by looking at me and saying to me, 'Well, Trace, would you rather me do nothing at all?' And knowing those three pieces I just mentioned, what we had become, and how cohesive as a group we were and the relationships that had been built in that clubhouse, I said, 'If that's the best you can do, just leave us alone.'"

Lo Duca, the catcher, was the heart of the Dodgers clubhouse. Mota was a vital setup man for Gagne. Encarnacion, just twenty-eight, had 13 homers and 43 RBI at the time but just a .289 on-base percentage. To a man who championed OBP in Oakland and may be the single most important person who lifted that particular statistic into its highly worshipped status today, sending the Artist Formerly Known as Batting Average into oblivion, that was an anathema.

So on Friday, July 30, as the Dodgers were traveling from Colorado to San Diego to open a series at Petco Park, DePodesta pulled the trigger and shipped Lo Duca, Mota, and Encarnacion to the Florida Marlins for first baseman Hee-seop Choi, starting pitcher Brad Penny, and a minor-league lefty named Bill Murphy who would never pitch for the Dodgers.

In 2004, the Digital Age was beginning to fully flower. The internet was fully operational. At Harvard that summer, DePodesta's alma mater, Mark Zuckerberg and friends founded Facebook. And though the introduction of the iPhone was still three years away, the BlackBerry was up and running and making texting so much more efficient than the old flip phones. Information traveled, if not at the speed of light, at least at the speed of gossip.

"I walked into the ballpark, and Jiminy Christmas," Tracy says. "You know the relationship I had with my players. I mean, I never lied to them. They knew that they could trust me. And Jesus, there's things going across the bottom line on ESPN in the clubhouse as these deals are going down. I've got kids that are already in the clubhouse for that night's game against the Padres.

"They're sticking their head into my office and they're going, 'Skip? Is this true?' And you knew at this point it was. I couldn't take it anymore. I had my bench coach, Jimmy Riggleman, close the door. He was sitting there with me, along with Jimmy Lett [the bullpen coach]. They're looking at me and I said, it was talked about. It was spoken about to me. And yet, I hadn't received any official word and there it is going across the screen."

GMs have been trading players and making roster moves against managers' wishes since the game was invented. But this was different. Instead of the collaborative give-and-take that is more normal in a winning season, it felt like a mad scientist had been turned loose in a laboratory. It would have been one thing if the team already was rebuilding, or struggling. But on that day, the Dodgers were 59-42 and led the NL West by 2.5 games. Yet the mood inside of that Dodgers clubhouse was funereal.

Even in real time, inside that clubhouse, it was clear that an epic battle between good, old-fashioned clubhouse chemistry and cold, hard stats had been waged, and chemistry had taken a clear TKO. This debate would be re-upped many more times over the following two decades as the Upstairs seized more turf from the Downstairs across the game, and continues to lead to great conversations today. But on July 30, 2004, it was stunning and decidedly quick.

"Obviously, it had happened," Tracy says. "It was a tough day, man. It was really, really tough. Mota didn't want to go. He came into my office and told me to tell them that. I mean, we had people crying in the clubhouse."

Tracy felt like what he and his staff had carefully planted and nurtured for the past few years had been rototilled. DePodesta, no doubt, felt like he was simply doing what he had been hired to do.

"Some of the circumstances that I came in under when I became manager, people didn't think I was going to be there too long," Tracy says. "I can understand that. Nobody knew who I was, or what my skill level was, or anything like that. So we were building up to what became something very, very special. And then, after 2004, it got broken. They broke it all up."

The key to the gut-wrenching trade deadline deal was Choi. DePodesta was enamored of him. Essentially, he was acquired to become the Dodgers' version of Scott Hatteberg, who gobbled up one full chapter in the book version of *Moneyball* as the prime example for

Oakland's laser focus on high on-base percentages, which the A's methodology had determined tied directly into runs scored. Choi, a big, burly (six five, 235 pounds), South Korean first baseman, had broken into the majors with the Cubs in 2002 and was traded to Florida in 2004. He was in his first season as a starter in Florida, and the Dodgers' new front office viewed him as a get, another player through whom it could exploit one of the game's inefficiencies. In just 80 games with the Cubs in 2003, he posted a .350 OBP. Over 95 games for the Marlins in 2004, his OBP was .388. At the trade deadline, for DePodesta, that was sugar to a picnic ground swarm of ants.

Mostly, Tracy's first career clash with the Analytics Revolution came with this roster maneuvering that he came to resent. In fairness to DePodesta, Tracy says, the GM did not attempt to foist lineups or pitching plans on him.

"There was just one incident during the time I was managing the Dodgers when here comes a sheet of paper from upstairs with a suggestion for tonight's lineup," Tracy says. "It didn't make it to the field. Hee-seop Choi was going to be our leadoff hitter. I don't know where the lineup came from. It was on a sheet of yellow legal paper and was brought down by one of the assistants. He handed it to me. I said, 'I'll take a pass on this.'"

Tracy took the sheet, tore it into several pieces, and handed it back to the assistant.

Today, Choi is simply a notable footnote during a tumultuous and disappointing Dodgers era. He played in 133 games in 2005, batting .253 with a .336 OBP, 15 homers, and 42 RBI. The club had lost Beltré to free agency, traded key setup man Mota and catcher Lo Duca, acquired troubled outfielder Milton Bradley, and gutted its bullpen. In 2004, four future big-league managers sprinkled into the Dodgers roster: Dave Roberts, Alex Cora, David Ross, and Robin Ventura. None remained in 2005. The chemistry was gone.

It was disastrous. The Dodgers finished 71-91, still their single worst season in more than three decades. While Tracy's exit came one day after the season, DePodesta was fired four weeks later by an owner, Frank McCourt, who was overmatched and underfunded. And Choi never played a game in the majors after that 2005 season. Instead, De-Podesta's replacement, Ned Colletti, signed veteran Nomar Garciaparra to play first base in 2006, prospect James Loney was on the way, and the club waived Choi during spring training. Though he did smash a three-run homer against Team USA in the 2006 World Baseball Classic, Choi spent the summer at Boston's Triple-A affiliate Pawtucket before returning to play in the Korea Baseball Organization in 2007. He remained there until he retired after the 2013 season.

Tracy found another job right away, in Pittsburgh, but lasted just two 90-plus-loss seasons before moving on to Colorado, where he would replace Clint Hurdle, have some early success, be named as the National League's Manager of the Year in 2009…and then collide head-on, again, one final time, with the Upstairs.

Beginning in 2012, Tracy's final season in Colorado, the paradigm for major-league managers would change as it never had before.

———

Mike Matheny was live on ESPN breaking down the Gold Glove Awards with Karl Ravech in Bristol, Connecticut, on the first day of November in 2011 when he was jarred by the sudden buzzing of the cell phone in his back pocket.

"I remember thinking, 'What a great time to have it on vibrate,'" Matheny says, chuckling.

Four days earlier, the Cardinals had defeated Texas in Game 7 of a thrilling World Series. Tony La Russa was retiring, bringing the era of One-Name Managers that much closer to extinction. Champagne and ticker tape still hung in the St. Louis air, but things were moving quickly.

When ESPN went into break, Matheny looked at his phone and saw that the vibration was a text from St. Louis general manager John Mozeliak: *I need you in my office on Friday to interview for the manager's job.*

At first, Matheny says, he thought somebody had grabbed Mozeliak's phone and was playing a joke. Though he was five years into his retirement and working for the organization as a special assistant to the GM and as a roving catching instructor, Matheny had never managed a game in his life. That is, unless you count his duty that summer managing his twelve-year-old son's Little League team.

But something else had happened that autumn foreshadowing a seismic change in the way managers were both viewed and valued. Four weeks before Mozeliak's text landed, the Chicago White Sox hired their former star, Robin Ventura, to replace Ozzie Guillen. Ventura, forty-four at the time, had zero experience managing anything. The previous spring, he had been an assistant coach for his son's high school baseball team in California.

Guillen had led the White Sox to the 2005 World Series title in his second season as manager and, increasingly, butted heads with president of baseball operations Kenny Williams over the following several seasons. Guillen was brash, outspoken, and beloved by White Sox fans. But after eight seasons with diminishing returns, it was clear that a new voice was needed. Ventura had joined the White Sox front office in June 2011 as a special adviser and was working closely with director of player development Buddy Bell. He had broken in with the White Sox as a player and spent the first ten years of his career there. And as evidenced by Guillen and so many others, Sox owner Jerry Reinsdorf always has been incredibly loyal to his team's alumni.

"Robin was a leader as a player," says Williams, who was fired in August 2023, after twenty years as the Sox's top baseball executive. "I saw that personally. I saw it from afar. He was, and this is one of the things people missed at the time, part of our front office prior to being named manager. So there were countless conversations with regards to our minor-league philosophy, our major-league philosophy, our way of going about things. He and Buddy spent a lot of time with each other. And so he was getting an education and managing. Did he manage in the minor leagues? No, but that's not a prerequisite. There is no prerequisite. If there were, you wouldn't see people getting jobs at the highest level in this game without any managerial experience of people. I reject the notion that you have to go through these different paths to get these positions."

From today's vantage point, where people no longer even blink when a man who has never before managed is named as a major-league manager, it is business as usual.

But in October 2011, this was an incredulous, controversial, and almost unimaginable decision. Throughout the industry there wasn't much middle ground: People viewed the White Sox's outside-the-box thinking one of two ways, as an astronomically arrogant and foolish decision…or as a stroke of genius.

It was a monumental move. And when the Cardinals followed suit with Matheny a few weeks later, it could not have been more clear: The old way of doing things was crumbling like the Berlin Wall. The old blueprint in which managers, like players, were required to serve an apprenticeship in the minor leagues before reaching the Holy Grail of the majors soon would be a pile of bricks and rubble.

"He had a communications skill that is above the rest, above average, well above average," Williams says of Ventura. "Someone who could walk right in there. And he's got presence. I think people sometimes discount presence. It was an easy presence that I felt the club needed at that time. You see sometimes the ebb and flow of one particular style of manager and then, you know, the club goes to a different style. I felt we needed that at the time. We had to do some rebuilding. We had to make the decision to not be in the middling area."

Brian Cashman, the longtime Yankees president of baseball operations, is one of Williams's oldest and dearest friends in the game. As the dust was settling from the Ventura announcement that autumn, he called Williams to commend him for the hiring, remarking that Ventura's skills and qualifications were "obvious." A few years later, Cashman and the Yankees would follow suit when they named Aaron Boone manager in 2018.

In St. Louis, Mozeliak did not view Matheny as a companion hire to Ventura despite the similarity. He had assumed the Cardinals' GM role in 2007, replacing Walt Jocketty, and had inherited the Hall of Famer La Russa. The two developed a good and successful working relationship, culminating in the most recent World Series title. La Russa had hinted in August that he would likely retire, so Mozeliak had some time to think about what a La Russa–less future would look like, both in the dugout and from the baseball operations perspective. La Russa was so good he didn't even need a bench coach. Without him, it would be a completely different look, indeed.

"I remember sitting there that night trying to just sort of soak in what just happened," Mozeliak says of the post–Game 7 emotions. "Yeah, we're world champions. But, OK, tomorrow Tony's going to step down as manager and we're going to have to address that. And then, obviously, we're going to have to go and hire a manager. And then ten days from now the free agent market is going to open and, guess what, Albert Pujols is going to be a free agent. In the back of my mind I knew we had to move quickly on the manager."

Following the mid-August conversation with La Russa about his future, Mozeliak had compiled a list of potential managers that ran some thirty-five deep. With the help of assistants Gary LaRocque and Mike Jorgensen, he whittled down the list over the following few months, knowing that what they were thinking in September likely would change by October and certainly November because organizations are fluid, and needs and viewpoints change.

Francona, fresh off his firing from Boston, was among those who interviewed for the job. So, too, did Ryne Sandberg and Jose Oquendo.

But it was Matheny upon whom Mozeliak settled. Similar to Ventura in Chicago, the move made perfect sense. La Russa's cleats were going to be impossible to fill anyway, so why not use this moment to be creative? Especially given that this was Mozeliak's first chance as an executive to actually shape things as he wanted?

Until the day of the text, the two had had no dialogue about Matheny managing the Cardinals. Matheny had retired as a player after the 2006 season and, since 2008, had done some coaching in the organization at spring training and as a roving catching instructor in the minor leagues. He was a special assistant of Mozeliak's. La Russa had been vocal when managing Matheny that his catcher one day would make a good manager. So, too, had Matheny's manager at the University of Michigan, the former Detroit Tigers All-Star Bill Freehan. In fact, Freehan was so adamant about it that he instructed Matheny to concentrate on taking Spanish-language classes during his time at Michigan. The catcher had planned to take some easy courses to boost his grade point average. Instead, he listened to his coach.

"What a prophetic thought," Matheny says. "It's still something I use every day."

Having played for the Cardinals and now working on their staff, Matheny had acquired an insider's knowledge and understanding of the organization, its culture, its people, and its young players. And from the club's point of view, La Russa's retirement offered an open canvas.

"It was almost like a blank whiteboard," Mozeliak says of Matheny. "Now, he certainly had his beliefs and communication and leadership and some of the other nuances of being a manager that are critical to have. But in terms of game experience, that was the biggest risk we were taking. Because, when you had somebody like Tony, the game didn't move too fast for him. He knew exactly what he was thinking. He was playing chess where a lot of other people were playing checkers."

Overall, it was clear that the game's landscape was changing, and with the Ventura and Matheny hires, Mozeliak and Williams were among the early revolutionaries.

"When you look at the sort of history of post-*Moneyball*, you use the word 'evolution,'" Mozeliak says. "All of a sudden, owners started to view the importance of the decision-making model and how you build a club. So all of a sudden, as player evaluations change, the modeling change to actually understand how to value players and do contracts, the shift on roster construction, and, architecturally speaking, how teams are being built, that was changing at a very fast pace. Whereas, you go back to the pre-*Moneyball* era, it was managers had a lot of say in what roster construction looked like. Now all of a sudden that was changing because there's actually, like, mathematical ways to think about valuations. And now you jump ahead to the 2011, 2012 time period, when teams were valuing decision-makers, and then we're looking at what kind of thought partners could go into that managerial role.

"The one thing I was very, very nervous about was someone trying to be the next Tony La Russa. I remember thinking about that, that gosh, this is a really tricky situation because those are Hall of Fame shoes to fill. And I felt it was going to be a huge burden on somebody."

That was an enormous part of the reason why the Cardinals zigged instead of zagged. In Matheny, because of his pliability and newness, there would be little comparison to La Russa. Together, he and the Cardinals would walk a different path. Mozeliak felt that Matheny understood leadership, people, and the big leagues, and he was both well liked and well respected by his teammates during his days in a St. Louis uniform.

"And so, when we're interviewing different people for the job, the one thing I kept coming back to was, Mike's going to be Mike," Mozeliak says. "He was young, he was impressionable, and I think what made his transition a little easier for me was that he was not stuck in his ways or had one way of doing things. He was much more open-minded."

That was how Matheny viewed it, too. He describes La Russa as maybe being "the only person I've been around in this game who could have possibly pulled off what Whitey Herzog pulled off as both a manager and a general manager, just having that kind of capacity. I would imagine if I were Mo, I would have wanted to do more than I was doing in that seat."

Matheny understood that there surely was some sort of template in place when Mozeliak took the job: This is how the job will go *with* La Russa, but when La Russa leaves, the GM role will expand. Which was exactly what happened.

"I always had a phrase that, look, I'm not looking to be a second-rate version of Tony La Russa, I want to be the best version of me," says Matheny, who instantly became the youngest manager in the majors when he took the job at forty-one. "My job was to continue to help the organization grow. I'm going to try and be me. I want to do my piece, and a big piece of that was listening to Mo, to [owner] Bill DeWitt, to the front office.

"It was obvious to me long before I interviewed for the position there was so much data and information and so many brilliant people we hired to find a competitive edge, that if you're so closed-minded not to embrace that, you're going to be a fossil in this game. I 100 percent believed that to be true, and still do. What Billy Beane and Oakland did certainly had a pioneering aspect to it, but every organization was exploring analytics in some way. We were doing it without that label before. Dave Duncan, our pitching coach, was doing it himself on smaller sample sizes. It was just that certain teams carried the banner and wanted everyone to know what they were doing, and that still goes on."

Matheny's first game managed came in Miami's Marlins Park on Wednesday, April 4, 2012. Over two hours and forty-two minutes, he went through about as unique an experience as he has ever had. After speed-learning the ropes of in-game managing during spring training, his first for-real experience was a 4–1 Opening Day Cardinals win. His lineup was stacked; the first six hitters were Rafael Furcal, Carlos Beltran, Matt Holliday, Lance Berkman, David Freese, and Yadier Molina. Starter Kyle Lohse breezed through 7.1 innings on ninety pitches, limiting Miami to two hits and one run. Matheny called upon Jason Motte in the ninth inning for the save. St. Louis scored twice in the first inning and never trailed. It was the first of eighty-eight wins and a second-place finish in the NL Central for the defending World Series champions.

"Especially early on, and it's not a great way to go about anything in life, but I took the medical mantra of 'Do no harm,'" Matheny says of his initial foray into managing. "That was my fear more than anything, doing something to get in the way of our guys. I was already a distraction, but you look down the lineup, those guys had been around the block a time or two. Those players understood the game and themselves."

Matheny was wise enough to know that even though he had played for thirteen years, won four Gold Gloves, and played under managers ranging from La Russa to Felipe Alou to Jim Fregosi and Phil Garner, he did not know everything—or even close to it, from the manager's chair. So he made sure to communicate openly and frequently with his players. He asked Furcal about his time in Atlanta: Tell me what you learned from Bobby Cox. Tell me how he handled you. It was Del Crandall's influence at work. The two encountered each other in Milwaukee when Crandall was coaching following a distinguished playing and managing career, and his lessons stayed with Matheny.

"These guys are just waiting to tell you how they're successful," Crandall, who would pass away in May 2021 at the age of ninety-one, told Matheny. "Ask them, and then shut up and listen."

It was sage advice.

"Taking over a young team without any managerial experience, I think, would be harder," Matheny says. "Veterans present a different set of challenges. Tony told me: Be conscientious enough to learn something new every day."

On his personal game card—the matchups and key statistics he kept in the dugout, four pages of stats condensed onto one card—Matheny scribbled nightly reminders to himself, as well. Different touch points—things he wanted to see from certain players, or say to certain players.

La Russa's advice to keep your eyes open and learn something new every day goes far beyond managing. It's a great life mantra for all of us.

"The other thing Tony said is that the hardest thing you're going to have to handle is how to handle a declining superstar," Matheny says. "I had never really thought about that before."

Here, Matheny got lucky. He had one of those on his first team in Chris Carpenter, whose right arm had no more to give after a sterling fifteen-year career during which he helped pitch St. Louis to two World Series titles while winning one Cy Young Award. He was a team leader, a star, a local legend, an inspiration. But in 2012, his glory was fading and he was able to make just three starts.

"Wow, did he handle it with wisdom and grace," Matheny says. "He was very self-aware. Your typical superstar is a superstar in his mind above all else, and it's so hard to unplug the 'I just don't have it anymore.' Carp bowed out with grace when he knew it was time."

Matheny viewed his new job through a wider lens than the singular duty of managing. He figured part of his charge was to help the Cardinals organization grow. And part of that was listening to Mozeliak and DeWitt. For his part, Mozeliak started traveling with the club more with Matheny in charge simply because he knew Matheny was learning and that there would be more questions. With La Russa, the feeling was that it wasn't always necessary to have an executive with the team in person because roster moves and other minutia could easily be discussed and accomplished in a phone call. But certainly, the volume of club-produced analytic reports and conversations increased, which led to more managerial conversations.

"I can't speak for the entire industry, I can only speak for the St. Louis Cardinals," Mozeliak says. "And we still believe that a manager needs to have the autonomy he needs to be able to do his job. All we try to do from a front-office standpoint is to increase the availability of modern tools. If they want to use them, we're here to help. If they don't, then we might sort of wonder why, but the idea is we still want them to be their own person. And even today, I still do that with Oli [Marmol, who followed Matheny and Mike Shildt in the Cards' lineage].

"We didn't really have to do a lot of things for Tony, because Tony was Tony. He had his confidence and he understood the decisions he was going to make. Whereas when we hired Mike, this was like that clean slate, and we could start building tools to help him with his in-game strategy, with how he wanted to think about advanced scouting or how to use those types of tools in his decision-making. And so that part was kind of exciting. It was fun. I think both sides learned a lot."

Soon, Matheny and Ventura would no longer be outliers. When Miami hired former catcher and recently retired (2010) Mike Redmond as skipper in 2013, he had no managerial experience. Neither did Brad Ausmus, who also retired in 2010, when Detroit hired him to replace Jim Leyland in 2014. Also in short order from the no-managerial-experience outlet, Washington hired Matt Williams (2014); Tampa Bay, Kevin Cash (2015); Minnesota, Paul Molitor (2015); Milwaukee, Craig Counsell (2016); the Dodgers, Dave Roberts (2016); Seattle, Scott Servais (2016); and the Yankees, Aaron Boone (2018).

"I thought it was creative," says Beane of his reaction as he watched the progress of the revolution that he and Alderson had started. "At that point, it was also recognized that the skills of a manager were more than just strategic, right? The people skills and leadership, the ability to be able to work with the press. At no point when a manager with no experience got hired was I actually thinking, 'Oh, that's crazy.' Because I sort of started to view the skill sets of a manager as being a lot more diverse than just being a guy who simply managed one thousand games in the minors.

"I think the job of the manager is much more dynamic than just being a guy who has basically punched a ten-year minor-league clock and now is suddenly evolved."

Now, two things became critical to the job of managers in the new century that their predecessors never faced: They were becoming the point men for implementing certain strategies concocted by the front office—limiting the workloads of starting pitchers, defensive shifts, platooning players, and more. And they were the ones who had to sell these new thoughts to the players.

Of artificial turf shortly after its invention and installation into Houston's Astrodome in 1966, the old rascal slugger Dick Allen quipped, "If a horse can't eat it, I don't want to play on it." Where their mental games and life outlook were concerned, this new world went far beyond artificial turf as the players navigated their careers, suspicious of anything new.

By 2015, MLB's Statcast was introduced, pouring more data and numbers into the game. Statcast is very specific and extremely accurate in measuring and analyzing player movements and athletic ability and is accessed by all thirty clubs. Exit velocity, launch angle, spin rate, sprint speed…all of this emanates from Statcast. It has changed coaching, making it more highly specific than ever. And it has allowed the Upstairs to gain a stronger upper hand than ever over the Downstairs.

"When Statcast started to happen, all the teams were getting all this data and they were hiring a bunch of smart people, and the managers and coaches all had access to this data," Beane says. "So over the next ten-year period, they were really involving themselves in the analytics and the game plans and things like that. Coaching staffs are very much involved in the creation of all this stuff now, especially game planning. That's why there's much more collaboration now."

Ventura finished third in the 2012 Manager of the Year voting, guiding the Sox to a surprising 85-77 record, just three games behind Leyland's powerful Tigers (88-74). But Chicago fell to under .500 over the following four seasons and, at the end of 2016, Ventura decided that he had enough. He was going through a trying time in his personal life (a tough divorce, among other things), and in January 2020 he went back to school—literally. He joined the staff at Oklahoma State as a student assistant, working under manager Josh Holliday, Matt's brother. And, more than three decades after his All-American career with the Cowboys—among other things, he compiled an NCAA record fifty-eight-game hitting streak—he officially graduated from the school in 2022 with a bachelor's degree in university studies.

Matheny managed for a decade, seven seasons in St. Louis before taking over the Kansas City Royals in 2020. Over his first four summers in St. Louis, the man who had prepped for the job by coaching his son's Little League team the summer before his big life change guided the Cardinals to one World Series (a loss to Boston in 2013), two NLCS, and one NL Division Series.

"Once that made it out there in public, then every twelve-year-old coach in the country thought they were equipped to manage an MLB team," Matheny jokes. "Especially after we took the Cardinals to the playoffs in our first four years."

———

The film *Moneyball*, released in September 2011, was in many ways a coda to the first stage of the Revolution before the Upstairs advanced even further into the Downstairs' turf, trampling acres and acres of heritage and tradition. The film also marked the end of the latest generation of a string of Hollywood baseball blockbusters in the 1980s and early 1990s: *The Natural* (1984), *Eight Men Out* (1988), *Bull Durham* (1988), *Field of Dreams* (1989), *A League of Their Own* (1992), and *The Sandlot* (1993). Baseball was good for the box office. Baseball was relatable to life. Depending upon one's taste, the movies ranged from good to great. They captured baseball's essence in so many ways: humor, soul, fantasy, childhood, love, romance, scandal.

Since *Moneyball*, nothing. Hollywood has chewed the last of the meat off that bone, packed up its cameras, and moved on. Movies need heroes. And as the game has changed, it is difficult to make heroes out of hard drives, spreadsheets, or the impersonal computer operators in windowless offices.

As the fight for baseball's soul raged at the management level, things were not going as well for the old, salty veteran Jim Tracy in Colorado during the summer of 2012 as they were for Matheny and Ventura in their debut seasons in St. Louis and Chicago. Just three seasons after Tracy earned the NL's Manager of the Year award, early in the summer of 2012, a front-office operative named Bill Geivett moved into the Rockies' clubhouse to offer direct input to the coaches and players and, essentially, observe. In a game that tilts paranoid in the most innocent of times, with managers, coaches, and players watching their backs while knowing the lines of those wanting their jobs are long, the red alarm lights figuratively began flashing: Essentially, Geivett also was serving as a direct pipeline to the front office. A clubhouse spy. In a competitive, emotional game that must allow players and staff areas to vent, exhale, and decompress, Tracy and his staff now had almost no privacy. Eventually, this practice of front-office types invading the clubhouse would become more common, if still unwanted. In *The Book of Joe: Trying Not to Suck at Baseball and Life*, Joe Maddon bitterly described how Los Angeles Angels general manager Perry Minasian and a top analyst, Alex Tamin, took lockers just off the coaches' locker room during his years there from 2020 to 2022, violating the field staff's inner sanctum. Geivett, who parted ways with the Rockies along with general manager Dan O'Dowd after the 2014 season and has not worked in baseball since, was the trailblazer.

That was off the field, but the timing coincided with an on-the-field directive that Tracy found every bit as difficult to stomach. Beginning that June, the front office unilaterally implemented a dramatic change that sprung from meetings to which Tracy says he initially was not even invited: As they continued attempting to unlock the secrets to successful pitching at mile-high altitude in Denver, the Rockies would move to a four-man rotation, the key being each starter would be on a seventy-five-pitch limit nightly.

"I was 100 percent against that," Tracy says, sitting comfortably in Colorado Rockies workout shorts during our visit in his Ohio basement all of these years later. "I was uncomfortable in my own skin with it. I wanted no part of it."

At the time, the rebuilding Rockies were stocking their five-man rotation with four rookies who were either twenty-three or twenty-four years old: Drew Pomeranz, Alex White, Christian Friedrich, and Jhoulys Chacín. Over his career in the dugout, Tracy had excelled with his knowledge of pitching. It had become one of his strengths. Yet now, in-season, he was stripped of much of that power. This was a radical enough move that would have made far more sense to implement in spring training. But now, nearly three months into the season?

By limiting starters to seventy-five pitches, the team would have to pay the tab elsewhere. And it was the Rockies' bullpen that would be forced to pick it up nightly.

"How many arms are we going to send to the surgery table, from a bullpen standpoint?" Tracy says. "Because at that time, the roster was still twenty-five men. And you still have an eleven- or twelve-man pitching staff. So how many innings are they going to have to cover? And seventy-five pitches, I mean, guys start fouling balls off and it's the third inning of the game and you're into your bullpen. How many days in a row do you think we can do that? You're going to hurt people. It's not going to work. I prided myself in what I did with pitching staffs."

Now the man who battled DePodesta on roster moves and team chemistry in 2005 as the Analytics Revolution began was on the front lines again, seven years later. Only this time, the Revolution was in Phase II, it was gaining momentum, and it was encroaching far beyond simple personnel discussions.

To Tracy, it was a chain-of-command issue. And the chain of command was being reorganized right in front of him, minimizing his own job—as it would with managers throughout the industry. This was only the beginning.

It was a far cry from the way things started with the Rockies, when he was hired as bench coach and then asked to take over for Clint Hurdle at the end of May 2009. The Rockies were 18-28 at the time, last in the NL West, and Tracy redirected them to a 92-70 record and an NL wild card spot. In 2010, things were going so well between Tracy and O'Dowd that the manager thought he had found nirvana. Over time, he had watched the game's best GM-manager combos—John Schuerholz and Bobby Cox in Atlanta, Walt Jocketty and Tony La Russa in St. Louis, Kevin Towers and Bruce Bochy in San Diego—with envy. Finally, he told his wife, Deb: This is what I've always envisioned.

"Oh my God, what a fabulous relationship we had," he says. "It was absolutely tremendous. But then as we got into year three, and into that fourth year, now it felt like everybody wanted to have their hands in the soup and tell me how to do my job."

The major change was a tragedy that shook the entire Colorado organization, a tragedy that in some respects the franchise never fully recovered from. The team was in Washington on April 20, 2010, when beloved club president Keli McGregor suddenly dropped dead of a rare virus that affected his heart muscle. He was only forty-seven. Tracy vividly remembers receiving the news in his hotel room in DC and collapsing to his knees in despair while taking the phone call.

"That's the biggest personnel loss I ever went through right there," Tracy says. At the time, he and O'Dowd were copacetic. He loved owner Dick Monfort ("To this day, I still like him").

"Things began to change dramatically," Tracy says. "And McGregor was unbelievable at keeping everybody in their own backyard. 'You have a job to do with a job title, stay in your own backyard and do your job. And when the season ends and there's opportunities available within the organization and your qualifications suggest you are capable of handling that position and want to talk about it, we'll discuss it then.' He was unbelievable at that. And when we lost him, the wheels started coming off. The lug nuts started to loosen and people are venturing into different places. People are starting to tell other people how to do their jobs and next thing you know, all hell is breaking loose."

The game that is etched in Tracy's memory came in Detroit's Comerica Park on June 15, 2012. The team was struggling, 24-38 at the time. There had been a meeting in O'Dowd's office in which orders were given to implement the new pitching strategy, during which Tracy learned there had been another meeting to which he had not been invited. And now, the Upstairs told Tracy to announce the change to the team in a clubhouse meeting because "they respect you, they trust you," Tracy says. "And I can't do it."

It is the fine, nuanced line that has become the norm today: The manager is asked to carry out the wishes of the front office and sell the plan to the players. And it is why clubs that lean hard into analytics hire inexperienced managers who simply are grateful to have the job and are willing to be the messengers for the Upstairs.

The veteran Jeff Francis, thirty-one, was the starter on this warm, eighty-three-degree Friday evening in Detroit. "And it was as uncomfortable a situation as I felt like I was involved in in eleven years of managing in the big leagues," Tracy says. "Because I had to walk out there and take that son of a bitch out of the game after seventy-five pitches, 4.2 innings, with the lead and a chance to get the decision and win the ball game."

Except, that was not what Tracy did. He simply couldn't bring himself to do it. With a 4–3 lead, he allowed Francis to finish the fifth inning—thus positioning the starter for the win—with eighty pitches. Then, as Tracy continued to squirm in the dugout, he sent Francis out to start the sixth. Leading off the inning, Detroit's Danny Worth promptly made things more uncomfortable for Tracy with an epic ten-pitch at bat before striking out. Now, Francis's pitch count was really running up.

Bryan Holaday followed with a base hit, bringing Tracy out to lift Francis in favor of reliever Adam Ottavino. Francis was done for the night at 5.1 innings and ninety-four pitches.

"When I put my hand out to signal to the bullpen, it was some kind of an embarrassing situation for me," Tracy says. "Because as much as I have prided myself in being strategically inclined, I had a reputation I think of being that good, there was just utter dismay. Like, what's he doing? It was so far off the grid from what I had been about for ten-plus years."

The bullpen did not hold the lead. Two batters later, Holaday came around to tie the game at 4–4. Francis would come away with a no-decision. The game went ten innings. Colorado exploded for eight runs in the top of the tenth to win the bizarre and memorable game 12–4.

Today, that evening in Detroit does not stand out to Francis as much as it does to his old manager. The lefty was in his second tour with Colorado in 2012 after pitching for Kansas City in 2011, and it was only his second start of the season.

"I did have conversations with Dan O'Dowd when he was thinking about doing it," Francis says of the seventy-five-pitch-limit implementation. "He explained to me the way we evaluate starting pitching can change, we were starting to use the Coors Field thing to our advantage and maybe keep people from pitching too much at home, maybe pitch more on the road. At the time, wins were still a big stat for pitchers, moreso than they are now."

Francis remembers O'Dowd explaining to him that personal wins wouldn't be as highly regarded, especially with the likelihood that Colorado's starting pitchers would not make it through five innings with the seventy-five-pitch limit.

"It was nine years removed from *Moneyball*, which completely changed the game and how we evaluate players and maybe now we were attempting to find something new," Francis says. "Did it work? No. But I can appreciate the attempt. It looked very different, which is why Jim said he was embarrassed to take pitchers out in the fourth inning of a one-run game."

Drew Pomeranz, then twenty-three, opened the 2012 season in the rotation for the first time. He was optioned back to Triple-A Colorado Springs for most of June and, upon his return to the bigs in July, the Rockies had embarked on their new four-man, seventy-five-pitch-limit rotation.

"When I look back on it, it's like, 'What the hell was that?'" Pomeranz says. "The system, assistant GM Bill Geivett moved his office into an adjoining conference room behind Tracy's office. Sometimes he would come in and talk with us after the game. It was a really weird dynamic. I was kind of young so I didn't know how it was all supposed to go. But normally the manager talks to us, so they had some funny stuff switching around over there. The four-man rotation was very strange. I was a younger guy and a lot of times I wouldn't even pitch on three days' rest, they would push me to the fifth day but still keep me on the pitch count. I particularly remember one outing against the Dodgers, I went four innings, had seven strikeouts, and gave up three hits and no runs and it was like, you're done, go ride the bike. It was a strange time to be around."

To Pomeranz, keeping the starters on a short leash and overworking the bullpen meant "you're kind of devaluing both sides. We always heard, 'Oh, it's a way to keep guys healthier.' But when I got to arbitration, I had all of these starts and yet I didn't have a lot of innings. It was weird."

Says Tracy: "I sat down with Dick Monfort in Detroit. I told Dick, I don't know if I can do this. I'm not comfortable with this. I said that I can't even perceive where those guys are mentally in relation to this. The only reason why I didn't walk away sooner was because of the respect I had for my players, and not only in Colorado but in Pittsburgh and Los

Angeles. The way they laid it out there for me over all those years and respected me. That's the only reason I made it to the finish line."

The Rockies cratered to 64-98, last in the NL West, and Tracy was done. He declined to trade his integrity for the $1.4 million dangling in front of him in 2013, the last year of his deal. Instead, he pushed the pile of money to the middle of the table, stood up, and walked away.

He was only fifty-six. He knew his stand would not sit well with certain organizations. He knew it might signal the end of the line. It was a chance he was willing to take. In the back of his mind, he could still hear his father's lifelong advice: Throw your shoulders back and stand up proud while accepting responsibility for this, that, whatever. Stand up for what you believe in. Otherwise, give it to the next guy and get the hell out.

So he got out and never looked back. A decade later, Tracy and his wife "chase the weather up and down Interstate 75." They have a place in Florida, and when the winter chill frosts Ohio a little too much, they jump in the car and head south. When golfing weather returns to the Midwest, it's back to Ohio. He had a few chances to go back to baseball over the years. When Dave Stewart and La Russa were running Arizona, they talked to him about becoming manager Chip Hale's bench coach. Texas did the same with him about becoming Ron Washington's bench coach. But that was how he had come to manage the Rockies, moving from bench coach to manager when Hurdle was fired, and he was wary of that happening again. He did not want to earn a reputation.

"When the curtain comes down, move on," he says. "Disappear. Nobody wants to hear what you have to say. Nobody cares what you have to say. And the last thing you want to do, especially as well as this game has treated you, is have people perceiving or interpreting that you're just sour grapes."

He and Debra have three sons, many of the family threads still held together as if by the red stitches of a baseball. All three boys played.

Middle son Chad has managed Boston's Triple-A affiliate in Worcester, Massachusetts, since 2022, and was voted as Best Managerial Prospect in a 2023 *Baseball America* survey of his peers. Jim Tracy still watches, though sometimes he remains perplexed and asks Chad to explain some of the modern thinking to him. He still considers the Dodgers, Pirates, and Rockies as "his" teams. He pays attention and roots for good things to happen to each of them.

He has no regrets about leaving when he did, not even over the extra million bucks that could be in his bank account today.

"But at what cost?" Tracy asks, voice rising. "I mean, what are you, a pawn in a chess game? Yeah, I'm not. I never have been. I wouldn't have been a very successful manager of the Los Angeles Dodgers if I would have been a pawn in the chess game."

A day after our Midwestern visit, Showalter would win his fourth Manager of the Year award for guiding the Mets to their first one-hundred-win season since 1988. The shine of that award lasted not much longer than Max Scherzer and Justin Verlander did in his rotation the following year as the Mets collapsed and Showalter was let go in favor of Carlos Mendoza, whose only managerial experience was two brief seasons in Class A. But Mendoza is pliable and entered the job willing to implement whatever president of baseball operations David Stearns wanted.

"The baseball world certainly has devalued that position," Matheny says of the manager, before noting how refreshing it was to watch Dusty Baker and Bruce Bochy go head-to-head in the 2023 ALCS. "Some people point at me and say you're one of the reasons why it changed. They think they can drag anybody in off the street now. I can't necessarily argue too much with that except the fact that I did spend a lot of years in a position that is probably as close to managing as any position could be. It doesn't say everything. It's not that you must play in MLB to have any kind of value. But I do believe there are some things that happen either from managing through the minor leagues or something you learn in uniform as a player. If you're using those opportunities to grow and learn and help develop strategies, then those are repetitions. But I get where people were going, and it certainly was looking that way, that we can put anybody in those positions, just put a warm body in those positions. But the game comes back around, to tell you the truth, and I think it's coming back around right now."

Even when he hired Ventura, Kenny Williams and the White Sox did not meddle as much as other clubs partly because of Williams's own experiences as an outfielder from 1986 to 1991.

"As a player in that locker room, if you know that the person sitting in the manager's chair has zero-to-limited influence in how the game is managed, how your career is being treated, that that person has all of the responsibility without the authority and then has to take the accountability, that's an unfair situation to put that person in," says Williams, the White Sox's third-round draft pick in 1982 out of Stanford. "And yet people are still taking these jobs knowing that because there are only thirty of them, you know? And so they try to navigate those waters, and none of them like it.

"And that segues into what potentially may be one of the biggest scams in sports, and that's the overreliance and overinfluence of analytics and the pushing aside of the human element of the game. There are so many more variables at play. You can put me in any room of analytic people and throw out various scenarios that keep them feeding you absolutes, and I can give you a variable or two or three or four that will make those projections nonrelevant."

Predictably, the Upstairs won the power grab. Managers' desks now come equipped with suggestion boxes. And the managers are expected to use them. Projections carry more currency than the human heartbeat. While Beane years ago found himself competing with nearby Silicon Valley for some of the best and brightest minds on the market, now the game is stacked with baseball operations men who have risen to authority not from the playing fields as they did a generation or more ago, but who have matriculated from Ivy League universities and other tony, private, East Coast colleges. Men such as the Mets' Stearns (Harvard), Baltimore's Mike Elias (Yale), Boston's Craig Breslow (Yale), Cleveland's Chris Antonetti (Georgetown University) and Mike Chernoff (Princeton), Detroit's Scott Harris (Columbia Business School), Oakland's David Forst (Harvard), Texas's Chris Young (Princeton), Toronto's Mark Shapiro (Princeton), Arizona's Mike Hazen (Princeton), San Diego's A. J. Preller (Cornell), San Francisco's Farhan Zaidi (Massachusetts Institute of Technology with a PhD in economics from Cal Berkeley), Pittsburgh's Ben Cherington (Amherst), and Miami's Peter Bendix (Tufts).

Williams makes a passionate case for the expertise of coaches, and for the ability of scouts to pick up on things through conversations with coaches and players that a computer cannot.

"It amplifies, I think, the importance of human interaction, communication, and the beauty in which our sports, and not just baseball, can and should be," he says. "You have people in the NBA now saying a player can only play for eight minutes. And then his production goes down and it's, like, wait a minute, so that means you'd never take him beyond eight minutes, he can't then condition well enough to play ten or twelve or twenty minutes? Come on. *Come on.*"

Six months after our visit in Arizona at White Sox spring training headquarters, in the midst of a historic, 121-loss season, owner Jerry Reinsdorf fired Williams to end an impressive two-decades-plus tenure of running baseball operations. Williams was the architect of the Sox's 2005 World Series title, their only championship in 106 years. As we speak in a quiet lobby on that early March day, before he was tossed overboard and made a free agent, Williams's eyes twinkle and he smiles as he winds to his conclusion regarding his thoughts on analytics.

"I think it's one of the biggest scams that are out there, but I respect it," he says. "And here's why I respect it: Because people who otherwise couldn't get in the game, the Ivy League analytic mindset, found a way.

"They not only found a way, they took this shit over."

CHAPTER 8

TANGLED UP
IN DODGER BLUE

Today's early still-of-the-morning beauty stands in stark contrast to the joyful and raucous din of the past week. Seven days after piloting the Dodgers to their eighth franchise World Series title, Dave Roberts graciously joins me at a beachside coffee shop in suburban San Diego, one more appointment in his vastly overstuffed calendar. Five days after he dances with the rapper Ice Cube during the championship celebration in Dodger Stadium, the high continues.

Reviews are in, and they are glowing. The postseason? He was brilliant. Bullpen usage? Masterful. Dance moves with Ice Cube?

Roberts sips his coffee and laughs. Well...

"Mixed reviews," he says. "From my son and daughter, I got, maybe, like a two or a three out of ten. But I will say there's some people who gave me, like, seven or eight. So I don't know."

This is a joyful man who long ago learned to tune out the critics. The knuckle-draggers on social media crushed him. A know-nothing, bottom-feeding president of the United States trashed his pitching moves in the middle of a freaking World Series game. Even his team's own fans in Los Angeles too often have been a little too quick to turn on him. Roberts has been skewered, grilled, dissected, roasted, toasted, second-guessed, third-fourth-fifth-and-sixth-guessed, analyzed, flayed, seventh-and-eighth-guessed, and everything in between.

Yet all he does is win—and keep returning for more. Entering 2025, the Dodgers were 851-506 under Roberts, a .627 winning percentage. That is the best winning percentage of any manager, ever, with one thousand or more games worked. *Ever.* You can argue that Roberts is the beneficiary of one of the game's most extravagant payrolls and foremost analytics operations. True. But unlike the Yankees, Red Sox, Cubs, Giants, Padres, and many more big spenders who have sat home in recent Octobers, the Dodgers under Roberts have advanced to postseason play in every one of his nine seasons.

David Ray "Doc" Roberts is the quintessential modern manager. He is pulled in so many directions every single day—by players, coaches, baseball operations officials, the Dodgers marketing department, public relations, ticket sales, community relations—that he seemingly is made partly of taffy. He stretches. He accommodates. He keeps smiling, and he keeps winning. He is one of the best in the business, and he is on a Hall of Fame trajectory.

Since his hiring by president of baseball operations Andrew Friedman before the 2016 season, Roberts in some quarters has been viewed as little more than a puppet of a cutting-edge, overbearing analytics machine that leaves little to chance and even less to manage. That's life today for modern managers as the Upstairs has seized more and more turf: They get all of the criticism and half (or less) of the credit. Say what you will, Roberts was never better than in 2023 when he held things together—and kept winning—despite a depleted rotation (Walker Buehler, Clayton Kershaw, Dustin May, and Tony Gonsolin were injured, Julio Urias was arrested late in the season on a felony domestic violence charge, and big-time free agent Trevor Bauer was pitching in Japan after sexual assault allegations by various women humiliated the Dodgers and their principles), no real shortstop, and other assorted injuries and holes.

Unless you go with 2024, when the Dodgers' rotation crumbled like a stale cookie with more injuries (Buehler, Kershaw, snazzy offseason acquisition Tyler Glasnow, snazzier offseason acquisition Yoshinobu Yamamoto, Gonsolin and May again, Gavin Stone, River Ryan), the bullpen was hit with injuries late in the season (Brusdar Graterol, Alex Vesia), superstar Mookie Betts missed two months with a fractured left hand, superstar Freddie Freeman suffered a high ankle sprain early in the postseason, shortstop Miguel Rojas was lost for most of the postseason with a groin injury, and second baseman Gavin Lux battled a hip flexor injury starting in the NLCS. Through all of this, Roberts kept the team together, spirits up, bad vibes down, and managed them straight into their fourth World Series in his nine years.

"There's never been a decision where the front office has told me, 'You need to play so-and-so here, you need to hit so-and-so here, you need to pitch so-and-so,'" says Roberts, directly addressing—at least, in regard to what happens in Dodger Stadium—the perpetual question that dogs nearly every modern manager. The question of who *really* is making the decisions is a constant annoyance for today's skippers, like the common cold and telemarketers.

From day one, Roberts has freely admitted that his is a collaborative effort with Los Angeles's baseball operations department. "Do I get information? The president of the United States gets a bunch of information and, ultimately, he's got to make a decision," he says. "On a smaller scale, that's what I get."

Over four days in September, he offered an unprecedented peek inside the day-to-day life of a modern manager. The Dodgers were zeroing in on another October, the brass was out in full force during batting practice, and the Dodgers brand was pumping on all cylinders. The year was 2022, but with the long-running Friedman-Roberts partnership, it could have been any September. The years and the players change, but the system and the methods remain the same.

Tuesday, Dodger Stadium, Los Angeles

Tonight's lineup is locked and loaded, the pitching plans for the week mostly are arranged, and as batting practice plays out, Roberts is all over the field. It is Tuesday afternoon, the day after a series-opening 7–4 loss to San Francisco, but things are in good shape anyway. The Dodgers are 92-42 and running away with another NL West title. They lead the NL West by 19 games and are just days away from wrapping up their tenth division title in eleven years.

After last night's game, as he often does, Roberts stayed late in his office and uncorked a bottle of wine. Along with former San Francisco teammate Rich Aurilia and his wife, Amy, and another couple, Roberts and his wife, Tricia, own the boutique wine label Red Stitch. Wine has been his passion for years. After the noise of the day and the roar of the evenings, these quiet moments afford Roberts, his coaches, and even front-office figures an informal chance to unwind and discuss whatever is on their minds, from baseball to world events. With the wine pouring and the office door open, bullpen coach Josh Bard—one of Roberts's confidants; their friendship dates back to when the two were teammates in San Diego in 2006—is a regular. Sometimes Friedman stops in and shares a glass, though not as often because, as the years pass, he naturally is empowering his staff more and more. Often, assistant GM Brandon Gomes joins for a debriefing of that night's game. Pitching coach Mark Prior sometimes pops in for a chat, though he does not classify himself as a wine guy.

"So then it gets to talking about our team, our players, over a glass of wine, which is great," Roberts says.

Earlier today, he took delivery of a new black Mercedes S500 right here in the Dodger Stadium parking lot. The not-so-publicized part of the baseball life is that, during the season, those in uniform—manager, coaches, players—typically spend eleven or twelve hours daily at the ballpark. There is barely time to brush their teeth at home, let alone knock off the mundane life errands for which we civilians must find the time. Roberts also typically gets his hair cut at the ballpark, keeps in touch with friends and colleagues via texts and emails, and, after games, catches up with his wife from his stadium office.

Typically, he arrives at the ballpark around one for a seven o'clock game. There are two chefs on duty each day in the clubhouse, so the players show up early, the food flows, and the day begins.

"When I played, guys didn't show up until two or three," Roberts says. "They would go grab lunch and then they would show up. But now we take care of their food, and it's really good food."

One of Roberts's guiding lights is that he believes it is vital to "touch" each of his players every single day. That means anything from a quick "Hey, what's up, how are you doing today?" to an informal chat on the field during batting practice to, if needed, a longer conversation with a struggling player in his office. It could be about that day's game. If it's near the trade deadline, it could be acquiring some intel about a rival player the Dodgers are targeting. By design, these touches are personally tailored. Families and kids are big and important subjects. Before he left via free agency for the Philadelphia Phillies, it wasn't unusual for shortstop Trea Turner to talk wine and tequila with Roberts. With Buehler, a Kentucky native, the chat veers toward bourbon or whiskey. In September, maybe it's something to do with Baylor football with Max Muncy, who played baseball collegiately for the Bears and remains a devoted alum. Before batting practice, Roberts bounces through the trainers' room, the kitchen, the clubhouse, wherever the path takes him as he looks for these touches. It is the complete opposite of his generational predecessors Sparky Anderson and Earl Weaver, who intentionally kept a distance from their players. Roberts wants relationships, strong ones, honest ones. It is his secret sauce, and it pays dividends when it comes time to remove a starting pitcher long before that pitcher thinks he should go, or when he must shuffle the bullpen deck and ruffle feathers.

"A lot of what I do is built on relationships," Roberts says. "Because I think this world is so analytics driven now, and data driven, and that's everywhere. I'm very mindful of not losing sight of the human element, the communication part of it. The trust, the loyalty. And so how do you do that? I believe that these are consistent conversations."

Few in the game are more skilled at this than Roberts. A naturally intelligent, inquisitive, empathetic man, he was the quarterback on his championship high school football team in San Diego and played baseball at UCLA before signing with the Detroit Tigers when they picked him in the twenty-eighth round of the 1994 amateur draft. He carved out a ten-year career as an outfielder with Cleveland, the Dodgers, Boston, San Diego, and San Francisco from 1999 to 2008, most famously stealing second base for Boston against Yankees Hall of Famer Mariano Rivera in the ninth inning of Game 4 of the 2004 ALCS to ignite a rally for the ages. The Red Sox came back that night, won four games in a row, and then won their first World Series since 1918. Upon retirement, Roberts, whose father was Black and whose mother is Asian American, spent one year as a Red Sox television analyst before going back home to become a special assistant to the Padres' baseball operations department. He hasn't left the West Coast since. Today, Roberts still gets regular mail from Red Sox fans, asking him to autograph this baseball card or that photo—so many of them of his famed theft.

He is media savvy, which feeds into his emphasis on the importance of honest and free-flowing communication with his players. He conducts his daily, pregame media briefing around 4 p.m. each afternoon. Like all managers, he periodically delivers a well-targeted message to his players through the media. But these occasions are rare. Mostly, the players hear what they need to hear from him directly, and the last thing he wants to do is either surprise a player or have the player see something taken out of context by the media. This dance—understanding the reporters' jobs and need for information while taking care of his players throughout—always is delicate.

"If we don't have that trust, there can be a lot of things I say that might be misconstrued or taken personally by the player," Roberts says. "And so the more we talk, the more I get the benefit of the doubt. And so nowadays with players, social media is everywhere. So for me, that's a big part of managing my day, making sure that me and the coaches and me and the players, we're on the same page."

There are times each week when Roberts is like the rest of us and a particular day will carry its own momentum, minor crises and interruptions will erode his time, and he doesn't make contact with everyone. He gets caught in his office for longer than he would like. He doesn't make it outside for batting practice, or he does but he's late and doesn't make the rounds he feels are important. Those are the days that make him uncomfortable.

"I don't feel great going into those games because I haven't connected to touch the players that day," Roberts says. "The days when I'm out there on the field, having conversations with the players, I feel so much better going into that night's ball game."

Today, the rounds are made, the touches are happening, and it is a good day. He talks with utility infielder Hanser Alberto, a productive, jovial veteran who was great for clubhouse chemistry when he was in Los Angeles, about spinning the ball when he hits it, much like a pitcher throwing it. The more backspin the bat can produce, the farther the ball goes. They discuss other hitting techniques, as well. Stan Kasten, the Dodgers' ubiquitous president and part owner, engages Roberts for several minutes on the grass just behind the plate as the team hits. Janet Marie Smith, the architectural wizard who was integral in planning Baltimore's Camden Yards and the refurbishing of Boston's Fenway Park (Green Monster seats!), and who now works for the Dodgers as they work to extend the life of the third-oldest stadium in the majors (Dodger Stadium opened in 1962), joins them for a bit. Moments later, Roberts is behind the batting cage comparing notes with Emilee Fragapane, a director in the club's analytics department. Gomes, the assistant GM, offers the manager a fist bump as he walks by.

With batting practice winding down, Roberts, as he does almost every day, walks over to visit with fans and special guests who are watching from behind velvet ropes in a makeshift holding pen on the warning track area behind home plate. As marketing departments have been turned loose across the game and the fan experience is emphasized (and every single possible revenue stream squeezed like the last bit of juice from an orange), almost every team now brings a group of fans onto the field for a personal, up-close view of batting practice. One brick at a time, the walls between the players—and manager—and the fans is lowered. Dick Williams would not have played so nice at this interruption.

Roberts? He interacts with the grace of a symphony orchestra conductor in full performance. He poses for selfies, signs jerseys, autographs baseballs, and joins in a group picture. Hopefully, he's got a tube of ChapStick tucked into his uniform pants, he smiles so big and so often. An excited fan is speaking on FaceTime to someone who couldn't make it to Dodger Stadium and asks Roberts if he will say hello. Of course he will.

"Hey, Lucas! Where you at, buddy?" Roberts says, voice projecting as if he's channeling Tommy Lasorda. "You're supposed to be here at Dodger Stadium!"

As Dodgers manager, Roberts is two parts baseball man and one part emcee. It's all just part of the job in today's world. When legendary broadcaster Vin Scully retired in 2016, Roberts was the one with the microphone leading the emotional postgame ceremony from the infield. He was the featured speaker at the unveiling of the Sandy Koufax and Jackie Robinson statues at Dodger Stadium in 2022. When the social justice movement hit overdrive in the United States during the COVID-19 pandemic after the murder of George Floyd in Minneapolis in 2020, followed by the murder of Jacob Blake, a Black man, in Kenosha, Wisconsin, Mookie Betts and other Dodgers opted to not play a game in protest. It was Roberts who addressed the issue on Zoom. ("It's not a political issue. I understand the election is coming up, but this is a human being issue," Roberts said. "We all need to be treated the same way, and a Black man being shot seven times in the back, it's just, we need to be better. That just can't happen.")

"It's all-consuming," Roberts says, before noting why it's easy to keep the smile on his face no matter how many requests flow his way: "I feel I have a job as a custodian for baseball because I want to do everything I can to promote this game. I had the good fortune of having Tommy Lasorda as a friend of mine. You could argue that Tommy was one of the biggest advocates, if not the biggest, for baseball in the entire world. And so, I saw the perfect blueprint."

Add to that the fact that Roberts played for the Dodgers, went to school in Los Angeles, and became great friends with Dodgers legends Maury Wills, Duke Snider, Don Newcombe, Manny Mota, and so many more over the years, as well as the club's Hall of Fame broadcasters Scully and Jaime Jarrín, and he feels all of this personally.

"I want this legacy to continue to live," he says. "There's not a day that goes by that I'm not asked to help cement the Dodgers legacy in some way. And I feel such a great responsibility, and I love it. So where someone else could look at this responsibility as too overwhelming, it's something I embrace. Because, again, I point back to Tommy. His whole life was around the Dodgers. He coined the terms 'Blue Heaven Here on Earth' and 'Bleed Dodger Blue.' I want our players to know, to understand, number one, how fortunate are we to play this game of baseball, all of us to be a part of this. And number two, what it means to be a Dodger. When you walk down the halls here at Dodger Stadium and you see all of these Dodgers greats, I want people to say when they see us play, 'This is how the Dodgers play baseball.' And I talk about that all the time."

The last of the fans greeted, Roberts heads inside for one of the key analytics gatherings of the day: About an hour before gametime, daily, the Dodgers conduct a "run prevention" meeting in Roberts's office. The group breaks down the opposing lineup coupled with the Dodgers' starter for that evening, what kind of game they envision from him, and the state of the bullpen—who's available, who's not, who's rested, who's not. Often, the team knows it will be making a roster move within a day or two or three—in today's game, relievers are on the move more than Amazon drivers—so that plays into strategy decisions, too. The group usually includes Roberts, Prior, Bard, the game planning and communications coach (Danny Lehmann for years before he was moved to bench coach in 2023), and, often, three or four assistant GMs and baseball operations staffers—Gomes, Jeff Kingston, or others. This included Farhan Zaidi, early in Roberts's tenure before Zaidi was hired as the Giants' president of baseball operations in 2019. When the team is on the road, the front-office rep normally is whoever is traveling on that particular trip.

"We meet, everybody gives options and thoughts on how we're going to prevent runs for that night," Roberts says. "I ask questions, they give me their thoughts regarding the best lanes for guys. So then I have an idea of how we can best use our guys. That's something that's really helped me in using our bullpen and being able to prevent runs."

Prior often starts the meeting with his thoughts on that night's starter—the pitcher's recent workload, where he's at physically and mentally, how he's feeling. A quick recap to make sure everyone is on the same page of understanding, OK, we're good, let's push this guy tonight, hard, through ninety or a hundred pitches. Or it may be that the starter was really stressed in his previous outing and the bullpen is fresh, the team has a day off tomorrow, so perhaps tonight is the night to cut twenty pitches off the workload and give the starter a break.

After that, the group runs through the relievers—aside from simple availability, who do they really want to pitch tonight? Maybe someone hasn't pitched in three days, so let's make sure to use him tonight.

After that, the group dives into specifics regarding that night's Dodgers lineup vs. the opposing lineup, formulating a template of preferred scenarios. Which batter vs. pitcher matchups they like and which ones they prefer to avoid. A few days ago, for example, Dodgers starter Dustin May was blown up by the Padres, surrendering six earned runs in five innings on a Friday night at Dodger Stadium. The Dodgers trailed 7–0 after six innings.

"So now it's more of a triage," Prior says. "Everyone that was on our board, now it's save them for tomorrow." On that Friday night, after May underperformed, the Dodgers essentially had to shift from win-tonight mode into a mode of sacrificing tonight in order to focus on winning the series (which they did, with decisive 12–1 and 9–4 triumphs on Saturday and Sunday).

"We get into some very granular stuff here and there, too," Prior says. "Maybe we really like this matchup, even though it looks weird on paper. Or there's something we've seen in game planning that we think we can exploit."

This is the second meeting of the day involving Roberts and the baseball operations group. Typically, some of them will pop into his office sometime around midafternoon, as well, to check on any updated thoughts he may have on what happened the night before, or if he has anything new regarding rotation plans six, seven days out. Or they may offer some of their own. Sometimes they'll talk about how he intends to manage playing time, particularly for veterans who are looking like they need a day off. Other times, they'll discuss players in the minor-league system.

Between the two meetings and making his rounds with players, Roberts typically spends about twenty minutes alone when he first gets the opposing lineup, studying it and playing out potential scenarios for that evening in his mind. Which relievers will he deploy, and when, as the game develops. What if disaster strikes early and the Dodgers' starting pitcher is hit with a comebacker? How is the team going to pivot, which relievers are available early? Roberts does this alone first because he wants to solidify his own thoughts and ideas for the evening. Then he will talk them over with Prior. Finally, after batting practice comes the group run prevention meeting.

A typical perception with analytics is that the manager is given reams and reams of data points and printouts and then spends each day cramming, as if for a final exam. The reality is that much of the information is disseminated and discussed during these meetings, and then Roberts and his staff digest the most pertinent points and take them into the game that evening. Nobody knows how the game will play out, and even the best projections regularly go offtrack. So the value in the information and discussions, for Roberts, is that if the game goes down one path, they've discussed various options for that and he is prepared and comfortable when he begins pulling whatever bullpen and pinch-hitting levers he feels are required. If the game goes down one of various other paths, those probably have been discussed, as well, and Roberts has a set of options there, too.

"That's where I get frustrated, when I hear it is all scripted," Roberts says. "There is no script. You don't know which way a game is going to go. I don't know if Clayton Kershaw is going to go seven innings, I don't know if he's going to go four. I don't know how the next guy into the game is going to throw. But you have to have an idea of how to put your players in the best position and, ultimately, that's my decision."

Wednesday, Dodger Stadium, Los Angeles

With an afternoon game today against the Giants, Roberts and the Dodgers cleared out of the clubhouse quickly the previous evening. The bottles of wine in the manager's office remained corked. Instead, Roberts drove the twenty or so minutes to his in-season home in Pasadena (he maintains his permanent residence in northern San Diego County) in his new Mercedes and took some ZzzQuil to aid in the quick turnaround.

After several seasons on the job and after piloting the Dodgers to the 2020 World Series title—their first since 1988—there is not much that keeps Roberts up at night anymore.

"Honestly, the thing that keeps me awake at night is when I don't feel totally connected to the players for whatever reason," Roberts says this morning, and with good reason: The previous night's 6–3 trimming of the Giants lifted the Dodgers to 93-42. "Whether they feel like they're not playing as much as they should play or their role isn't what it should be, just to try to keep everybody on board. You understand the short-term view that players have, but as a manager you really appreciate the long term."

He appreciates the emotions because Roberts was a lefty-swinging platoon outfielder for much of his career. When he played in this stadium, wearing this uniform, that was his role under Jim Tracy. He did not appreciate it. He felt he should have been on the field more, felt he had earned it, felt he was better than the limitations placed upon him. But he never questioned his manager and, in his current role today, he can look back and appreciate Tracy's work.

In his own work, he is so focused on keeping players on track that it isn't even so much about winning and losing for Roberts. Of course, that's much easier for him to voice than, say, the skipper of the Kansas City Royals or Chicago White Sox, given how much winning these Dodgers have done since Roberts took charge in 2016.

"We can go on a losing streak for a little bit and it doesn't really bother me because if I feel everybody's on board and playing the right way, it will turn," he says. "There are moments in time where I feel we're not focused. That bothers me. I wouldn't say it keeps me up at night. I don't know if it's because we won the World Series in 2020, to be honest with you. But then, there was a little bit of a need to win. In '16 there was a honeymoon, '17 we don't win the World Series, '18 and '19, it was like, 'Are we going to become the Buffalo Bills?' After we won in '20, I do believe that removed a lot of the anxiousness to win a World Series."

But in an ever-changing game, first-round playoff knockouts by San Diego (2022) and Arizona (2023) embarrassed the Dodgers and caused an extraordinary spending spree when they signed free agents Shohei Ohtani ($700 million over ten years) and Japanese right-hander Yoshinobu Yamamoto ($325 million over twelve years) before the 2024 season. Anxiety and pressure always will live in the Dodger Stadium manager's office, regardless. The job never gets easier.

Two misconnections that probably were inevitable for Roberts came with outfielder Joc Pederson, who bounced from the Dodgers to the Cubs and Atlanta in 2021 and then San Francisco in 2022, and Kiké Hernández, who signed with Boston as a free agent in 2021.

"They were very good baseball players, but their strengths were they were platoon players," Roberts says. "As a player, you want them to feel that they always are the best option and an everyday player. Our relationship to this day isn't great because they felt it was a personal attack for me not playing them in everyday roles. It's unfortunate, because they are two good guys. But because of how I chose to play them and value them as players, it became personal. Those are things where, as a manager, you want everyone on board and it's unfortunate that our relationship is strained because of that. That sucks." That Hernández returned to the Dodgers in 2023 and 2024 and both parties made it work is a testament to not burning bridges and, especially, to the flexibility and control a successful manager in today's game must exhibit.

When Friedman and Roberts discussed adding Hernández at the 2023 trade deadline, each felt that Hernández was one of the best current postseason players in the game and that re-obtaining him would aid both the team's depth and increase the Dodgers' chances of winning eleven games in October. They had a similar conversation before re-signing Hernández as a free agent before the 2024 season. Hernández bought in to the Dodgers' proposed role for him both times.

"So, for me, that shows a lot of growth in him, because there were many years in the past where we just didn't see eye to eye," Roberts says of Hernández, who rewarded the Dodgers by batting .375 during their brief 2023 postseason and then .294 with two big homers and six RBI during the 2024 championship postseason. "And it's not a personal thing for me, because players feel they have certain capabilities. But I do believe that as time has gone on, he's seen how valuable he can be in a certain type of role." And, today? "Kiké and I couldn't be closer," Roberts says.

Yasiel Puig "took a lot of bandwidth" because of how his outrageous behavior and tendency toward tardiness affected the team. Roberts clicked with Puig, personally, and probably that connection helped extend Puig's time in Los Angeles longer than it otherwise would have. "The problem was when it affected the team where he showed up late or might not hustle," Roberts says. "His culture was different than our culture, and I'm sympathetic towards that, where players feel you should treat everybody the same, and that's just not always the case."

Conversely, Max Muncy is an example of a player whom the Dodgers pulled off the scrap heap after Oakland released him at the end of spring training in 2017. He went through the platoon battle, scrapped for playing time, and, to an extent, still does. But unlike Pederson and Hernández, Muncy has stayed and thrived, and he came to respect Roberts.

"It's easier to accept when you know you're not being lied to right to your face," Muncy says. "I know there are a lot of teams and a lot of organizations that do that, and that's when you start getting turmoil in the clubhouse because so-and-so is bad-mouthing someone behind their back. It doesn't happen here because, hey, why aren't I playing today? And he explains well, there's option A, option B, and option C, and all of these things need to be happening, and that's why you're not playing today. And you're like, 'OK, hmmm, fair enough.'"

One of the keys to Roberts is his authenticity. Generally speaking, players are more adept at sniffing out phonies than they are at cashing their own paychecks. Like children who see right through their parents when Mom and Dad are uncertain of something or are not prepared to follow through on their promises, players, too, see this instantaneously with managers.

"What makes Doc a good manager is his ability to interact with guys and get on everybody's level," Kershaw says. "That's the biggest thing. He has the ability to talk one on one and sit down with you and at the same time be the energy guy. We need that. Something I could never do that he does a great job with is he talks to the media every day and is the same guy. He has to do it twice a day, answer questions, give people time. I know that's something I would be really bad at, and he's great at it. And that doesn't seem like a huge part of the job, but at the same time, handling that and weathering that storm is good because it takes the burden off of us.

"Public speaking, all that stuff. Because managing now with the DH is really just bullpen managing. That is challenging, but other than that, there's not a whole lot there anymore with the DH. But all the other stuff that goes into it. The biggest thing is managing the personalities. And we've had a lot of personalities come through this clubhouse, all ends of the spectrum. We have a saying in here, 'No rules, just win the game.' And Doc really helps with that. He really embraces that. He doesn't care. He's not micromanaging. He's not, like, 'Oh, this guy's not working hard.' Whatever. It's, 'Is this guy preparing to win the game tonight?' That's it. Helping guys do that. He's good at that."

At fifty-two, Roberts is still young enough to relate to today's players; he is a skilled communicator who relays exceptionally well what the organization wants the public to know while also figuring ways to convey the organization's messaging both to players and the media. He's got plenty of street cred from his own playing career. He has managed some of the biggest stars in the game: Kershaw, Cody Bellinger, Buehler, Ohtani, Max Scherzer, Mookie Betts, Adrian Gonzalez, Yasiel

Puig, Corey Seager, Albert Pujols, Justin Turner, Trea Turner, Jason Heyward, Kenley Jansen, Chase Utley, Freddie Freeman, and, now, Yamamoto and Glasnow among them.

Before he left Los Angeles as a free agent for Boston following the 2022 season, as the Dodgers were restructuring their roster and player payroll preparing for Ohtani's free agency a year down the road, Justin Turner and his wife, Kourtney, developed close relationships with Dave and Tricia Roberts. They got to know the Robertses' two kids: Cole, who played baseball at Loyola Marymount University; and younger sister, Emme, who is at Stanford. It is a lasting friendship, the kind that goes well beyond baseball—and the kind that never would have happened in the black-and-white world of 1977 between Billy Martin and one of his players.

The relationship was built over their seven years together. Turner would sit in Roberts's office and the conversations would veer far beyond baseball, to life in general. Turner would ask about something that was going on with Emme, or check how Cole was playing.

"It's not necessarily a conversation just about baseball," Turner says. "It's a conversation about digging a little deeper."

One thing Turner always has appreciated is that even as Roberts's internal thermostat is naturally set to even-tempered and good-natured, he doesn't flinch when tough conversations are needed. Personally, Turner says, there have been "plenty of times" when he was struggling and Roberts assured him that the confidence and trust are still there and he would keep putting Turner in the lineup.

"If he sees something he doesn't like or thinks something needs to be addressed, he has those conversations right away," Turner says. "He nips them in the bud, doesn't let things fester or turn into anything bigger. It's not always what guys want to hear, but guys respect the fact that he comes up and tells you how he feels. And it doesn't really hamper the relationship. He can tell you that you need to do something better or do it a certain way, and the next day he comes up and is checking on your family and asking how you're doing. It doesn't carry over. I think that sets him apart."

Roberts also is secure enough to allow various forms of input from players. On the eve of Betts's first spring training after the blockbuster deal sending him from Boston to Los Angeles on February 10, 2020, he phoned Roberts and asked if it would be OK if he addressed the team. Betts, coming off of winning the 2018 World Series with the Red Sox—over the Dodgers—had a few things he wanted to say regarding work ethic and seriousness of purpose. Roberts could have viewed that as a personal indictment and deterred Betts. Instead, Roberts thought it was a great idea and gave Betts the floor in the team meeting as camp opened.

Betts's move to the infield from the outfield also emanated from a conversation with Roberts, just talking about the outfielder's health and some nagging injuries, and brainstorming a way to do something differently.

"He's not scared to try things," Betts says. "He's not scared to fail. He understands that's part of it. He just is a guy who goes to work. He doesn't think about the negatives of things. He's always looking at the positive side. He spins things to be positive. And he is really good at his job."

The greatest reward in his job, Roberts says, is when struggling players approach him instead of the other way around.

"Whether it's personal, whether it's professional," Roberts says. "I can easily say winning the World Series…but that's a by-product of the relationships I've been able to build. To see players feel vulnerable toward me, and also these guys are growing as men. And that's what my number one goal is, because I feel if we can grow these guys as men, they're going to be better baseball players for us."

Conversely, his biggest challenge isn't necessarily the end goal of winning another World Series. It comes within the scenarios that develop during the season that become pressure points.

"The team is not winning, so Rome is burning," Roberts says. "The team is not hitting, you've got to change the hitters. You're not pitching well, the bullpen is not performing, so you've gotta blow the whole thing up. The most important thing is to remain steadfast because we are still playing 162 and I can look back many times when people thought I should have benched Justin Turner, Max Muncy, released Kenley Jansen. There are always those people having a rough go of it and fans and the media think it is the end of this player. A lot of this is managing people. The game itself is the easy part. Managing the people, the players, their minds, their hearts, is the most gratifying and fulfilling, but it's also the most challenging."

Behind Kershaw, who holds the Giants to two runs over six innings before Justin Bruihl, Evan Phillips, and Alex Vesia cover the final three frames, the Dodgers take the series from San Francisco with a 7–3 afternoon romp. Life is good. The team is heading into an off day tomorrow before opening a series in San Diego on Friday. For the Dodgers, it will be another measuring-stick series against an improved team looking to take their crown. For the manager, it will be a nice homecoming and a chance to sleep in his own bed.

Saturday, Petco Park, San Diego

Gabe Kapler was supposed to be the next Dodgers manager when Don Mattingly left to take over the Miami Marlins in 2016. At least, given Kapler's theoretical inside track at the time as the Dodgers' director of player development and heavy industry and public speculation. Conventional wisdom had it as a stacked interview that would end with Kapler's coronation.

Nine years later, Kapler has come and gone as the Philadelphia manager (2018–2019), risen and fallen as the San Francisco Giants skipper (2020–2023), and landed in a third organization as an assistant general manager of the Miami Marlins. Bags packed, unpacked, packed again, unpacked…

Roberts, then forty-three, was the Dodgers' surprise choice after he absolutely crushed the exhausting, laborious Dodgers interview process, wowing the ownership group in particular. It was his second interview that winter after a visit with the Seattle Mariners. But speaking of a stacked interview process, there, GM Jerry Dipoto picked his longtime friend and colleague Scott Servais. Dipoto had hired Servais as his assistant GM in 2011 when Dipoto was running the Los Angeles Angels. Then, after a falling out with manager Mike Scioscia and failing to gain the support of owner Arte Moreno, Dipoto resigned in July 2015 and was named to run the Mariners that September.

"It went great," Roberts says of the Mariners interview. "And I think that they let the Dodgers know that I was kind of out there, that I showed well."

Following three years in San Diego's baseball operations department and after overcoming a battle with Hodgkin's lymphoma, Roberts moved back into uniform in 2013 as Bud Black's bench coach. But he was badly snubbed when new GM A. J. Preller fired Black in June 2015. Not only was he not even considered for the Padres' managerial opening, but Preller named Pat Murphy as the manager to finish out the season and left Roberts as bench coach. Black and former Angels outfielder Darin Erstad were among the finalists in the Dodgers' interview process, along with Roberts and Kapler.

"It was arduous," Roberts says. "It was long. It was detailed. Ultimately, the best advice I got was from my wife. She said, 'If you're going to do this job, you can't fool these people. You have to be yourself.' So this weeklong, two-week process, I was myself the entire time. I'm sure in the beginning there were things they agreed with and things they didn't agree with, but I think my authenticity showed through. I could have an overall managing philosophy or try to pattern how I do my job from this manager, that manager, whoever. But ultimately, if it's not who I am and what I believe in, it's just not going to hold water. It's not going to sustain itself."

The Dodgers' interview process was more in-depth and far longer than Seattle's. By the end, Roberts figures, he interviewed with about eight people in Seattle and at least twenty, perhaps more, in Los Angeles. He talked with controlling owner Mark Walter and with minority owners Peter Guber and Magic Johnson. There were sessions with Kasten, Friedman, and a half dozen or so of his baseball operations staff. Vice presidents, scouts, and more.

"It was like a corporate interview," Roberts says. "It wasn't like you're a baseball manager and what the job entails. That makes sense. Because it's not just managing on the field. It's managing up. It's managing the entire staff. This is a $4 billion organization, so you're basically interviewing for a CEO position."

Reminders of that have occurred every single day in his near decade on the job. They come during his daily media briefings. His live television interviews. His visits to community hospitals. His response to every victory, every defeat, every controversial brushfire that threatens to rage out of control if he gives the wrong answer or uses the wrong word.

Along with the Dodgers' continued domination on the field, his record for handling all of this with aplomb undoubtedly plays into his growing longevity. His biggest faux pas, in his own estimation, came when the Dodgers placed right-hander Trevor Bauer on administrative leave in early July 2021, when sexual assault allegations first came to light. It was the very beginning of an incredibly sensitive (and revolting) story, and the Dodgers and MLB were scrambling to track down details as the court of public opinion was moving at light speed. Roberts, as usual in his role as manager, became the franchise's public spokesman.

"I said something pretty benign, like, we're going to wait and see," Roberts says. "I thought it was benign. That was what I was told to say, because we didn't have all the information. I was being sensitive toward the situation. I was told by MLB and by the Dodgers to say we're going to wait, we're going to hold off and not suspend the player right now. And then, it was like a media storm."

Then there was Game 4 of the 2018 World Series against Boston. The Dodgers had been beaten by the scandalous Houston Astros in the 2017 Fall Classic and now they were trailing Boston two games to one in a pivotal moment in Dodger Stadium a year later. Veteran lefty Rich Hill was pitching with a 4–0 lead into the seventh. He was filthy, having fanned six and surrendered just one hit. But when he walked Xander Bogaerts to lead off the seventh and then struck out Eduardo Núñez, Roberts decisively headed to the mound to remove Hill. Two relievers and three batters later, Boston's Mitch Moreland blasted a three-run homer to ignite a comeback that would end with Boston scoring five in the ninth for a 9–6 win. Six Dodgers relievers combined to surrender eight runs and seven hits, issuing three walks and striking out only one batter. The Sox would win it all the following night.

It was the second World Series in a row that a game turned when the Dodgers hooked Hill too early. In Game 2 against Houston, Hill was dealing through four innings (one run, three hits, seven strikeouts, and three walks) but was replaced by Kenta Maeda entering the fifth. The Dodgers trailed 1–0 at the time. Though they came back in the middle innings to take the lead, the game spun into the eleventh inning before Houston won 7–6. By removing Hill so early, even more was required from a Dodgers bullpen that burned through eight relievers that night.

All of this is what emerges on the other side of the data and analytics that get fed into the Dodgers' extensive run prevention meetings. In the case of Hill vs. Boston in Game 4 in 2018, the Dodgers' initial idea was to go with an "opener" and then bring Hill into the game next as the "bulk innings guy." When Roberts discussed it with Hill in the lead-up to Game 4, the veteran was reluctant. He was thirty-eight and had worked out of the bullpen only once in the previous four years. With the manager having failed to sell Hill, the pitcher took a phone call from Friedman on the morning of Game 4 with the same pitch.

"I wasn't thrilled about that," Hill says. "Especially at the time. The opener was a newer concept. Now you're starting to see a lot of teams go to a six-man rotation and you're seeing a lot of openers. They're actually valued more. Talking now, at this point in my career, it would be something I would be more open to, just understanding where I'm at, physically."

There is reasonable criticism here that the Dodgers at times get too cute with their pitching in October, that they have been too proactive and made moves too soon and it has backfired. The more relievers used, the more the odds increase that at least one of them is not going to be on his A game that night. And it's anybody's guess which one. Had they made different or more successful pitching decisions, particularly in those two games with Hill, perhaps the Dodgers would have more than one World Series title since 1988.

"If we weren't cheated out of the World Series in '17 this would be moot," Roberts says, referring, of course, to losing to a Houston team that later was found to be using an illegal, video-driven sign-stealing scheme that stained their title. "If we'd have won that World Series, this whole 'I took Rich Hill out,' then it would have been the complete right decision. So that's something that I'm very sensitive towards, in the sense that because the world is very results driven, because we didn't win and I know we got cheated."

Media, fans, and social media trolls traditionally blast Roberts whenever these moves backfire in October—as second-guessers do with every manager in every game when things go wrong in the postseason. It is the easiest second-guess in sports: When a reliever doesn't do the job, well, the manager shouldn't have called for him. It mostly is a lazy and knee-jerk reaction, especially in an age when managers are making these moves based in large part on the detailed information emanating from pregame meetings and discussions. The manager is the one who calls for the reliever and then is the front man postgame explaining what he was thinking, while the anonymous analytics experts remain, Oz-like, behind the curtain and are not required to take public accountability for anything.

And so, in the ninth inning of Game 4 against Boston, as the Dodgers pen was blowing the game, then-President Donald Trump took to Twitter: "Watching the Dodgers/Red Sox final innings. It is amazing how a manager takes out a pitcher who is loose & dominating through almost 7 innings, Rich Hill of Dodgers, and brings in nervous reliever(s) who get shellacked. 4 run lead gone. Managers do it all the time, big mistake!"

Within an hour afterward, now one game away from elimination, Roberts was facing the press when my old colleague, Tyler Kepner of the *New York Times*, did what nobody else had yet done but what was required in the moment: He read the president's tweet to Roberts and asked his reaction. Because he was, um, managing and not on social media, this was the first Roberts learned that the White House had ripped him.

"I'm happy he was tuning in," Roberts said in a pitch-perfect response, before adding: "I don't think he was privy to the conversation. That's one man's opinion."

"I thought that was more comedic, considering the source," Roberts says. "Now, things are so much in real time to where I don't take things personally, and I encourage managers I talk to and mentor to not take things personally because not everyone has all of the information we have."

Not taking things personally is easier said than done. The biggest difference between Roberts's expectations of what managing would be like when he took the job in 2016 and the reality he saw had nothing to do with the baseball, the dynamics between him and the front office, or anything else Dodgers related. No, it is the toxicity of social media.

"I didn't expect the social media criticism, the cynicism, the hate," he says. "That's something I didn't appreciate coming into this job. And like it or not, certain narratives land with people and it bleeds into people's thoughts. The anger these people have, it's sad. It's absolutely bananas."

What the knee-jerkers on the Platform Formerly Known as Twitter—introduced in March 2006—continually miss is that, in the Information Revolution, nobody surpasses the Dodgers in terms of sheer volume and precision. No manager is better equipped than Roberts when the first pitch arrives at 7:05 p.m. each evening.

"The front office and Doc have the same goal, to win the game," says Kershaw, who, of course, has been with Roberts since the beginning. "I think our front office does a great job with providing him with information. Now, if they do disagree, and I know Andrew has said this before, he's the on-field manager, he gets to make those decisions because he has to live with them. I think Andrew and Gomer [assistant GM Gomes] and all those guys upstairs do a great job of giving their input, giving him all the information but not micromanaging in-game, like you should have done this or you should have done that. I think they have a good relationship, as far as I can tell. But I can see where that definitely would be a problem for some teams."

Before he even started managing, his good friend Black—who had pitched in the majors for fifteen years before becoming the pitching coach of the 2002 champion Angels and then moving on to manage San Diego and Colorado for seventeen more years—told him: If you ever want to manage, you'd better learn to like pitchers and understand them. Roberts has taken that to heart. He normally does not attend the daily hitters' meetings, leaving those to the hitting coaches. He does make it a point to frequently watch the between-starts bullpen sessions of his rotation in the early afternoons. He also spends serious time with his relievers as they throw their flat-ground sessions before games or, simply, conversing with them during batting practice. The more collateral he builds with them, the more understanding they are when he makes the hard decisions to pull them during games.

Be it a pitching move he makes in May or one under the hot glare of October, Roberts from his first days in Los Angeles has been very public that his work is a collaboration with the front office. It is the way it has to be in today's game, and that was what he voiced in his interview that blew away so many over those two weeks in the autumn of 2015. The days of a powerful manager who molds the team in his image—Whitey Herzog and his team of jackrabbits tailor-made for St. Louis's Busch Stadium in the 1980s—are history.

"I made it very clear from the get-go that my job was to manage the players that are given to me," he says. "My job is not to put together the roster. I was a gritty base stealer, a slash-and-run-type guy who bunted. We don't have those types of players. And so for me to want to impose the way I played the game with this roster makes no sense. But just because I didn't hit home runs or I didn't have Freddie Freeman's skill set doesn't mean I can't manage the player. I didn't pitch, but that doesn't mean I can't manage a pitching staff. I say a prayer every day, don't make it about me."

Even as his playing career ended in San Francisco in 2008, Roberts had no aspirations to manage. But after a few years away, working in broadcasting and baseball operations, the desire to get back in uniform returned. He wanted to coach. It went from there, and now the managing extends to all hours of the day and night, and he's a natural.

In fact, he may be the only man in his position today who doubles as a manager and a shuttle driver. On the drive to San Diego on Wednesday night in his brand-new Mercedes, Roberts ferried reliever Blake Treinen most of the way from Los Angeles before exiting to his house and leaving the right-hander to Uber the last twenty-five or so miles. Treinen had family in town, so instead of waiting for the off-day bus ride on Thursday, he asked the manager if he could hitch a ride a night earlier.

"Phenomenal Uber driver," Treinen says. "The car practically drives itself, though. It's really nice."

The ninety-minute drive sped by.

"He and I are both cut from a similar cloth from the aspect that we both believe that Jesus Christ is our Lord and Savior, and so we had a good conversation about life and just kind of as believers, what's going on in today's world," Treinen continues. "He's a good dude. There's always good things to talk about, and he's got a good ear."

That extended all the way into a chilly Wednesday evening in the Bronx on the World Series stage two years later. But now, it was the eyes and heart of Treinen that came into play. Five outs away from the title, with two Yankees aboard and the Dodgers clinging to a 7-6 lead, Treinen was the team's seventh pitcher of the evening. There wasn't much left in the bullpen, save for starter Walker Buehler's soon-to-be-unforgettable volunteer work to close out the ninth inning and clinch the championship. But, before Buehler, Treinen had thrown thirty-seven pitches and the tying and go-ahead runs were aboard with slugger Giancarlo Stanton up next.

Looking to slow the momentum, Roberts went to the mound himself while deciding whether to send Treinen after Stanton or call for Buehler. The manager looked hard into the pitcher's eyes to see what was there. He placed both hands on Treinen's chest, feeling for his heartbeat. Taking his pulse, literally.

Though nearly twenty-five months had passed since that simple, late-night ride down the freeway from Los Angeles to San Diego, that very private and this very public moment nevertheless were connected over the years, not unlike a baseball stitched together with red yarn.

"We built a relationship that was way beyond player-coach. That moment, among others, allowed for him to trust me and anything I asked of him," Roberts says, recalling that carpool evening with Treinen. "I do think that our connection that we had, on the mound in that moment, gave him just enough to get those next couple of hitters. And it started years ago."

Roberts had barely returned to the dugout when Treinen fired a sinker that Stanton popped to right field. Then, Treinen finished off Anthony Rizzo on four pitches, tossing an eighty-five-mile-per-hour sweeper past a flailing Rizzo for strike three. An inning later, the Dodgers had their first full-season title since 1988. The party was on.

Sunday, Petco Park, San Diego

Following a series-opening loss, the Dodgers bounce back with an 8–4 win on Saturday night, followed by an 11–2 trouncing on Sunday. Today's win moves the Dodgers' record to 96-43 and clinches their tenth consecutive postseason berth. Afterward, Roberts presides over a simple champagne toast as the club packs for the flight to Arizona. The point is to acknowledge the achievement while understanding that there are bigger things ahead.

Standards are high with this organization, and history is understood and appreciated. Walter Alston managed the Dodgers for twenty-three years, winning four World Series. Lasorda managed the next twenty-one years and won three more titles. The days of any club, even one of the game's jewel franchises like the Dodgers, employing just two managers over a forty-four-year period are long gone. Bookended by Lasorda and Roberts, Bill Russell, Davey Johnson, Jim Tracy, Grady Little, Joe Torre, and Don Mattingly managed the Dodgers from 1997 to 2015. The lineage going back to Alston and Lasorda is impressive, and Roberts feels a deep responsibility to maintain and nurture the rich history.

"With those two guys in particular, the longevity and the consistency really speaks to me," Roberts says. "When you're talking about guys who have managed for twenty years each, it's remarkable. For me, there's no telling what the future holds. But I look at those two guys and what they meant for this organization, and I try to follow that mold in the sense of the Dodger way, and what it means to be a Dodger."

Which is?

"There's a professionalism. The Dodgers are a very traditional, classic franchise, and I think how that translates on the field, for me, is how we go about playing the game. How our players interact with fans, understanding the responsibility of what it means to be a Dodger. And that aligns with the brand name Los Angeles Dodgers."

In the days of Alston and Lasorda, it was far more baseball than "brand." Evolution, both within the sport and within the culture, has changed things immensely. Lasorda arguably might have been the best ambassador for baseball who ever lived. Between his enthusiasm and passion, he was a one-man marketing department in addition to being a Hall of Fame manager. But he also had wide-ranging freedom that Roberts does not: He did not have to worry about every off-color joke and expletive going viral.

Lasorda worked under a single owner, Walter O'Malley, in the days when things were so simple that O'Malley provided free ice cream to employees on days when the Dodgers were in first place. There was a *Leave It to Beaver*–style wholesomeness. The iPhone, introduced in 2007, was still eleven years away when Lasorda managed his last game in 1996. Conversely, two years before Roberts replaced Mattingly, the Dodgers formed their own TV network, SportsNetLA—as the Yankees had done with YES a few years earlier. Regional sports networks contributed to the exploding worth of teams and money coming into the game during the early 2000s—and changed the job descriptions of managers as well as pressures and priorities for clubs. Now, managers are on these club-owned networks before and after every game and are asked to be the face of the franchise PR-wise, which arguably is as important as working the dugout during the games. Roberts, and others, must take everything in stride and project a calmness and likability.

Though several bootleg recordings of Lasorda rants have circulated underground for years, in his era, they never made it on the air and there was nowhere to take them viral. One such classic was his postgame diatribe on May 14, 1978, following a 10–7 loss to the Cubs when a reporter asked a particularly lazy question, wanting his "opinion" of Dave Kingman's three home runs for the Cubs.

"What's my opinion of Kingman's performance?" Lasorda replied, the wick of the dynamite stick starting to sizzle toward explosion. "What the fuck do you think my opinion of it is? I think it was fucking bullshit. Put that in. I don't fucking care. What's my opinion of his performance? Shit. He beat us with three fucking home runs. What the fuck do you mean, 'What is my opinion of his performance?' How can you ask me a question like that?

"What is my opinion of his performance? Shit. He hit three home runs. Shit. I'm fucking pissed off to lose a fucking game, and you ask me my opinion of his performance? Shit. I mean, that's a tough question to ask me, 'What is my opinion of his performance?'!"

No way something like that stays private today, and no way any of today's managers even have something like that in them. Clubs are way too cautious with whom they hire.

Today, what passes for controversial sometimes seems incredibly benign. At the winter meetings in Nashville, Tennessee, in December 2023, Roberts stirred the pot when he actually confirmed to reporters that the club had met with then–free agent Ohtani and that Ohtani was their top target. Anybody who even knows that a baseball is round and not oval knew that. But Ohtani's camp wanted radio silence, and Roberts quickly was upbraided by his bosses for daring to be truthful. To his credit, Roberts's response was that he wasn't going to lie.

That incident aside, Roberts, who has never undergone any formal media training, understands that media and fans love a passionate reaction and outlandish quotes. And he is skilled at understanding that any overly emotional reaction is going to benefit neither himself nor the Dodgers.

"I wouldn't say it's pressure," Roberts says. "It's mindfulness. Anything I say is going to affect this $4 billion machine. From Mark Walter to the clubhouse attendant. It affects everyone. And so I can laugh and say that Tommy was a good friend of mine and a great manager, but the way he sounded off and reacted, in this culture nowadays, it just won't age well. It's funny, it's one of those things where I count on my players to be dependable, and that's what Mark Walters, Stan Kasten, and Andrew Friedman count on from me, as well, to be dependable."

Eric Karros, who played fourteen seasons in the majors, broke in with the Dodgers in 1991 and played his first five and a half years under Lasorda before the legend had to leave managing in the middle of the 1996 season with health problems. He became close to Lasorda over the years and admired the way he did his job.

"There was a Herm Edwards line I heard one time, and I would characterize this for Tommy: 'I don't treat every player the same, but I treat them all fair,'" Karros says, speaking of the old NFL coach. "There were guys where Tommy would get in their faces, other guys no way he ever got in their faces, he'd try to lift them up. That's what made Tommy so good, his ability to understand what made each guy tick. I think that's what Doc is great at. I played for Dusty in '03 and I'd run through a frickin' brick wall for that man, for anything, *anything*. That's not analytics, that's not statistics, it's not something measurable. That's a feeling created between two human beings. Tommy could do it, Dusty did it, and I think it's one of Doc's strengths."

One of Karros's most memorable moments with Lasorda came during his rookie season when he was still learning both his manager and the majors. The team was in Philadelphia, Lasorda's home area, and he had participated in one of Lasorda's classic, big Italian dinners on Saturday night.

"We're at this family's house, we're eating at midnight or whatever, day game the next day, and I make an error," Karros says. "Ground ball to me, and I overthrow Mike Scioscia at home. Our dugout is on the third-base side and I can see in there and I can see that Tommy is livid. He's pointing at me, he's talking with [coach] Joey Amalfitano, so I know I'm going to get an earful when I get in there. It's my rookie year and I'm just trying to prove I can play in the big leagues. So I come off the field and Tommy is like, 'What the fuck is going on out there? Jesus almighty, you're better than that!' I started to say, 'Tommy, I was trying,' and I didn't even get the word 'try' out. He was like, 'Try? *Try?!* I can get any of these blankety-blanks in the stands out here to try. I don't want triers, I want doers!' I wasn't going to make that mistake again."

Understanding that television cameras are everywhere today, if there is an animated conversation to be had, Roberts makes sure to bring the player a few steps down the runway behind the dugout and out of public view because he does not want to embarrass anyone. Yet as he projects an outer calm in the moment, many wonder why he is not reacting more directly.

"I'm not going to react right there because, now, with the media, it's the players' wives or spouses, their kids, their moms, their dads, all these people are saying, 'Hey, Dave did this when you did this,' and that's not going to end well," he says. "So those difficult conversations happen all the time."

They just do not happen in the dugout or on the bench.

While their personalities are different, Karros, who remains in the game today as a television analyst on the Dodgers' network and for Fox, sees at least some of Lasorda in Roberts.

"Tommy is always going to be a bit more boisterous, but I think both are Players' Managers," Karros says. "Both are guys who try to understand the guys who are in uniform, know their wives, know their families, make it more of a personal relationship. It's weird, I'm trying to figure out which is more difficult: Tommy did all that while he was also making all the decisions. Where Doc is in a spot where he's ultimately making the decision but there is a heck of a lot of input. I don't know, is that more difficult or not as difficult? I would think it would be more difficult in that you've got to consider a lot of other things other than what you're feeling right there on the bench in that moment."

From the extreme pressure points in a corporate game with owners looking for returns on their investments to the conference room discussions that can leave the walls closing in on managers to the social media vitriol, the shelf life of today's skippers almost certainly will be less than was their predecessors'. Alston lasted nearly a quarter of a century. Lasorda worked for more than two decades. Roberts is still a young man who possesses, as his former manager Tracy says, "the energy of ten men." But even at that, few are built to last the way some of the lions of the past were. Mike Scioscia, who managed the Angels for nineteen seasons from 2000 to 2018, may be the last one who comes close to two decades.

"I would say, for me, if I could do this somewhere between ten and fifteen years, and if I could just stay with the Dodgers, that would be ideal," Roberts says. "Because in ten years, you can kind of make a mark where you've done it, you've got some longevity there. Of course, it's more of a conversation with my wife."

The ironic thing, Roberts has learned, is that he got back into coaching because of his affinity for both the game and the players. But as manager, there is precious little time in the day to actually coach. It is far more administrative.

"But that's kind of the manager job these days," he says. "Because it's not an autonomous job anymore. So there's a lot of factions or groups that have input, and this business is a multi-multi-billion-dollar industry, let alone organization. So being one of the faces of the organization calls for a lot. And I think the easiest part of it, which is probably the most critical, is the Xs and Os of the game. That's where I'm most criticized, but that's the easiest, right? The hardest part is managing my time and being able to fulfill all the responsibilities that I have outside of a baseball game."

In his own way, and with a modern twist, Roberts carries on Lasorda's deep belief in the Dodgers with one of his favorite messages to his players.

"In this world, there is so much gray," he says. "So much gray. But in this case, as far as the Dodgers and what we want to be, there is no gray. It's black and white. You're either in or you're out. You're on board with what we're doing, or you're not."

Roberts thinks back to when he took charge in 2016, how the lineup was not completely set, how analytics drove many of the Dodgers' platoon and roster decisions, and some of the outside noise that came with that.

"Seven years later, that's what teams are doing now," he says. "So that's where it's like, for me, I have a lot of confidence in that. There's always resistance, and I'm very grateful for what the Dodgers are, very forward-thinking. Now, there are thirty teams that are using analytics, and the teams that don't are at the bottom."

Even at that, it does not come with a guarantee of championships. Alston won all four of his World Series titles before the playoffs even existed. Then, the champion of the NL simply advanced to play the AL champion in the World Series. Lasorda won each of his two titles in the infancy of the playoffs, when the leagues were broken into Eastern and Western Divisions, and the champions of each met in the ALCS and NLCS, the winner in each advancing to the World Series.

Today, fans gripe about wasted seasons if their team doesn't win it all. Yet October has become a full-on obstacle course, with a team having to win as many as three playoff series before reaching the World Series. In Alston's day, there were sixteen MLB teams total, and two played in the World Series. During most of Lasorda's run, there were twenty-four teams and four made the playoffs. Today, twelve of thirty teams qualify for the playoffs.

"That's the truth, I just don't think people want to hear it," Roberts says. "They look at the format, at the structure of the postseason, which is completely different than it was fifty, forty, twenty, ten years ago. They don't want to hear structure as the reason the Dodgers don't win the World Series. In the old days, when you won the NL or AL pennant, you had a fifty-fifty chance to win the World Series. I understand the way it is now, there's more revenue, I absolutely understand that. But the fact is the way you get to the World Series and win the World Series is completely different."

It still does not change the fact that the Dodgers annually field a team they believe can win another World Series. And in 2022, they fueled their hopes with an MLB-record player payroll of $285 million. Yet a month after today's champagne toast, during a return trip to San

Diego, the upstart Padres will bounce them during an NL Division Series. And Roberts will pass the rest of the month by taking his wife on an impromptu trip to London. After another season of pouring his heart and soul into this Dodgers ethos, no way is he going to stay at his home in San Diego as well-meaning friends and neighbors cheer for the home team.

Postscript: November 2024, Cardiff, California, Starbucks

The difference between the Dodgers' latest title and the pandemic-induced short-season championship in 2020, Roberts explains during our early-morning chat, is contained within the range of emotions.

The first World Series title in 2020 softened the naysayers. This one should shut them up for good—well, at least until next season.

"This is like pure joy, with a little bit of relief because no one can say anything else, you know?" he says. "What else are they going to say, right? I still stand by the fact that 2020 was harder than this year, because of the circumstances. Then, people were just living lives that were completely different."

That doesn't mean 2024 was easy, or anything close. It never is. The fact that the Dodgers had been bounced early in the Division Series in each of the past two seasons, by San Diego and Arizona, hung over them early in this postseason like the gloomy Southern California marine layer. A third consecutive early exit and Roberts felt, even given his consistent winning, that outside noise might force internal change.

"You can replace some players but at the end of the day, you're the one who's going to be held accountable, and your job is on the line," says Roberts, whose contract at the moment ran for just one more year, through 2025. "And for me, I never got any assurance going into my last season, or even after the regular season, and we had a great year, that regardless of how the postseason goes, you're coming back and you're our guy. I never got any assurance.

"So, for me, the noise starts to get louder. Also, living in San Diego and being so close to it when we played the Padres, yeah, that bleeds in. I do everything I can to block that stuff out."

Things turned not only because the Dodgers dumped the Padres in an exhilarating five-game series, but in *how* they did it. The Dodgers showed more fight, grit, and character. They exhibited more depth. Essentially, Roberts says, the team "took off our boxing gloves and got into a bare-knuckle fight." It was that or else, the manager says of the Padres, because "that's the way that team operates."

At one point during the postseason, Roberts noted that superstar Mookie Betts had become like a son to him during their five years together. One of Roberts's stops during his victory lap after the title was for a visit on Betts's podcast. Among other things, they spoke of how this particular team had taken on the skipper's personality: Gritty. Scrappy. A fighter.

"I had to be that way because I didn't have all that talent as a player," Roberts tells me of the shared traits between himself and his 2024 team. "And that's something I'm very proud of. And Mookie and I, we have, like, this father-son relationship where we go a lot deeper than baseball. We talk hours at a time."

The addition of Ohtani also escalated both the eyeballs and pressure on the 2024 Dodgers simply "because of signing the best player in the world," Roberts says. "But managing him was a piece of cake. Really. I really believe that, once we got rid of that interpreter, he became his own man and we got to see the real Shohei: vulnerable, open, and joyful. He got along with the players and staff real well. And he and I have a great, simple relationship. It's a great relationship."

The fact that Ohtani played the last three games of the World Series with what turned out to be a torn labrum in his left shoulder that required surgery five days after it ended is somewhere between head-shakingly incredible and heroic. Though he didn't do much with the bat, his presence soothed Roberts and the Dodgers like a favorite blanket because they knew he would still intimidate the Yankees in the box.

Meanwhile, because of the pitching injuries (the legend Clayton Kershaw, would-be ace Tyler Glasnow, onetime starters Gavin Stone, Dustin May, and Tony Gonsolin all were injured), the Dodgers had to maneuver through a bullpen game in Game 4 of the World Series and, essentially, another one in Game 5 when inconsistent starter Jack Flaherty spit the bit and surrendered four runs in just 1.1 innings. Roberts used twelve pitchers over those final two games after successfully navigating through two more bullpen games against the Mets in the NLCS.

Those by far are the most taxing and stressful games for a postseason manager, especially for one who has been there many times before, as Roberts has, enough times to have some experience with it backfiring.

"The more decisions you have to make, the more chances you have to be wrong," Roberts says. "And in a case like that, a lot of times if you're wrong, quote, unquote, or it doesn't work out, then it's your fault. So it just goes to the point that that's where we were at."

He picked the pieces up and put them down like a master chessman. Most impressive was Game 5 when, as a 3-0 series lead for the Dodgers was threatening to melt to 3-2 and force a return trip to Los Angeles, he recognized every dip and twist of the roller coaster. When the Yankees crushed Flaherty en route to a 5–0 lead, Roberts went with his lower-leverage relievers Anthony Banda and Ryan Brasier because he recognized that he could not risk burning his high-leverage relievers when there likely would be at least one more game, and possibly two, as the high wire he was walking moved even higher.

But when the Dodgers popped for five runs to tie the game in a sloppy fifth inning for the Yankees, the Los Angeles skipper immediately made a sharp turn and deployed big gun Michael Kopech, followed by high-leverage arms Vesia, Brusdar Graterol, Treinen, and Buehler. The script had changed—one of so many reasons why those scripts that are plotted pregame in the age of analytics turn to toilet paper as the game actually plays out. Back in it, Roberts opted to go for the jugular because he wanted no part of the Yankees forcing more games in Los Angeles. See, what happened in 2004 was loosening up in his own mind's bullpen, er, eye. That's when his Red Sox trailed the Yankees three games to none, he swiped that base to key a ninth-inning rally in Game 4, and Boston became the only team ever to erase a three-game deficit and win four consecutive games in a seven-game postseason series.

Because of that, Roberts knows the psyche.

"Then what happens is you go back to the next stadium, there is a large part of the fan base and players that are, 'We're at home and excited,' but then there's a part that starts to get anxious and nervous and that bleeds in and in baseball, anything can happen," Roberts says as the sun shines and pedestrians who have no idea who this man is in a nondescript ballcap, sunglasses, and an oversized white hoodie walk by to get their morning caffeine fix. "And then when you start getting anxious and tense, you never know.

"So I wanted to end it right there. And once our guys showed to get back into the ballgame, I just felt that I had to exhaust every resource."

Earlier in this chapter, I wrote that Roberts's best managing job came in 2023 when he maneuvered through injuries and drama to lead a division titlist. That remains impressive, but he surpassed that in 2024, what with the early-season distraction of the gambling scandal that snared Ohtani's interpreter, losing Betts for three months to a fractured hand, the regular assorted pitching injuries that included Yamamoto missing two months, would-be ace Glasnow being shut down, and Kershaw's season ending, sadly, with another injury.

Asked to compare the two, Roberts thinks for a beat but really doesn't hesitate long before answering.

"I just feel that I haven't done anything different," he says. "I think that I didn't work any harder. I didn't lean into the players any more. Every single year, there are different circumstances that you have to deal with to keep the ship moving forward."

It is a spot-on answer because, beyond so many other traits, one of the most important aspects of a manager's job is to be consistent, to be the same guy his players expect to see every day, no matter what is happening—while at the same time making every adjustment he needs to make as things happen and anticipating other things before they do happen. It is the classic description of a duck: so beautiful, still, graceful, and calm while moving across the lake, but below the water his legs are paddling like hell.

He still loves every bit of it. And regarding his earlier thoughts on hoping to manage the Dodgers for ten to fifteen years and let it be the only place he ever works, now entering his tenth season, he's nowhere ready to stop.

"I think it's more on the back end now," Roberts says. "I think fifteen seems like a nice round number." His hope is to do a contract extension this winter that at least takes him to within range of a fifteenth year. He not only deserves the years, he deserves the money, somewhere north of the record-setting five-year, $40 million deal Counsell earned from the Cubs in 2023.

In the immediate aftermath of joining Alston and Lasorda as the only Dodgers managers ever to lead the team to multiple World Series titles, Roberts received especially meaningful congratulatory calls from, among others, President Joe Biden, Vice President Kamala Harris, Dodgers legendary Hall of Famer Sandy Koufax, World Series–winning managers Dusty Baker and Cito Gaston, and executives with whom he once worked—Larry Baer (San Francisco), and Mark Shapiro (Toronto). By the day after the title, Roberts's cell phone was stocked with some six hundred texts. Because it is who he is, as we sit here a week after the World Series, he's already answered every one of them.

Later tonight, Roberts will fly to Madrid, Spain, with wife Tricia and son Cole for an eagerly anticipated family vacation with daughter Emme. Now in her third year at Stanford in prelaw, Emme, twenty-two, is studying abroad this quarter while Cole, twenty-four, is a minor-league free agent after playing in Arizona's organization for the past two summers. In Europe, the sweet family time will allow Roberts, however briefly, to step away from the noise and constant interruptions that his job entails. Soon enough, 2025 will be here. And the critics undoubtedly will be closely tracking his decree to Dodgers' fans during the Dodger Stadium celebration to "run it back."

CHAPTER 9

THE NEW NORM

If there was any question that the San Francisco Giants, who won three World Series championships in five seasons, were a wholly different group a mere six years after winning their third title in 2014, proof positive was found in a simple snapshot of then-manager Gabe Kapler's coaching staff.

Before the 2020 season, he approached Farhan Zaidi, the club's president of baseball operations, with a novel ask. He wanted to increase the size of his staff. Significantly. When Zaidi heard the number, his first reaction was that his New Age manager perhaps was burning a few too many incense candles in his office.

But Zaidi heard Kapler out, then ran the request through the Upstairs. And, presto change-o, the Giants opened the 2020 season with thirteen coaches, including MLB's first-ever female coach, Alyssa Nakken.

"It may be a little bit outside the box, but outside the box increasingly is inside the box," Larry Baer, then San Francisco's president and chief executive, told me.

Outside the box increasingly is inside the box. That covers so many aspects of today's game. Starting off the field, and trickling onto the field via the lack of strategy that once was: Hit-and-runs. Sacrifice bunts. Stolen bases for a period of years, until MLB changed rules for the 2023 season to inject more action into what was becoming a stiflingly stationary game devoid of action, suffocated by the analytics movement. Where the seeds of victory once sprouted from the mind of a manager—the reason why the ballpark snapped and crackled for those great old Tom Kelly–Tony La Russa and Sparky Anderson–Billy Martin matchups—you win a game differently now: by lessening the odds of making outs, and by increasing probabilities in other ways.

When Kapler's predecessor in San Francisco, the decidedly old-school Bruce Bochy, was piloting the Giants to World Series titles in 2010, 2012, and 2014, he worked with what had been the standard in baseball for decades: six coaches. They were bench, hitting, pitching, first base, third base, and bullpen. By Bochy's final season in 2019 under Zaidi, the Giants had added an assistant hitting coach and, reflecting one significant change in the game, a "coach–video replay analyst" who aided in deciding when an umpire erred and the manager should ask for instant replay intervention.

The changes in San Francisco reflect the rapid-fire changes that have come to MLB in recent years. It is where computers, millennials, specialization, and changed media, including the rise and fall of regional sports networks, merge and intersect. Managers must be patient, nice guys. They must have a soft touch. How they communicate is as important—and often moreso—as the strategic part of a manager's toolbox. They are leading a generation of players who have grown up with travel ball and private coaches—and many players retreat to their private hitting and pitching gurus in the offseasons, which can complicate the job of a major-league staff when they return the next spring. Or even in-season, when a slumping hitter reaches for his cell phone to seek advice from his private hitting coach back home when he doesn't get immediate results from the instruction of the team hitting coaches.

"Where it's changed a little bit from the Lasordas and Billy Martins, that style of management was more telling than selling," Bochy says. "You told players, 'This is how it is.' Now, with how the game is being run, a lot of it is you have to sell what you're doing. For example, we're platooning, and this is why. Or this is why you're pitching four or five innings, because of your numbers the third time around the lineup. When I first started, we made the lineups and we made the changes without having to explain reasons to the player."

Throw in today's fractured political landscape and righteous social justice concerns, and there are more land mines both on and off the field than ever before. Kapler, in fact, wrote publicly on his *Kaplifestyle* blog in May 2022 that he was going to stop coming onto the field for the national anthem after one of the more recent school massacres, in Texas, because he was uncomfortable with the direction the country is headed. It was a far cry from when Billy Martin managed Oakland and in the spring of 1980 introduced newly acquired Glenn Burke to the team with a homophobic slur.

With many players revealing more of themselves personally than ever before via their own social media channels, Kapler, who was more prolific on *Kaplifestyle* in the years before he became a manager, gently treaded down that path, as well. But for a skipper, there are complications: the line between speaking for himself and representing the organization is somewhere between razor thin and nonexistent. While personal opinions about off-the-field events routinely are both given and demanded by so many others, it remains different for a manager. Always, he is on duty, even in his off-hours. Sometimes, even before he technically is on duty. When La Russa came back to manage the White Sox in 2021, one of the first things he had to do was talk to some of the team's Black leaders—Tim Anderson chief among them—to explain how his views of blackballed NFL quarterback Colin Kaepernick had evolved. During his hiatus from the game while he was retired, La Russa said that he thought Kaepernick and other athletes who knelt for the national anthem were disrespecting the flag, the country, and the anthem. His previous comments were immediately brought up when the Sox hired him five years later, and even before he spoke with his players, the organization made sure he was prepped at his introductory press conference.

"I know in 2016, when the first issue occurred, my initial instincts were all about respecting the flag and the anthem and what America stands for," La Russa said then. "A lot has gone on in a very healthy way since 2016, and not only do I respect but I applaud the awareness that has come into not just society but especially in sports.

"And what I'm learning more and more, like with the Players Alliance and especially with the White Sox, when your protests actually have action-oriented results, the way you are going to impact, make things better, I'm all for it. There is not a racist bone in my body. I do not like injustice...anything peacefully done and sincerely thought of and especially with an action at the end of it will not be a problem."

Addressing very public events about which he has a strong opinion always has come naturally to Kapler—until he became a manager. Both of his parents were educators, and they raised him to pay attention, understand society around him, and have a sharp worldview. So when he sees the steady flow of racial injustice, social injustice, and gun violence in today's world, he has sharp opinions. It can be argued that part of having a platform where an entire city hears you talk, as managers do, is not being down the middle about things. Yet organizations are designed, from baseball to restaurant chains to the Boy Scouts, in a manner in which leaders are discouraged from speaking up. Saying the wrong thing will lose customers, especially in these divisive times. And nobody wants that, whether you are the San Francisco Giants, the New York Yankees, or Disney World. In today's ferociously competitive entertainment market, you cannot risk alienating even a part of your fan base.

Before he was fired in San Francisco near the end of the 2023 season, Kapler ranged to the extreme of most managers sorting their way through today's cultural chasms. Kapler and Roberts ("Anything I say is going to affect this $4 billion machine") both spoke out on racial and social injustices, but the line behind them to do so wasn't exactly spilling around the block. Most others are not comfortable edging so close to that cliff. Blowback can be fierce and most don't want to deal with it, let alone bring unasked-for vitriol and negativity to the team. In fairness, Earl Weaver and Dick Williams in their day went nowhere near expounding on the president of the United States and his policies.

Things have become so much more complicated today. Big, sprawling, at times messy, informed with multicultural points of view… emblematic of the Giants' expanded coaching staff. Though some across the game are skeptical of many of Kapler's motives and methods—anything or anybody unique and out of the norm is a lightning rod for opinions in all walks of life—his reasoning behind this specific topic was deceptively simple and made all the sense in the world.

During his conversation with Zaidi, he likened it to the importance of having a healthy pupil-to-teacher ratio in school. The smaller the class size, the more the students benefit.

"And I thought, this isn't grade school, this is the major leagues," Zaidi told me, smiling, in the autumn of 2021 following San Francisco's 107-win season to eject the Dodgers from the NL West throne room (though the Dodgers soon would claw back and eliminate the Giants in a riveting Division Series).

But it made eminent sense. So instead of one hitting and one pitching coach, the Giants employed three each: a hitting coach, a director of hitting–assistant hitting coach, and an assistant hitting coach, and a pitching coach, a director of pitching, and an assistant pitching coach. They kept the traditional roles (bench-infield coach, and first- and third-base coaches) and added a nontraditional one (quality assurance coach). There was a bullpen-catching coach, plus two more assistant coaches, one of whom was Nakken. Notably, when the Giants replaced Kapler with the veteran Bob Melvin for the 2024 season, Nakken went through the interview process for manager—another first for a female—and then was retained as a member of Melvin's coaching staff.

Shortly after the Giants lapped everyone during one of the best NL West races in years, by 2022 thirteen teams were listing coaching staffs in double digits (not including the manager). Cincinnati matched the Giants with thirteen. The Phillies, Cubs, and Diamondbacks were at twelve each; the Red Sox and Angels were each at eleven. And by 2024? Copycatting across the game was nearly complete. Twenty-nine of the thirty clubs listed at least a double-digits number of coaches. The outlier was Washington, the cheapest club this side of Oakland, with eight. Even the lame-duck Athletics, who were Las Vegas bound, listed a game-high seventeen coaches.

There was a "lead strategist–bullpen catcher" in Kansas City (Parker Morin) under manager Matt Quatraro, a "strategy coach" (Danny Barnes) with the Mets under Carlos Mendoza, a "run prevention coordinator" in Milwaukee under Pat Murphy, a "Major League Coach, Data Development and Process" (Alex Smith) with the Cubs under Craig Counsell, an "assistant hitting coach–Integrated Performance Coach" (Tim LaMonte) in Cincinnati under David Bell in 2024, before staff changes led to LaMonte's firing, and a plethora of "bench coach–offensive coordinators." Never before have "teacher-pupil" ratios been so focused on individual attention at the major-league level. In an age of specialization, it makes sense. But some of these made-up titles and their accompanying corporate-speak also are distressing reminders that our pastoral game is moving far too close to the NFL in terms of volume, attitude, and overanalysis. As the late, great political columnist Mary McGrory once wrote of the country, "Baseball is what we were, and football is what we've become." She did not mean it as a compliment.

"Teams are paying a lot of attention to the support they can provide players and recognize that there are a lot more resources at our disposal as organizations than there were fifteen years ago," Chris Antonetti, Cleveland's longtime president of baseball operations, told me in the spring of 2021.

More often than not, as the old generation fades into the new, today's younger, modern managers desire all of it, too.

"Mark Kotsay came up in the analytics world as a player and, as a manager, he's been developed in that world to the point where, weirdly, they're now like, 'I want an analytics coach on the bench with me' instead of having an analytics guy be with them before the game or even every few series," says Beane, whose A's hired Kotsay when Bob Melvin left for San Diego in 2022. "Now, they want analytics guys with them full-time on the road. Whereas, before, it was seen as this sort of us vs. them."

———

In San Francisco, things fell apart between Kapler and the Giants just two seasons after that 107-win high-water mark. They went 81-81 for an encore in 2022 and then fell to 79-83 in 2023. Zaidi fired Kapler, forty-eight, with just three games left in the season. The axing came after a couple of players, notably ace Logan Webb, publicly complained about the direction of the team, with Webb remarking, "We have to make some big changes here to create that winning culture that we want to show up every single year and try to win the whole thing." Not directly addressed by the Giants but also of note: Following nine consecutive seasons of drawing three million or more fans, the franchise dropped to 2.7 million in 2019, Bochy's last season, 2.4 million in the 107-win season of 2022, and 2.5 million in 2023. The disconnect between the fans and the team appeared wider than any disconnect between the clubhouse and Kapler. Part of the attendance decline undoubtedly related to the rough, postpandemic times the city of San Francisco was suffering through, with a skyrocketing homeless population and with the city itself hollowed out by so much of the workforce now laboring from home. That meant less walkup to night games from those eager to finish their workdays with a meal in the city and a short walk to a beautiful ballpark to catch a ball game.

That the attendance decline also was related to the Giants' shrinking star power via a raggedy Scrabble-board lineup steeped in analytics clearly was evident, as well. Where the Giants once boasted A-listers like Barry Bonds, Tim Lincecum, Barry Zito, Madison Bumgarner, Matt Cain, and Brian Wilson, now the last vestiges of the World Series titles were a trio of gamers near the end of their careers: Buster Posey, Brandon Crawford, and Brandon Belt.

Kapler immediately was tasked with tackling the advice La Russa delivered to Matheny in St. Louis: There is nothing more difficult for a manager than handling a declining superstar. In particular, he moved Crawford into a platoon role following the shortstop's subpar 2019 during which he batted just .228 (.236 vs. left-handers) with a .304 on-base percentage. Both were career worsts for Crawford over an entire season but, at thirty-three, and with a changed swing heading into 2020, the shortstop felt he had earned the opportunity to at least start the season playing every day. Part of it with Crawford, Posey, and Belt in 2020 was "load management." Crawford in particular had some very tense discussions with Kapler behind the scenes.

"I had worked all offseason on a new swing and I'd been hitting well with it in spring training," Crawford says. "So my thing was, give me the benefit of the doubt. I've hit lefties in the past, I have a new swing, let me at least try it before we talk about platooning. The more analytical thinking was we're going to play the righty against lefty pitchers. And coming off of '19, I didn't have a very good year and then 2020 was [a pandemic-shortened sixty-game season] so they were thinking that every game matters more in a sixty-game season. So there were reasons on both sides, and that's why we went back and forth on it. And fortunately, I kind of played my way into more playing time. I definitely commend Kap on having those discussions even if there were discussions I didn't want to have with him."

As the stars faded away, it was clear when Zaidi replaced Brian Sabean as San Francisco's top baseball man that the Giants were diving far deeper into analytics, and on many nights the Giants' lineup became an anonymous rotation of who's-thats and never-heard-of-hims.

"When I saw four utility guys starting on Opening Day, I was doing the pregame and postgame show in San Francisco, and on Twitter I said that the Russians have hacked the Giants' computers," says Tim Flannery, who served Bochy as a coach on all three World Series–winning teams and played in the majors for eleven seasons. "Farhan immediately calls me. I told him, 'I'm all with you, man, I'm totally with you. But I'm a utility player, and if I'm playing on Opening Day, there's something fishy going on. I played ten Opening Days and I started only one. I'm a utility player. You're not giving guys rests already.' He was pissed, but he laughed his ass off."

That was on Bochy's last Opening Day in San Francisco, in 2019. The star power only lessened as the Giants swung and missed at Bryce Harper, Aaron Judge, Trea Turner, Shohei Ohtani, and many others in recent winters on the free agent market. And given the direction of the game and the reduction of the onetime strong manager to the role of middle manager, you cannot name one manager today whose hire or presence will affect ticket sales. As compared to when installing Billy Martin as skipper gave the Twins and A's immediate and noticeable bumps at the box office.

No doubt, Kapler paid for some of this as the Giants sank into a malaise that went far deeper than simply his managing of the ball club. But this all falls under the New Normal as some organizations long ago figured out the Information Age while others are discovering that it is not simply a magic trick, and a quick expansion of the analytics department alone does not guarantee wins. With all thirty clubs subscribing to analytics to varying degrees today…well, not everybody can win. Some clubs still have to finish below .500.

"I don't think we fully understand as an industry how to use all of the technology and data that we have now," Kapler says. "We're still trying to figure all of that out. As a manager, needing a front office to get me all in on the information train, or asking have you checked out this new technology train, personally speaking, I didn't need that. I was naturally interested myself. I still think there are managers around the game, and definitely when I came up, who didn't appreciate the level of engagement and then weren't comfortable with or interested in using the new technologies and applying data to their decision-making and player evaluation. It's about style, it's about curiosity, and, I cannot stress this enough, as I evolve and change and grow as a manager, I am more inclined to listen to a less progressive, more traditional, more intuitive style of front office, manager, or player than I ever have been."

Much of that comes from his own experiences. Kapler's first managing job came in Philadelphia in 2018. He was forty-two, brash and not too far away from his playing days (he retired after the 2010 season). The Phillies led Atlanta on his very first Opening Day 5–0 in the sixth, when he yanked starter Aaron Nola after only sixty-eight pitches, a decision that backfired badly as the Braves roared back to win 8–5. Nola told reporters afterward that he had plenty left, and other players were surprised at the move. It was a horrible first impression that, despite some good moments along the way, set the tone for a rocky two seasons and out in Philadelphia.

"Some of the mistakes I made early on were just managing too aggressively," says Kapler. He adds that while he had solid reasons behind the move, he would do things differently knowing what he now knows because on that Opening Day stage, the quick move with Nola "was surprising. And when something is surprising and aggressive, it doesn't work. People feel like it's a gut punch."

Though his time in Philadelphia was brief, Kapler fared better in his two seasons there than you might remember, finishing 80-82 and then 81-81. But Philadelphia and the East Coast is tough. Already suspicious of Kapler's New Age methods—the *Kaplifestyle* blog, for example, was well known when he started in Philadelphia—it was not a place willing to wait and watch a new manager grow into his cleats.

"Gabe was a good manager for us," says Andy MacPhail, Philadelphia's team president at the time. "Matt Klentak, our GM, didn't want to fire him and neither did I. At the end of the day, John Middleton insisted on it, and that was his right as he owned the team. Gabe managed the talent level as much as you could expect. The first year there, the club improved fourteen games."

In each of his seasons of managing in both Philadelphia and San Francisco, Kapler's teams finished with better records than the preseason computer projections. Yet he was fired twice, another example of the inexact nature of the job, especially in today's world.

"I was a fan, but what I didn't understand was just how bad a fit it was with Philly, and that's what John understood—he's a Philly guy," MacPhail says. "In some respects in Philly, Gabe brought it on himself. He went overboard in praising players even when it was clear they didn't have a good game. He was way too positive, so the ultimate outcome is the press knowing he's going to be super-positive and walking into that interview room loaded with negative questions. It got to be too much, and it was hurting his credibility with the media and fans even though he knew bloody well what was going on. He thought he was protecting the players. Finally, I had dinner with him and said, 'Gabe, you're going to say Jake Arrieta was good and the media is going to go to Arrieta and he's going to say, "I sucked."'"

San Francisco appeared to be a perfect fit to start, Kapler being a West Coast native. His progressive thinking matched the Bay Area's progressive ways, as did his interest in analytics, and he had a preexisting relationship with Zaidi from when they both worked for the Dodgers. But as Kapler will be the first to tell you, while certain managers' personalities may be a better match with certain cities, the bottom line for a manager is still this: If you win, you fit in anywhere.

"The most important experiences I've had were as the farm director of the Dodgers," Kapler says during a conversation in a San Diego coffee shop about a month before he was fired in the summer of 2023.

"Although Philadelphia, and to some degree, every moment that passes is teaching us all lessons, right? The one that stands out to me is my time as farm director of the Dodgers. In my first year doing it, I thought I knew exactly what needed to be done to change player development with the Dodgers. That meant, essentially, turning the page and bringing player development into another era by becoming more progressive, more analytical, more data driven.

"In doing so, I think I came at it in a pretty cold way. That meant blowing past some of that really rich experience that a lot of the staff in player development had had. It meant just making moves, making changes, and not listening first. I don't think I was really hearing people out. I felt like I had a lot of answers, and I didn't. I started making changes very quickly, and sometimes things need to happen more slowly."

It is why Kapler strongly believes diversity of background, race, socioeconomic upbringing, and perspective is crucial for baseball operations staffs and managers today. It is a competitive advantage, he believes, "in how we make decisions and how we apply our experiences. I think if you get, let's say, ten people in a room trying to solve a problem and all ten are very data-driven, very progressive, and very cut-and-dried," then you end up missing something because every one of them is studying the issue from the same vantage point.

It plays into the big, wide, diverse coaching staff that he and the Giants built together. It plays into competition. It plays into life.

"Sometimes we call that application of experience as gut instinct or intuition when, really, it's a collection of things you've seen over a long period of time and you're using that to try and get the best outcome by making the best decision," he says. "I just don't think problem-solving—and that's really what organizations are, they're solving problems, with one vantage point from the progressive, analytical, traditional—is the best way to win baseball games. That's how I've evolved."

After six seasons of managing during which he guided his teams to a very respectable 456-411 (.526) overall record, Kapler in the winter of 2023–2024 decided to bring those ideas to the Marlins in another of his career reinventions: He was named as Miami's assistant general manager. Whether he goes back into uniform to manage again, stay tuned. Things change rapidly today, with people and organizations both evolving more quickly than ever.

———

In a consignment store in Sacramento, California, in the summer of 2022, a dog slowly ambles around greeting customers, lolls about behind the cash register, and is generally being irresistible. The boxer's name tag reads "Bochy," and it belongs, of course, to the shop's owner—one of the legions of Giants fans in the area and, in particular, a fan of the world champion manager.

"His name is Bochy, or Boch," the shop owner says, offering a choice for the multi-threat pooch, before wryly adding, "But we call him Bruce when he's bad."

Bruce Bochy has been many things throughout his nearly five decades in the game: four-time World Series winner, future Hall of Famer, beloved teammate, respected manager, cult hero, and much more. And yes, he's had dozens and dozens of people tell him that they've named their dogs after him. But he himself rarely has been bad.

Despite the fact that they are on your local television and radio airwaves far more than any of their predecessors, most of today's milquetoast managers wouldn't inspire a ferret to be named after them, let alone man's best friend. And it did not go unnoted as the 2023 postseason played out that, as so many other inexperienced, flavor-of-the-month managers came and went, the sturdy veterans Bochy and Dusty Baker matched up against each other in the ALCS. In the end, Texas eliminated Houston. It was an inspirational story all the way through with Bochy: Following three years of "retirement," he was lured back by one of his former pitchers, Chris Young, now the president of baseball operations for the Texas Rangers, and he led Texas to its first-ever World Series title in his first year back.

Only three managers in history now have won more World Series than Bochy: Casey Stengel (seven), Joe McCarthy (seven), and Connie Mack (five). Walter Alston, Joe Torre, and Bochy are next at four each.

It was the founder of Facebook, Mark Zuckerberg, who famously advised in an interview with *Business Insider* years ago to "move fast and break things. Unless you are breaking stuff, you are not moving fast enough." He was speaking on the topic of innovation in business, and he was speaking the language of Silicon Valley. Zuckerberg founded Facebook in his Harvard dormitory room in 2004 and, like so many cocksure entrepreneurs, he had swag and a blithe view of norms. "Disruptive innovation" was the buzz phrase used throughout so much of business—particularly in Silicon Valley—over the first couple of decades of this century, and it swept across the corners of baseball, too. It was evident in the changes in the way the game was played on the field, in the new look in managers' offices, and in the willingness of management to move quickly to dismantle methods of doing things—some of them tried-and-true—that had lasted one hundred or more years in the game.

The departures of Bochy and Brian Sabean, San Francisco's former general manager, from the Giants organization are illustrative of the whiplike changes that continue to occur in today's game. Until 2010, the Giants had not won a World Series in the Bay Area since moving from New York to San Francisco in 1958. After winning three in five years, there was a time in this game when the two would have been given lifetime contracts and been allowed to stick around as long as they wanted. But that time was not now, not in an age of, yes, disruptive innovation. Sabean stepped back, took a role upstairs, and ceded day-to-day baseball operations to Bobby Evans for the 2015 season—then was marginalized in 2019 when the Giants named

Zaidi as their president of baseball operations. With no give-and-take and almost never asked for any input whatsoever, the man who lorded over the organization for eighteen years as general manager, the longest such tenure in club history, left to take a job as a special adviser to Brian Cashman with the Yankees.

The impersonal numbers revolution led Sabean to a point where he no longer even roots for the Giants, he told the *Krueg Show* podcast in October 2023, as Bochy's legend was expanding in Texas. Furthermore, he said of Bochy's "retirement" in San Francisco in 2019, "He did not go out on his own terms. The whole world knows that."

Zaidi denies that Bochy was pushed out, and Bochy maintains that his relationship with Zaidi always has been good. It was different, of course, in that Sabean was a lot like Bochy's longtime boss in San Diego, the late Kevin Towers. Both men were old-school, direct, and swashbuckling. So is Bochy. The Giants used analytics under Sabean—I can still remember him muttering pointedly in the dugout before a postseason game that San Francisco is so close to Silicon Valley and what do people think, the Giants are so stupid as to not take advantage of that? We use analytics, Sabean said then. We just don't advertise it like the A's do. By the time a few years passed and Zaidi took charge, of course, the numbers trickle had become a full-blown avalanche.

"The best way I can say it is, it wasn't in the front yard, it was a little more in the backyard," Bochy says of analytics in the pre-Zaidi days. "Now the balance of that has changed so much. The decisions now, for the most part with these clubs, are data driven. That's just the way it is. Even a lot of coaching has to do with the information you can get through analytics. The biggest difference was the information I was provided."

During the Giants' three World Series runs, Bochy recalls, he met with Sabean and Dick Tidrow, the former pitcher who had a brilliant mind and had become Sabean's top adviser.

"We would talk about the game and, of course, we had information from advance scouts," Bochy says. "I didn't have that when I first started managing. It evolved quite a bit there from '95 through 2010, let's say. You had your advance scouts, but we had more data. They were sending us information down to help us making decisions. Now, they weren't driving every decision. It's just a case of, hey, the world's changing and so you have to adapt how you do things. Getting more information is going to help you adapt.

"With that said, your leadership has changed, too, because you don't have the authoritarian type of manager quite like you used to, the Dick Williamses, the Billy Martins. There's more balance with decision-making from the front office on down to the manager and coaches."

And has that made Bochy's job easier, harder, or both?

"Great question," he says. "I think at times a little bit of both. Why I'm saying that is because you welcome the information because we were all used to doing it ourselves. We all used to have our own spray charts. I remember after games getting out the colored pencils and charting where hitters hit the ball. Every hitter had his own spray chart. We did that on our own. Every hitter versus every pitcher. Now, everything is available to you, you hit a button and pull up BATS, Tru-Media, or whatever.

"But the other side is, managers now are scrutinized a little more because there is information out there on every decision made and you're going with your instincts on how a pitcher is throwing. Let's say you don't walk a guy intentionally but the numbers say you should. You're more open to criticisms now than ever."

TruMedia advertises that it "integrates MLB's Statcast data for MLB clubs and provides them with turnkey product that allows them to analyze the data using key metrics and custom visualizations, many of which were developed by TruMedia's Analytics team." According to the company, twenty-one MLB clubs in 2021 and "several major media organizations" licensed TruMedia's analytics platform, which provides teams and media the ability to "quickly analyze multiple data sources within one intuitive user interface."

Where three or four analysts were doing "the lion's share of the work" during the first part of Bochy's tenure with the Giants, "by the time I retired we probably had a dozen. Now, you have clubs with twenty or thirty analysts. Teams have bought into it so much." But the trick, and what's changed over time, is to boil down all of the information into bite-size pieces that the players can digest.

"I still remember the first advance report we got," Bochy says of what in the early days essentially was a novella. "Buster Posey came into my office and said, 'I'm supposed to read this before every series?' We talked, and then they condensed it into two or three sheets of paper."

Beyond that, the analysts weigh in during trade negotiations. They study the amateur draft, breaking down which pitchers and hitters are controlling the strike zone to the nth degree.

"It used to be batting average, then it was OPS [on-base percentage plus slugging], then slugging, and now they've got so many I don't even know what some of them are," Bochy says.

Two things are instructive here. This is a manager who continues to lead his teams to World Series titles. And this is a manager who always has wanted every piece of information he could acquire.

Case in point: Theo Epstein, then twenty-eight, was a young executive cutting his teeth as San Diego's director of baseball operations in April 2001, when the Padres, off to a poor 6-11 start, were in Los Angeles facing a sweep following a tough loss on Saturday night. Epstein, at the time, was wading into the shallow end of the analytics pool.

"We had a real small early analytics department at the Padres," he says. "It was just a couple of guys sort of mixing in some numbers in addition to our other responsibilities."

They would look at righty-lefty splits, how some of the Padres' hitters fared against four-seam, fly ball pitchers vs. two-seam, ground ball pitchers, that sort of thing. Bochy showed interest, so Epstein would hand him a chart before each series.

After the Saturday night game in Dodger Stadium, with a then-healthy and formidable Darren Dreifort slated to face the Padres the next day, a young and still-raw Epstein was in Bochy's office reviewing the latest loss.

"We're getting our asses kicked, he's in a bad mood, and I brought up a split, maybe a lineup tweak he might want to make based on the numbers," Epstein says. "We had a great relationship, still do. But that night he goes, 'Tomorrow, fuck, you think this is that easy, *you* just make up the lineup.'"

Epstein apologized for overstepping, immediately realizing in the raw emotions of another loss, he should have done a better job of reading the room. "I should have waited for a better time," he told the manager.

"Well, fuck, what I'm doing isn't working so you fucking do it," Bochy responded. "You make up the lineup."

"You're serious?" Epstein asked.

"Yes."

So Epstein went to work that night, ran some numbers, and made some changes. He put a speedy outfielder, Santiago Perez, in the leadoff slot. Moved the outfielder Mike Darr to second from fifth. He handed his lineup to Bochy. The manager glanced at it and said, "All right, this is what we're going with."

"So I'm sitting in the scouts' section at Dodger Stadium that Sunday afternoon and here we go," Epstein says. "First inning, one-two-three. Second inning, one-two-three. Third inning, one-two-three. Fourth inning, one-two-three. Fifth inning, one-two-three. Dreifort's got a fucking perfect game.

"Boch keeps looking over at me and shaking his head and staring at me. I'm trying to avoid his eye contact. I'm dying on the inside. We ended up winning the game, but we were getting dominated."

It took eleven innings, but the Padres won 7–6. Bubba Trammell belted an RBI double in the eleventh that held as the winning run.

"We laughed about it after the game," Epstein says. "It was an early example of all of these good-natured tension moments between the front office putting its hand on the scale a little bit on some lineup stuff based on numbers and a manager, especially at that point, who knew more about baseball in his pinky finger than I did then or probably ever will."

More than two decades later, Bochy absolutely remembers that afternoon.

"First of all, we're all working together," he says. "You know, I'll work with anybody as long as we're working together. We all want to win, so I'll have some fun with it. Obviously, I wasn't doing too good a job at the time."

Bochy pauses and, with a wry grin, reveals that that wasn't the last time he told a smart front-office staffer to write the lineup himself.

"I did it with Larry Baer in San Francisco," Bochy says, eyes twinkling, of the Giants president. "He gave me a lineup once when we were in Oakland. But he forgot to put a DH in there, so I had to fire him."

Bochy figured when he stepped away at sixty-four following the 2019 season that he probably was finished. But as much as he enjoyed retirement in the Nashville area, with the grandkids nearby, the fishing excellent, and plenty of time to savor good wine, he missed the competition. There were very few jobs that he would have taken, and the plethora of hires that made major-league managing look increasingly like an entry-level job was insulting.

"I'll be honest, there have been a couple of hires where I even raised my eyebrows with the decision," he says. "But you also understand now where the game is going. A lot of the decisions are dictated by analytics, so teams are looking for somebody who, first of all, you still have somebody to keep harmony with the club and someone to be able to work with the front office and analysts and is going to be OK with the analysts driving most of the decisions that are made on the field."

When Texas reached out, Bochy knew it would not be that way. In Young, the Rangers top baseball executive, and his special assistant

Nick Hundley, Bochy saw two men who once played for him in San Diego and, accordingly, understood his methodology and his skills. Young flew to Nashville first on what essentially was a recruiting mission and spent seven hours talking baseball with his old manager. Texas owner Ray Davis flew out a couple of days later for more hours of conversation. They laid out both the support they would have for Bochy—spending big money on pitching that winter, hiring a skilled coaching staff, and, yes, providing him with plenty of analytical information. But they also promised to afford him plenty of latitude to manage as he wanted. He trusted them enough to accept. In his first year, it worked out far beyond what anybody could have imagined.

Now, despite what the Zuckerbergs of the world say, disrupt things too quickly, and, while some good may come of it, unintended consequences, chaos, and bad things also emerge. The Giants broke things. Bochy won. The Giants with Bob Melvin in 2024 were beginning anew with their second manager in the post-Bochy era. Bochy in 2023 won it all in his first year back for Texas. Though Melvin and Zaidi had a good, comfortable working relationship from their years together in Oakland, the move in San Francisco also is an admission that maybe a more experienced hand at the helm matters.

In Major League Baseball, the question of whether things ever will swing back to the more traditional-style manager is always hanging in the air. The successes of Bochy, Dusty Baker, and Brian Snitker in the years from 2021 to 2023 begs that question even more. While the New Normal remains, replacing veterans such as Terry Francona and Buck Showalter with a wet-behind-the-ears Stephen Vogt or the raw Carlos Mendoza—both big, attractive pieces of clay just waiting to be molded—it has been old-school managers steeped in decades of experience who guided their teams to three consecutive World Series wins before the Yankees' Aaron Boone and the Dodgers' Dave Roberts met in the 2024 World Series.

Besides pliability, there is one other enormous driving force that leads organizations to tilt toward hiring neophytes to manage.

Money.

MLB managers generally are and have been criminally underpaid, and the steady influx of inexperienced hires is one avenue toward keeping it that way.

At the peak of his time with the Yankees in 2008, Joe Torre earned $7.5 million annually in salary. Fifteen years later, according to research from my lifelong friend and former colleague Bob Nightengale of *USA Today*, the winningest manager in Dodgers history, Dave Roberts, was earning less than half of that at $3.25 million.

In fact, until Craig Counsell leveraged his free agency into an eight-year, $40 million deal in leaving Milwaukee and taking over the Chicago Cubs, there were only six managers guaranteed to earn at least $3 million in 2024: Bochy, Melvin, Showalter, Roberts, Boston's Alex Cora, and Washington's Dave Martinez. And Showalter was collecting that from the sidelines after his firing. His replacement, rookie manager Carlos Mendoza, signed a three-year deal worth $4.5 million total, barely half of what Showalter made annually. In today's landscape, that's a win-win for both manager and team: Mendoza was able to land his first managerial job, and the Mets were able to significantly reduce that line item on their overall budget.

Compare all of this with the top 2023 salaries in the NFL (New England's Bill Belichick, who at the time was at $20 million annually), NBA (Detroit's Monty Williams, $13.05 million), college football (Alabama's Nick Saban, $11.4 million before his retirement), college basketball (Kentucky's John Calipari, $8.5 million), and NHL (Los Angeles's Todd McLellan, $5 million), and it is embarrassing. Especially when you toss in the fact that these managers are the frontmen for their organizations, with Counsell still shaking his head at the incredulity of his professional peers when he was in Milwaukee—the Packers and Bucks coaches—who could not believe his staggering media commitments in isolation, let alone everything else that is a part of his job. Even when Boston awarded Alex Cora a three-year extension worth more than $7 million per season on July 24, 2024, while joining Counsell in raising the bar for modern manager salaries, it still fell far short of the top coach salaries in other sports.

When Snitker managed Atlanta to its first World Series title in twenty-six years in 2021, he earned just $1.2 million. In 2023, six MLB managers earned less than $1 million in salary, and fifteen earned $1.75 million or less. Even many college baseball coaches earn more: According to USA Today Sports' research in 2023, there were ten college managers earning $1.2 million or more annually, topped by Vanderbilt's Tim Corbin ($2.47 million).

Despite MLB revenues checking in at around a record $11 billion, manager salaries are shrinking—both in the long view and recently. In 2018, three managers earned $6 million a year: Bochy in San Francisco, the Angels' Mike Scioscia, and the Cubs' Joe Maddon.

Some blame ever-swelling analytics departments for gobbling up outsized pieces of the financial pie and leaving less for managers. Indeed, baseball operations staffs have increased in sheer volume over the past decade or so. Where there once was a general manager, now there is a president of baseball operations, generally with two or three special assistants, followed by a general manager and more assistants in organizational flow charts. That's one factor. Another is, in an age of specialization, salaries for pitching and hitting coaches have increased and another financial pressure point is the expansion in coaching staffs via sheer numbers. Instead of one pitching coach and one hitting coach, today there are at least two and often three of each.

"So when you think about your overall cost of running your coaching staff, I don't think we're spending less today than we were in 1999, for example," says one high-ranking executive with a National League team who declined to speak publicly on the topic. "Less might be going to the manager, but the pie has gotten bigger."

The executive refutes the idea that stagnant manager salaries are a result of the industry devaluing decisions being made on the field. Over the past fifty years or so, he says, "I would argue that revenue and payroll had a pretty reasonable correlation. What we know right now is, baseball revenues are at an all-time high. So, as an owner, you want somebody who understands fiscal responsibility and fiscal management skills, because all of a sudden, when you're adding an extra column or more zeroes, the importance of how you think about decision-making is critical on the business front."

Indeed, just as the pay gap between CEOs and the typical worker in the United States has widened significantly, key executives who keep the owners' fiscal house in order are paid handsomely, too. In 2022, according to the Economic Policy Institute, CEOs were paid 344 times as much as a typical worker, in contrast to 1965, when they were paid twenty-one times as much as a typical worker. Similarly, there was a time in the game when it was not uncommon for a field manager to earn more than a general manager. Those days are long gone. Andrew Friedman, the Dodgers' president of baseball operations who is believed to be the game's highest-paid executive, earns a reported $10 million annually.

Regardless, baseball managers historically have been underpaid, and they are reminded of this every time they glance over to another sport and see a new coach's contract there. And Counsell, for one, does not think it has anything to do with extra money getting funneled to analytics departments or to baseball operations officials or to coaching staffs.

"With the league in general, manager salaries have not risen comparative to other sports," Counsell told me during an extended conversation at the winter meetings in San Diego in December 2022, as he headed into what would be his free agency walk year in Milwaukee. "But I don't think it's a function of baseball operations."

What it is, Counsell explained, "is just contract structure. There's very few free agent managers."

And fewer still are the *desirable* free agent managers. The list is loaded with those who have been fired and are hoping for a second or third chance. Rare is it that a winning manager, like Counsell, works through the end of his deal and then can test the free agent waters while at the top of both his game and earning potential.

When he became one of the hottest free agent skippers in recent years following the 2023 season, he leveraged it into a record-setting deal with the Cubs. There were strong hints that he would leave Milwaukee, but conventional wisdom had him following David Stearns to the New York Mets. The two had worked beautifully together with Milwaukee's limited resources to squeeze more out of several Brewers teams than reasonably could have been expected. But when his contract expired after the 2023 season, Stearns was wooed by Steven A. Cohen, the Mets' owner, to run baseball operations there. With Counsell also free, the Cubs, quarterbacked by Jed Hoyer, their president of baseball operations, moved to strike quietly and quickly. The result was a stunning deal for one of the game's best and most respected managers. And maybe it was no coincidence that not long after the Cubs snapped him up, one of Counsell's biggest managerial influences, Jim Leyland, was voted into the Hall of Fame.

"He just had this wonderful sense of patience, patience, patience," Counsell says. "It was the right time to do things. I always felt he had patience and then, oh, yeah, *that's* why he did that. The game would unfold for him and he had the right strategic move to play when he needed it.

"On the other side, so many people are confused today, they think a manager's job is 90 percent strategy and it's not. It's probably the other way. Managing people is the bigger part of your job, and the strategy part is a smaller part."

Two things remain vivid from his playing days that continue to influence the way he does things today. In Colorado in 1997, after he had played in just four major-league games, the Rockies traded Counsell to the Marlins in July. Counsell did not know then—Colorado manager Don Baylor well because, as he said, "I was, like, the thirty-fifth player on the team," yet the manager sat him down to explain the trade. It was the opposite of most deals. Usually, young players are sent to lousy teams where there is more playing time. The Marlins were loaded and headed for the playoffs.

"He crystallized it a little for me, thankfully," says Counsell, who would score the winning run in the bottom of the eleventh inning of Game 7 of that year's thrilling World Series to win it for Florida. "I was naive to the whole thing. It wasn't long, but that little bit put me at ease. A lot of times, that's a small snippet of what you do as a manager. You help put a player's mind at ease so he can go out and perform."

Melvin, Counsell's manager in Arizona, was the first person who explained why, from a manager's perspective, he made some of the moves he made. It intrigued Counsell's already inquisitive mind. Too, Melvin influenced Counsell on how to allow a player certain freedoms.

"It doesn't mean I could do whatever I want," Counsell says. "He was still boss. But a great example was, we were playing Kansas City one day with Zack Greinke on the mound. We were doing the advance scouting meeting. Bob came in and gave a talk about, hey, this is a really, really good young pitcher. I kind of interrupted him and said something to the effect of, 'This is bullshit. So we don't have a chance today, huh? Skip, we're not going to beat this guy? We're going to *crush* this guy.' He was really mad at me. I don't blame him. I don't know why I did it. We won the game, we crushed Greinke, and then after the game he called me into his office and yelled at me again."

Melvin smiles, his memory of the incident a little different: "He popped his head in my office after the game and asked, 'Are we good?' And then we talked some more."

"He yelled at me, but he also kind of respected me because he understood what I did," Counsell says. "He wasn't emotional enough not to accept why I did it. I wanted us to believe we could beat the guy.

So he gave me that back. And I think that's what managing is. The guy is the boss, but he's not always right. I respect him, he respects me, and he gives me the freedom to go out and be the best player I can be. That's how I think it works. But I don't believe the manager is always right. I don't believe that. Although he told me he didn't like it, he was actually listening to me, too. Maybe that's how managing has changed, in the era of Earl Weaver it was more this is how it works. But you can be successful at this and have it be a two-way street with your players. Because we have players with brilliant baseball minds. I'm not above that. And I learn from them. That's probably where I would say if the job has changed a little, it's right there."

What Counsell argues has not changed is the players. It is a unique and refreshing point of view in today's world because the typical take of most in the game who are north of fifty years old is that the players today are different, they're more self-absorbed, they don't listen, and they are more difficult to reach.

"I don't like the notion that players are different today," Counsell says. "I really don't think they are. I think that's wrong. Players today have the same dreams. The bond to their teammates is the same. We all have more information at our fingertips, and that's not always good."

Modern players, Counsell says, simply have "different things that you have to help them with. They have different stimuli you have to be concerned about, like social media. It's maybe a different set of problems than maybe tripped-up players of my generation."

As great and convenient as today's devices are, Counsell points out, "they are dangerous devices, and instead of the media being one voice now the media is millions of voices. And that's challenging."

He does not address social media in any sort of teamwide talk, but he keeps his antennae up all summer, especially when he sees a struggling player or a noticeable mood change.

"You give them credit," he says. "If you've made it into a major-league clubhouse in spring training, you're pretty sharp, man.

You've navigated a lot of potholes in your career. You've got your head on pretty straight."

At the same time, when a player is clearly bothered by something or perhaps when a coach approaches Counsell and says so-and-so is particularly down today, the manager is ready to move.

"There are no rules for that," he says. "There aren't. That's why communication, I think, is a tougher skill to get a handle on who's good and who's not good at it. There are no set parameters to me when this player needs to be picked up and when he needs to be pushed. There's not a playbook there. You've got to feel it."

CHAPTER 10

THE NEW RULES

What the Digital Age has given in terms of big data and instant replay, the Digital Age has taken away in terms of the emotion and the soul of the game. Managers rarely put on a show arguing with umpires anymore because they can simply call for replay. Home-plate collisions have been legislated out of the game as catchers no longer are allowed to block the plate. The wipeout slide at second base to break up a potential double play is out. A player on a hot streak may nevertheless find himself on the bench simply because a computer doesn't like a matchup with that evening's pitcher.

The end result is that the New Normal emanating from the New Rules, in many instances, makes for a softer, less edgy, less emotional, and more robotic game.

Some new rules were installed simply because with contracts having soared to today's heights, the powers that be don't want the rough-and-tumble game that baseball once was so that expensive superstars don't get hurt. Others were installed because of pace-of-play issues.

"They've taken a lot of strategy out of the game," acknowledges Bochy, the former catcher who took his share of collisions at the plate and also was managing San Francisco when he lost his catcher for an extended period of time—and by the next season the so-called Buster Posey Rule eliminating home-plate collisions was in place. "The rule where your pitcher has to face a minimum of three hitters, that changed the game. The biggest game changer in the NL was when they brought in the DH. That changed a lot because a lot of your moves with pitchers were dictated on whether he was coming up to bat and you're down a run or two in the fifth."

Economics and an overall paucity of pitching have removed pinch-hit specialists. Used to be, teams got by with nine-man pitching staffs. Now, it's twelve or thirteen, which limits the number of bench players on a roster. Furthermore, in most cases for all but the richest teams, clubs choose to carry younger players on the bench because they are cheaper. The legendary pinch-hitters such as Manny Mota (Dodgers), Terry Crowley (Orioles), and Gates Brown (Tigers) are few and far between anymore.

Mark Sweeney, who ranks second all-time with 175 pinch hits (Lenny Harris leads with 212), carved out a fourteen-year career with this skill. Though he had no idea what his future held when he was young, breaking in under La Russa in St. Louis helped shape him.

"He was the most nerve-racking manager because he would take chances at random times," Sweeney says. "He wanted to be a mystery as a manager. And one time he caught me without knowing where my bat, batting gloves, and helmet were. The story resonates with me to this day because of how nervous I was when I went up there. I'm going into the batter's box scared that my manager knows I wasn't ready."

Never again, through stops in San Diego, Cincinnati, Milwaukee, Colorado, and Los Angeles, did Sweeney allow that to happen. That moment made enough of an impression on him that he always paid close attention to his managers, what they were doing, and what their next moves were going to be. For a pinch-hitter, it was a survival skill.

"Tony knew everything, and you knew he had the pulse of everything going on around him," Sweeney says. "If you were taking grounders during batting practice, you had a feeling that he was watching you. He gave the sense of, I don't know if it was fear, there was some of that probably, but there was also an awareness he had that most managers don't have. I actually thanked him at the end of my career. I said, 'Thank you for molding and giving me the structure to adapt to all kinds of different managers.'"

The infamous brushback pitches or beanballs that were commonplace with Bob Gibson, Don Drysdale, Sal "the Barber" Maglie, and so many others from the black-and-white-television generation, thankfully, are a relic of a bygone era. Umpires, some more jumpy than others, are encouraged by the commissioner's office today to issue warnings at the very first hint of trouble with an inside pitch before anything has even started. Given today's hard throwers, most of the time—but not always—the game is better off to be proactive rather than reactive.

It certainly has reduced many of the beloved-by-some, hated-by-others bench-clearing brawls that gave managers another platform to deliver blood-oath loyalty to their players. Though, truthfully, the game probably couldn't have withstood many more brawls like in the Padres-Braves game in Atlanta on August 12, 1984, during which seventeen players were ejected. It was so ugly that injured Braves third baseman Bob Horner, who was watching the game from the press box, stormed down to join the fisticuffs for the second or third round of an afternoon of persistent guerilla warfare. Things deteriorated so badly that plate umpire John McSherry at one point ordered all remaining players who had not been ejected to clear the benches and bullpens and watch the game from the clubhouse until they were needed, at which point the manager would designate someone to summon them. Kurt Bevacqua was hit by a beer while standing in the dugout during one of the skirmishes and charged into the stands.

Two future Hall of Famers were managing that day, Atlanta's Joe Torre and San Diego's Dick Williams. Williams wound up suspended for ten days and fined $10,000; Torre was suspended for three days and fined $1,000. As is the case with many brawls, the seeds were planted by an incident earlier in the series. The Padres had a big lead and Alan Wiggins kept working to lay down bunts. Atlanta starter Pascual Perez was charting pitches in the dugout and, along with many of his teammates, became increasingly angry with Wiggins's attempts.

So on Sunday afternoon, Wiggins stepped in to bat and Perez hit him with the first pitch. Most everyone expected that and Wiggins took first. But when Perez came to bat in the second inning, Padres starter Ed Whitson tried to hit him and missed. Then, during Perez's at bat in the fourth, Whitson tried to hit him three more times. The entire afternoon devolved into an ugly beanball war. Atlanta police stood atop each dugout for the final few innings.

Afterward, Torre told reporters, "Dick Williams is an idiot. Spell that with a capital *I* and a small *w*."

Retorted Williams: "At least he's learning how to spell better."

"I don't remember the quote, but I'll tell you, I don't doubt anything," Torre says today, chuckling. "That damn game probably was the longest one of my life. It went all the way into the eighth inning when I brought in Donnie Moore. I told him, 'We need to win this game, just get this guy.' He looked me in the eye, and when I went back to the dugout, I said, uh-oh, no chance."

Moore drilled the first batter he faced, Graig Nettles, earning ejections for both himself and Torre, who had been warned by the umpires several innings earlier.

"That was torture," Torre says. "It was really torture."

Wouldn't you know it, when the Yankees hired Torre to manage in 1996, Williams had landed in the organization as a special adviser to Steinbrenner.

"After my first meeting with the team, he came up to me to tell me how much he thought it was a great meeting," Torre says. "Baseball, the one thing about it, it's just like arguing with the umpires. Once you leave the day and come back the next, it's all brand-new."

Much of the emotion, unfortunately, now has transferred out of the game and onto social media. As Counsell says, he does not issue any teamwide proclamations for social media because if a player is skilled enough to make it to the majors, he's generally smart enough to navigate social media. But perhaps this is the one area where instead of managers needing to make sure they have the backs of their players, on many occasions maybe it is the players who need to rise up and show their manager that they can reciprocate the favor.

"You've always had to have thick skin to manage," Bochy says. "You can't get caught up in it. We're probably like the guy who wins the presidency—half the people like you, half don't. You could get caught up reading social media and because you had a bad day, you're reading all about how bad you are. Bobby Cox gave me probably the best advice I could get when I started managing. He said, 'Bruce, if there's any advice I can give you, don't listen to the talk shows. People call in and say do this, don't do that, they're not going to like you. Do it your way.'"

October is the worst time on social media for managers because even those fans who don't bother watching baseball until the playoffs become instant pitching experts and, increasingly in today's Conference Room Managing era, have little understanding of the way things work. It's true even of some segments of the media. In 2018, I was mentoring a young colleague during the Dodgers–Red Sox World Series, and Game 1 hadn't even ended before he texted me that Dave Roberts's bullpen choices were awful and going to cost the Dodgers. The young writer, gifted in many ways but still raw enough to not know what he didn't know, was assigned to write a lead column for Game 2, and sure enough, midway through, informed me that he was going to rip Roberts. I emailed back that, respectfully, maybe that isn't the best angle because it is too simple. If you are going to go that route, I wrote, here is an off-the-record, for-background explanation of how the Dodgers do things. I didn't mention their pregame run prevention meetings specifically, but I explained that Roberts was not making these decisions with full autonomy, at least not in the old way of a Tommy Lasorda or a Walter Alston. There were strategy meetings, and baseball operations was involved. Didn't matter. The column was published, and it shredded Roberts and Roberts alone without any context. My colleague had not been covering baseball more than two or three years at that point; it was his very first World Series column, and he felt his knowledge was superior enough to take on an experienced manager. Or, sadly, as is the case too often in today's media world, maybe he was just looking for clicks.

But by far the most egregious example of this brave new world came during the 2014 American League wild card game between Kansas City and Oakland. It was a crazy, wild, back-and-forth game in which the Royals took full advantage of Oakland starter Jon Lester's inability to throw to first base to keep the runners close. The Royals stole seven bases total, revving up with their first three while Lester was in the game. But the Royals still almost blew it when James Shields, Yordano Ventura, and Kelvin Herrera surrendered five runs in the sixth inning.

Shields started the inning by allowing a Sam Fuld single and then walking Josh Donaldson. Manager Ned Yost immediately called for Ventura, a starter unaccustomed to entering a game after an inning started and with men already on base. Furthermore, this was Tuesday, and Ventura had started the season finale two days earlier in Chicago. He threw seventy-three pitches before being removed after the fourth inning.

From his perch on the desk for the TBS pre- and postgame shows, the Hall of Fame pitcher Pedro Martinez sprang into action, crushing Yost in comments that bordered on character assassination. Martinez tweeted, "I think Ned Yost was trying to give this game away, in any way possible," and "I think Ned Yost had a panic move and almost gave the game away again." Pedro was just as strident on the postgame show.

"It really didn't bother me because it is really easy to second-guess after the fact, right?" Yost says. "Two, that decision Pedro Martinez was crushing us on, we had talked about for a month. We had started, as a group, planning. We knew we were close to making the playoffs and we started talking about situations a month out on what we would do in a big game. We had talked about a lot of situations, one of them being that if we got toward the middle innings and we've got guys who are really good hitters coming up, Yordano Ventura coming in throwing ninety-eight miles per hour with a really good breaking ball could bridge us from the fifth to the seventh innings. It just so happened in that game, in the sixth inning, that situation came up. We had talked about it and talked about it and talked about it. It didn't work out. But I didn't just sit there in the sixth inning and go, 'Well, hey, let's put Yordano Ventura in.' I understood what we had done and how it was thought out. It just didn't work out. But I understood how easy it is to second-guess."

Ironically, Martinez had been at the eye of the Grady Little storm eleven years earlier, another all-time second-guess for fans. As in this case, the team had every bit of information to make the smart decision. With Pedro, the numbers that year showed how significantly he deteriorated in a game after his ninety-fifth pitch—something Theo Epstein tried to impress upon Little, but the Sox analytics apparatus was not yet in full force, and baseball operations pulled its punch and allowed Little full autonomy. By 2014, the Royals, like most everyone else, were deep into analytics and, as Yost points out, the Ventura decision was more than a month in the works thanks to collaborative planning between the baseball operations department and the manager.

That an all-timer like Martinez, who also works for MLB Network, an arm of the league itself, would absolutely kill Yost on national television without a full understanding of the behind-the-scenes collaboration speaks to how misunderstood the job of today's manager remains.

Led by Martinez, Yost took a beating that autumn. After escaping the wild card game, the Royals took it to Mike Scioscia's Angels in a three-game Division Series sweep. Nevertheless, on the eve of the AL Championship Series against Buck Showalter's Orioles, the *Wall Street Journal* ran this headline over a preview column: "Ned Yost and Buck Showalter: The Dunce and the Chessmaster." By now, Yost was being portrayed nationally as a clueless hillbilly despite the fact that he had done something no Kansas City manager had done since 1985: lead the Royals into postseason play.

"I'm thinking to myself, whoever wrote this article never came in and sat in my office, I don't know him from Adam, he never asked one question, has he ever even been around what we've done?" Yost says. "Now if you come in and interview me, talk to me, ask me some questions, and come out thinking, 'That guy is stupid as hell,' if that's your opinion, then OK, at least you did your homework. To me, it was pure ignorance."

Of course, the Royals delivered a four-game sweep of Baltimore to advance to a World Series they nearly won but for Madison Bumgarner's Game 7 heroics. Then, Yost led the Royals to a second consecutive World Series in 2015 and a world title over the New York Mets. Who was the dunce now? Well, there were a few...and Yost was not among them.

To this day, Yost says, he's never spoken with Martinez.

"I wasn't interested in talking to him about that," Yost says. "I never heard what he said, but you always hear what he said from your buddies and your friends. I laughed because I didn't understand the extent of it and because you're so into what you're doing at the time."

When Yost returned home for the winter, he went hunting over at his buddy Jeff Foxworthy's place.

"I want to show you this deer I've named Pedro Martinez," the comedian told the manager.

"Pedro Martinez…why?" Yost asked.

"Because he's the fattest, ugliest deer on the farm," Foxworth replied.

Yost laughs as he tells the story. And as far as he knows, Pedro Martinez, the deer, remains alive today. (And, in another excellent development, so is good guy Pedro Martinez, the human.)

Meanwhile, Yost felt no need for vindication, then or now.

"I never did," he says. "I've always had a real good sense of who I am and what I am and how I go about my business and how prepared we are as a staff. I didn't care what anybody said. I've never had Facebook. I don't have one social media thing on my phone. Never have. I never paid attention to message boards, any of the team stuff. I always had a real good sense that what we were doing was right based on the work we were putting in. And we would have won two World Series if it wasn't for Madison Bumgarner. One guy."

The now-retired manager's farm is about thirty-five miles out of Columbus, Georgia, not far from Greenville, population 794. He spends his time fishing, hunting, looking for arrowheads, "and when the spring comes, we start cutting the grass again." He and his wife, Deborah, enjoy their four children and five grandchildren.

Yost was very close with the late NASCAR legend Dale Earnhardt Sr., and remains so with Dale Earnhardt Jr. When Yost retired, Junior told him, "The important part is if you're retiring to something, not from something."

Without question, it was the former. And what terrific advice.

One safe space in which Yost knew the sharpshooters would stand down was upstairs in the Kansas City Royals' general manager suite. Dayton Moore held that job from 2006 to 2022 and in that time worked with Buddy Bell, Trey Hillman, Yost, and Mike Matheny as his field managers.

"So we had a rule," Moore says. "I'm not saying we're perfect, right? We're human beings. But one fundamental rule we had as a front office that I implemented is that we don't second-guess the manager and the coaching staff up in the suite. We never second-guessed the manager, the coaches, or the staff."

Privately, Moore told his managers, I am not going to debate your strategy or your pitching moves. I'm not going to come downstairs and discuss whether you should have hit-and-run in a particular situation.

"But I told them that I will ask questions from time to time because the owner is going to call me tonight or tomorrow and he'll ask me things about your bullpen usage or perhaps why someone wasn't in the game or how come this particular player didn't play or why was he taken out of the game," Moore says. "So I don't ask those questions because I'm second-guessing you. I'm asking those questions to inform the owner in a way where he continues to have confidence in you as the manager."

As respect for managers erodes with every new addition of an Ivy Leaguer to a front office, Moore worked to celebrate the manager in Kansas City. All relationships that a general manager forges within an organization are important, but the two that are the most vital, he says, are those with the owner and manager.

"You're constantly looking and trying to create pathways for those relationships to thrive, especially an owner and the manager," says Moore. "I always encouraged our owner to just, once or twice a homestand, go into the manager's office. Spend time with him. Just you and him, get to know each other. Learn about each other's families. So they're not up there in that suite being overly judgmental or overly critical about what's going on on the field. Because it's very difficult to explain a lot of things that happen on a baseball field."

As Buddy Bell says with a wry chuckle, "If you want a job where everyone thinks they know more than you do, managing is what you need to do."

Moore, a graduate of George Mason University, joined Texas as a special adviser to president of baseball operations Chris Young in 2023 after an ownership change in Kansas City resulted in his firing. His feeling throughout his time as a chief executive was that the more the front office is involved, the less chance the manager has to be successful. The job of the front office, he believes, is that it should do everything possible to support the efforts of the manager, the coaching staff, and the players, allowing them to operate in a way in which they're freed up to make the decisions to push the right buttons.

That certainly is not the way most postmodern front offices work.

"I think what's important today is the ability of the manager to incorporate what the front office is telling him and then repackage it and communicate it to the players in a way that's not offensive to the players," Alderson says. "That's an important skill. That's not a skill that had to exist twenty, twenty-five years ago. So managing that perception of control by the front office over control over the decisions made on the field is important. I think that's why Bob Melvin had success in Oakland as long as he did. He had a strong front office but was able to take input and utilize it in a way that motivated players rather than dehumanized players."

Today's managers do more—even including in-game, live television interviews—but because of various modern pressure points, expectations, and rules changes, reveal less.

So, while arguing with umpires and many similar theatrics have been diluted by the Digital Age, so, too, has the overall Show—the way the game is played and managed. Baseball operations departments direct managers to run the game according to probabilities—one example of why the stolen base had become an endangered species before recent rules changes—and it is why we saw so many position players pitching in the garbage time of routs before, again, baseball had to step in and legislate that. As Showalter told me, it used to be that if a team was forced to use a position player in a blowout, the manager returned to his hotel feeling awful that night because he had mismanaged or misused his bullpen. Then, it became all based on probabilities and, given the shortage of pitching, even with thirteen-man pitching staffs, it suddenly wasn't about mismanaging. Rather, when a score reached a certain point, probabilities took over and some managers simply did what the Upstairs asked of them to save the arms of their relievers. To the detriment of the game.

"The other way that front-office dynamic is muted somewhat is when a manager understands analytics as well as the front office does and is able to not only absorb information but request it and cause the front office to have to go back and respond," Alderson says. "The reason that is important is it gives the manager a certain leverage with the front office."

Increasingly, younger, New Age managers who recently played, such as Mark Kotsay, Rocco Baldelli, and Torey Lovullo, are well versed in the numbers and want more of them. All-timers like Cox, Bochy, and Leyland surely could manage in any era—as Bochy proved in 2023—though in certain situations, sparks could fly.

"The only situation where I would try to balance things out is what is not enough information and what is too much information," Leyland says. "Some of it is very valuable information. I would assume some of it is just reading material."

Leyland's old boss, Dave Dombrowski, continues to give managers space while running the Phillies. And the value of a manager was proven again in 2022 when the Phillies replaced Joe Girardi with Rob Thomson in early June. Just 22-29 at the time and playing uptight under Girardi, the Phillies immediately relaxed and won eight in a row under the looser Thomson, then galloped all the way to that fall's World Series before losing in six games to Houston.

"I think the manager's position is extremely important," Dombrowski says. "This is just me speaking, but I think a manager can make a difference between first and last place. And when I say that, not to the point of strategically during the game, because I'm going to assume that most managers, when they get to the big-league level, understand strategy. Maybe you outmaneuver somebody a few times a year, but just the overall way they set the tempo for an organization, for their players, the relationship of how the players can perform for them versus somebody else, that aggressive mindset. I think managers are as important as they've ever been."

Dombrowski always has believed in giving his managers latitude without dictating to them. One illustrative example came in the 1997 World Series after the Marlins lost Game 6 to Cleveland. With Game 7 looming, cleanup man Bobby Bonilla was scuffling. Dombrowski was sitting in Leyland's office postgame along with several coaches when Leyland quizzed the group about Bonilla, asking what they would do with tomorrow's Game 7 lineup.

"And I remember I went home and we're talking about it, my parents were there, and my dad said, 'Well, so what are you going to do tomorrow?'" Dombrowski says. "And I said, 'I don't know. We'll see tomorrow what he decides to do. That's his decision.'"

Tomorrow came. Leyland dropped Bonilla from fourth to sixth in the lineup, and Bonilla smashed a solo homer against Jaret Wright in the seventh inning, the first blow in what became a 3–2, eleven-inning win for the Marlins. The way Dombrowski figured it, Leyland should have a far better pulse of the clubhouse and the team than the GM.

"Really, if you don't have confidence in the manager to do that, you probably have the wrong manager," Dombrowski says.

Leyland formed a brilliant tandem with Dombrowski for key parts of their careers. An owner-ordered fire sale wound up driving both men to eventually move on from Florida. They reunited in Detroit in 2006—Leyland replaced Alan Trammell—and worked together eight more years and through two more World Series runs (St. Louis beat the Tigers in 2006 and the Giants swept them in 2012).

"I was told the story that when he took the job, he was told by Dave Dombrowski that he would be able to take the players that he wanted, and there wouldn't be a lot of pushback," says Justin Verlander, the three-time Cy Young Award winner and onetime Most Valuable Player who broke in as a rookie during Leyland's first season in Detroit in 2006. "And then comes spring training and he saw a couple of kids, myself and Joel Zumaya, super young but threw the shit out of the ball, and he was like, 'I'm going to take those guys.'"

Verlander pauses and says he feels bad saying that because he doesn't recall who was on the team before and whose jobs he and Zumaya took, and he doesn't want to appear callous.

"And the way I heard the story was that Dave goes, well, they're so young, and we don't know what we're going to get from them," Verlander continues. "And Jim says, well, respectfully, I know who the other guys are and I'd rather see what we're going to get from these guys. Let's just use our eyes. I've watched them pitch.

"He really advocated for me right out of the gate. Who knows the ripple effect of that, but just the confidence of breaking with the team and being there right away and getting off on the right foot like I did that season. Then it was off to the races."

Two decades later, Verlander now realizes some things that he took for granted as a young player.

"I love Jim and, you know, I almost wish I could go back and relive those days as a veteran now, and understand a little more about what made him so great," Verlander says. "I think his ability to have a feel for the locker room and for the players, and to get the best from his guys, is something I didn't quite realize back then. But looking back, I see that he had a great feel for the pulse of the team. A good leader who knew how to manage different personalities. And on the field, he was one of the last managers, there aren't many of them left now, who just trust their instincts. I mean, we didn't have analytics back then, so there was a lot of instinctual stuff going on. He had great instincts, just brilliant."

Sharp instincts are still allowed to flourish today in the manager's chair in Atlanta, where Brian Snitker honed his while managing 2,714 games in the minors before finally being named as the Braves' manager at the age of sixty in 2016. Unlike many other teams in what has become an increasing trend in professional sports, Atlanta does not worship at the altar of "load management." Instead, Snitker believes that players stay healthy, stay strong, and get better by playing.

Shortstop Dansby Swanson, in his walk year in Atlanta in 2022 before signing a free-agent deal with the Chicago Cubs, played in 162 games. The year before, he played 160. Freddie Freeman under Snitker played in 162 games, 158, and 159 before signing as a free agent with the Los Angeles Dodgers. Third baseman Austin Riley played in 160 games in 2021 and 159 in both 2022 and 2023. First baseman Matt Olson played all 162 games in his first two seasons in Atlanta (he also played all 162 during one of his seasons in Oakland, in 2018).

Snitker is the only manager working today who was hired by the legendary Hank Aaron. Then Atlanta's farm director, Aaron released Snitker as a player in 1980 because the Home Run King saw more potential in him as a manager than as a player. Aaron hired Snitker as a roving instructor in 1981, then made him the manager at Class A Anderson, South Carolina, in 1982. Snitker was twenty-six.

"I asked Hank one time, 'Hey, how many games did you play in spring training?'" Snitker, the NL Manager of the Year in 2018, says. "He said, 'All of them.'

"Our guys don't do that. But we are different here, I think, because we do have guys who play 162 games a year. The heat maps, where a lot of teams make you rest players, I think players get stronger by playing every day. To me, if they're healthy, they're stronger. They don't wear out. They get sleepy, they don't get tired. I think it makes them stronger, and that's why guys have good years."

After a lifetime in the game, part of Snitker's reasoning is that players are going to miss enough time when they get banged up, so a manager doesn't need to give them extra days off. Rather, those will occur naturally—as needed. And Snitker, sixty-nine, would rather keep a struggling player on the field as long as possible so he can fight his way out of it, rather than sit him down in the midst of a slump.

"As a player, they have to believe in themselves and they have to allow themselves to come out of a struggle," Snitker says. "I'm always looking down that bench to see what guys are doing, how a guy who is struggling is handling it, how he's sitting there. You know? And if they allow themselves to come out of something, they will."

After the Braves won the 2021 World Series, Riley sought out his manager with a heartfelt thank-you for keeping him on the field. Respect, gratitude, and love oozed from that moment. After hitting .226 over eighty games as a rookie in 2019 and .239 during the COVID-shortened 2020 season, the third baseman was colder than a garage freezer to begin 2021. He was hitting .188 on April 12 and .190 six days later. He didn't crack his first home run until the season's eighteenth game. Snitker never blinked. He wrote Riley's name into the lineup on April 17. Wrote his name again on April 18. Wrote it again on April 20 and April 21 after the Braves had a scheduled day off on April 19. And he kept on sticking with Riley.

The third baseman finally heated up in May and finished the season hitting .303 with thirty-three homers and 107 RBI. He hit .320 with three RBI to help push Atlanta past Houston in the World Series, the Braves' first title since 1995. He was seventh in the MVP voting.

"I started off about as cold as you could," Riley says. "And he just kept putting me out there, kept putting me out there, kept putting me out there. And, you know, just sharing that moment after the World Series, he was like, 'I always knew you had it. It was just that we gotta give you some time.' So that, that was the coolest moment. Him having that faith in me and, next thing you know, we won the World Series. It was awesome."

What also was awesome was the old-school Snitker finally getting to enjoy baseball's greatest moment in the spotlight after the game tried to toss him overboard so many times over the years. He managed at various levels of Atlanta's farm system through three decades in outposts such as Sumter, South Carolina; Macon, Georgia; Greenville, South Carolina; and Jackson, Mississippi. He was managing Triple-A Durham when Ron Shelton was filming the classic movie *Bull Durham* at the Durham (North Carolina) Athletic Park in October 1987 and that was how his old catcher's mitt got a star turn, going from Snitker's office to actor Kevin Costner's left hand and into celluloid history.

Three times he was added to the Atlanta major-league staff: as a bullpen coach in 1985, again from 1988 to 1990, and then as a third-base coach under Bobby Cox and Fredi González from 2007 to 2013. Snitker faced a significant career crossroads when, after the Braves won the NL East title but were beaten by the Dodgers in a Division Series, he was part of a shakeup of the major-league staff and banished back to the minor leagues to manage Triple-A Gwinnett. He was fifty-eight, and doors were closing. Essentially, Snitker was scapegoated by then–general manager Frank Wren.

This is one of those moments in a career where joy and optimism often exit stage right, replaced by bitterness and toxicity. But Snitker refused to sour.

"I could be pissed off," Snitker says. "But then, if I didn't like it, I needed to check out and go do something else. And I wasn't going to. It was kind of like, this is my chosen path, and I just kind of accepted it. I said, well, I'm just going to do the best job I can wherever I'm at. I never felt like I needed to validate what I did in my career. I got the opportunity to stay in the organization and I sure wasn't going to turn it down. And it actually worked out pretty good for me."

But he couldn't have known that at the time. In fact, as he was heading south in his career, a whole new crop of big-league managers was heading north, men who had recently played the game but had never managed. It was the latest incarnation of analytics, a concept that now was standard enough that many baseball operations men around the game decided they wanted eager, blank-canvas skippers who would implement baseball operations "suggestions" without any pushback. So in 2013 and 2014, men who had scattered parts of their souls across the game for decades, paying their dues as minor-league managers and major-league coaches, were not being rewarded. Instead, former players who had never managed at any level, such as Robin Ventura (White Sox), Mike Matheny (Cardinals), Walt Weiss (Rockies), and Mike Redmond (Marlins), glided into managers' offices across the game.

"I just figured, well, that's the way it's trending right now," Snitker says. "The industry is going that route. But all of a sudden, now, since I've been back in this, they're going back the other way."

Snitker chuckles.

"It's like your dad's ties," he says. "He had the skinny ties and the fat ties, and they would roll around and come back in style after a few years."

The game rolled around and came back to Snitker. And when it did, the years had seasoned him perfectly. With his wife, Veronica, he had raised two kids, daughter Erin (thirty-eight) and son Troy (thirty-six and a hitting coach for the Astros). Patience had softened his youthful temper. Where he once flashed the precociousness of a young man, he now carried the wisdom of an old man.

"Johnny Sain used to tell me when I was a first-year manager, when things are getting hairy, just back off and let the players take care of it," Snitker says. "So the first game I ever managed, I ordered an intentional walk to load the bases. I had no idea. I had no idea of the situation. So the next guy came up and hit the ball off the wall, cleared the bases.

"So I'm in my shower after the game and I'm thinking, 'You did exactly what Johnny told you not to do.' I tried to create the action instead of just backing off and letting the players handle it.

"The biggest thing I've learned over time is that this is a really hard game to play. And these guys make it look really easy."

Oh, and the *Bull Durham* connection? It wasn't only Snitker's glove that made an appearance. In the opening credits, as the camera pans

Annie Savoy's home, there is a baseball card tucked into the frame of her mirror. Snitker. Perfect. The ultimate "lifer" in the best baseball movie ever made. One in which Hollywood accurately depicts its version of the ultimate lifer, Crash Davis.

The only thing more Hollywood than Hollywood was Snitker managing Atlanta to the World Series title in 2021.

"Yeah, keep the ties," Snitker says, chuckling. "They may come back in style. Maybe one of those thick ties, you know. They tried the skinny ones and I'm the thicker one again."

———

In Kansas City, when Moore hired Matheny to replace Yost upon Yost's retirement following the 2019 season, the Royals obtained a manager who had guided St. Louis to three division titles, one World Series appearance, and two second-place finishes, and was well versed in analytics. He seemed a good fit for an organization that skillfully blended old-school scouting and modern Sabermetrics.

And, for an organization that valued managers, Moore did what he had done for those who previously held the job under his watch: He had his people produce a slick, eighteen-page document for distribution throughout the organization so that all Royals employees immediately could feel like they were welcoming a new family member. There was a note from Matheny describing how excited he was to take the job. There was a beautiful family photo from daughter Katie's wedding complete with a who's who diagram putting names with the faces of all of Mike and Kristin Matheny's children, followed by a page listing Mike and Kristin's wedding date and the entire family tree—their children's ages and schools attended, the name of their one grandson and noting "2 more grandsons on the way!" There were a couple pages listing influential moments in Matheny's life (along with books that most influenced him), career highlights, and awards, along with a couple of pages listing what Matheny had most learned from being a manager and some highlights of his coaching philosophy.

As a companion piece, the Royals issued a three-page document of Moore's personal thoughts about each manager he had worked with, along with the new guy Matheny.

The point of this exercise, in Moore's words, was "to honor the legacy of the manager position. Whoever we hired, we did our best to honor who had been there before, as well."

The document went to the front office, business operations, the ownership group, and more.

"If baseball is an integral part of the institutions of the United States, if it is important to our culture, to our city, to our region, to our fan base, then you have to make it important and you have to celebrate it," Moore says. "Like families sit and talk about their heritage and their genealogy, we put a packet together on Matheny and his family and sent it to our front office, the media. And we had a luncheon for the entire group to celebrate the manager.

"Every leader, no matter what level, you've got to have the support of everybody. All aspects of the organization. But not to the point where you devalue the manager—he's not going to answer to the business operations."

Moore shared it with Young when the winning pitcher of Game 1 of the 2015 World Series began his journey as an executive with Texas.

"If we want this game to continue to be America's pastime, and I still believe it is, there are 162 games a year that provide entertainment, drama, learning opportunities, growth, connecting generations," Moore says, "then I think the manager position should always be honored."

EPILOGUE

THE FUTURE

In January 2022, Apple became the world's first company to be valued at more than $3 trillion. Following a brief dip in the markets, Apple soared past that milestone for a second time in June 2023.

Seven months later and buoyed by its deep dive into artificial intelligence services, Microsoft followed Apple in becoming the world's second company to surpass $3 trillion in valuation. With this, in January 2024, Microsoft also surged past Apple as the world's most valuable company.

Individually, both Microsoft and Apple had surpassed Saudi Aramco (the Saudi Arabian Oil Company), Alphabet (the world's third-largest technology company and parent company of Google), and Amazon. Ours is a world completely unrecognizable from 1977, when the Commodore Personal Electronic Transactor first began shipping to the public. Floppy disks and audiocassette tapes have yielded to AI, GPS, and Alexa setting your home thermostat and turning your lights on and off in the evenings.

Time was, Red Smith, the sprightly old *New York Times* sports columnist, wrote in the 1950s that rooting for the Yankees was like rooting for U.S. Steel. Then, U.S. Steel was the world's most valuable company. As 2023 turned into 2024, it was set to be acquired by Nippon Steel.

There is no stopping progress, which was how it came to be during this time that in a dugout in Hillsboro, Oregon, the Arizona Diamondbacks' high Class A affiliate, the manager flashed signs, hollered encouragement, and consulted with the pitching coach. It looked just like any other professional baseball game in any other locale on a September evening. Except as the Spokane Indians came to bat, the manager in Hillsboro's dugout was easily identifiable by the long, blond ponytail flowing from beneath the back of her baseball cap.

Ronnie Gajownik was a highly respected coach in Arizona's system who was named by the club as the second female manager in the history of professional baseball in 2023. She followed Rachel Balkovec, who was completing her second year as manager in Tampa, the Yankees' low Class A affiliate in the Florida State League. Also on this same evening, Alyssa Nakken, the first female coach in major-league history, was in uniform with San Francisco as the Giants played the Cubs in Wrigley Field.

Each is very aware of time and place.

"For me, I represent any female who works in baseball," Gajownik says. "Men, you just represent yourself. But the people who come into an experience with me, if they go to another organization, I'm going to be the expectation or standard of a female coach over there."

By all accounts except the won-loss record—which usually is an improper gauge, anyway, in minor-league baseball—Gajownik's first season as manager was an unmitigated success.

"It's gone really well," Gajownik says as we talk over sandwiches early on a brilliant September afternoon at Longbottom Coffeehouse, just a short pop fly down the road from Hillsboro Ballpark in lovely

Hillsboro. "The D-backs are wanting to get a good product from Class A to Double-A and Triple-A and the big leagues, so I feel like if there was ever any problems when it came to how I manage or just conversations, the clubhouse, and whatnot, then that would have been addressed and it never has been. Two of the things I told the guys is always be on time, because time is the one thing you can't get back. You can get back food, money, clothes, but time, that's me investing in you and I can't get that back. And also, actions speak louder than words. I can come in here and say whatever I say, but then if I go out on the field and I'm an asshole, who you really are is how you act."

Messages received. The affinity and respect between Gajownik and the young Hops is genuine and true. She often calls the players "Poppy," and they reciprocate by calling her "Mama." Sometimes when a player is called into her office, he's nervous simply because he's being summoned to the manager's office. Male or female has nothing to do with it.

"It's been cool seeing the relationships develop with them," Gajownik says. "Not even as a female, but just as a manager."

One of the most unique relationships developed with an infielder-turned-outfielder named Andrew Pintar. A fifth-round pick out of Brigham Young University in 2022, Pintar started the season in rookie ball, was moved to low-A Visalia, and now had been in Hillsboro for nearly two months. But he was coming off two shoulder surgeries. One day a few weeks earlier, while playing second base, he threw to first and badly misfired. Then it happened again. The yips had him.

Pintar approached Gajownik in the dugout in the middle of the game, panicked.

"I can't throw!" he told her. "I don't know what's going on! I don't know what to do."

Gajownik calmly told him, OK, let's not think about this right now. Let's just get through the game. Whatever you need to think to get through it, think that, and then don't worry, we'll figure it out.

What they figured out, in part through consultations with Josh Barfield, who at the time was Arizona's director of player development, and Jeff Gardner, a key Diamondbacks big-league scout, was a way to transition Pintar to the outfield.

"When we told him he was moving to the outfield, his face was like, thank you," Gajownik says. "Because it allowed him to free up his mind again. His first thing was like, 'My girlfriend is really going to like me now because all I talk about is my throwing. So she's going to love this news and it's her birthday, so this is a great birthday present for her, too.' So that's the thing. People think of them as just players, and I think that's what's frustrating, too. When I hear some of the stuff fans say to the players, it's like, you're not at the zoo. These are human beings."

Veronica Rose Gajownik, thirty-two, was part of the gold medal–winning United States women's national baseball team at the Pan Am Games in 2015. Yes, *baseball*. She played softball at the University of South Florida and, following that and the Pan Am Games, she was hired on as an assistant softball coach at Liberty University (2016–2017) and then at the University of Massachusetts (2018–2020). It was during the worldwide COVID-19 pandemic that USA Baseball put together some Zooms for alumni from the women's national baseball team, bringing on ex-scouts, umpires, coaches, and front-office personnel as guests. One of those was Elizabeth Benn, who would become the director of major league baseball operations for the New York Mets from 2022 to 2024 but at the time was working in the commissioner's office. During the course of the Zooms, Gajownik's questions impressed several people, and soon Benn emailed asking whether she had any interest in working in professional baseball. The thought had never crossed Gajownik's mind. She does, however, recall standing in her kitchen when news came over ESPN that the Chicago Cubs had hired Rachel Folden as an organizational hitting coach in November 2019.

"I remember seeing that and I was like, 'That is so sick,'" Gajownik says.

She grew up in Florida going to Tampa Bay Rays games, always had an affinity for Chicago teams because of her Illinois-born father, loved the White Sox's Magglio Ordonez and Frank Thomas, and today wears No. 34 because it was the number of another of her heroes, former Cubs ace Kerry Wood.

Three organizations reached out when she responded to the email from the commissioner's office that, by all means, she would love to have an opportunity to work in professional baseball. She accepted an offer from the Diamondbacks because the conversations with them were comfortable and she felt the people were genuine. The club hired her as a video assistant in Hillsboro for the 2021 season and moved her to coaching Double-A Amarillo in 2022 when another coach was lost for the season to injury. She impressed enough in that role that by 2023, she was back in Hillsboro as the manager.

Throughout, the Diamondbacks loved her knowledge, attention to detail, creativity, and force of personality.

"I'm telling you, she's going to be a major-league field staff member here one of these days, and pretty soon," Arizona manager Torey Lovullo says. "She's a great teacher. She's fearless. Her ideas and her knowledge and her ability to teach."

During spring training, Lovullo says, "when I need a new drill, I search her out. And she's like, 'Let's do this.' Her ability to teach is pretty impressive."

Treading into a man's world mostly has left Gajownik nonplussed. Naturally, when she was starting her first season as manager, there were jitters. She had recurring nightmares that she was not writing the correct names on the lineup card. The first two weeks of the season, the WHOOP Fitness Tracker she wears on her wrist was regularly reporting that her recovery rate from the previous day's stress stood at only about 25 percent.

"It was terrible because I was so stressed out internally, but thankfully no one saw it and I like that a lot of people said, 'You seem self-confident,'" Gajownik says. "So I think I did a good job of keeping it internal."

By the end of the first month, the stress had dissipated. She began to feel her groove. She wielded her fungo bat, a touching gift from Rockies third-base coach Warren Schaeffer, like she meant it.

"I loved working with her," says Schaeffer, who was managing the Arizona Fall League's Salt River club in 2022 with Gajownik as a coach when they learned that she would be managing Hillsboro in 2023. "She's very smart. She loves the game. She's got a good mind for it."

By September, among many other things, Gajownik had learned the value of talking with her pitchers daily so she could gauge where they were emotionally. She was on the field early every day conducting individual drills before batting practice. She had been ejected from a couple of games, sending a charge through her roster as her players loved the sight of their five-foot-seven, ponytailed manager going nose to nose with umpires. One of the ejections came with an automatic one-game suspension because the ump deemed that a Hops pitcher threw at a batter's head—which Gajownik thought was a ridiculous charge. The team was at home during her suspension. "So I went in the stands and ate a hot dog" during the game, she says.

There wasn't really an "earning her stripes" moment with the guys, but there were a couple of humorous incidents that came close. Coaching third base during games (as minor-league managers do), she refrained from that time-honored baseball ritual of slapping a teammate on the rear end.

"I haven't done that yet. Because I want them to feel comfortable with me and understand who I am as a person. Like, I'm married. I'm married to a woman. I'm very happily married," says Gajownik, who wed Andrea in December 2020 and stood as the first openly LGBTQ manager in minor- or major-league history.

But when Shane Loux, one of the Diamondbacks' minor-league pitching coordinators, was in town, there was a play on which the base-runner slid into third and popped up more quickly than Gajownik expected. She went to pat him on the back but, suddenly, it became an awkward butt pat.

"So Shane was like, you need to make an announcement and say at the beginning of next spring training, 'Hey, guys, you have a year with me so I'm going to slap your ass now,'" Gajownik says, chuckling. "So that'll be a fun announcement, whenever that does come."

To her players, she was simply one of the guys—albeit with a different rank.

"It's definitely a little different, but she knows her stuff," says outfielder Jack Hurley, Arizona's third-round draft pick in 2023. "It feels like any manager you build a relationship with."

Catcher Christian Cerda, one of the most jovial and generous players on the team (he insisted, after a pregame clubhouse chat, that I help myself to the spread of chicken and rice; I declined—I can't take food from the minor leaguers!), admits to some initial skepticism when he found out he would be playing under a female manager.

"I think everybody can say the same thing," Cerda says. "But like they say, you can never judge a book by its cover. She gave me another view than I thought it would be."

As LuJames Groover, Arizona's second-round pick in 2023, says, "They wouldn't have hired her if she didn't know what she was doing. So there's a trust factor there."

After finishing 24-42 during the first half of the Northwest League season while playing as the youngest team in the league, the Hops went 32-34 in the second half. Longtime owner Mike McMurray professed to being "amazed" at Gajownik's ability to keep the team together and make sure things stayed positive during some of the summer's more difficult times. Barfield, who left Arizona to join the White Sox as their assistant general manager in 2024, acknowledged the same.

"You see it sometimes in the minor leagues," Barfield says as we sit together in the stands during that evening's Hillsboro-Spokane game. "It's a grind, and when you have a losing season, it can take a toll on guys. And when it starts to take a toll, you see the quality of the work and quality of the compete go down. That's when it gets concerning, from my perspective. And she's done a really good job of keeping the focus every day on guys getting their work in and finding ways to get better competing every day, win or lose. And I think that's what you look for in every manager."

In the late 1970s, that minor-league manager might have been gruff Jim Leyland, chain-smoking his way through games and overturning food spreads afterward if the compete wasn't there. Tonight, following Meriwether Lewis and William Clark's grand expedition through the Pacific Northwest in the early 1800s, this manager is blazing more trails, blond ponytail and all.

When I ask Gajownik if she considered trimming her hair just so she wouldn't be so noticeable—she already had enough of a spotlight and pressure on her—she went for the history books. There was a female umpire in the 1970s who worked in the Northwest League, she says, referencing Christine Wren, who chopped off her long hair for that reason, just to fit in. Maybe in 1975 that was a necessity. But here in the summer of *Barbie* and Taylor Swift, not so much.

"I think it's sad," Gajownik says of Wren feeling the need to cut her hair. "Because if we all look at the rainbow only being able to see the color purple, we're not going to be able to see yellow and we're not going to be able to see red and green. So even though I am in this male world, I'm here because I bring a different perspective. And that's not a bad thing."

In fact, it is just the opposite, she says, getting all fired up. She brings up the vitriol on social media giving women hell for daring to step into the male sports realm.

"Do you know how many men who have never played softball in their lives, they've just played baseball, are coaching at top softball programs?" she says. "So what the hell is the difference when you have all these men in women's sports that they've never played, especially in baseball and softball? Why am I any different? It's just because, again, they're just used to seeing a man everywhere and you're not used to seeing women everywhere. And that's where we're finally getting the point, we're starting to see women everywhere. That's always been my biggest gripe, there's so many males in women's sports, coaching, and they've never played, so why do I have to deal with the shit?"

Balkovec, who preceded Gajownik as the first female manager in professional baseball, piloted the Yankees' low Class A team in Tampa in 2022 and 2023 before being named as director of player development for the Miami Marlins in 2024. A native of Omaha, Nebraska, Balkovec, thirty-seven, played college softball at Creighton and New Mexico.

"I've got to credit Kevin Reese, he's the one who brought her to me," Yankees general manager Brian Cashman says of the club's director of player development. "In terms of knowledge, leadership, and strength, in terms of having a really strong process of holding people accountable, every one of those boxes is easily checked with her. If you're going to be working under Rachel, whether you are a player or a coach, you'd better bring your A game because she's going to demand it. That's how she's wired. The sky is the limit for her and I continue to look forward to watching her career and where it takes her and how far it goes."

Nakken, thirty-four, was named to San Francisco's coaching staff in 2020 following a stellar softball career at Sacramento State University, where she was named to the All-Pacific Coast Softball Conference team four years running. She hit .304 and in 2012 was the conference's Scholar-Athlete of the Year. She joined the Giants in 2014 as an analytical intern. In 2022, she became the first woman to coach on the field in an MLB regular-season game when she took over first-base duties after Antoan Richardson was ejected in the third inning of a game against San Diego.

The Giants interviewed Nakken for the managing job in October 2023, after firing Kapler and just before hiring Bob Melvin. They retained her on Melvin's twelve-person staff for 2024, but in 2025 she left the Giants to become an assistant director for player development with the Cleveland Guardians. For her part, Nakken, who is a Sacramento-area native and had been affiliated with the Giants for a decade, loved her work in that organization but remained open-minded as to what might be next.

"I can see myself trying to do a lot of things," Nakken says. "Life is full of opportunities. Each career you embark on and the path you take, every day there's something new out there. That's really interesting."

So she says she simply focuses on wanting to just "dominate the role, the responsibilities I'm given, and be a leader in my own right in the position that I'm in. If you bring people together who know how to lead, but also know how to follow, really good things happen."

Opportunities that once were unavailable now exist for women in Major League Baseball. Jen Pawol was named as a full-time umpire for spring training in 2024, putting her on track to possibly become MLB's first regular-season female umpire. In addition to roles filled by Nakken, Gajownik, and Balkovec, more women than ever are traveling with clubs in support roles: coaches, trainers, strength and conditioning, video support staff, and more. MLB in May 2023 sent a memo to all thirty clubs ordering adequate facilities for traveling female staffers. As the sole female coach in the game, this is just one of the obstacles Nakken fought to overcome daily. Private locker rooms or dressing quarters have been OK, Nakken says, but the bathroom situations in some places are difficult. She knew things would be different when she was hired in 2020, and the COVID-19 pandemic ensured that by shutting down her first spring training and delaying the start of the season until July. She limited her media appearances because she knew the challenge of getting to know the players would be heavy enough and she did not want them to see her all over the television in interviews before they had a chance to see what she was about for themselves. Into her fifth season when we spoke, helping out with everything from baserunning to infield shifts to running numbers on opposing relievers so Giants pinch-hitters were prepared when entering a game, Nakken hoped to remain in uniform rather than transition into a baseball operations role. Still, in her perfect world, she one day will become a bench coach and, maybe, a manager.

Following her one season managing Hillsboro, the Diamondbacks in 2024 promoted Gajownik to bench coach at Double-A Amarillo. Absolutely it was viewed as a promotion, says Arizona general manager Mike Hazen—even though it wasn't a managing role.

"It's part of our responsibility to develop our players, and we try to develop our staff, too," Hazen says. "Part of our responsibility is developing their skills to make sure they're ready to work on an MLB staff."

One thing for certain is, one way or another, the old boy network is being broken up. Where once managers were recycled as quickly as aluminum cans and newsprint, now the advertisements for open jobs come with the tag "No Experience Necessary." And with women entering the ranks at the Class A level, as much as the job has changed over the past two decades, the future of managing is more of an open question than ever. If anything over the past several years, we've seen teams look for new ways of thinking, and new ways of doing things, in the manager's chair. With the Black Lives Matter and #MeToo movements as this country finally and belatedly arrived at a hard reckoning with social justice issues, managers must behave better than their predecessors, too. Look at Mickey Callaway, the former Mets manager whose career was torpedoed when, following two seasons of leading the Mets before being fired, he justifiably was fired again as the Angels' pitching coach in the spring of 2020 when sexual harassment allegations were revealed both in New York and dating back to his days as a Cleveland pitching coach before that.

Managers are coming and going more rapidly than ever as front offices turn over and philosophies change. Suddenly, Mike Scioscia's nineteen-year run managing the Angels looks as formidable as Connie Mack's fifty-two-year managing career. Will another manager ever come close to reaching three thousand wins? Doubtful. Tony La Russa finished at 2,884, and even the venerable Bruce Bochy is far away from that mark, standing at 2,093 career victories after his rousing comeback with Texas in 2023. Will someone even reach two thousand wins, or will Dusty Baker be the last of that group? Francona was the closest at 1,950 before retiring following the 2023 season, but now his return to Cincinnati in 2025 should easily bring him to the two thousand club. And as numbers change, managers face the same shifting markers as players in one sense: Who are the Hall of Famers working among us today? Francona certainly. After that, it's a difficult call. Roberts is certainly on pace in Los Angeles with a few more seasons in charge.

It took her far too many interviews over far too many years, but Kim Ng finally broke the glass ceiling for female general managers when she was named as the Miami Marlins' head of baseball ops before the 2021 season. It was such a momentous occasion that she received congratulations from, among many others, Michelle Obama, Billie Jean King, and Martina Navratilova. Over the next three summers, she left her mark—particularly with shrewd trades at the deadline in 2023 that helped push the Marlins into the playoffs. With that, Ng became the first female GM ever to lead a team into the postseason. But, baseball being baseball, she left the Marlins after the season due to philosophical differences with owner Bruce Sherman. He planned to hire a president of baseball operations, which would bump her down to second-in-command. Even after she constructed a playoff team.

Nevertheless, after Ng, many in the game are predicting that we will see a female field manager in the not-too-distant future.

"I could see a future where MLB has a woman commissioner," Cashman, the Yankees GM, told me in February 2024. "We've already checked the box of a woman GM, and I can see a woman manager. I don't see why a woman can't be in any capacity in the game. They're just as talented, if not more talented, in many cases.

"We almost had a president of the United States who was a woman," Cashman said, referring to Hillary Clinton, "and we've got a vice president who is a woman" in Kamala Harris. "I would think if you could be a vice president of the United States, you certainly could manage a Major League Baseball team," he said.

Gabe Kapler, who was instrumental in hiring Nakken as MLB's first female coach, predicts it will happen in the next five to seven years and adds, "I'd be shocked if there's not a woman managing a major-league team in the next ten years."

Says Arizona's Hazen: "I absolutely think it's going to happen. I think the game is changing, front offices are changing, now Kim broke ground as the first female GM...it's going to happen. The next step for me is that you're going to see more and more coaches coming up through the ranks on MLB staffs. I might be wrong. To me, it's about the person in that position: what type of leader, communicator, how players feel they are treated, respect for that person, all of that I think is agnostic to the gender."

Even heretofore crusty old-schoolers whom you may assume would be guardians of baseball's traditions and locker rooms may surprise you with some of their views. Part of it, perhaps, is, once you become the father of a daughter, you have a far better understanding when conversations turn toward, if not "smashing the patriarchy" then at least questioning the patriarchy.

"Maybe it's something that should have happened a long time ago," says Buck Showalter, who has come a long way since his days of being bothered by something as simple as Ken Griffey Jr. wearing a cap backward during batting practice. "I have a daughter. And I just think that if there is some door closed to her just because she's female, it just doesn't sit right with me. Like someone who might be gay. Life's just too short. Can't we all just get along and create the same opportunities whether somebody is Black, white, Hispanic, woman, gay, I don't care. I couldn't care less. I just want to know if you can help us win."

Showalter, whose daughter reviewed his last few contracts before he signed them ("She knows the rules better than I do"), cites some enlightening conversations he had with Benn when he was with the Mets.

"If you can help us win, I don't care if you are man, woman, or child," Showalter says. "She liked that. I said, 'You've gotta bring something.'"

The playing field, so to speak, is never going to be equal. One indisputable fact within the growing discussion regarding whether a woman will ever manage an MLB team, and when, is that while those conversations are occurring, we're still not even square with minority hirings in the game. There remain fewer Black managers today than there were five years after Al Campanis's ignorant statements on that ill-fated *Nightline* interview in 1987. And, as Dusty Baker points out, age discrimination is something that most folks prefer not to discuss, either.

"I might have helped Tony La Russa get back in Chicago or I might have helped Bucky Showalter get a job in New York. I might have helped Bruce Bochy when everyone was talking about we're too old," says Baker, who was hired by the Astros to help save their postscandal reputation in 2020 when he was seventy-one, and then helped continue their success. "And I might have helped some senior citizens of the world when everybody's trying to push all the senior citizens out for cheaper, younger, inexperienced people."

Bosses are looking for younger and younger people not just to manage, but for leadership roles across the board in various industries, Baker notes, which also lends itself to early retirement and then people getting "dementia at fifty-five or sixty because they're not doing anything." Both managers and the influx of Ivy Leaguers into front-office roles have brought down the average ages of those running ball clubs.

"I've always thought, why does baseball try to push the older guys out when the musicians try to bring them in?" Baker continues. "Know what I mean? When I see the Rolling Stones playing with Muddy Waters or Santana playing with John Lee Hooker, or you got this guy playing with James Brown or David Bowie playing with so-and-so, it's like how come musicians try to learn from each other? Edgar Winter and Johnny Winter were singing with Albert King. Why do the young try to learn from the elderly in music, but in most walks of life they're pushing the elderly out instead of trying to learn from them and take from their experience in order to get better?"

It's a fine line, just as we've seen in the past couple of presidential elections. Experience and wisdom are not valued nearly as much as they should be in our youth-oriented culture. Yet, where is that line when someone is too old, especially in leadership positions in which it is important to project strength and mental acuity?

Joe Maddon nearly became a manager a decade before he took over Tampa Bay in 2006. The Angels were scrounging for a new skipper after blowing a sizable AL West lead in 1995 and then following that up with a lousy 1996. Bill Bavasi was the general manager and had what could have been a brilliant idea: He identified Maddon, then forty-two and an Angels coach, as a future manager but did not think he was quite seasoned enough. Sparky Anderson, sixty-two at the time, was home in Southern California following his well-decorated career managing Cincinnati and Detroit. Bavasi wanted to convince Anderson to add one more chapter to his legacy by managing the Angels, with Maddon as his bench coach. Anderson wouldn't be there very long, and Maddon would be the manager-in-waiting serving his apprenticeship while Sparky led.

Anderson was intrigued, and the idea went as far as a lunch date with Sparky, Bavasi, and then–Angels president Tony Tavares.

But then Sparky ordered soup.

And as he drew his hand to his mouth during lunch, his arm shook and some soup splashed.

That was the end of that idea. The Angels at the time were owned by the Walt Disney Company, and Tavares was president of Disney

Sports Enterprises. Not only was Tavares responsible for overseeing the ball club, but he had a corporate image to maintain. And despite Anderson's Hall of Fame career, an older man with the shakes as manager did not fit that image. Bavasi says Tavares initially loved the idea but could not get past the shaking arm and the soup spoon.

"I've seen a lot more people have their soup spoons shake a lot worse who have led huge companies to success and have started other careers in their lives," Bavasi told me in 2019. "I think it was just somebody who didn't know Sparky and saw him for the first time, or close to the first time.

"You can't blame Tony. If you were in the same spot Tony was in, you'd have done the same thing. You've had to have known Sparky to say, 'I'm not worried about this, it's been this way for ten years.'"

It is one of the most intriguing what-ifs in recent baseball history: Had Anderson gotten the job and then Maddon succeeded him, likely, Scioscia's nineteen-year career as Angels manager, which started in 2000, never would have achieved liftoff. And in that chain reaction, had his career gone in that direction, Maddon likely would have never teamed with the Cubs for that 2016 World Series title.

Many veterans in the industry think—and hope—that with Brian Snitker, Dusty Baker, and Bruce Bochy leading their teams to consecutive World Series wins in 2021, 2022, and 2023, it will redirect the game back toward recognizing the value of managers, especially experienced managers, and maybe throttle back some of the analytics and reemphasize the value of the human touch, managing with the eyes, ears, and mind in addition to the raw data. Given the investment in analytics, not just in expanded baseball operations departments but in Digital Era advances like Statcast, Rapsodo (the pitch-tracking device that measures spin rate, movement, and command, and can break down pitching mechanics), and Trackman (a device that measures exit speed, launch angle, and spin rate off the bat for hitters), there is no going back from where we are today. Nor, in many respects, should there be.

From here, there also are so many more avenues down which managing could travel. Fan Controlled Football, a seven-on-seven league that operated in 2021 and 2022, was created as the first sports league controlled entirely by fans. Might something like that eventually develop in baseball? Interesting to fantasize about wild theories like that, but do you think teams closing in on $300 million payrolls like the Dodgers, Yankees, and Mets would cede control of any aspect of the organization? No chance. With today's economics, what once were players are now "assets," and that is no small part of the reason why baseball operations have seized some of the manager's turf. It's like managing a corporation: When the finances reach a certain level, a board of directors and layers of management become involved. (Though it would be entertaining to watch fans manage bullpens in October and be forced to come to the begrudging conclusion that perhaps today's managers actually *do* know far more than they do.)

Meanwhile, the Independent League Sonoma Stompers turned their operations over to a couple of analytic authors, Ben Lindbergh and Sam Miller, who were allowed to run all aspects of the team during the 2015 season according to advanced statistics. The results are found in the entertaining book *The Only Rule Is It Has to Work*. Results? The book was better than the on-field results, as the Stompers finished second in a four-team league and lost the championship game.

What's more realistic than either of these novel approaches sometime in the future may be artificial intelligence managing, simply because some of the AI methods already have seeped into the sport in the form of the analytics reports run before every game that help dictate a strategy blueprint for that night's contest. Already, baseball has become all about projection systems and probabilities. But as Torre, Maddon, and others keep reminding us, this game has a heartbeat, and as much as the statistics crowd attempts to reduce it to a numbers game, the human element always will keep the pendulum from swinging too far toward calculators and spreadsheets.

Heck, there may be a better chance of seeing the return of the player-manager in the future than so many of the previous ideas (the game's last player-manager was Pete Rose, with Cincinnati from 1984 to 1986; the last to do it in the AL was Don Kessinger for the Chicago White Sox in 1979). While most in the industry long ago left that idea for dead, left-hander Rich Hill, one of the game's more thoughtful veterans, thinks there again is a place today for this relic from the past, given the sport's evolution. The key, Hill says, would be having a strong bench coach who could sift through the analytics information. (Memo to the Cleveland Guardians: You may want to consider this. The last two times Cleveland won the World Series, the then-Indians were led by player-managers—Lou Boudreau in 1948 and Tris Speaker in 1920. Hint hint.)

Hill's ideal candidate for a modern player-manager is either a position player or a starting pitcher, someone who has a good handle on the overall pulse of the team. For this reason, relievers wouldn't qualify as they spend so much time each game isolated in the bullpen. But Hill's general pitch is, so many clubs already have moved toward hiring a recently retired player who has never before managed that it wouldn't be much of a leap to go a couple of years younger and simply name as manager a current player who commands respect.

That respect, Hill believes, would benefit everyone. The particulars, he adds, would have to be with a team whose lineup is very set, an understanding of who's on the bench and their roles, and where platoons may be in effect. This would eliminate any potentially negative feelings regarding how much the manager plays; it mostly would be pretty obvious and there would be no accusations of playing favorites.

Analytics, Hill believes, actually is a large reason as to why a player-manager would work today. The bench coach would handle most of that, which means his (or her) role would be expanded. And that ties into salary.

"I think figuring out how that payment works, as far as how much you're going to be paying the player-manager, it would maybe be a little bit of a subsidized contract leading into the bench coach," Hill says. "He would probably get a higher salary than most bench coaches, which would be deservedly so. Because if the manager is going to be going out there and performing every fifth day on the mound, or possibly playing maybe not every day, but, say, three days a week…you're on second base, something happens and, hey, we need a pinch-runner, who's it going to be? You need a solid bench coach, somebody who's going to understand, someone with the same, like-minded thoughts as the manager. And that's the other thing as far as managing, for me, if we're ever going to have something like that again, which I highly doubt, but everyone would be on the same page. The communication would be seamless."

Player-manager or no, that word "seamless," tied in with "communication," plays into Hill's modern-day Utopia as far as the perfect team. Scouts are forever looking for five-tool players—someone who can hit for average, hit for power, run, throw, and field.

"When you take a sixth tool, which is camaraderie, and have an understanding of what it means in the clubhouse to be a glue guy or something like that, in that sense, how much benefit on the budget is that?" Hill asks. "It's a small investment for that type of push."

Bottom line, disruption has wreaked chaos in so many industries, and those in leadership roles are still working to put the pieces back together in ways that make sense. That even includes something as historical and durable as Major League Baseball, and its positions within. Squeezed by the Ivy Leaguers and analytics power grab above them and the everybody-gets-a-trophy generation of players playing for them, so many managers today have been reduced to middle managers in a corporate game that often seems as if it has fallen into an identity crisis.

"I think the manager is still an incredibly valuable role, it should go without saying," Theo Epstein says. "'Middle manager' is a bit of a condescending term and not accurate, in my opinion. Part of it is, if your GM is looking for someone just to carry out his wishes, it's designed to fail. It's probably not going to work in the long run. You see examples of that from time to time, and for the most part those are not winning organizations. It doesn't work in the long haul.

"A better term is collaborator, thought leader, somebody responsible for creating culture in a clubhouse, an expectation of excellence. If you think about what goes on in a big-league clubhouse now, the role of the manager has almost expanded because there is a lot more happening. It's really important that the manager be capable of helping to lead the effort that helps players become the best version of themselves. That's an organization-wide effort now. It used to be the domain of development in the minor leagues, and then when players came up it was time to sink or swim. Now, it's a constant push to grow. It's almost a defining characteristic of the best major-league clubhouses now. It comes from everywhere. It's not just a major-league coach, like a pitching coach. It's the manager, the coaching staff, everyone in player development. You have analysts, sports scientists, biokinetic experts, guys who never played with opinions and, in a lot of cases, informed opinions. While the GM might be who hired them, it all has to run through the manager and coaching staff. The manager has to be the one who buys in, engages, streamlines information, validates information, applies information, and executes with it.

"And that's just for the players, to help them be the best versions of themselves. Then everything that goes into the manager's in-game decision-making. That's a massive responsibility. Making players their best, establishing the right culture, make the right decisions every night, and then, oh yeah, on top of that you have to be the spokesperson for the entire organization twice a day, every day. Yes, these days it's probably the GM setting the philosophy and direction of the organization where forty years ago it was the manager. You hired the manager then and how he did things was how you did things. Top-down. Now, it bubbles up. But it's the manager who is in the trenches every day and that becomes a huge part of what the organization is really about, its philosophy and direction."

No matter how much they've been defaced, devalued, and detached from so many things they once did, managers continue to matter and always will. The most perfect algorithm still is incapable of spitting out a flawless blueprint for tonight's game, and somebody in that dugout is going to have to read and recognize those moments when things fly off script and either steer them back on script or make decisions in the moment that create a new script. The most hands-on executive still is not going to touch as many players in that clubhouse, daily, as his manager.

In many ham-handed organizations, there are too many cooks in the kitchen, too many fingers in the pie, which results in mixed messages and crossed wires. Anything less than perfect and (mostly) genial communication between the manager's office and baseball operations, ownership, the coaching staff, player development, training and nutrition, sports science, and more threatens the manager's authority. And the minute players recognize that is compromised, respect dissipates and he's finished. Authenticity is real, and it is impossible to fake.

"I followed Lou Piniella in Seattle, and I was well aware how all of those players, his players, thought things should be run," Bob Melvin says. "There was a time I realized, yeah, but no. You've got to be yourself. You can't be somebody else. I went out and got thrown out for about the third time, and I raised a big fuss that was more choreographed. I think I threw my hat. And later I'm just going, 'What did I do that for?' Players have to know your emotions are authentic. They just have to."

The position may no longer come with the autonomy it once had, but there are ways to set the manager up to succeed—and, also, unwittingly, to fail. The best, most successful organizations have structured a system in which all of these departments work together harmoniously. There is a reason why the Los Angeles Dodgers, Tampa Bay, Houston, Milwaukee, Baltimore, Cleveland, and Minnesota are among those analytically inclined teams who consistently win. The Andrew Friedman–Dave Roberts combination in LA, Derek Falvey–Rocco Baldelli in Minnesota, Erik Neander–Kevin Cash in Tampa Bay… there is not a disconnect between the manager's office and other departments, or between the various departments themselves. There is cohesion. It is far more difficult to build and maintain than it sounds, and the number of organizations that fail at this most basic operating tenet is astounding. There are so many tentacles reaching out to players daily within each organization, so many more than there once were, and players have come to expect and be comforted by this. When those tentacles deliver to players what they need, more often than not the results are successful. When the player gets pulled in too many directions—when the various departments are not working together cohesively, in sync—the players become overwhelmed and lost. Language is different today in many cases, as well. A few years ago, with an analytics-based hitting coach on board, one of the most traditional organizations in the game internally banned the term "situational hitting." The hitting coach demanded that the approach to each at bat be the same no matter what the scoreboard said or how many runners were on base—or on which bases they stood. Some of that is just crazy—and unless every department is in sync with very New Age ideas like that, then more likely than not, things will devolve into chaos and grumbling.

In some ways, these changes are like Apple's IOS updates on the iPhone: As things develop and evolve over time, they become necessary for optimal performance, privacy, and security. Ignoring them can lead to sluggish performance and security risks.

As Sandy Alderson says, today's manager must possess tools within his skill set that those of thirty and forty years ago never even had to consider. As Phillies president of baseball operations Dave Dombrowski believes, a manager can be the difference between a team finishing in first place and last place. The Phillies witnessed that dramatically, of course, when Rob Thomson replaced Joe Girardi in June 2022. There were no significant player personnel changes, the schedule didn't suddenly break in their favor…but the Phillies turned sharply and started winning—and carried it all the way to the World Series, where they were beaten by Houston.

Despite evidence to the contrary regarding the diminishing role of managers, Cashman, the game's longest-tenured GM, believes they are equally as important today as they were fifty years ago—no more, no less. He likens it to NASA. When Neil Armstrong first walked on the moon in 1969, the game's longest-tenured GM says, Armstrong was the face of the space program—like managers were the face of their organizations.

"But in reality, the manager works six months," Cashman says. "Then they go off. In Joe Torre's case, he went off to Hawaii in the wintertime. So NASA has a space program that has all of these different experts in various different fields working twelve months a year, 24/7. To put it together and translate it into our world, we have an amateur scouting program, domestic and international, you have an analytics department, a player development department, a pro scouting department, a physiology department which is your athletic training staff, your strength and conditioning program, your mental skills program, your performance science team, all of which are twelve months, 24/7, nonstop. That's mission control, from GM all the way down. So managers are not the space program. But we build—I equate it to the space shuttle—we build this $300 million space shuttle which happens to be your player payroll. We're picking the players, drafting them, developing them, signing them as free agents or minor-league free agents, international free agents, waiver-claiming them, and we've got a forty-man roster you turn over to this guy who works six months.

"So none of us can do what a manager is charged to do, which is manage a baseball team, manage a clubhouse, manage pre- and postgame with the media, none of us can do that. Just like nobody at

NASA can fly a space shuttle. You still need that expert pilot skill set that's second to none that can do things very few people can do. So they're vitally important now as they were then. Whitey Herzog wasn't drafting players and developing them in the minor leagues when he ran the Cardinals, and neither was Bobby Cox in Atlanta. They're not in the draft room in the summer. Aaron Boone is managing the team in Toronto or wherever when we have our third-round pick."

The Braves of the '90s and early 2000s were incredibly successful, Cashman points out, not just because of Cox, but because men like Roy Clark, who was Atlanta's scouting director, were finding and developing players like Chipper Jones. The last Yankees dynasty, the one Torre managed, benefited from the acumen of, among others, GM Gene "Stick" Michael and superstar scouts like Bill Livesey and Brian Sabean, who landed and then developed Derek Jeter, Andy Pettitte, Jorge Posada, and others.

But if the organization delivers talent like that to an ineffectual manager, then...*pffft*. Like air escaping a balloon.

"Managers are vitally important, necessary, they have a unique skill set that no one else can do," Cashman continues. "They have the rare ability to blend intelligence, leadership, intuition, information-processing abilities, and communication skills. What they do and have to employ on a daily basis to continue to command that room, it's an impossible job that only a unique few can do. It's just as important today as it was yesterday and generations beyond. But the game has exploded and grown."

Beane likens the modern manager to an altogether different entity than NASA.

"The manager today is a little bit like the White House's press secretary," the Athletics executive says. "The manager every single day is absolutely the face of the organization, and his ability to project, whether you win or lose, a very positive, transparent face to the organization is just so critical. And nobody's better at that than Bob Melvin.

I never had to wake up in the morning, I would never get a call, saying, 'Can you believe what Bob said in the paper?' He was brilliant. His ability to maintain relationships with the press, with the players, we had an incredible representation to the organization on a daily basis. To me, that's a very important part of the job today. And our job is to give him the information so that when you're in the dugout, you've got all the information you want, but the game is going really fast. And the managers who have the ability to process that information again and again and then use it in a real-time basis, those are the great managers who can do that. And Bob to me is as good as anybody."

Peeling back the layers to ascertain where a manager's territory begins and where the baseball ops' ends, the picture is more blurry than ever. Asking managers and top officials in an organization where the lineups come from today is as awkward a conversation as those with kids who want to know where babies come from. "Collaboration" is the word of choice, and there is a reason. In today's group-think world, by the time the computer spits out matchup numbers and probabilities, as Melvin says, it becomes pretty clear who should be in the lineup that night, anyway. And given the Age of Enlightenment thinking that your best hitters should come to the plate most often, it becomes pretty obvious where most of those hitters should be slotted in the lineup.

"Who the author of that lineup is is irrelevant if all you care about is the ends justify the means," Beane says. "So that's the way I look at it. And any sort of pushback on that, really, it's pushback on ego, I think, as much as anything. It's bruising to the ego and, quite frankly, that can really restrict the growth of any leader, company, or business if the ego overwrites what are, in many cases, very good ideas."

But to view a manager only as one spoke in the Big Wheel is counterproductive, as well, if respect erodes and players tune him out. The New York Mets won a game against Arizona in April 2022 because they "stole" a run: A Mets baserunner tagged up early from third base and as the Diamondbacks appealed, the runner certainly would have been called out. But that was when J. D. Davis, the heads-up runner on first base, broke to steal second. It distracted the Arizona pitcher enough that he made a throw to second—which immediately nullified the appeal. It was something that the cagey veteran Buck Showalter, a rules wonk, had talked with his players about during spring training, an angle they could one day play if it came up. And it did. Had the Mets won the NL East by one game in 2022, Showalter's veteran acumen would have been one of the deciding factors. Alas, instead the Mets lost steam down the stretch and wound up in a tie with Atlanta for first place at 101-61. When they fired Showalter a year later and named neophyte Carlos Mendoza as his replacement, a blank piece of paper onto which president of baseball operations David Stearns and his numbers people could paint their masterpiece, while the payback may come in the overall execution of the computer plans, it's difficult to believe Mendoza or any other inexperienced manager will be savvy enough to affect things like Showalter did within the framework of a nine-inning game.

The website 538 did a study in 2014 in which the author determined over 162 games that a manager is worth somewhere between –2 and +2 wins in a season. It is a razor-thin margin, but it also is another example of why the sharpest managers always will matter.

The difference today is that information flows from so many sources and the most astute of skippers—old-school such as Bochy, new-school like Cash—keep their minds open and remain eager to take what they need. The brainpower in today's game is higher than ever, so, as Cash says, shame on him if he doesn't soak in what he can by listening to the smart people around him. But, as for the notion that today's skippers are simply middle managers?

"I don't know if that's fair," Cash says. "I can definitely appreciate that it's changed. But I would almost say it's evolved more. I'm not knocking any manager from the past there. But as players evolve, we, as managers, better evolve with them. You've got to be able to connect with the players, you have to be able to be a part of creating an atmosphere where the players want to come to the ballpark, want to perform. I mean, those are big tasks put on coaching staffs, and they're certainly led by managers."

By any standard, Cash is one of the finest managers working today. Perhaps if there is any justice, the future one day will include him managing his Tampa Bay club to a World Series title. That may not completely erase the memories of Blake Snell and what could have been on that long-ago night in 2020, but it certainly at least would ease some of the sting.

Moments come and go so quickly, and the big ones, whether they work out or backfire, remain burned into a manager's soul for eternity. As the evolution continues and the game changes, the only constant is that what the future holds, in both digital and human terms, is unknowable.

One of Tom Kelly's most enduring memories from the Jack Morris Game 7 in 1991 is of the quiet before the storm on that Sunday of the clincher, just before he left his home for Minnesota's Metrodome.

"My father called," Kelly says. "And I remember saying to him, 'I sure hope the players will decide the game, whether we win or lose. I really don't want to get involved. I want to stay out of the way.' It became anything but that. I had more decisions that game than in the first six combined. Trying to figure out how to score a run, I tried bunting, I tried the hit-and-run, and then I remember letting Shane Mack swing and he hits into a double play, which was really agonizing. Then the decisions to walk David Justice to try to get Sid Bream and, of course, Jack threw him a splitter and it worked out, he hit it to Hrbek to start a double play. Unbelievable.

"There were things that worked out, and some things I tried to do didn't work out. Letting Jack pitch the tenth inning certainly worked out. I've thought about that quite a few times. Then you're involved in every inning, almost making some kind of decision. It was excruciating.

I'm sure Bobby Cox felt the same. He had to pull Smoltz out of there. Jesus. Those fellas were dealing. My God."

The game's unpredictability by design and humanity by nature is the Great Equalizer, which is what continually fuels the intrigue. It also is why the manager remains integral to the game—and to the success of a winning team. What the job looks like now is vastly different from what it was fifty years ago. And what his job—her job?—will look like in the near future is certain to undergo more change. Again, and again, and probably yet again.

Some years after that 1991 World Series, Kelly was on a golf course with Eric Curry, one of the NCAA's top basketball referees. As they were approaching a green, Curry's cell phone buzzed, which teed off Kelly to begin with, because Kelly remains old-school in every respect. Curry answered, because the moment was just too delicious: On the other end was his longtime buddy, John Smoltz. And sure enough, within moments, Curry handed his phone to the old manager, saying someone wanted to say hello.

"So I got on the phone with Smoltz," Kelly says. "And I said, 'Listen, I gave you enough due, you pitched your ass off. But I've got to make this putt, so I've got to go.'"

ACKNOWLEDGMENTS

I didn't realize it at the time, but this book started some three decades ago. And it continued through hundreds of rental cars, thousands of miles through Florida and Arizona springs, across the country during sweltering summers, and through the endless airplane flights of October playoff baseball. It was fueled along the way by Kansas City barbecue, Chicago deep-dish pizza, New York steaks, Boston seafood, Southern California tacos, a few Waffle Houses, and many other stops. As you read in these pages, so much of a modern manager's job is about relationships, and what I didn't know then but do now is that I, too, was building relationships. And that was the most enjoyable aspect of this project, reaching out to some of the baseball people I've had the privilege to work with over these years to have them help tell this tale of what a manager's job was then, what it is now, how we got from then to now, and why we got from then to now. To those who think baseball writing is simply a few characters at a time on the Platform Formerly Known as Twitter, you're missing out. It's the relationships you develop and nourish over the years. That's where the fun, and the meaning, is.

Grateful doesn't begin to describe my feeling toward all who carved out the time to talk, be it in person or on the phone, and the list is longer than a Red Sox–Yankees game circa 2004. Baseball people love to talk baseball, and before you know it, you are reeled in. I talked to some two hundred people for this project over the past two and a half years. I thank all of them, but especially those who went above and beyond in sharing with me the greatest gift of all, their time:

Searching the archives, the first time I ever quoted Dodgers manager Dave Roberts was way back in November 1989, when he was a senior quarterback leading Rancho Buena Vista High School to the San Diego Section championship and I was covering high schools for the San Diego edition of the *Los Angeles Times*. More than three decades later, in the spring of 2022, I approached him on a back field at the Dodgers' Camelback Ranch spring training complex, told him about this project, and asked if he would be OK with me shadowing him for a few days for what hopefully would be a revealing chapter going behind the scenes with all the stuff that is required of a modern MLB manager today. Roberts immediately was intrigued by the subject and agreed, and later that summer he generously allowed me to hang around with him for four days (see chapter 8). Then, in an incredibly fortuitous bit of timing—at least, for this book—he led the Dodgers to the World Series title last fall. So, of course, with the final deadline for revisions to the manuscript due just a week after the series, I pestered him again. And once more, despite being exhausted and coming off of a post–championship parade illness, he cheerfully agreed to meet again. That was the final interview for the book (promise, Dave. Get some rest. See ya again soon!).

That was just the start. I covered the Twins for six seasons in the 1990s, and though gruff manager Tom Kelly suffered no fools and was quick to bark, somehow he came to tolerate me. My initial idea was to visit him in Minnesota, and perhaps talk over lunch. I had so much to ask. Imagine my exuberance when I phoned him and learned he had not changed one bit. "Scotty, I don't even talk to my wife that much," he growled. "I'm not interested in lunch. And I don't know why I would want to help anybody with a book, anyway." So we chatted a bit more, and finally he agreed to a phone interview if I would keep it reasonably short. Call me Monday, he said. So I did. We talked for three and a half hours, and he was tremendous. As I said, baseball people cannot resist talking baseball. All you have to do is ask a reasonable question or two and sit back and listen.

Dusty Baker welcomed me into his house for a *New York Times* story, won his first World Series in Houston later that year, and then spent more time with me on the phone that winter for this project. Jim Tracy hosted me in his home outside of Cincinnati one afternoon for a wide-ranging discussion on his time in the dugout as analytics blasted into the game like a freight train. Bob and Sue Boone graciously invited me into their home to discuss Bob's managing career—and Aaron's—as we watched a Yankees telecast with Aaron managing. Watching his postgame news conference with them may have been more fun than analyzing his in-game work. (The whole thing was carried out with Aaron's full knowledge and blessing.) Back in 2015, when I was working for Bleacher Report, Kirk Gibson was as fierce as you would guess when I visited him at home in Michigan and, for the first time, he spoke about his Parkinson's disease diagnosis. While that wasn't for this project, you'll read some of his insights about his tempestuous but ultimately loving relationship with Sparky Anderson from that visit in these pages. On a picnic table at the Cincinnati complex in Glendale, Arizona, in 2023, Buddy Bell and I talked for an hour and a half. At one point, old friend Walt Jocketty, who was waiting for his lunch partner, walked by and chided me with, "Scott, what are you doing, writing a book?" Well, um, as a matter of fact...

So many others were so generous at ballparks and on the telephone (hey, I couldn't get to everyone's home, plus, word probably would have started to spread and these folks would have begun shutting me down!).

Kevin Cash had to be long past tired of talking about hooking Blake Snell early in Game 6 of the 2020 World Series but nevertheless was incredibly invested and thoughtful during our conversation about that and the Rays' overall way of doing things. Hall of Famer Jim Palmer, as you would expect, was a kick while remembering Earl Weaver.

Also, special thanks in particular to: Sandy Alderson, Josh Barfield, Billy Beane, Paul Beeston, David Bell, Bruce Bochy, Bret Boone, Brian Cashman, Craig Counsell, Dave Dombrowski, Theo Epstein, Jeff Francis, Terry Francona, Cito Gaston, Mike Hazen, Rich Hill, Art Howe, Kent Hrbek, Jacque Jones, Gabe Kapler, Eric Karros, Jim Leyland, Grady Little, Andy MacPhail, Jerry Manuel, Mike Matheny, Lloyd McClendon, Bob Melvin, Paul Molitor, Dayton Moore, John Mozeliak, Mark Prior, Mike Shildt, Buck Showalter, John Smoltz, Brian Snitker, Dr. Charles Steinberg, Charley Steiner, Mark Sweeney, Joe Torre, Justin Verlander, Kenny Williams, and Ned Yost.

Two impressive ladies were extremely helpful, as well, a sentence that would never have appeared in a book about managers in, say, the 1970s or 1980s. Ronny Gajownik was the second-ever female professional manager in 2023, working at Class A Hillsboro in the Arizona organization. So I visited her in Oregon and watched her manage, and it was so educational watching the young men playing for the Hops relate to a female manager—with total respect, professionalism, and humor—before, during, and after the game. Ronny and I talked over lunch, at the ballpark, and then back in her office over a glass of postgame wine after that night's game. And Alyssa Nakken, who became the first MLB coach ever while working on Gabe Kapler's Giants staff, was a helpful resource, too.

Thanks to John Blundell, MLB's terrific vice president for communications, for his patience and help in connecting me with Joe Torre. To Jon Shestakofsky, vice president of communications and content at the Baseball Hall of Fame, for giving Jack Morris a nudge to return my call when Morris was a little slow on the deal after giving me his phone number and telling me to call anytime. To Rob Butcher, the retired Reds media relations director, for simply being one of the best ever and for his help with Buddy and David Bell and myriad other things over the years. And to Bob Tewksbury, the lead to my coauthor on *Ninety Percent Mental*. What a tremendous partnership we had—and still have—and it was fun to get his insights on managers for this book. Even though I think he owes me something like ten lunches by now (just kidding, Retired Pitcher!).

A sort of odd thank-you to two folks who, unfortunately, didn't make it into the book. For a time, I was going to do a chapter diving into the history of the old concept of player-managers. In that vein, the late Pete Rose and Don Kessinger—the last of that breed in the National League and American League—were tremendously insightful during long telephone interviews. But the manuscript was getting too long and, while it was sort of a fun detour, it didn't quite fit into the book's overall theme. Perhaps one day, somewhere, I'll resurface those interviews.

When I hear authors discussing their "next project," I've come to understand the meaning of that term very well. Tewksbury and I published *Ninety Percent Mental* in 2018. My ace literary agent Rob Kirkpatrick and I periodically discussed over the next few years what would be next. *The...next...project.* It is such a long process that you'd better settle on something you want to do...but something you hope people will like...and something you are happy to live with for two or three years—or more—as it consumes you. Then when you do, you write a proposal, your agent kicks it back to you and says it needs to be fleshed out more, so you do, and then your agent kicks it back to you again with more demands and...well, thanks, Rob. You're the best. And I mean that.

At Hachette, this book started under editor Dan Ambrosio, who also edited *Ninety Percent Mental*. I loved the continuity. But then things changed and I inherited Brant Rumble as my editor. And he's terrific. How lucky am I that the switch was seamless. Thank you both,

Dan and Brant. You're both big league. My thanks to Niyati Patel, Mark Steven Long, Carolyn Kurek, and Albert Tang, as well.

USA Today's brilliant, longtime baseball writer Bob Nightengale and I first worked together at the *Los Angeles Times* in 1989, and we quickly advanced from colleagues to friends to, really, him becoming my baseball brother: sidekick, confidant, sounding board, travel partner, Cooperstown Hall of Fame housemate, steakhouse pal, barbecue buddy, and so many other things. To Jerry Crasnick and Jayson Stark, my lifelong friends, baseball colleagues, dinner partners, press box mates...thank you for being by my side, always. I miss you, Jim Caple, and love you, Vicki Schuman. To my beloved *New York Times* baseball team—until the paper shut down its sports section—what a fantastic time working with great talent who became great friends. Tyler Kepner—also for a time my sometimes partner on MLB Network Radio—Ben Hoffman, James Wagner, David Waldstein, and Ben Shpigel, you are awesome. And to my old Fox Sports San Diego television buddies, Mike Pomeranz and Mark Sweeney. Boy, did we have some fun together.

For me, it all started in Michigan, and I've got the friends to prove it: I first met Greg Althaver, Sam Bellestri, Dr. Dan Eby, Matt "Wildman" Miller, and Jerry Walsh around the time we were fifteen, and we've stuck together ever since, sharing hopes, dreams, ups, and downs, through marriages, kids, and careers. Then a couple years later, along came Tim Hoffman, who, with his fabulous wife, Maira, would become godparents to our daughter and, well, without the lifelong support system of all these guys, life wouldn't be nearly as rich as I sit and write this. And it's always good to have a fan in Australia: Karl Taylor has been over to see several World Series, and I know one day he actually will see his beloved Yankees win again.

One thing I do not recommend while in the middle of writing a book is being diagnosed with a life-altering medical condition. You always hear that life can change in an instant and, hoo, boy. To those on the home front who have stepped in with love and support to take care of my wife and me when we've needed it over the past year and a half, unending gratitude, especially to my sister-in-law Charissa Gray, my original "Sister Wives," Kirsten, Liz, and Jennifer (sorry, it isn't nearly as scandalous as it may sound), my cousin Pam (and her husband Bill) Zilligen, Bruce and Sandi Meyer, Don and Kendal Patterson, Gary and Paulette Phillips, Wendy Traber, Wade and Lara Walker, Steve and Ada Wilder, and Frank and Joanne Volpe. And, especially, to Dr. Darren Sigal and nurses Kerri, Adria, Inja, Angela, Jamie, and Felicia: Thank you for all you are doing, you beautiful, beautiful people.

I have been blessed with the most supportive parents you can imagine in Alan and Rosemary. If you don't believe it, check this out: 1972, Game 5 of the ALCS, Oakland at Detroit, an afternoon start, and they wrote a note that I could stay home from fourth grade to watch the telecast. Then, they wound up reading every word I think I've ever written ever since. Love you, Mom and Dad. And the same to my brother, Greg, and his wife, Marit, and my nieces Delia and Cleo, and my sister, Jennifer, and her husband, Ernest, and my nephews Ethan and Jacob and niece Piper.

Finally, to the loves of my life: my wife, Kim, and daughter, Gretchen. You know things are a little different at home when a baseball game is on television and, from the time Gretchen was six or seven, if she wanted to watch something, she would preface it before attempting to change the channel by asking, "Dad, do you need to watch this baseball game?" The patience, love, and understanding over the years that both of you have given continues to fuel and inspire me. And it explains the periodic lump in my throat. I love you both more today than yesterday. To borrow and turn a phrase that Zac Brown sings, it's a sweet, sweet life with you two, living by the salty sea.

Scott Miller
Autumn 2024
Carlsbad, California

INDEX